AF559968

UNDERSTANDING PAKISTAN

UNDERSTANDING PAKISTAN

Emerging Voices from India

Edited by
MATHEW JOSEPH C.

MANOHAR
2015

First published 2015

ISBN 978-93-5098-094-1

Published by
Ajay Kumar Jain *for*
Manohar Publishers & Distributors
4753/23 Ansari Road, Daryaganj,
New Delhi 110 002

Typeset by
Ravi Shanker
Delhi 110 095

Printed at
Salasar Imaging Systems
Delhi 110 035

Contents

V. PAKISTAN AND JAMMU & KASHMIR

Acknowledgements

THIS VOLUME IS the outcome of a national level seminar conducted by the Centre for Pakistan Studies, MMAJ Academy of International Studies, Jamia Millia Islamia, New Delhi for research scholars on the theme *Understanding Pakistan*. The articles in this volume reflect the thinking of young India on the polity, society, culture and foreign policy of Pakistan.

In the three days seminar research scholars from all over India participated. Eight working sessions were conducted and 25 papers were presented. The keynote address was delivered by M.J. Akbar and renowned political scientist from Pakistan, Prof. Mohammad Waseem delivered a Special address. Prof. Rajen Harshe gave the valedictory address. Eminent scholars like Prof. Ashwini K. Ray, Prof. Kalim Bahadur, Prof. Rashmi Doraiswamy, Dr. Dileep Padgaonkar, Amb. T.C.A. Rangachari, Commodore C. Uday Bhaskar, Dr. E. Sreedharan and Captain Alok Bansal chaired various sessions. I thank all of them for their eager participation and support for this academic endeavour.

I am grateful to the Vice-Chancellor of Jamia Millia Islamia and the Director of the MMAJ Academy of International Studies for their encouragement and tremendous support for this venture. My colleagues, the office staff and the students at the MMAJ Academy of International Studies also rendered a great deal of help and support to the seminar. I sincerely thank all of them.

I owe a deep sense of gratitude to Prof. Ajay Darshan Behera, Coordinator, the Centre for Pakistan Studies, without whose vision and leadership, the seminar and this volume would not have been possible. Dr. Tasawwur Husain Zaidi, Project Associate with the Centre for Pakistan Studies needs a special word of thanks for his assistance in organizing the seminar.

I am thankful to Shiraz Sheikh, Tarun Mathur, Azad Ahmad Khan and Azhar Ali for their help in the editing process of this volume at various stages. Lastly, I would like to thank Manohar Publishers for readily agreeing to publish this volume.

New Delhi MATHEW JOSEPH C.

Contributors

Anwesha Ghosh is a Doctoral Candidate at Willy Brandt School of Public Policy, University of Erfurt, Germany.

Ashish Shukla is an ICSSR Doctoral Fellow at Centre for South Asian Studies, School of International Studies, Jawaharlal Nehru University, New Delhi.

Azad Ahmad Khan is a Doctoral Candidate at MMAJ Academy of International Studies, Jamia Millia Islamia, New Delhi.

Azhar Ali is a Doctoral Candidate at MMAJ Academy of International Studies, Jamia Millia Islamia, New Delhi.

Bidisha Mukherjee is a Research Scholar at Institute of Foreign Policy Studies, Calcutta University, Kolkata.

Deepali Raghunath Khaire is a Doctoral Candidate at Centre for Security Studies, School of International Studies, Central University of Gujarat, Gandhinagar.

Dipanwita Roy Ghatak is a Doctoral Candidate at Department of International Relations, Jadavpur University, Kolkata.

Dheeraj Kumar is a Doctoral Fellow at Department of Electronic Media and Mass Communication, School of Media and Communication, Pondicherry University, Puducherry.

T.K. Jabir is Lecturer at Department of Political Science, MES College, Nedumkandam, Idukki District, Kerala.

Nishu Sharma is a Doctoral Candidate at Centre for South Asian Studies, School of International Studies, Jawaharlal Nehru University, New Delhi.

Puyesh Kant Sharma is a Doctoral Candidate at Centre for West Asian Studies, School of International Studies, Jawaharlal Nehru University, New Delhi.

Samir Ahmad Bhat is a Doctoral Candidate at Department of Political Science, University of Kashmir, Srinagar, Jammu & Kashmir.

Shalmaly Mukherjee is a Doctoral Candidate at Department of History, University of Delhi, Delhi.

Shashi Kant is a Doctoral Candidate at Department of Political Science, University of Delhi, Delhi.

Shiraz Sheikh is a Doctoral Candidate at MMAJ Academy of International Studies, Jamia Millia Islamia, New Delhi.

Sumit Kumar Jha is an ICSSR Doctoral Fellow at UGC Centre for Southern Asia Studies, School of Social Sciences and International Studies, Pondicherry University, Puducherry.

Tarun Mathur is a Doctoral Candidate at MMAJ Academy of International Studies, Jamia Millia Islamia, New Delhi.

Urvashi Sabu is an Associate Professor at Department of English, PGDAV College, University of Delhi, Delhi.

Yaqoob-Ul-Hassan is a Research Assistant, Institute for Defence Studies and Analyses, New Delhi.

Zarine Khan is a Doctoral Candidate at Centre for International Politics and Diplomacy, School of International Studies, Jawaharlal Nehru University, New Delhi.

CHAPTER 1

Introduction

Mathew Joseph C.

PAKISTAN IS AN enigma for many in India. Scholars, political observers and analysts, politicians and civil society activists generally view Pakistan through a prism which is coloured by suspicion and fear. Pakistan is not considered as a normal state by many in India.[1] In the general Indian imagination, Pakistan is a creation of the unholy alliance between British imperialism and Muslim nationalism. Muslim nationalism is mainly understood as nothing but Muslim communalism or separatism.[2] Muslim nationalism and the consequent movement for Pakistan are always described in the Indian narrative of anti-colonial freedom movement as a tool in the hands of the British Empire to divide the national movement and prolong the achievement of independence from the alien rule.

The incident of Partition which divided the 'unified' India into two, i.e. India and Pakistan still looms large in the Indian narratives on the freedom movement. The very ideology which was used to divide 'unified' India – the Two Nation Theory could not preserve the unity of Pakistan.[3] The unity of Pakistan proved to be a mirage within a period of 24 years. The country got divided into two countries, Pakistan and Bangladesh, in 1971 following a very violent conflict between the two wings of the erstwhile Pakistan. The collapse of 'unified Pakistan' was a blow to the assumption that religion can be a potent force in uniting people who belong to different ethnic groups, cultures, traditions and customs.

The articles in this volume are written by young research scholars from various universities in India, who are interested in studies related to Pakistan. One can observe in these writings a clear departure from the existing Indian scholarship on Pakistan, which is mainly concerned with strategic and security issues and India-Pakistan relations. The domestic politics of Pakistan also figures in a minor way in the existing Indian scholarship on Pakistan. Pakistan's culture, literature and cinema are very rarely taken up for study by Indian scholars. However, the young scholars who have contributed to this volume have taken up issues related to culture, literature and cinema along with conventional issues like strategic and security matters and domestic politics. The young scholars assembled here have in that sense initiated a welcome change in the nature of Indian scholarship on Pakistan.

I

Politics and economy are the dominant spheres of activity in any given polity. Despite the difference in the level of development this is true in the case of both the developed and developing worlds. Pakistan cannot be an exception in this regard. The politics in Pakistan is largely shaped by the level of economic development of the country. The class nature of the political elite, which is a combination of the military-bureaucratic elite and the landed aristocracy, and the institution of state will not be fully understood without a threadbare analysis of the economy of Pakistan. The retardation that happened to the natural growth of various social forces under long years of colonialism, the status of Pakistan as a client state in the periphery of capitalism and the perpetuation of existing power hierarchy by forces from within and without have played their role in shaping the kind of modernization happening in the country.

To many social analysts Pakistan portrays herself as a society which is reluctant to accept the norms of modernization and modern values in everyday life.[4] Dipanwita Roy Ghatak in her article 'Pakistan through the Kaleidoscope of Modernization' questions that very notion and argues on the contrary that Pakistan's path of modernization presents a complex and contradictory picture simultaneously. What is important to understand is that the timeframe prescribed by the existing successful Western models of modernization is not applicable in the case of Pakistan. This is true in the case of the process of modernization of the post-colonial world. Apart from the timeframe, the nature and pattern of Pakistan's modernization are also different from the universally acceptable models. Deepanwita argues that, anchoring around Islam Pakistan is modernizing herself on her own terms and in at her own pace. Her argument reaffirms the futility of applying Eurocentric or Western notions of socio-political evolution in the non-Western world.

One of the issues which Pakistan encounters in her nation-building process is ethnic nationalism.[5] The Pashtun ethnic nationalism which threatened the very integrity of Pakistan as a nation state has been managed by accommodating the Pashtun elite in the national mainstream. This model was not effective in Baluchistan. Shashi Kant in his article 'Ethno-nationalism in Pakistan: The Case of Baluchistan' points out that the sheer exploitation of the natural and mineral wealth of Baluchistan by the Punjabi dominated Pakistan state has almost completely alienated the people of Baluchistan from the idea of Pakistan. Pakistan treats Baluchistan as an internal colony. The Baluchi resistance against this discriminatory treatment has now developed into a full-fledged conflict between the Baluchi people and the Pakistan state. The severity of the conflict in Baluchistan provides ample insights into how Pakistan state deals with movements for ethnic assertion and national self-determination.

The port city of Karachi witnesses the ill-effects of the overplay of identity politics around ethnicity. After Partition the Mohajirs from India had resettled themselves in Karachi, changing the city's nature, appearance and ethos.[6] Apart from the Mohajirs, people belonging to other ethnicities also migrated to Karachi as it was the capital then and the economic and industrial hub of Pakistan. The increasing population and the inability of the native Sindhis to reassert themselves in the city has made it a theatre of ethnic violence over the last thirty years. Tarun Mathur in his article 'Ethnic Transformation of Karachi and its Implications' argues that the politics which governs Karachi is all about ethnicity. The problems in governing the city pose peculiar challenges to the provincial administration of Sindh and it is ill-equipped to meet those challenges. Hence violence has become the norm of everyday life in Karachi.

The emergence of new social movements around environmental concerns in Pakistan is a less known and discussed subject in the literature on Pakistan. The Indian scholarship on Pakistan is certainly not concerned much about this. However, issues related to environment and other livelihood issues are getting important in contemporary

Pakistan.[7] Puyesh Kant Sharma in his article 'Environmental Movements in Pakistan: A Case Study of Mangala Dam in Mirpur' maps out the various new social movements that have emerged in Pakistan over a period of time and brings out the arguments put forth by these various movements ranging from e-waste management in Karachi to the construction of new dams in Pakistan. The traditional image of Pakistan as a country where politics is nothing but the dominance of military and the movements against it is subtly questioned here. The possibility of environmental politics cannot be ruled out in a country like Pakistan which is known for the absence of micropolitics generally.

II

The system of education in Pakistan, the nature, organization and functions of the media both in English and in Urdu and various manifestations of popular culture are always considered to be sites of political contestations between various interests is a widely accepted truth. As these spheres are directly connected to civil society, they are all the more important. Any serious analysis about Pakistani politics has to take the activities in these spheres as important because they represent in a way the tensions in the politics of Pakistan.

The medium of instruction in Pakistan has always been a contentious issue. Politics over the medium of instruction is always linked to the power position of various social classes. Pakistan was conceived as a homeland of Muslims in the Indian subcontinent. At the first instance Urdu was declared as the national language of Pakistan, though it was the mother tongue of less than 10 per cent of the population.[8] Following this declaration it was important for the state elite to impose Urdu as the medium of instruction along with English and other provincial languages like Punjabi and Sindhi. Azad Ahmad Khan in his article 'Language Controversy and Education in Pakistan' describes the process in which English and Urdu established their importance over other provincial languages as the medium of instruction and the problems it created for the students who were mainly proficient in their mother tongues. Khan argues that the prestige and status associated with English-medium schools and education ensures the continuation of the socio-political hierarchy established in the colonial period.

Apart from the issues related to language, the construction of the history of Pakistan is also a major issue of concern in the context of the education system. The official history constructed by the ruling elite is widely disseminated through the history textbooks written for various levels of students. These textbooks in every sense distort the history of the Indian subcontinent and thereby justify the creation of Pakistan as an inevitable step in the preservation of Islamic faith, customs and traditions.[9] Zarine Khan in her article 'Construction of History in Pakistani Textbooks' points out how these textbooks emphasize the stereotypes of Muslims and Hindus created by the colonial authorities and strengthened by the communalists of both the communities. This official narrative of history rejects the commonalities of the people of India and Pakistan as a mere illusion and portrays the minorities in Pakistan as second-class citizens.

The public consciousness of any society is largely shaped by the media in its various forms. In the case of Pakistan the military regimes over the years exerted tremendous control over the media in order to keep their domination over the polity intact. Under Gen. Pervez Musharraf's regime (1999-2008), contrary to the usual practice, the media was allowed to spread in breadth and depth and it marked a turning point in Pakistan's history. The liberal attitude of Gen. Musharraf's regime towards media activism led to the proliferation and penetration of both print and electronic media to every nook and corner of the country. Now media in Pakistan has achieved the capability of determining the contours of politics in the country. Dheeraj Kumar in his article 'Media Agenda Setting in Pakistan: Prospects for Socio-Political Transformation' elaborates and explains this development in the context of the happenings in the recent history of Pakistan. Both the media and judiciary act as strong pillars supporting the efforts towards the institutionalization of democracy in contemporary Pakistan.

The different kinds of tensions individuals and communities face in their everyday lives are generally not reflected in academic and scholarly writings. Rather these are not considered to be important in the process of the political and historical evolution and transformation of societies. In the case of Pakistan, this is all the more true. In the writings on Pakistan more attention is given to the Two Nation Theory – the foundational principle of Pakistan – the issues related to Partition, civil-military relations and so on. The everyday life of

Pakistani society and the citizens of the country never figures in the mainstream writings on Pakistan. Their lives are extremely political yet they do not get the attention of conventional scholarship. However, they are the main themes of literary expressions, paintings, music and films. Literature and products of popular culture are great sources of information to map out the workings of contemporary Pakistan. So far Indian scholarship on Pakistan has paid no attention to this aspect. Some of the articles in this volume try to address literature and popular culture in contemporary Pakistan.

Literature reflects what socio-political and historical writings could not do. Among the different genres of literature, poetry is more expressive in depicting the political and philosophical dimensions of everyday life. Urvashi Sabu in her article 'Pakistani Women Poets and the Dynamics of Religion, Politics and Society: A Comparative Study of Kishwar Naheed and Zehra Nigah' vividly illustrates how poetry reflected the issue of religion and social control over individuals. As feminists both Kishwar Naheed and Zehra Nigah challenged the oppressive mores of religion and society in their own poetic ways. Their poetry is both artistic expressions of high value and a fine document of the Pakistani women's resistance towards repression of all kinds.

The importance of culture in evolving distinct identity for nation states is an established fact. Culture is a broad term which encompasses a whole lot of creative aspects of individuals and communities. Music is a major aspect of national culture which determines the identity of any nation state. Of late the multi-national companies (MNCs) in order to expand their business have started using aspects of national culture to penetrate into new territories. Apart from other aspects of culture, music is used in a big way in this regard. The musical programme *Coke Studio* is one of its kinds. Bidisha Mukherjee in her article 'Coke Studio: A Musical Identity' argues that the Pakistani version of *Coke Studio* is playing more than the role of a contemporary musical programme. According to her it is imparting a sense of pride to the urban youth of Pakistan about their country's rich and diverse culture. It has also tried to create a positive image for Pakistan in the eyes of the international community.

Among the popular art forms cinema is the most influential one. Though the roots of Indian (Bollywood) and Pakistani (Lollywood) cinema have many commonalities, Pakistani cinema has acquired a distinct identity of its own over a period of time. Unfortunately, not much academic attention has been paid to Pakistani cinema unlike its Indian counterpart. Shalmaly Mukherjee's article 'Understanding Pakistani Cinema: A Peek from Across the Border' is an attempt on the part of a young Indian scholar to address this. Mukherjee has constructed a history of Pakistani cinema and mapped out the various trends in it thematically and otherwise.

III

The question of minorities is a vexed political issue in all of the countries in South Asia. In Pakistan it has assumed significance in the context of the division of the country into Bangladesh and Pakistan. The separation of Bangladesh (erstwhile East Pakistan), significantly reduced the percentage of minorities in the population of Pakistan. Post-1971, the Muslim population of Pakistan almost reached 97 per cent and the minorities, including Hindus, Christians, Sikhs, Parsis, Bahais, and so on became a negligible section of the population. In 1974, under Z.A. Bhutto, through a declaration of the National Assembly, Ahmadis were excluded from the community of Muslims.[10] Automatically they became part of the category of minorities. The Islamization drive initiated by Gen. Zia ul-Haq (1977-88) further marginalized the minorities. The anti-Shia thrust of the Islamization process alienated the Shia community in Pakistan, which forms almost 20 per cent of the population, from the mainstream.[11]

Sectarianism is another menace unleashed by the process of Islamization. The Islamization drive has triggered the formation of many Sunni sectarian organizations and they systematically carry out anti-Shia and anti-minority activities in connivance with the state.[12] This has led to the creation of sectarian organizations among the Shia community. Apart from the Shia-Sunni divide in the Muslim world, domestic reasons like the political economy of the Shia-Sunni relations in Pakistan has played a role in precipitating the sectarian violence.[13] This violence which started in the 1980s has acquired many dimensions and has now became one of the major challenges threatening the stability of the social fabric of Pakistan.

Pakistan as a nation state came into being on the basis of the aspirations of the Muslim minority in British India. The demand for Pakistan was raised citing the minority status of Muslims compared to

Hindus in British India and its future implications. When Pakistan was created, Hindus, Christians and Sikhs became prominent minorities in the country. But these minorities were treated by the majority Muslims the same way they were expecting them to be treated by the majority Hindus in undivided India. Shiraz Sheikh in his article 'Religious Minorities in Pakistan: Aspirations and Challenges' elaborates the sad plight of minorities politically, socially and legally. Despite differences in their nature and character all governments, be they military or civilian, have treated minorities in the same manner. As a result of this minorities are a marginalized lot in the national life of Pakistan and their status will remain the same in the near future.

The Blasphemy Laws are the main tool with which the minorities in Pakistan are targeted. These draconian laws empower anybody to take legal action against anyone who disregards Prophet Muhammad. In a broader sense these laws are applicable to all citizens of Pakistan. However, in practice they are mainly used against people from the minority communities, mainly Christians.[14] The Blasphemy Laws are the legacy of Gen. Zia ul-Haq's military regime. In the post-Zia period no government could revoke the Blasphemy Laws though political parties except the religio-political parties are of the opinion that they should be withdrawn. T.K. Jabir in his article 'The Blasphemy Laws and the Minorities in Pakistan' explains how severely the Blasphemy Laws have affected the minorities in Pakistan. People who have supported the demand for the revocation of these laws have either been killed or terrorized. The killing of Salman Taseer, the erstwhile Governor of Punjab, became a chilling example of how the critics of Blasphemy Laws would be treated.

Religious extremism and sectarianism in Pakistan largely strengthened under the Islamization process during the regime of Gen. Zia. The seeds of these social ills were there earlier; however, they got state patronage under Gen. Zia whose priority was to secure political legitimacy for his usurpation of power.[15] The beneficiaries of the state patronage of religious extremism and sectarianism were the religio-political parties like the Jamaat-e-Islami, Jamiatul Ulema-e-Islam and the likes. The religious elite for the first time got an opportunity to dictate terms to the state and they used and enjoyed it tremendously. These religious elite were supported by the social classes which were adversely affected by the policy of nationalization initiated by the regime of Z.A. Bhutto. Azhar Ali in his article 'Religious Extremism and Sectarian Violence in Pakistan: Revisiting Islamization' brings out the role played by the Islamization drive of Gen. Zia in creating the twin evils of religious extremism and sectarianism in Pakistan and its consequent fall-out of the fragmentation of socio-political fabric of the country.

IV

Afghanistan has always been a problem for Pakistan. In 1949 the former opposed Pakistan's entry into the United Nations Organization[16] and later challenged its very existence by supporting the movement for the establishment of an independent Pashtunistan.[17] The intervention of the erstwhile USSR in Afghanistan in 1979 further complicated the relations between the two countries. It also triggered the second phase of the Cold War and suddenly Pakistan became a frontline state for the Western world in confronting the USSR.[18] The notion of *jihad* was invoked in this confrontation. The military regime of Gen. Zia which was ruling Pakistan at that time seized this opportunity to buttress its sagging legitimacy.

The withdrawal of the USSR from Afghanistan and the consequent collapse of it ended the Cold War forever. After the Soviet withdrawal, the USA and her Western allies lost interest in Afghanistan,[19] they only considered Afghanistan as a theatre to fight the USSR. Once the Soviet forces left Afghanistan cracks appeared in the unified opposition to the Soviet occupation. Chaos and political anarchy dominated in the post-occupation Afghanistan. Pakistan made use of this instability to create the Taliban and eventually succeeded in establishing a Pakistan-controlled regime there. Establishing a client regime in Afghanistan as part of the policy of creating 'strategic depth' *vis-à-vis* India was a long-held dream of Pakistani strategic planners.[20] They realized this dream when the Taliban took control of Kabul.

The events of 9/11 had changed this 'strategic gain' upside down. The ensued regime change in Afghanistan once again made Pakistan a frontline state in the American-sponsored 'War on Terror' in Afghanistan.[21] Pakistan had no option but to go with the US in this. As a result it had to abandon whatever strategic assets it had created in Afghanistan. However, Pakistan maintained her secret contacts with the forces that they openly encountered as an ally of the US in her 'War on Terror'. Anwesha Ghosh's article 'Pakistan's

Afghan Policy: The Dynamics of Continuity and Change' discusses the various dimensions of Pakistan's Afghan policy. In the context of the withdrawal of the Western forces from Afghanistan in 2014 one can expect dramatic shifts in Pakistan's policy towards Afghanistan.

From the beginning, Pakistan has been suffering from an identity crisis. Mohammad Ali Jinnah, the founding father of Pakistan, wanted the country to be a modern, democratic Muslim country.[22] However, this idea was criticized by the conservative sections in the country. They wanted Pakistan to be an Islamic country without which there would be no justification for its creation and very existence. The tussle between these two perspectives about Pakistan largely shaped the history of the country. It is important to note that the sections who stood for making Pakistan an Islamic country have established sufficient influence in Pakistan over these years. The 'War on Terror' has further increased the influence of these sections. Yaqoob-Ul-Hassan's article 'Pakistan: Islamic Identity, Jihadist Upsurge and the War on Terror' argues that the US-led 'War on Terror' undoubtedly augmented the Islamic extremist elements and provided legitimacy for their clamour for *jihad*.

The immediate casualty of the 'War on Terror' is democracy and democratic public space in Pakistan. The anti-US sentiment created by the 'War on Terror' has increased radicalization in Pakistan in general and in the Federally Administered Tribal Areas (FATA) and Khyber Pakhtunkhwa in particular. The increased radicalization in turn has reduced the already shrinking democratic space in Pakistan. The beneficiaries of this development are the Islamic political parties, their feeder organizations and Islamic extremist and sectarian forces. Though these organizations have not been able to establish their complete hegemony over the public space, they have achieved the capability of setting the politico-moral agenda of everyday politics in Pakistan. Ashish Shukla's article 'War on Terror and Democracy in Pakistan' elaborates how the 'War on Terror' has affected the process of democratization of Pakistan negatively. He argues that it has strengthened authoritarian elements and the military and led to countless human rights abuses.

In the post-9/11 period, as part of the 'War on Terror', Pakistan was compelled to act against the extremist forces which were created by her. It became necessary to act in the context of the radicalization of the FATA and bordering areas with Afghanistan. The Pakistan army reluctantly took up this task and achieved limited success.[23] The Pakistan army is not trained to undertake counter-terrorism operations. On the contrary, adventurously the army has been helping the extremist and radical elements to carry out covert activities in both India and Afghanistan. When it faced the very same radical elements as enemies it could not perform the task of carrying out counter-terrorism operations as expected. Nishu Sharma's article 'Terrorism in Pakistan and Fragile Counter-terrorism Strategy' outlines the above-mentioned dilemma of Pakistan army and the pitfalls of the counter-terrorism strategy pursued by it.

Like any other country in the world, Pakistan also conducts her foreign policy and relations on the basis of fulfilling her national interests in both the short and long term. Among her relations with foreign countries, relations with the US and China are of prime importance. Pakistan-India relation is an adversarial one and extremely complex. Pakistan's relationship with Afghanistan is also problematic. According to many Pakistani strategic planners, the country is surrounded by enemies and it is important to have alliances from within and without the region. Pakistan's relations with the US and China are to be viewed in this regard. While for Pakistan China is an all-weather friend,[24] the relationship with the US is smooth and complex at times. It is largely because the Pakistan-US relations are not based on Pakistan's terms, America's larger strategic calculations shape it from time to time.

The relations between the US and Pakistan according to some scholars determine the domestic politics and external behaviour of Pakistan. The famous dictum that Pakistan is dominated/controlled by three As (Allah, Army and America) is an illustration of this notion.[25] This notion is not completely baseless. Pakistan has all through functioned as an outpost and a client state for the US in protecting and augmenting the latter's strategic interests in Asia. The Pakistani elite has immensely benefitted from this patron-client relations between the US and Pakistan. In the changed strategic context of post-9/11, strains have appeared in it yet it will continue in the near future as it is. Sumit Kumar Jha in his article 'US-Pakistan Relations: Retrospect and Prospect' elaborates and explains the complexities in the US-Pakistan relations and provides some valuable insights regarding its future. In the existing politico-strategic environment both countries need each other and it might remain so for some time to come.

V

The single most important issue which is hampering the normalization of relations between India and Pakistan is related to Jammu & Kashmir (J&K). Pakistan is not ready to accept the finality of J&K's accession to India in 1947.[26] According to various Pakistani narratives, J&K was forced to accede to India. Pakistani narratives point out that being a Muslim majority princely state J&K should have been a part of Pakistan, as the country is formed on the basis of the Two Nation Theory. India counters this argument by pointing out that Maharaja Hari Singh of J&K, the legitimate political authority in J&K during the time of British withdrawal from India, had decided to accede to India in the event of the Pakistan-sponsored tribal attack. The decision of the Maharaja was endorsed by the people of J&K under the leadership of the National Conference and Sheikh Abdullah.[27] For Pakistan, the accession of J&K with India symbolizes the incompleteness of Partition.[28] On the contrary, India considers the accession of the Muslim majority J&K as a validation of the superiority of 'secular and composite' Indian nationalism over the 'communal' Muslim nationalism of Pakistan.

President Gen. Pervez Musharraf, despite the Pakistan military's position on the J&K issue, moved forward and put forth some proposals for the resolution of the problem of J&K.[29] The American pressure on Pakistan and the deteriorating economic and internal security situations within the country compelled Gen. Musharaff to move in this direction. When Asif Ali Zardari became the President of Pakistan in 2008 the peace overtures from Pakistan assumed more seriousness. The strategy was twofold: weaken the forces of reaction (military and religious extremists) internally and build a new relationship with India based on trust and friendship. According to President Zardari 'destinies of the people of both Pakistan and India and the development of the entire region lies in friendly, cooperative and good neighbourly relations between the two countries'.[30] The regime changes in Pakistan have influenced Pakistan's Kashmir policy too. Samir Ahmad Bhat in his article titled 'Pakistan's Changing Policy on Kashmir: Dimensions and Determinants' describes the changes which have taken place in Pakistan's policy towards J&K over a period of time and its possible fallouts.

The centre of the 'Ideology of Pakistan' is Islam. The wide variety of Islamic practices in the landmass of Pakistan is not allowing homogenization of Islam despite the attempts of the religio-political elite in the country. According to the Pakistani position, since J&K is a Muslim majority state it should be part of Pakistan. Here Pakistanis are only going by the Muslim majority character of J&K. The Islamic practices in J&K and the rest of Pakistan are radically different. Kashmiri Islam is anchored around Sufi traditions of syncretism and coexistence. Also it exhibits certain characters peculiar to Kashmir. The difference in the way Kashmiris and Pakistanis understand, practice and experience Islam became one of the main reasons for the people of J&K to accede to India than Pakistan. Deepali Raghunath Khaire in her article titled 'Pakistan's Incoherent Claim on Kashmir' explains this difference convincingly and argues that this aspect has made Pakistan's claim over the territory of Kashmir is weak and incoherent. Unless Pakistan looks at J&K as an area where majority of the people practice Islam in a manner which is evolved according to the historical advancement specific to it and that makes Pakistan's claim over J&K illogical and baseless would help Pakistan to device sensible policies towards the resolution of the problem.

As mentioned in the beginning, the contributions in this volume on Pakistan by young scholars in India clearly show the diverse academic concerns of them. These scholars are willing to take up hitherto untouched issues related to Pakistan as their subjects of analysis and study. Thereby these scholars are trying to open a new path in the studies on Pakistan in India. The existing Indian scholarship on Pakistan is largely accused of hyper-nationalist and perception-driven attitude. This can be said in equal measure about the existing Pakistani scholarship on India.

It is important to note that though the articles in this volume mark a rupture in the tone and tenor of the existing Indian scholarship on Pakistan, they maintain aspects of continuity too. As scholars living in the Indian milieu it is quite natural that they have to imbibe elements of the existing body of knowledge about Pakistan. However, these young new scholars are not stopping there. They are moving forward in their quest to understand Pakistan equipped with new methodologies, sources and tools of analysis. In this process they have explored hitherto unfamiliar terrain which their predecessors never dared to tread.

Notes

1. The innumerable numbers of op-ed articles appearing in the mainstream newspapers in India are examples of this pattern of thinking.
2. For details see Shabnum Tejani, *Indian Secularism: A Social and Intellectual History, 1890-1950*, Bloomington: Indiana University Press, 2008.
3. Ashok Kapur, *Pakistan in Crisis*, London: Routledge, 1991, p. 93.
4. Most of the works on Pakistan by Westerners give this idea. The themes of their writings revolve around the inability of the 'backward Muslim dominated polities' to modernize and secularize. See Stephen P. Cohen et al., *The Future of Pakistan*, Washington D.C.: The Brookings Institution, 2011, p. 57.
5. See Farhan Hanif Siddiqi, *The Politics of Ethnicity in Pakistan: The Baloch, Sindhi and Mohajir Ethnic Movements*, New York: Routledge, 2012.
6. Oskar Verkaaik, 'Muhajir Politics: Ethnicity, Islam and the Muhajir Quami Movement', in Ravi Kalia (ed.), *Pakistan: From the Rhetoric of Democracy to the Rise of Militancy*, New Delhi: Routledge, 2011, pp. 49-51.
7. See Khawar Mumtaz, Yameema Mitha and Bilquis Tahira, *Pakistan: Tradition and Change*, Oxford: Oxfam GB, 2003, pp. 53-8.
8. Stephen Alter, *Amritsar to Lahore: A Journey Across the India-Pakistan Border*, Philadelphia: University of Pennsylvania Press, 2001, p. 79.
9. See K.K. Aziz, *The Murder of History: A Critique of History Textbooks Used in Pakistan*, Lahore: Vanguard Books, 1993.
10. Sadia Saeed, 'Political Fields and Religious Movements: The Exclusion of the Ahmadiyya Community in Pakistan', p. 190, URL: http://sociology.yale.edu/sites/default/files/saeed_ppst.pdf (accessed on 19 August 2013).
11. Iftikhar H. Malik, *Religious Minorities in Pakistan* (Report), p. 13, URL: http://www.minorityrights.org/admin/Download/pdf/MRGPPakistanReport.pdf (accessed on 19 August 2013).
12. Mariam Abou Zahab, 'The Regional Dimension of Sectarian Conflicts in Pakistan', in Christophe Jaffrelot (ed.), *Pakistan: Nationalism without a Nation?*, New Delhi: Manohar, 2002, p. 115.
13. For details see Frédéric Grare, 'Pakistan: The Myth of an Islamist Peril', Policy Brief, Carnegie Endowment for International Peace,

February 2006, URL: http://www.carnegieendowment.org/files/45.grare.final.pdf (accessed on 19 August 2013).

14. Hassan Abbas, *Pakistan's Drift to Extremism: Allah, the Army and the America's War on Terror*, New York: M.E. Sharpe Inc., 2005, p. 104.
15. Tahir Wasti, *The Application of Islamic Criminal Law in Pakistan: Sharia in Practice*, Leiden: Brill, 2009, p. 283.
16. Shahid Javed Burki, *South Asia in the New World Order: The Role of Regional Cooperation*, Oxon: Routledge, 2011, p. 24.
17. Chrisophe Jaffrelot, 'Islamic Identity and Ethnic Tensions', in Christophe Jaffrelot (ed.), *A History of Pakistan and its Origins*, London: Anthem Press, 2004, p. 31.
18. Robert G. Sutter, *The United States in Asia*, Plymouth: Rowman and Littlefield Publishers, 2009, p. 131.
19. Larry P. Goodson, *Afghanistan's Endless War: State Failure, Regional Politics and the Rise of the Taliban*, Washington: University of Washington Press, 2001, p. 147.
20. Aparna Pande, *Explaining Pakistan's Foreign Policy: Escaping India*, New York: Routledge, 2011, p. 59.
21. Thomas P. Thornton, 'The Ongoing Conflict: Pakistan and India', in Craig Baxter (ed.), *Pakistan on the Brink: Politics, Economics and Society*, Oxford: Lexington Books, 2004, p. 28.
22. Stephen Philip Cohen, *The Idea of Pakistan*, Washington: Brookings Institution, 2004, p. 42.
23. For details see Seth G. Jones and C. Christine Fair, *Counterinsurgency in Pakistan*, Santa Monica: Rand Corporation, 2010.
24. Teresita C. Schaffer, 'India Next Door, China Over the Horizon: View from South Asia' in Ashley J. Tellis, Travis Tanner and Jessica Keough (eds.), *Asia Responds to its Rising Powers: China and India*, Seattle: The National Bureau of Asian Research, 2011, p. 287.
25. Samina Ahmad, 'Reviving State Legitimacy in Pakistan', in Simon Chesterman, Michael Ignatieff and Ramesh Chandra Thakur (eds.), *Making States Work: State Failure and Crisis of Governance*, Tokyo: United Nations University Press, 2005, p. 156.
26. Anne Noronha dos Santos, *Military Intervention and Secession in South Asia: The Cases of Bangladesh, Sri Lanka, Kashmir and Punjab*, Westport: Pareger, 2007, p. 69.
27. Amitabh Mattoo, 'India's International Relations: The Search for Stability, Space and Strength', in Alyssa Ayres and Philip K. Oldenburg (eds.), *India Briefing: Takeoff at Last?* New York: M.E. Sharpe, Inc., 2005, p. 100.

28. Aparna Pande, *Explaining Pakistan's Foreign Policy: Escaping India*, New York: Routledge, 2011, p. 39.
29. S. Riffat Hussain, 'Resolving the Kashmir Dispute: Blending Realism with Justice', *The Pakistan Development Review*, vol. 48, no. 4, pt. II, Winter 2009, pp. 1023-4.
30. Cited in the official website of the President of the Islamic Republic of Pakistan, URL: http://www.presidentofpakistan.gov.pk/index.php?lang=en&opc=6 (accessed on 19 August 2013).

POLITICS AND ECONOMY

CHAPTER 2

Pakistan through the Kaleidoscope of Modernization

Dipanwita Roy Ghatak

Modernization and modernity have been core concepts in analysing and understanding societies of the developing world, especially ever since decolonization came to be the accepted norm around the globe. The indicators of modernization have been essentially Western. A degree of uniformity when it comes to social structures and values, institutionalization and a way of social and political life, came to be the desired 'modern' world across states. Modernization theory's most influential proponent, Karl Marx, claimed that economically developed societies show the future to less developed societies. Not only Marx but also Friedrich Nietzsche, and everyone from Lerner to Bell, predicted the decline of religion in the wake of modernization. However, religion and spiritual beliefs have not faded. Instead, social and political debates on religious and emotionally charged issues such as euthanasia have grown increasingly salient and a resurgence of fundamentalist Islam has established a major cleavage in international politics. The process of modernization is not simple. It means taking in the new but not always throwing out the old. Thus a coexistence of tradition and modernity in a completely new identity is often the end product in the process. Even though today the Western developed economies and societies are not held as superior models everywhere, a core concept of the modernization theory seems valid today. Industrialization produces pervasive social and cultural consequences, from rising educational levels to changing gender roles. Industrialization is seen as the central element of modernization process that affects most other elements of society.

In recent years, research and theory on socio-economic development have given rise to two contending schools of thought on the process of modernizing a society. One school emphasizes the convergence of values as a result of 'modernization', the overwhelming economic and political forces that drive cultural change. This school predicts the decline of traditional values and their replacement with 'modern' values. The other school of thought emphasizes the persistence of traditional values despite economic and political changes. This school assumes that values are relatively independent of economic conditions and industrial development. Consequently, this school of thought predicts that convergence around some set of 'modern' values is quite unlikely and that traditional values will continue to exert an independent influence on the cultural changes caused by economic development.[1]

In the post-war United States, a version of modernization theory emerged that viewed underdevelopment as a direct consequence of a country's internal characteristics: traditional economies, traditional psychological and cultural traits, and traditional institutions.[2] From this perspective, traditional values were not only mutable but could and should be replaced by modern values, enabling these societies to follow the virtually inevitable path of capitalist development. The causal agents in this developmental process were naturally the rich, developed nations that stimulate the modernization of 'backward' nations through economic, cultural, and military assistance. These arguments were criticized as blaming the victim, because modernization theorists assumed that underdeveloped societies needed to adopt 'modern' values and institutions to become developed societies.[3] Modernization theory gradually came to be criticized, and eventually it was pronounced dead.[4] The post-war version of the modernization theory tended to neglect external factors, such as colonialism, imperialism, and newer forms of economic and political domination. The emerging neo-Marxist and World Systems theorists emphasized the extent to which rich countries exploited poor countries, locking them in positions of powerlessness and structural dependence. Andre Gunder Frank and Immanuel Wallerstein's works especially propounded this view vehemently in the international academic field. Underdevelopment, as Frank put it, is developed.[5] This new school of thought conveyed the message to poor countries that poverty has nothing to do with internal problems, it is, in fact the fault of global capitalism, and consequently modernization or the lack of it too. World System theorists have not been immune from criticism, especially from those who claim that the international economic order enables more than it constrains nascent economies to grow and prosper and that foreign investment does trigger growth and stimulate competition; that is however another debate. Evidence from around the world indicates that economic development tends to propel societies in a roughly predictable direction. Industrialization leads to occupational specialization, rising educational levels, rising income levels, and eventually brings unforeseen changes in gender roles, attitudes toward authority and sexual norms; declining fertility rates; broader political participation; and a less easily led public. Determined elites in control of the state and the military sometimes have tried to resist these changes, but in the long run, it becomes increasingly costly to do so and the probability of change rises. Paradoxically, it has come into observation that modernization can actually strengthen traditional values. Elites in underdeveloped nations who attempt to mobilize a population for social change often use traditional cultural appeals, as in Japan's Meiji Restoration. More recently radical reformist groups in Algeria used Islam to gain peasant support, but as an unintended result strengthened fundamentalist religious values.[6] Thus, cultural identity can be used to promote the interests of a group and in the process may strengthen cultural diversity. Generally, 'as global integration intensifies, the currents of multiculturalism swirl faster. Under these conditions, which include the juxtaposition of ethnically distinct labour forces and communities, the politics of identity tends to substitute for the civic politics of nation building.'[7]

Different societies follow different trajectories of modernization and growth even when they are subjected to the same forces of economic development, in part because situation-specific factors, such as cultural heritage, also shape how a particular society develops. Max Weber argued that traditional religious values have an enduring influence on the institutions of a society.[8] Following this tradition, Samuel P. Huntington argues that the world is divided into eight major civilizations or 'cultural zones' based on cultural differences that have persisted for centuries.[9] These zones were shaped by religious traditions that are still powerful today, despite the forces of modernization. The zones are Western Christianity, the Orthodox world, the Islamic world, and the Confucian, Japanese, Hindu, African, and Latin American zones.

Scholars from various disciplines have observed that distinctive cultural traits endure over long periods of time in the face of the forces of modernity, and continue to shape a society's political and economic performance. In this context I would like to cite as example the case of modernization in Pakistan. Pakistan's modernization has taken a distinct form. It is manifestly employing Western norms and institutionalizing them without essentially realizing modernization ideals. The Western forms, in practice are often adopted on the surface but often they end up serving traditional functions. In some cases, one part of an institution may be seen to lean towards modern norms while the other parts may be swept by Islamic revivalist fervour. The result more often than not is imbalanced development. Islamic revivalism has emerged as a parallel force of social change in Pakistan. Three major trends are influencing social discourses in Pakistan: Indigenization, Modernization and Islamization. These processes do affect, change and give rise to new social norms and institutions that affect everyday life and policy making too.

Pakistani society has been slowly but surely moving along the path of modernism. The mode of production has fundamentally changed. Pakistan is no longer an agrarian society except in some remote rural pockets, and is no longer steeped in occupational castes and the obligatory barter of goods and the *seypi* system. Monetization of the economy has really proved to be the main catalyst in transforming social relations.[10] The heart of the problem of imbalanced modernization lies in the uneven state of economic modernization. While some industries have leapt into the post-industrial state, some are still stuck in traditional modes of production. Pakistan is a nuclear state but hardly any city has an adequate sewerage treatment plant. Pakistan is a strategic partner of the US in the Cold War and in the 'war against terrorism', and all other anti-terrorism drives, yet ethnic strife divide the policy-making minds of Pakistan. Millions of Pakistanis live or work abroad. The Pakistan diaspora today links remote Pakistani villages with Europe, North America and the Middle East. Globalization has visibly reached and flourished in Pakistan and yet cultural norms, beliefs and values remain anchored to traditions and customs, in fact they are very much prioritized.

Historically, a state has a critical role in the processes of development and modernization. In the developed and modern societies of today, for example, Britain and Germany, it was the state that led the transformation from a feudal to a modern society, particularly through the legislative initiatives of the nineteenth century and early twentieth centuries. In Pakistan, like in other Third World countries, the state is the only institution that can effectively lead orderly social transformation and cultural change. The Pakistani state has steadily failed to succeed in this role. From the beginning, more than one idea of Pakistan has defined the state and society, contributing to an ideological incoherence and political instability. Pakistan is a pluralist society nestling plural ethnic and linguistic identities but when it comes to the state it follows unitary and centrist policies.[11] Islam has come to be employed to justify this feature. Thus state and ideology have inherently been in opposition to the essentially pluralistic society of Pakistan. Islamic organizations operate almost like estates within the state. *Ulema* issue *fatwa*s that are binding on the government to follow on secular, temporal issues like the issue of Kashmir, whether or not to trade with India or send a women's sports team to the Olympics. General Musharraf's government denied any role in sending *jehadi*s into 'India-held' Kashmir but the leader of Lashkar-e-Tayyba, Hafiz Saeed proclaimed that the Kashmir *jehad* will continue. The state ignores these challenges to its authority. Pakistani state and society have gone through periods of political and social turmoil punctuated by zones of peace. Military coups have swung the country from periods of strong state and weak society to short phases of strong society and weak state. Pakistan is gradually turning into a weak state and weak society. The state's authority has steadily diffused since the 1980s.

Pakistan's society has gradually evolved from a dualistic to a tripartite structure since its inception. The so-called traditional and modern divide dates back to its colonial history but the third component, that is, institutionalized Islam has evolved after independence. In essence these three are parallel sub-cultures each with distinct values and lifestyle. This division has visibly permeated many social institutions. Education has come to have three separate curricula, approaches and institutions, i.e. schools whose medium of instruction is English and schools which instruct in vernacular languages and the third one being centres of religious (Islamic) education, *madrasa*s. Vernacular schools essentially cater to the lower classes and traditionalists especially in the rural sectors, whereas English-medium schools are suited to the rich segment of the populace. The Islamic institutions have historically trained Imams, but they have evolved with the state's patronage to provide not only training for religious leaders but also temporal education.

Three parallel but distinct trends corresponding to these three streams of social change have also affected femininity and gender roles.[12] It is very visible in the public space. The modern Westernized woman earns her daily bread alongside men while the traditional woman is expected to stay at home. Islamic women take part in the public sphere, but they carve out segregated institutions by wearing full body *burqa*, head covering *hijab* and taking up jobs and social leadership roles. This tripartite division in the process of social change is also visible in the realms of class.

The above clearly reflect that modernization in such diverse societies like that of Pakistan can never be a uniform process. While some segments will gallop ahead, others will fall behind and yet some will simply refuse to budge and cling on to the glories of the past. Such tripartition of the Pakistani social structure and its segmentation into sub-cultural groups are indications of the growing internal differentiation of society and culture. The processes of modernization coupled with social change are carving parallel tracks within the economy and society, laying separate paths of development by class, mode of living, ideology and occupation.

One distinct characteristic that separates Pakistan's process of modernization and social change from many Third World countries is its cultural roots in Islam and Muslim nationalism. Pakistan's national discourse has one constant, namely its commitment to Islamic identity. A puritanical model of Islam is being promoted and advocated in Pakistan as an alternative to Westernization. The Islamic mode of living has grown into a lifestyle in Pakistani society.

Islamization has taken two forms in Pakistan. First, Pakistani society has been visibly Islamized. Television and radio devote many hours everyday to sermons and prayers. During the month of Ramadan, the stricture on fasting is followed strictly and rarely is anyone seeing eating publicly. *Zakat,* a wealth tax, has been deducted compulsorily from Muslims' savings accounts since 1979.[13] What is queer is that this process of Islamization of public life has proceeded with the adoption of material culture and economic globalization.

Second is the acceptance of Islamism as a normative way of life. Islam was offered as the third alternative, in contrast with capitalism and socialism. In Pakistan some class segments have adopted the Islamic way of life, creating an Islamic sector within society. An Islamic mode of life was institutionalized during General Zia's rule.[14] When he assumed power after removing Bhutto, he behaved like a despot. When a mass movement led by religious leaders started in 1977, he almost panicked and went on making concession after concession to please the *ulema* and other fundamentalists. Pakistan went through its most conservative period during Zia-ul-Haq's time. Zia, both on account of his beliefs and political needs, sought to impose conservative Islam. He made Islam his main political constituency. He did so by introducing *hudood* punishments, cutting off hands of thieves, stoning adulterers to death. On the contrary, the Koran says that an ideal Islamic society will be just and equitable. According to Koran, the dynamics of social structure work on dialectical interaction between the *mustakbirin* and *mustad'ifin* (i.e. the powerful and arrogant, and the weak and the oppressed).[15] The key Koranic terms in this respect are *adl* and *ihsan* (i.e., justice and benevolence). Pakistan from its very inception has favoured the rich, powerful, influential, feudal, bureaucratic and military elite. The poor and oppressed have always been on the receiving end in the Pakistani society like in any other developing society. Though the Prophet had prohibited absentee landlords sharing crop with cultivators (*muhaliqa* or *mukhabira*) it has been rampant in Pakistan since its formation. The feudal elite have always enjoyed positions of power and influence in Pakistani politics and society and no government has neither tried nor succeeded in breaking feudalism, ironically when no Islamic society can be feudal. The government has in fact tried to reinforce it regardless of its political rhetoric. The Pakistani society has proved to be like any other society, exploitative and unjust with formal strictures of Islamization laid down by the *ulema* under the influence of their own social context.

Islamization as a way of life parallel to the actors of normal secular, modern life. Islamic banks presumably offer interest-free services and cater to large segments of the population. Islamic studies are a compulsory part of the educational curricula even in medicine and engineering. In education the effect is quite large; Islamic history, theology and ideology have permeated almost all the courses. Sharia laws and Shariat courts function as separate yet parallel systems of justice.[16] They include the *hudood* punishments for drinking and theft as well as the *qisas* and *diyat* legistations, which is blood money to compensate for murder.[17] Islamic cultural institutions, administrative boards and research bodies have multiplied. The bitter side of this parallel realm of life is that vigilantism has increased, especially targeting minorities and harassing small sects. Local *maulvi*s empowered by the Islamic creed declare *fatwa*s and dispense justice. Such institutions could flourish only because the state has allowed them to. Pakistan today has turned into a county of anxieties. Branded a terrorist state, it often finds itself the victim of terrorist acts. Jehadist outfits originally born to fight the USSR have morphed into a number of terrorist outfits sabotaging Kashmir's internal strife for freedom, which in turn convolutes the tensions between Pakistan and its biggest immediate neighbour India.

How can a state which relies on religious normative views to organize its public order embrace modernization? Social life in Pakistan has been simultaneously evolving along two tracks: Islamization of the public sphere and modernization of the private sphere and also the economy. It's not that orthodox Islamists ban the use of modern products of technology, in fact they liberally use them within the limits of affordability. They have been readily adopting air travel, recent advances in medicine, television, cell phones or the pursuit of riches for that matter. It is plain to see that Pakistani moral order is cracking up under the pressures of all these contradictory theories on right and wrong.

The Islamic mode of living is a system of rules and values. An idealized Islamic society has always been one of the ideas of Pakistan. After Independence the *ulema* and Islamic political parties, Jamaat-e-Islami, being in the forefront, first pressed for the formal enactment of Islamic laws. They did not really have anything missing from their agenda, be it electoral politics, agitations or even violence, whatever the situation called for. Moulana Mawdudi, the head of this organization, has been the propounder of the ideology and the theoretician behind this movement. His speeches and his vision of Pakistani society based on puritanical Islam appealed to the rising middle class, who were still trying to grasp the meaning of modernization and cope with the strong currents of social change. The subsequent defeat of the Islamists in the elections combined with General Ayub's military rule did restrain this trend. However, the failure in electoral politics redirected Jamaat towards capturing the attention of the youth. Its student wing the Islami Jamiat-e-Talaba (IJT) became the nursery for young Islamists. It also organzed a sort of standing force to mount agitations against ideological opponents. It even followed a well-tested military approach of binding new recruits into small groups which in turn gives them a sense of belonging. This proved to be very effective in attracting village boys and girls lost in the city colleges. Surprisingly this body has been very popular in the student elections of colleges and universities, particularly in engineering, medicine and science faculties. This is how Islamic segments of the urban middle class have been built from bottom up.[18] It is these segements that are the driving force behind Islamic revivalism. The students of the *madrasas* are not the vanguards of this trend as many believe; they mostly belong to the rural sectors of society with not much influence in the affluent public sector. Another agency that has served to build Islamic structures in the public domain is the Tablighis. As a social movement it has contributed greatly to observances of Islamic tenets. General Zia's military rule did quite a lot to institutionalize Islamic laws and practices.

The issue of Islamization of Pakistani society is not only an internal matter, many external stimuli have contributed in leading up to the state of affairs that is today. The USA encouraged Islamic groups in Pakistan during the Cold War as counterweights to the socialist influences of Soviet Union. Fearing domino effect, the Afghan *jehad* against Soviet Union was lavishly funded and armed by USA through Pakistan. Gradually Afghani tribal interpretation of Islam seeped through the borders and entered Pakistan, planting in its wake terrorism and sectarian violence. Also, even though the effect has been subtle, Pakistani workers in Saudi Arabia and the Gulf brought back not only Islamist conservatism but also modern consumerism. The oil wealth-driven Wahhabism, together with the influences of the Iranian revolution have together created a mix of staunch Islamist lifestyle combined with the edge of competitiveness brought in by globalization and modernity, making for a unique stage in the process of modernization of Pakistan. Islamic extremism is the unintended consequence of the privatization of *jehad*. Social life in Pakistan at the beginning of the twenty-first century is deficient in peace, security and harmony.

Social change often erodes established norms bringing about a period of uncertainty. New beliefs and value systems eventually do fill such a normative void, but they are seldom altogether new. More often than not, they grow out of traditions with new understandings of meanings and symbols attached to them. That tradition and modernity are not mutually exclusive but in fact complementary as has been repeatedly demonstrated by the history of social change. In Pakistan, caste, clan or tribal titles have been resurrected as surnames after they had begun to be abandoned in the 1950s and 1960s. The flip side of this trend has been nepotism and corruption in modern bureaucracies reflecting the incorporation of family values and kinship obligations in public activities. Islamic revivalism has proved to be the most pervasive form of tradition that has been reinvented. It promotes a puritanical vision of society organized around Shariat laws. What is to be taken note of here is that traditional or modern versions of Pakistani culture are not un-Islamic but they have their roots in the folk or spiritual Islamic traditions of rural origins.[19] The envisioned Islamic order is believed to be modern and urban in its essence, but it is also to be legalistic and textual in approach. It basically calls for resurrecting institutions that its proponents interpret to be 'original and eternal' in values.

Islamic revivalism is the ideology of those climbing out of an agrarian or feudal milieu into an urban, commercial order. It offers a belief system for the recently prospering and largely urban class segments of professionals and small-scale entrepreneurs. As a social movement Islamic revivalism in Paksitan parallels the contemporaray evangelism of Europe and the USA and the messianic Judaism of Israel. This project in Pakistan promotes social conservatism, emphasizing ritual piety, women's segregation, rigid dress code, ascetic life and a collectivist ethos. All in all, Islamic class segments in the Pakistani society combine modern material culture with traditional norms and conservative values in an attempt to forge an Islamic model for an urbanizing society that badly needs a new social and moral order. It has incorporated notions such as welfarism, social justice, and human rights within its puritanical philosophy. Puritanical Islam is displacing folk beliefs and spiritual traditions of historic Islam in Pakistan.[20] So far this model has delivered little to improve everyday life. Islamists observe social norms such as punctuality, efficiency or respect for rules just as laxly as modernists and traditionalists. All these paradoxes have given rise to a characteristic phase in social change whose contradictions are apparent in public as well as private life.

However, two basic questions arise from the acknowledgement of Islam's undeniable presence and role in Pakistani society.

- How Islam affects areas of social life that are outside the ecclesiastical realms of the religion, i.e. other than spiritual beliefs, practices, beliefs, experiences and solidarity?
- How social life in turn affects Islam as a functioning institution in spheres of its ideology, patterned behaviour and practices?

As for the former the story of the impact of Islamic discourse on social life can be characterized as transformative, almost revolutionary when it comes to public behaviour. A very visible impact has been on the increased religious piety in everyday life. Up to the late 1970s a very sizeable minority, predominantly the elderly population, performed obligatory *namaz* daily. The Islamization of the 1980s saw a culture of public observance of prayers and pieties slowly evolve into a norm. Today no one is surprised if during a flight someone starts to get down on their knees to pray on the aisles. Pakistani cricket team was photographed lining up to pray on the grounds at a match with India in March 2004, a practice almost unthinkable in the 1970s and the 1980s. Even during meetings and conferences, the call to *namaz* makes even the most unorthodox of Muslims suspend their duties and line up for prayers. Earlier the religiously inclined would choose to pray in private and mostly refrain from public demonstration.

What is queer to note is that Islamic observances have swept large sections of the middle and upper classes in the city but in comparison the poor and illiterate have not become more religious than they were in the past. Islamic revivalism has mostly been an urban phenomenon. It is in the cities where the ideas and actions of Islamization are essentially formulated, discussed and enacted. Islamic parties and their student, youth wings are based in cities, although there are pockets of rural or tribal revivalism in the Khyber Pakhtunkhwa tribal and northern belt.

The basic difference between urban and rural Islam in Pakistan is that the former tends to be more puritanical and textual compared to the spiritual or folk thrust of beliefs and practices in rural or tribal areas. In the urban areas Islam is interpreted to the people and led by *ulema* while in the rural areas it is more inspired by *sufi*s and saints. The rural version of Islam in Pakistan is more easygoing and tolerant. What is interesting to note is that the upwardly mobile village families who are educated and switch to industrial and service occupations are drawn to relatively more exegeses-driven Islamic discourse. The personal-salvation Islam infused by *sufi*s yields to Sharia norms and denominationally defined practices. Essentially veiling has been a lower middle-class custom but in the 1990s it has materialized into the *niqaab* with face covered but eyes visible, mostly among conservative Muslim women, many of whom fully participate in public life. Farm women work in fields and go about without covering their faces, but when their sons become clerks or overseers, the young women of the family begin to observe *purdah* and wear a *burqa* covering both body and face. When a family becomes rich and rises to the upper echelons of society its women may discard *burqa*.[21] The custom of wearing a *hijab* among female students and professionals is quite recent and a modern form of the *burqa* which covers the head leaving the face open.

Norms regarding women's modesty vary across social, geographical and class divides. The boys and girls coming to study in the big cities often fervently vote for Islamic student bodies in the college or university elections, while back home, in national or local elections they vote for the Pakistan People's Party. Thus strangely the social context has a strong bearing on commitment to Islam.[22] The rural-urban differences become even starker when it comes to examining whether the issue of Islamization in Pakistan is for the sake of the religion of Islam or for Muslims. Visibly the seat of political, economic and social power, the urbanite population is more steeped in the puritanical, vigilantist version of Islam rather than the more liberal *sufi* variant popular in rural Pakistan. Thus as a family moves up into the upper stratas of society or gets a respectable job in the city, behavioural patterns change, it all becomes contextualized.

The Islamic discourse has also given rise to various social service organizations, universities, schools, associations, clubs, labour unions, student bodies and professional societies. Islamic organizations have multiplied to a point where they constitute a distinct sector within civil society. Even with data limitations it is safe to say that *madrasa*s and seminaries have increased manifold since the 1980s. With introduction of Islamic studies at all educational levels, including engineering and medical study programmes, teaching opportunities have opened for graduates of seminaries. *Madrasa*s and seminaries issue juridical opinions on people's behaviour, social trends and public policies. General Musharraf during his term in office accepted seminary diplomas as equivalent to college degrees for eligibility to contest the 2002 elections.[23] Such measures undoubtedly enhanced the importance and influence of theological schools. Almost every social institution today has developed an Islamic stream, organized formally as well as informally as a club, circle and networks. A deep fissure runs through the landscape of Pakistan's civil society dividing Islamic and secular organizations.

Islamization has affected people's images and views about how they live. This is the imagined culture which has been suffused with Islamic imagery. Many deliberate efforts have contributed to this phenomenon. Be it the portrayal of history to make a case for the new state of Pakistan as a nation or the shadow of such efforts in literature, art and cinema. Yet, the lived culture, which is how people actually live, is quite different and continues to be driven by secular socio-economic factors. Although Pakistani television, and print media often portrays a picture that Islam is the chief preoccupation of the people it is not the case. Individuals are very much driven by acquisitive interests and material considerations with strong inclinations to disregard laws and obligations in everyday life like in any other country. Ethnic and religious ties have repeatedly clashed with the process of Islamization and Islam has often lost. For example the Jamaat's hold over Karachi's voters broke down with the rise of Muhajir (the refugee) consciousness. Pashtoon or Balochi solidarity has repeatedly swept aside appeals to Islamic unity in elections. In universities and colleges the IJT faces stiff competition from ethnic or caste/clan organizations.

While Islamic discourse has had its impact on society, the changing socio-political patterns and trends of Pakistani society too, in turn have had their impact on the ideology of Islam. In the early years of Pakistan, the Islamic narrative emphasized on fostering righteous behaviour among individuals and creating an Islamic constitution for the state. The Islamists believed that the righteous Muslims would vote them into power and hence put their faith in democracy. In this period the Islamic discourse was anti-communist and steered a middle path between capitalism and socialism.

Then emerged the doctrine of populist socialism. In this era the Islamic welfare state and *musawat-i-Muhammadi* (Muhammad's social justice) became ideals for the Islamic order.[24] It was quite a notable reformulation of earlier concepts and goals. During the period of Islamization of the Pakistani society under Zia's rule, cultural transformation was viewed as the path to Islamic order. This programme attempted to reorder social relations and cultural transformations through *hudood* and other laws, thus bringing in the power of the Koran and Sharia to operate side by side secular, temporal matters of the society and even override secular powers and actions of the state. This led to the downplay of democracy as an element of Islamic order. The support garnered by Zia's government from Islamic parties had a feedback effect on the Islamic narrative. It was argued that authoritarianism came to be accepted if used to advance Islamic goals. Liberal Islamic viewpoints were gradually driven off the public platform as a shift emerged towards conservatism in Islamic discourse. Segregation of women came to be idealized. Sectarian differences were highlighted. Militancy for Islam was justified as a necessary means for bringing about Islamic order. Cultural traditions were often invested with Islamic legitimacy.

Another trend that has come to be in this search for identity amidst social change in Islamized Pakistan is the invention of traditions. The Islamic discourse of Pakistan legitimizes its political objectives on the sacred traditions of the early days of Islam in Arabia and reinforces practices that emerged in Iran or medieval India. The patriarchal family, arranged marriage or landlordism are examples of social practices legitimized as elements of Islamic tradition by a majority of *ulema* although these have been questioned by the liberal-reformist interpreters of Islam.

The rise of Taliban in Afghanistan (1996) had its effect in Pakistan. Many urban Islamists were seduced by the so-called purity of the Taliban traditions. The Taliban's staunch anti-Westernism made them all the more popular among various conservative sections of the population. Green has for a long time been the Islamic colour. People wear green turbans or scarves as a mark of their faith and devotion. The Taliban wore black turbans which became a mark of resurgent Islam. Soon the black turban came to be associated with the tradition of the Prophet.[25] Thus again a new tradition was invented.

The question that arises here is how the process of Islamization affects modernization in Pakistan. The two processes, curiously, have largely been compartmentalized in their respective spheres: material and legal or cultural. They clash as well as complement each other in various ways. The result is a state of moral uncertainty and social cleavage. The Islamic discourse lays claim to its own form of modernity.

It locates the origins of human rights, social justice and even scientific progress in Islam and the civilization it spawned. It espouses these values and ideals in abstract and maintains that they have been appropriated by the West. Yet while translating these values into institutions the Islamic discourse diverges significantly from modernity. It vehemently rejects Western individualism, gender relations, personal liberties and consumerism but accepts individual enterprise and a kind of capitalism restrained by 'interest free transactions'. It stands for a morally guided social order that turns out to be a hollow enactment of many tribal/agrarian practices bound together in a collectivist polity. What ensues is an imbalance between what is said and what is actually practiced.

What are the factors and institutions that provide the balancing ground and prevent the Pakistani civil society from disintegrating? Pakistan has often been described as a failed state. However, to this Stephen P. Cohen's word can be aptly quoted, who is not only a long-standing observer of Pakistani politics but also a firm critic: 'This is a state that is not likely to disappear soon.'[26] The divergences and tensions evident in Pakistani society are not typical to only Pakistan; they are common to many Third World nations. What is characteristic to Pakistan is the expression of such divisions and the challenge of managing them.

There are many institutions that hold this society together. Family and kinship come first. One derives their identity, security, opportunity initially from family or kin, even from tribe. Both these institutions have incorporated demands of urbanism and development. Like any other social institutions this too carries the social cost of nepotism, in spite of that they are a potent source of social cohesion.

Nationalism is another such potent force which holds the balance against the strong confusing surge of modernism and social change. It ties together people of all sects and sections of society to a common destiny. Nationalism in everyday life may not be that apparent but it comes through and displays its raw power during times of crisis. Be it 1947 when refugees came streaming into Pakistan, the war of 1965, the inglorious defeat of 1971 or periodic upheavals that brought down failing governments such as 1969, 1971, 1977 and 1998. It is the Pakistani society that ultimately rescues the state in crisis. The people's nationalist commitment explains to a large extent why predictions of Pakistan's demise have so far been ill founded.[27] Islam is also a source of cohesion. It unites all Muslims spiritually and emotionally despite divides and differences in beliefs and practices. Islam also underpins Pakistan's moral order, which despite being under strain form the challenges of modernization, nevertheless lays the common groundwork in Pakistani society.

There is an ideological and moral resistance to modernization that smacks of Westernization. Preserving the indigenous culture and identity is a strongly held value and Islamic revival promises the rediscovery of equality, human rights, democracy and scientific thinking. This pattern of modernization is not unique to Pakistan; its form is influenced by cultural particularities, but its structure is not much unlike others.

Samir Khalaf cites similar patterns of modernization and social change in Lebanon as 'adaptive modernization', where traditional institutions are seen to be realigning themselves in response to the challenges of material and economic changes. The resurgence of cultural identities and religious revivalism is one way of coping with the tensions and discontinuities of social change. They are essentially expressions on indigenization of modernity. Traditions are not static and they do not act as brakes to social change but they do evolve to maintain structural continuity.

Eric J. Hobsbawm's term, 'invention of tradition' and Manaul Castell's notion of reflexivity, conscious reconstruction of institutions and identities point to the ways in which traditions promote their form of change. Most theorists of modernization envisage a dialectical interplay between traditions and modernity. Social change is supposed to be full of contradictions. It is only the view propounded by the media that paints social change as a one-dimensional, smooth process that sweeps away long established norms and values. Deliberate reconstruction of institutions is necessary to cushion against such confusing sweeping changes in the society. Social legislation and public reforms are the tools for such reconstruction. The Pakistani society has grossly lagged behind in this aspect.

The narrative of social change in Pakistan suggests that two parallel processes have unfolded:[28]

- The diffusion of modern materialism and consumerism.
- Indigenization of technologies, products and institutions.

Islamization can be interpreted as a process of indigenizing political ideologies and moral values under the gamut of Islam. A traditionally organic society is being segmented into sharply differentiated groups of divergent lifestyles. Social distances are increasing and institutions succumbing to the contradictory pulls of social change and splitting. The fragmentation of society without the common ground of an integrative moral order is the challenge posed by the rapid social change in Pakistan.

A moral and ideological gap has appeared with the increasing differentiation of society. Modernization and globalization do not offer a moral purpose and a fulfilling ideology, they in turn threaten national identity. Islamic revivalism and the indigenization process draws such validation only because it has the essence of a purposeful life. Although the potential for such a life hasn't been realized yet they succeed in feeding the people's need for a national identity. The conflation of Westernization and modernization in Islamic critiques of modernity allows Islamists to play on Pakistani nationalism. In Pakistan no other alternative has emerged yet to satisfy the demands for national identity and modernity at Pakistan's own terms. A moral order that balances material modernism with cultural continuity is needed. This national agenda remains unattended leaving cultural development and modernization grossly vulnerable to revivalism. This challenge in the pace of modernity is essentially moral in nature and has so far not been sufficiently dealt with or addressed.

Notes

1. Paul DiMaggio, John Evans and Bethany Bryson, 'Have Americans' Social Attitudes Become More Polarized?', *American Journal of Sociology*, 1996, 690-755.
2. Daniel Lerner, *The Passing of Traditional Society: Modernizing the Middle East*, New York: Free Press, 1958; Myron Weiner, ed., *Modernization: The Dynamics of Growth*, New York: Basic, 1966.
3. York W. Bradshaw and Michael Wallace, *Global Inequalities*, Thousand Oaks, CA: Pine Forge, 1996.
4. Immanuel Wallerstein, *The Modern World System*, vol. 1, New York: Academic Press, 1974; idem, 'Modernization: Requiescat in Pace', in *The Uses of Controversy in Sociology*, ed. L.A. Coser and O.N. Larsen, New York: Free Press, 1976, pp. 131-5.
5. Andre Gunder Frank, 'The Development of Underdevelopment', *Monthly Review*, 18 (September 1966), pp. 17-30.

6. Randall G. Stokes, and Susan Marshall, 'Tradition and the Veil: Female Status in Tunisia and Algeria', *Journal of Modern African Studies*, 1981, pp. 625-46.
7. Philip McMichael, 'Globalization: Myths and Realities', *Rural Sociology*, 1996, pp. 25-56.
8. Max Weber, *The Protestant Ethic and the Spirit of Capitalism*, tr. T. Parsons, rpt., New York: Charles Scribner's Sons, [1904] 1958.
9. Samuel P. Huntington, 'The Clash of Civilizations?', *Foreign Affairs*, 1993, pp. 22-49; *The Clash of Civilizations and the Remaking of World Order*, New York: Simon and Schuster, 1996.
10. Shahid Javed Burki, 'The State and the Political Economy of Redistribution in Pakistan', in *The Politics of Social Transformation in Afghanistan, Iran and Pakistan*, ed. Myron Weiner and Ali Banuazizi, New York: Syracruse University Press, 1994, pp. 274-308.
11. I.H. Malik, *State and Civil Society in Pakistan: Politics of Authority, Ideology and Ethnicity*, Basingstoke, 1997.
12. Therese Saliba, Carolyn Allen and Judith A. Howard, eds., *Gender Politics and Islam*, Chicago: University of Chicago Press, 2002, pp. 65-71.
13. Mohammed A. Qadeer, *Social and Cultural Transformations in a Muslim Nation*, New York: Routeledge, 2006, pp. 266-9.
14. Vali Nasr, 'Military Rule, Islamism and Democracy in Pakistan', *Middle East Journal,* vol. 58, no. 2 (Spring 2004), pp. 195-209. http://www.jstor.org/stable/4330001
15. Asghar Ali Engineer, 'Pakistan: Religion, Politics and Society', *Economic and Political Weekly*, vol. 31, nos. 41/2, 12-19 October 1996, pp. 2800-3.
16. Asghar Ali Engineer, *Islam in Contemporary World*, Berkshire: New Dawn Press Group, 2007, p. 100.
17. Ibid., p. 109.
18. Ian Talbot, *Pakistan a Modern History*, London: C. Hurst and Co., 2009, pp. 67-80.
19. Mohammed Arkoun, 'Present Day Islam Between its Tradition and Globalization', in *The New Voices of Islam: Rethinking Politics and Modernity*, Mehran Kamrava, California: University of California Press, 2006, pp. 29-65.
20. Tariq Ramadan, 'The Way (Al Sharia) of Islam', in *The New Voices of Islam: Rethinking Politics and Modernity*, Mehran Kamrava, California: University of California Press, 2006, pp. 65-99.

21. Therese Saliba, Carolyn Allen and Judith A.Howard, eds., *Gender Politics and Islam*, Chicago: University of Chicago Press, 2002, pp. 65–71.
22. Arkoun, op. cit., 2006.
23. Nasr, op. cit., 2004.
24. Engineer, op. cit., 1996.
25. Talbot, op. cit., 2009.
26. Stephen Philip Cohen, *The Idea of Pakistan*, Washington D.C.: The Brookings Institution, 2004.
27. Qadeer, op. cit., pp. 275–6.
28. Ibid.

CHAPTER 3

Ethno-nationalism in Pakistan: The Case of Baluchistan

Shashi Kant

Ethnicity is a presumed identity of a group derived from common descent and shared pasts. The essence of ethnic group is the concept of 'ethnie' and the ethnic community. Myths of common ancestry, shared memories, cultural values and historical pasts define an 'ethnie'. It is a collective self-consciousness which separates ethnic communities from ethnic categories. All ethnic communities, it is important to note, do not become a nation because of the pressures of assimilation and absorption in the larger societies.

Etymologically speaking, the word 'ethnic' is derived from Greek word 'ethnikos'; which referred to non-Christian 'pagans' or group of the population sharing common cultural and racial traits and primitive cultures.[1] Talcott Parsons defines an ethnic group as a group, the members of which have distinctive sense of history.[2] On the other hand, Yusuf Bangera defines it in terms of 'ethnic consciousness'. According to him, 'concrete social experiences are often important in the construction of such consciousness'.[3] Max Weber also underlines ethnic groups as those 'human groups that entertain subjective belief in their common descent and shared past'.[4] Certainly an understanding that comes out of Weber's thought is that of 'consciousness'. Unlike race, which is hereditary, ethnic membership is a presumed identity. Benedict Anderson refers to it as an 'imagined community'.[5] Common descent, therefore, does not create but facilitates the formation of groups in a specific political environment.

Karl Marx differed from Weber as he viewed 'groups' as social classes based on the relations of production. The economic aspect is understood in terms of the base which divides capitalist society broadly into two: the bourgeoisie or the owner of the means of production, and the proletariat or the working class. The inherent contradictions in social relations create conflicts in society where conflicts become inevitable. When these conflicts reach a stage where the 'class in itself', that is the 'working class', becomes a 'class for itself', it leads to a revolutionary change in redistribution of resources. Three elements can be identified in the Marxist understanding: first, consciousness transforms the group into action, economic determinant distinguishes between different groups and three, ethnic and economic factors encourage the group into action.

In the contemporary scholarship, Paul Brass defines ethnic groups in terms of objective attributes. It believes in certain distinguishing cultural features that separate one group of people from another and these features may be language, territory, religion, colour, diet, dress or any of them.[6] Ethnicity is a sense of ethnic identity, which has been defined by George De Vos as consisting of the 'subjective, symbolic or emblematic use' by 'a group of people ... of any aspect of culture, in order to differentiate themselves from other groups'.[7] Ethnicity or ethnic identity also involves subjective self-consciousness. It demands status and recognition. In other words, ethnicity to ethnic category is what class consciousness is to class. Theodorson and Theodorson define an ethnic group as one which enjoys a common cultural tradition and a sense of identity of being a sub-group within a larger society.[8] Fredrik Barth emphasized the role of cultural factors in the formation of ethnic groups.[9] Barth explains the limitations of subjective factors by showing how they change over a period of time, due to interaction with other groups. The sense of separateness in terms of identity may be replaced by a distinct ethnic identity, like Bengali Muslims who fought as Muslims for Pakistan in 1947 and then fought against Pakistan as Bengalis in 1970–1. Barth, therefore, suggests that the focus had shifted from cultural traits to the process of creation and maintenance of ethnic boundaries, and 'continuing dichotomization' between members and outsiders. Barth holds the view that ethnic groups may become behaviourally assimilated in terms of ethnic markers like language, lifestyle, dress code, etc., yet maintain their sense of ethnic identity. An ethnic group is therefore a form of social organization in which the members make use of certain cultural traits from their past which may not be historically verifiable.[10]

Ethnic conflicts seem to have increased as a consequence of diffusion of 'modernity'. What is, perhaps, more striking about ethno-politics is that the resurgence of ethnicity as a political force has been all but ignored by mainstream literature. Modernization and Marxist school of thought had portrayed ethnic identity as a primordial sentiment whose relevance would diminish with the expansion and penetration of modern industrial society. However, it has been a surprising phenomenon to see the rise of the ethno-nationalism at this particular juncture, when the global political economy and the diffusion of modern culture are deeply entrenched in all corners of the globe.

The world has witnessed the revival, intensification and stubborn persistence of ethnicity as an issue in politics. It has become a focal point of popular mobilization, and at the same time source of domestic and interstate conflict. The political salience of ethnicity has endured not just in former colonial territories of the Third World but also in post-industrial democracies of Europe and America as well as in major communist countries such as China and former Soviet Union. The big question arises is why has ethno-nationalism remained such a powerful force in modern world? Why have ethnic identities not declined despite modernization of societies? What are the structural, cultural and individual factors which are responsible for the rise and persistence of ethno-nationalist movements? How have these movements been characterized and what is the basis of ethno-nationalist movements?

Ethno-nationalist Movements

Ethno-nationalist movements today constitute one of the most widespread, protracted and violent forms of conflict in the modern world. Ethno-nationalist movements are viewed as transitory movements towards full-scale nationalism. Generally, states experience divisive conflicts over the terms of incorporation of ethnic minorities, religious sects and ethno-nationalists. The available literature suggests that ethno-nationalism falls into two major categories that are primordial and instrumentalist. The first treats 'ethno-nationalism' as a manifestation of persisting cultural identity based on primordial sense of ethnic identity. The second regards ethnicity as an exercise in 'boundary maintenance'.[11] But the fundamental question has been left unanswered by both schools which is how the culture, which forms the core of 'ethinie' according to *primordialists* seemingly begins to metamorphose into a conscious group, demanding a nation? Instrumentalists, on the other hand, are unable to explain as to how certain cultural variables become autonomous agents for political transformation at such a large scale. Therefore a broad theoretical issue involved in ethno-nationalism needs to be re-examined. The following section would examine the relationship between ethnic groups and nationalism.

Anthony D. Smith distinguishes between *ethnic categories* and *ethnic communities*. There are innumerable ethnic categories based on cultural factors like language, custom, religion, etc. The essence of an ethnic group, according to Smith, is the concept of 'ethnie', or ethnic community. It is a collective level of identity. It is in such communities that the power of social conflicts can be located.[12] Myth of common ancestry, shared memories, cultural elements and link with a historical territory or homeland define an 'ethnie'.[13] But only rarely do these categories become ethnic and ethnic nations. These formations take place only when these categories become self-aware of their collective identity. The process of assimilation and absorption into larger society is so intense that only a small number of ethnic categories are able to survive it.[14]

According to Thomas Erikson, since ethnicity itself is a wide ranging phenomenon, the definition of ethnic groups also reflects this variation. Erikson identifies four different kinds of ethnic groups to explain this variation.[15]

i. *Urban ethnic minorities:* Non-European immigrants in European cities or non-Americans in the United States. Although aware of their distinctive origin, these groups are assimilated in the nation state system and, therefore, make no demands for independence or statehood or separate territory.
ii. *Indigenous people:* They are aboriginal inhabitants of a territory who are partially integrated in the capitalist system of production and consumption. They are relatively politically powerless.
iii. *Proto-nations:* They have a definite leadership and claim to be separate nation state. They are territorially based, differentiated according to class and education and are large groups. Such groups are covered most by media and have all the characteristics of a nation except a state and could, therefore, be called 'nation without a state'. Erikson includes the Kurds of Iraq, Palestinians, Sikhs and Sri Lankan Tamils in this category.

iv. *Ethnic groups:* In plural societies these are normally groups residing in colonially created states that are culturally diverse. Although they participate in the political and economic system of the state, they consider themselves distinct and are also considered so by the society. The different caste or religious groups in independent India could be examples of this category. Secessionism is not their goal and their distinctiveness is asserted in the form of group competition.

The above analysis highlights the basic tenets of ethnicity, which is a very complex phenomenon and which defies a clear-cut definition. These definitions offer subjective, objective as well as behavioural characteristics of ethnic groups. The phenomenon can be explained in political, sociological and anthropological terms. We can sum up the characteristics of ethnic groups in the following points:

- Identity or self-perception as distinct social entity
- Recognition by other groups
- Cultural traits to build upon this identity
- Shared memories of disadvantage within plural societies, and
- Focused towards the achievement of certain material goals in the future.

Group identity or consciousness is a key element of an ethnic group. Identity and ethnic groups are, therefore closely related.

Nationalism, according to Ernest Gellner, is 'the political principal which holds that political and national unit should be congruent'.[16] Although it may present itself as the awakening of the latent force, it is a modern phenomenon, a new form of social organization, which uses some of the pre-existent cultures and sometimes invents them.[17] Marxist thinker Tom Nairn combines Gellner's modernization perspective with Gramscian, to provide a materialist explanation of nationalism, which appeals to an educated middle class and is able to mobilize support cutting across class. Nationalism, according to Nairn, arises in threatened and underdeveloped peripheral societies whose intelligentsia mobilize the people along cultural lines around the development goals of the local bourgeoisie.[18] Following the instrumentalist perspective, Eric J. Hobsbawm sees nationalism as an 'invented tradition' of political elites to legitimize their power in an age of democratization and revolution.[19]

Anderson agrees that nation is an artefact and defines it as 'an imagined political community', imagined as both inherently limited and sovereign.[20] In fact, two rival conceptions of modern nationalism have emerged. The first identifies the nation with all the citizens who are part of the territorial sovereign state. The other viewpoint conceives the nation along ethnic lines in which membership is inherited and not based on formal citizenship. Ethnic conflicts express the underlying tensions between these two notions of the nation.[21]

The idea of nation and nationalism is wide and varied. Keeping this fact in mind, for the purpose of the present article, it would be relevant to note three points:

- A nation state is a territorial and political unit.
- A nation is a community of people who share a common culture, real or 'imagined'.
- Nationalism is the sentiment, the idea that creates or aspires to create nation states out of nations.

In other words, a nation shares most of the attributes of a group, but is more territorially and politically integrated. Nation has a vibrant political leadership that articulates its aspirations in the shape of a territorially carved out nation state. An ethnic group or nation emerges as conflict in society unfolds. As most scholars have pointed out, nations and ethnic groups are an 'imagination', based on identity or consciousness of people. The group emerges as a distinct social entity when strains are felt in a plural society. The two points which are evident from the above analysis are: one, ethnic groups or nations are dynamic actors in society. Two, their formation and existence revolve around identity or awareness. Collective identity is, therefore, crucial to ethnic groups.

II

Ethno-nationalism in Pakistan

South Asia, home to eight different countries (Afghanistan, Bangladesh, Bhutan, India, Nepal, Maldives, Pakistan and Sri Lanka) constitutes one-fifth of the world's population. It is home to divergent ethnic groups based on multidimensional mixture of various linguistic, religious, sub-regional cultures and tribal identities. Demarcations of territorial boundaries drawn by the British while withdrawing from the subcontinent in 1947 left some ethnic groups residing among others in newly-independent multi-ethnic states. These newly-independent states in the subcontinent have found themselves engulfed in the herculean task of national integration and state building.[22] The purpose of this task was to extend the writ of central political institutions and rules of governance into peripheral regions of these countries and to attempt to build a sense of common national identity and generate loyalty around specific culture and iconic symbols preferred by the central state. But this very process of creating loyalty by suppressing distinct identities based on different cultures, ethnicity, language, religion and others, often caused friction, leading to potentially violent tussle between central political elites and various ethnic groups.[23]

The Case of Pakistan

Pakistan became a state in 1947 as a result of the Partition of India. The state was carved out on the basis of the two-nation theory, that is India and Pakistan are two separate nations on the basis of religion that are Hinduism and Islam. Pakistan is linguistically and ethnically a diverse state. There exist numerous difficulties in determining the various ethnic groups, languages and cultural diversities in Pakistan. Distribution pattern of languages in Pakistan differ widely. Six major languages cover about 98 per cent of the country's population: Urdu is spoken by 7.57 per cent, Punjabi by 44.15 per cent, Sindhi by 14.1 per cent, Pashto by 15.42 per cent, Baluchi by 3.57 per cent, Siraiki by 10.53 per cent people.[24] Urdu was never the dominant language of any of the peoples of Pakistan excluding an insignificant number. It was the Muslim nobility, the big Muslim businessmen, a section of the Punjabi Muslim intelligentsia educated in the tradition of the Aligarh colleges and the Muslim immigrants from the United and Central Provinces of British India that spoke Urdu (Table 3.1).

As far as ethno-national identities are concerned, five separate groups draw our attention namely, Pashtun/Pakhtun, Punjabi, Sindhi, Mohajir, and Baluch. The oldest ethno-nationalism in Pakistan is Pakhtun/Pashtun nationalism – the Pakhtuns believe that ethnically they are from the same Aryan stock that originated in Central Asia.

TABLE 3.1: THE SIX LEADING LANGUAGES SPOKEN IN PAKISTAN

		Census (in per cent)			
Rank	*Language*	*1998*	*1982*	*1961*	*1951*
1	Punjabi	44.15	48.17	66.39	67.08
2	Pashto	15.42	13.15	8.47	8.16
3	Sindhi	14.10	11.70	12.59	12.85
4	Siraiki*	10.53	9.54	–	–
5	Urdu	7.57	7.60	7.57	7.05
6	Baluchi	3.57	3.02	2.49	3.04

Note: * Siraiki was included with Punjabi in the 1951 and 1961 census.[25]

Pakhtun nationalism has always found resonance and response from Pakhtun parts of Afghanistan. Before 1992, all governments in Afghanistan supported the old demand of Pakhtunistan that envisaged a united state of Pakhtuns involving Pakhtun areas of Pakistan and Afghanistan.[26]

Second major nationalism is of the Sindhis, which combines both regional and ethnic dimensions. This is a community living in Karachi, Hyderabad and various other cities of Sindh. Its nationalism is based on Sindhi language, culture and history. Sindhi nationalism does not find the same kind of overlap with India as in the case with Pakhtun nationalism *vis-à-vis* Afghanistan or Baluch nationalism *vis-à-vis* Iran.[27]

Immigrants from India in the post-Independence period have emerged as a separate ethnic entity, calling themselves Mohajirs. The people originally hailed mainly from the Hindi belt of northern India. They speak Urdu and are proud of their language and culture.[28]

The largest element of the Pakistani population comprises the people of Punjab. However, they do not claim nationality. They identify themselves as Muslims or Pakistanis. Baluchis are present not only on the side of Pakistan but in Iran and Afghanistan as well. The Afghan portion contains numerically fewer Baluchis. The Baluch tribe in Iran regards itself a small and dissident minority who would rather be united with the Baluch people of Pakistan and look up to them to take the lead.[29]

The Case of Baluchistan

History underlines that Pakistan seems to be unable to tackle the problem of ethno-nationalism. Its most spectacular failure was to reconcile the ethno-national identity of Bengalis, who succeeded in 1971 to form a separate nation that is Bangladesh. Similar ethno-nationalism has been simmering in Baluchistan, a frontier, strategically located and the largest province of Pakistan.

Origin and Language

Baluchistan contains nearly half the landmass of Pakistan that is around 40 per cent of the county's territory. The total population of ethnic Baluch people is estimated to be around 9 million worldwide. However, the exact number of those who are Baluch or claim to be of Baluch ancestry is difficult to determine. As of 2010, the Baluch are 4.97 per cent of Pakistan's 177,276,594 people.[30] Historically, the origin of the Baluchis goes back to distant history around 2,000 years back. Most of them claim that their ancestors came from Aleppo in modern Syria at the time of Arab conquest in ninth century. However, Western investigations reveal that historically the Baluchis are inhabitants of north-western Iran, adjunct to the southern coast of the Caspian Sea. In thirteenth and fourteenth centuries the Baluch people, who settled there, came into contact with the Pashtuns, Punjabis, Sindhis and some Dravidian groups. It was during this period of settlement that they were faced with repeated attempts at subjugation by the Persian, Sindhi, Afghan, Sikh and other conquering armies who could only succeed in establishing limited suzerainty over them.

Culturally, the Baluchi ethno-linguistic group is far from homogeneous. Diversity, in terms of historical origins, geographic isolation of individual tribes, intermingling and wider integration and the result of the recent partitioning of their homeland into separate states has changed in their lifestyles and social patterns.[31] Some have adopted regional vernaculars depending upon where they have settled. Iranian Baluchis, for example, have assimilated to a certain extent into Persian culture. Similarly the Afghan Baluchis have begun to speak Pashto in addition to their own dialect. However, the greatest difficulty in ascertaining Baluch cultural boundaries in Pakistan lies in its relation with the Brahuis.[32] According to the 2008 Pakistan Statistical Year Book, households whose primary language is Baluchi represent 40 per cent of Baluchistan's population, 20 per cent of households speak Brahui, and up to 25 per cent speaks Pashto, making Baluchi, Brahui, and Pashto the three dominant languages in the province.[33]

The Baluchi language has descended from a lost language linked with Parthian or Median civilizations, which flourished in the Caspian and adjunct areas in the pre-Christian era.[34] It is one of the oldest living languages classified as a member of the Iranian group of the Indo-European language family amongst which it is closest to Kurdish. There have been some borrowings from Persian, Sindhi, Arabic and other languages. Until a century and a half the Baluch did not have any recorded literature. Of late, Baluch people have evolved a Baluchi script known as Nastaliq, a variant of the Arabic script. However, the script may have been borrowed to a certain extent and the Baluch culture as such has faced with continual pressure from strong well-developed neighbouring cultures, the Baluchis have been remarkably successful in preserving a distinct identity of their own. The Baluchi language and a relatively uniform folklore and value system have provided a common platform for the various scattered tribes.

Topography

Agriculture is pursued only in regions where facilities of irrigation exist. Due to the lack of irrigation facility, only about 4.5 million acres out of 47 million acres of plain land is used for cultivation purpose. Fruits are grown at higher altitudes. Generally, wheat, barley, rice, tobacco and cotton are cultivated. Cattle rearing seems to be the primary source of livelihood for most of the population and almost 90 per cent of land is used as pasture land. The province is highly rich in natural resources. Besides natural gas it has large reserves of minerals. The province is full of marble and limestone reserves and contains 95 per cent of world's asbestos. It has significant reserves of chromites, silica, gypsum, manganese, graphite, sulphur, fluorite and iron ore. The region is known for its vast oil reserves also. Baluch copper fields at Saindok are being exploited with the assistance of the Chinese company MRDL. Saindok has assumed importance after gold and silver were struck here. Sharig is a coal-mining town in which Chinese presence is significant. Recently a huge deposit of gas was confirmed from Sharig exploration site. Besides copper, oil and natural gas reserves, large deposits of coal, silver, gold, platinum, aluminium and deposits of uranium have also been found in the Baluch tract. Nature has endowed the province with sea, mountains and plains which have immense natural wealth. But the important fact is that Baluchistan is not only self-sufficient but also supports the federal government with its valuable resources.[35]

The Baluch homeland is strategically important to Pakistan. Baluchistan is the main base for space programme and rocket experimentation facilities of Pakistan. Important strategic airports in Baluchistan are at Gwadar, Pasni, Turbat, Juzzak and Robray. Situated near Iran and Afghanistan borders these airports are valued by the USA for strategic use against Iran, if such a situation arises in near future.

Religion

The Baluchi tribal groups are almost entirely Muslim and adhere to Hanafi School of Sunni sect of Islam which is in harmony with the state of Pakistan which is also predominantly Sunni. This may seem to place them in unity with Pakistan state and its Islamic ideology. However, religious uniformity is not complete and to overstate the strength of Islamic bond between the two can be deceptive. Moreover, the powerful loyalty to clan and tribe continues to claim the highest allegiance.[36] It poses a big question about the utility of *Islam* as an 'integrative force'. Moreover, religion has been used and exploited maximum by the Pakistani state to suppress any form of protest. Though Pakistan was created as a Muslim state in 1947 and became an Islamic republic in 1964, steps towards greater 'Islamization' have been taken after 1978 only.

Phases of Insurgency

The north-west regions, including North West Frontier Province/ Khyber Pakhtunkhwa and Baluchistan have always been a cause of discomfort for Pakistan. Even before the creation of Pakistan in 1947, the erstwhile colonial master Britain tried to pacify the tribesmen for many years.[37] However, they succeeded in subduing most of Baluchistan. With the departure of the British from India and the creation of Pakistan, the problem of the tribal area was transferred to the three governments of Pakistan, Iran and Afghanistan under which the Baluchis lived. Pakistan inherited the bulk of the Baluch and Pathan population and consequently inherited the most problematic issue that it has to live with it and proved most frustrating to the ruling Punjabi dominated circles. Religion with which they sought to bind the whole population failed in its function. The policies of the new state accentuated the dissatisfaction of living within Pakistan. It resulted in a restive population which not only continuously tried to assert itself politically or otherwise, but also tried to claim ties with their co-ethnic groups beyond the border.

There have been four insurgencies in Baluchistan since the creation of Pakistan. These were in 1948, 1958-9, 1963-9 and in 1973-7 (see Table 3.2). The current crisis is being called as the fifth insurgency.[38] The roots of the crisis in Baluchistan go back to the early years of Pakistan.

The state of Kalat which was a princely state, declared independence on 15 August 1947. Jinnah had asked the Khan of Kalat to accede to Pakistan. The Khan laid several conditions for the accession. In 1947, the Khan of Kalat asked his assembly to decide the question of accession. The House of the People of Kalat state was dominated by three main political parties, i.e. Kalat National Party led by Ghaus Bakhsh Bizenjo, Anjuman-e-Watan Party led by Abdul Samad Achakzai and Jamiatul Ulema-e-Hind voted against accession to Pakistan. In spite of this, the state of Kalat was coerced by Pakistan in 1948 to accede to it. The second Baluch insurgency was led by Nawroz Khan in 1958 who opposed the occupation of Baluchistan by Pakistan. The 1973-7 insurgency was provoked by the dismissal of the coalition government of National Awami Party (NAP), Jamiatul Ulema-i-Islam (JUI) parties

TABLE 3.2: INSURGENCIES IN BALUCHISTAN

Insurgency	*Date*	*Leaders*
First Conflict	1948	Mir Ahmad Yar Khan
Second Conflict	1958-9	Nawab Nawroz Khan
Third Conflict	1963-9	Sher Mohammad Bijarani Marri
Fourth Conflict	1973-7	Nawab Khair Bakhsh Marri
Fifth Conflict	2005 to date	Nawab Akbar Khan Bugti and Mir Balach Marri

Source: http://www.globalsecurity.org/military/world/war/pakistan1.html

in the province headed by Attaullah Mengal. In the 1970 elections, the National Awami Party and the JUI which won a majority, were called upon by Z.A. Bhutto to form the government in the province. The NAP succeeded as the largest single group in the provincial assemblies of NWFP and Baluchistan. With the help of JUI, the government was formed in April, 1972 and federal government appointed, the Baluch nationalist leader Ghaus Bakhsh Bizenjo, as governor of Baluchistan and Attaullah Mengal became the chief minister and Khair Bakhsh Marri became the chairperson of NAP parliamentary party. However, the sudden decision of Z.A. Bhutto to dismiss provincial government on 12 February 1973, invited varieties of interpretations. The official version was that Soviet arms and ammunition ordered by Baluch leaders had been found in Iraq embassy in Islamabad. As the insurgency gained momentum between 1973 and 1975, Bhutto made three offers of amnesty but no agreement was reached on ending the war.

Since December 2005, Pakistani Army has once again been fighting its own people in Baluchistan. It has launched operations in the area killing people indiscriminately. This is the fifth time the Pakistani Army has launched an armed assault in Baluchistan during the past six decades.

Case of Internal Colonialism

These insurgencies were the results of economic, social and political marginalization which had led to a sense of alienation and discontent among the people of the province. The Baluch people saw that their rich resources were being held by the outsiders and they were being deprived of benefits from them. The paradox is that Baluchistan is considered to be the poorest province though it is rich in natural resources and minerals. Pakistan gets its 36 per cent of total gas production from Baluchistan. This is again a surprising fact that only 17 per cent of the gas is used by Baluchistan and 83 per cent by the rest of the country.[39]

People also had memories of forcible annexation of their province which had embittered them. Ever since the inception of Pakistan, the political leaders, military or civilian, have never cared to redress their grievances. Baluchi political culture has been secular and had no influence of the two-nation theory on it. Ghaus Bakhsh Bizenjo, leader of Kalat echoed this sentiment when he said: 'They say we must join Pakistan for economic reasons. Yet we have minerals, we have petroleum and we have ports. The question is what would be Pakistan without us?'[40]

The people of Baluchistan have constantly been the victim of gross negligence and apathy of the federal governments of Pakistan. The literacy rate of the province is 26.6 per cent as against the national average of 47 per cent. The unemployment rate is highest at 33.48 per cent against 19.68 for Pakistan in general. With 47 per cent people living below the poverty line in the province, unemployment in the region has been compelling the Baluchi youth to involve themselves in criminal activities, smuggling, and drug peddling. With no roads, no electricity, no safe drinking water and meagre health facility, Baluchis are nursing grievances against Pakistani establishment.[41]

The Baluchi people have very negligible presence in administration, police and economy. Even the Baluch regiment has hardly any Baluch officers and soldiers. Pakistan Petroleum which is responsible for extraction and distribution of Sui gas does not give employment to Baluch youth as a matter of policy.

Gwadar Port Issue

The coast of Pakistan has got numerous natural harbours, namely Jiwani, Gwadar, Pasni and Ormara. Out of these, Gwadar has the potential to boost economic development in the region which has remained most backward in Pakistan. A study conducted by the Asian Development Bank (ADB) on ports found Gwadar to be the best alternative to the Persian Gulf Ports in terms of location, which could handle more ships and larger oil tankers. The port is connected by a newly-constructed Makran coastal highway from Sheikh Raj, approximately 105 km north of Karachi which has the potential to boost trade between Pakistan and Iran.

A new wave of ethno-nationalist militancy was aroused after the announcement in 2001 that the central government will build a port on the south-west coast of Baluchistan. This project was signed between Gen. Musharraf and the then Chinese premier on 24 March 2002.[42] Gwadar Port is designed as a regional hub for transit and transhipment of goods for Afghanistan, Central Asia and West Asia. China is paying $198 million out of the total construction cost of $248 million and providing substantial numbers of engineers and workers. Almost all the construction contracts have been awarded to non-Baluchis, mainly Punjabis. There is great suspicion among the locals that without local participation, the project has been launched by the central government to colonize them. This feeling has been echoed in the following lines:

Some observers share the view that the Gwadar port is one of the biggest land boondoggles in Pakistan's history. The local people owned the land through generations but lacked documents of ownership. The elites have bribed revenue clerks to register Gwadar land in their names; the land was then resold at rock-bottom prices to developers from Karachi, Lahore and other major cities . . . illegally allotted to civilian and military bureaucrats living elsewhere. . . . The poor and uneducated Baluch population had been shut out . . . Gwadar has become a lightning rod for Baluch hatred of Punjabi-ruled Pakistan.[43]

Baluch nationalists believe that Pakistan Army dominated by Punjabis is the biggest land grabber. In Gwadar, the army is operating as a mafia, falsifying land records. Hussain Ashraf, a two-time minister of Baluchistan in an interview with Adeel Khan said:

Central government claims that Baloch *sardars* (tribal chief) are anti-development. It is laughable for Gwadar because we do not have any *sardars*. We are not tribal people. We are fishermen. The question is: what do they mean by development? Building cantonment and naval bases? That's not development. That's colonization. For the last 55 years we were not allowed benefit from our resources. Sui gas resource goes to rest of Pakistan but we do not have it. Frankly, they want to eliminate us. We did not see a better future yesterday. We do not see a better future today. The only future that we can see is that Gwadar town will become Lyari of the new Gwadar town. We are the Kurds of Pakistan.[44]

Conclusion

The above analysis suggests that the tension between the Baluchi people and the central government has grown because of Islamabad's heavy-handed armed response to Baluchi militancy and its refusal to negotiate demands for political and economic autonomy. The central authorities, more so the army which plays a dominant role in the power structure of Pakistan has always been inclined to finding military solutions to political problems. A Senate Committee that was constituted in 2004 to look into this problem made some recommendations, the important ones being the abolition of Sardari system, implementation of the constitutional scheme of centre-province relations, restoration of the rights of provincial assembly to legislate on local laws, participation of Baluchis in the developmental process, job quota for Baluchis in federal ministries, corporations and departments, maximum representation in Pakistan Petroleum, oil and gas development and participation of locals in developmental projects of the province.

In a nutshell, the main issue in Baluchistan is political and economic. Pakistan's civil-military establishment seems incessantly reluctant to accommodate minority ethnic groups in the broader democratic framework of the nation. Military in Pakistan is so deep seated in the power structure of the state that it is hard to imagine that it would ever give way to civil and democratic control.

Insurgency finds fertile ground when population feels aggrieved and neglected. There is no better antidote for the politics of insurgency than the politics of development. Developmental welfare should be initiated in the region. On the other hand, the resources of the region should be used in such a manner that it could lead the betterment of the people of the region. History reminds us that if the authorities sitting in Islamabad don't pay heed to the genuine grievances of the Baluchis, then Pakistan may in the near future become further Balkanized.

Notes

1. Sudhir K. Singh, 'Ethnicity and Religious Aspect in Pakistan', URL: www.jammu-kashmir.com/insight20020101d.html.
2. Talcott Parsons, 'Some Theoretical Considerations on the Nature and Trends of Change of Ethnicity', in N. Glazer and D.P. Moynihan, eds., *Ethnicity: Theory and Experience*, Harvard: Harvard University Press, 1975, p. 56.
3. Yusuf Bangera, *The Search for Identity, Ethnicity, Religion and Political Violence*, UNRISD Occasional Papers, no. 6, Geneva, November 1994, p. 6.
4. Max Weber, 'What is an Ethnic Group' in Monserrat Guibernau and John Rex, eds., *The Ethnicity Reader: Nationalism, Multiculturalism and Migration*, Cambridge: Polity Press, 1997, p. 15.
5. Benedict Anderson, *Imagined Communities*, London: Verso, 1991, pp. 1-9.

6. Paul R. Brass, *Ethnicity and Nationalism*, New Delhi: Sage, 1991, pp. 1-11.
7. George de Vos, 'Ethnic Pluralism', in George de Vos and Lola Romanucci-Ross, eds., *Ethnic Identity: Cultural Continuities and Change*, Palo Alto: Mayfield Publishing Company, 1975, p. 16.
8. George Theodorson and Schiller G. Theodorson, eds., *A Modern Dictionary of Sociology*, New York: Thomas Crowell, 1969.
9. Fredrik Barth, 'Ethnic Groups and Boundaries', in Fredrik Barth, ed., *Ethnic Groups and Boundaries: The Social Organization of Culture Difference*, Oslo: Scandinavian University Press, 1969, pp. 14-15.
10. Ibid.
11. Ted Robert Gurr, 'Why Minorities Rebel: A Global Analysis of Communal Mobilization and Conflict since 1945', *International Political Science Review*, vol. 14, no. 2, 1993, p. 167.
12. Ibid.
13. Anthony D. Smith, *The Ethnic Revival in the Modern World*, Cambridge: Cambridge University Press, 1989, pp. 33-7.
14. Anthony Smith, 'The Ethnic Sources of Nationalism', *Survival*, vol. 35, no. 1, Spring 1993, p. 52.
15. Thomas H. Erikson, *Ethnicity and Nationalism: Anthropological Perspectives*, London: Pluto Press, 1993, pp. 12-14.
16. Ernest Gellner, *Nation and Nationalism*, Oxford: Blackwell, 1983, p. 1.
17. Ibid., pp. 48-50.
18. Tom Nairn, *The Break-up of Britain: Crisis and Neo-nationalism*, London: New Left Books, 1977, pp. 332-41.
19. Eric J. Hobsbawm, 'Introduction: Inventing Traditions and Mass Producing Traditions: Europe 1870-1914', in Eric J. Hobsbawm and Terence Ranger, eds., *The Invention of Tradition*, Cambridge: Cambridge University Press, 1983. See also, Eric J. Hobsbawm, *Nations and Nationalism Since 1780: Programme, Myth, Reality*, Cambridge: Cambridge University Press, 1990. Even Paul Brass shares the same view as Hobsbawm.
20. Benedict Anderson, *Imagined Communities: Reflections on the Origin and Spread of Nationalism*, London: Verso, 1991, p. 6.
21. Rodolfo Stavenhagen, *Ethnic Conflicts and the Nation State*, New York: Macmillan, 1996, pp. 3-4.
22. Paul R. Brass, *The Politics of India Since Independence*, Cambridge: Cambridge University Press, 1990, pp. 31-2.
23. Jugdeep S. Chima, 'Ethnic Sub-nationalist Movements in Contemporary South Asia', *Asian Survey*, vol. 39, no. 6, November-December 2009, pp. 915-16.

24. URL: http://www.census.gov.pk/MotherTongue.html.
25. Ibid.
26. M.B. Naqvi, 'Ethno-Nationalism in Pakistan: Cross Border Laps', *South Asian Survey*, 1997, vol. 4, no. 213, pp. 213-20.
27. Ibid.
28. Ibid.
29. Ibid.
30. The World Fact Book, Central Intelligence Agency (CIA), URL: https://www.cia.gov/library/publications/the-world-factbook/fields/2075.ml?countryName=Afghanistan&countryCode=af®ionCode=sas&#af
31. Robert G. Wirsing, 'The Baluchis and the Pathans', *Minority Right Group Report*, no. 48, p. 3.
32. Nina Swidler, 'Brahuis Political Organization and the National State', in Ainslie T. Embree, ed., *Pakistan's Western Borderlands*, Durham: Carolina Academic Press, 1977, p. 112.
33. Percentage Distribution of Household by Language usually Spoken and Region, 1998 Census, *Pakistan Statistical Year Book 2008*, Federal Bureau of Statistics, Government of Pakistan.
34. Richard N. Frye, 'Remarks on Baluchi History', *Central Asiatic Journal*, no. 1, 1961.
35. Ibid.
36. Stephen L. Pastner, 'Lords of the Desert Borderlands: Frontier Feudalism in Southern Baluchistan and Eastern Ethiopia', *International Journal of Middle-East Studies*, no. 10, 1979. pp. 34-42.
37. Robert G. Wirsing, 'The Baluchis and the Pathans', *Minority Rights Groups*, Report no. 11, Chapter II, p. 14.
38. Kalim Bahadur, 'The Crisis in Baluchistan', *World Focus*, vol. 27, no. 10, October 2006, pp. 23-5.
39. International Crisis Group (ICG), 'Pakistan: The Worsening Conflict in Baluchistan', *South Asia Report*, no. 119, 14 September 2006, p. 16, URL: http://www.crisisgroup.org/home/index.cfm?id=4373.
40. Ghaus Bakhsh Bizenjo, leader of Kalat State National Party in Lower House of Parliament of State of Kalat in 1948. Quoted from Alok Bansal, 'Baluchistan: Strategic Importance and a Tale of Ethnic Marginalization', *World Focus*, vol. 27, no. 9, October 2006, p. 3.
41. Population Census Organization, Pakistan, URL: www.census.gov.pk/DemocraticIndecator.html.
42. Frederic Grare, 'Pakistan: The Resurgence of Baluch Nationalism', *Carnegie Endowment's South Asia Report*, no. 65, Washington, D.C, 2006, pp. 6-9.

43. Robert D. Kaplan, 'Pakistan's Fatal Shore', *Atlantic,* May 2009, *Herald* (Karachi), June 2008, URL: http://www.theatlantic.com/doc/print200905/Kaplan-Pakistan.
44. Hussain Ashraf, in an interview with Adeel Khan in Gwadar, January 2008. Quoted from Adeel Khan, 'Renewed Ethno-nationalist Insurgency in Balochistan, Pakistan: The Militarized State and Continuing Economic Deprivation', *Asian Survey*, vol. 49, no. 6, November-December 2009, p. 1080.

CHAPTER 4

Ethnic Transformation of Karachi and Its Implications

Tarun Mathur

PAKISTAN IS A COUNTRY with vivid identities. People here are as diverse as in any other country. It is a multi-religious, multilingual and multi-ethnic country. People speaking different languages and following different sects within Islam are considered to be people of different ethnicities. People concern themselves with ethnic identity and not so much with national identity. Thus this kind of diversity often leads to ethnic politics or rather ethnic conflicts within a particular country. And this possibility increases if these ethnic groups are geographically concentrated. This is exactly what has happened in the case of Pakistan.

In Pakistan, Karachi is a diverse city, where numerous South and West Asian ethnicities live cheek by jowl. There are more Baluch living in just one area of Lyari in Karachi than are currently living in the entire province of Baluchistan, and the city supersedes Peshawar as the largest Pashtun city in the world. The sizeable numbers of Punjabis and Sindhis, all competing for housing, jobs and transport, have prompted the emergence of ethnic-based political parties that often overshadow former mainstream national or religio-political parties such as the Muslim League, the Pakistan People's Party, Jamaat-i-Islami and Jamiatul-Ulema-e-Islam. Here, the politics of ideology and class often seem to have been replaced by the urban ethnic mix where political patterns remain anchored in tribal/ethnic hierarchical patronage. Karachi has offered greater opportunities to the young self-confident *Muhajireen*, yet the influx of Baluch, Sindhi, Pathan, Kashmiri and

Punjabi migrants, often from rural and tribal backgrounds, has created a high level of competition.[1]

Theoretical Interpretations

The modern usage of 'ethnic group' has come to reflect the different kinds of encounters industrialized states have had with external groups, such as immigrants and indigenous peoples; 'ethnic' thus has come to stand in opposition to 'national', to refer to people with distinct cultural identities who, through migration or conquest, have become subject to a state or 'nation' with a different cultural mainstream. Donald Horowitz argues that all conflicts based on ascriptive group identities – race, language, religion, tribe, or caste – can be called ethnic.[2] Thus ethnicity can be defined in terms of (i) religious, (ii) racial, (iii) linguistic-cum-religious and (iv) sectarian ways.

In any ethnically plural society that allows free expression of political demands, some ethnic conflict is more or less inevitable, but it may not necessarily lead to violence. When there are different ethnic groups that are free to organize, there are likely to be conflicts over resources, identities, patronage, and policies. If ethnic protest takes an institutionalized form – in parliaments, in assemblies, in bureaucratic corridors, and as non-violent mobilization on the streets – it is conflict but not violence. Such institutionalized conflict must be distinguished from a situation in which protest takes violent forms, rioting breaks out on the streets, and in its most extreme form civil war ensues or pogroms are initiated against some ethnic groups with the complicity of state authorities.[3]

Stanley Tambiah notes,

> Ethnic identity above all is a collective identity: we are self-proclaimed Sinhalese, Malays, Ibos, Thais and so on. It is a self-consciousness that substantializes and naturalizes one or more attributes – the usual ones being skin colour, language, religion, territorial occupation – and attaches them to collectivities as their innate possession and their mytho-historical legacy. The central components in this description of identity are ideas of inheritance, ancestry and descent, place or territory of origin, and the sharing of kinship, any one or combination of which may be invoked as a claim according to context and calculation of advantages. These ethnic collectivities are believed to be bounded and to be self-producing and enduring through time.[4]

Migration often leads to ethnic transformation of a particular space. And this often leads to ethnic conflicts among different communities. People tend to migrate for better economic opportunities, resources and jobs. In many Third World political systems, this ethnic transformation of population quite often leads to ethnic conflicts and that too of violent nature.[5] Another factor influencing the mobilizing of some groups and not others has been an unevenness in rates of social change among different social groups, leading in turn to imbalances in their relative access to jobs, educational advantages, and political power.[6] The phenomenon of refugees played a decisive role in shaping the general political attitudes in Pakistan. The trauma of migration involved sacrifices of life and property and generally raised the level of political consciousness of the refugees.[7]

Karachi: A City of Migrants

Pakistan has suffered since its birth from disabilities associated with regional differences and resultant competing national demands. Pakistan has adopted policies of ethnic preference formulated to address the demands of disaffected groups. Pakistan, a multi-ethnic state, since the dismemberment of East Pakistan (Bangladesh), has contained five major ethnic groups. In numbers, the largest of these are the Punjabis, followed by the Sindhis, the Pathans, the Baluch, and the Mohajirs (people who migrated from the then British India to the newly-created state of Pakistan during Partition). There is also a significant 'tribal population'. Each of these groups is defined by an admixture of linguistic and political attributes – Punjabis in Punjab speak Punjabi as their mother language, Sindhis in Sindh speak Sindhi, Pathans in the Khyber Pakhtunkhwa speak Pashto, Baluch in the Baluchistan speak Baluch, and Mohajirs in Sindh speak Urdu.[8] However, there is a significant slippage in such definitions of ethnic identity. Considerable numbers of Punjabis, Pathans, and Sindhis live outside their respective provinces. This is particularly true in regard to the ethnically diverse major urban areas of Pakistan, like Karachi.

Karachi, the city whose municipality was the oldest in India and which had become the capital of Sindh in 1937 after the province was separated from Bombay, 'could also boast of a nucleus of administrative buildings, which was what a central government suddenly faced with the problem of housing the offices of an entire state needed'.[9] Karachi was officially made the capital of Pakistan on 22 May 1948, when the constituent assembly decided that it would be separated from Sindh to become a federally administered area. The seeds of ethnic strife were thus planted in Sindh, which would soon become a battleground for aggrieved 'ethnic groups' constructing their identities through their confrontation with the other(s). Karachi's modern history is thus marked by apparent economic success mitigated by violent 'ethnic' and more recently, 'sectarian' conflicts.

Karachi's predicament can be explained through a mismanaged, misunderstood, and misrepresented demography.[10] The land which earlier was occupied by Hindus has been taken over by the Muslim refugees who came in large numbers after Partition. The city struggled to come to terms with its troubled demography and migrant population. The largest city in the country is itself a mini-Pakistan with the peoples of numerous regional and linguistic backgrounds strenuously competing for jobs, housing and, in some cases, political power. Irrespective of contested statistics and census reports, Karachi accounts for every tenth Pakistani and is the largest Mohajir, Baluch, Sindhi, Pashtun and Kashmiri city. It is the fifth or sixth largest Punjabi city besides having the biggest concentration of the Afghans and a sizeable number of several other South Asian communities. Unlike many other countries with negligible or zero migration, Pakistan still has a visible element of migration fashioning its socio-political and economic contours. The external as well as internal migrations have made Sindh in general, and Karachi in particular, the most plural region in a young country already characterized by an unprecedented mobility.[11]

Karachi's Ethnic Transformation

Karachi was the first capital of Pakistan. It has been termed the 'Glory of the East', the 'Liverpool of India and Pakistan' and the 'Croydon of the East'.[12] It rose to be the first air port and the third sea port of undivided India within a brief period of hundred years, after being established by Sir Charles Napier in 1843. It is a city grown to be Sindh's metropolis amidst the innumerable villages in the province. Karachi is the only city to grow at such a rapid rate that no other city in the subcontinent has been able to match its speed. In this article, I have dealt with the post-Partition ethnic transformation of the city.

Lord Mountbatten announced his plan for the withdrawal of the British from India on 3 June 1947. He gave 15 August 1947 as the date for this momentous event; this date was nine months earlier than the previously announced date of withdrawal, June 1948. The states of India and Pakistan had to start functioning even before their boundaries were known to them. There was no clear cut idea of what the parameters of territory or powers the new states were to have. Pakistan had to find a new capital as well. The Quaid-i-Azam, faced with such problems, asked the premier of Sindh, Sir Ghulam Hussain Hidayatullah if Karachi could be the temporary capital of the newly-established state.[13]

On the eve of independence, Karachi, the capital of Sindh, had a population of about 4,50,000. Slightly over 60 per cent of this population was Sindhi speaking. The other languages spoken by different communities living in the city were, in order of importance, Baluchi, Urdu, Hindi, Punjabi, Gujarati, Kutchi, Brahui and Marathi. Nearly 51 per cent of the population was Hindu, 42 per cent Muslim, 3.5 per cent Christian and 1.1 per cent Parsi.[14] A significant change in the demography of Karachi occurred after Partition. Within a few months after it became the capital of Pakistan, it received 6,00,000 refugees from India. In addition, it received a large number of government servants and support staff from other provinces of Pakistan. This huge influx was accompanied by an out-migration of the Hindu population from the city.

In Pakistan, Muslim refugees came to be officially called Mohajirs. Although the specific Urdu word for refugees is *panahgir* (the seeker of *panah* or refuge), the word Mohajir, which means both migrant and refugee, invoked the migration of Prophet Muhammad and his followers from Mecca to Medina in AD 622. Naming Muslim refugees who came to Pakistan Mohajir has been interpreted as an attempt to ideologically reinforce Muslim League's broad claim that Pakistan would be a home for Muslims, imbue a sense of religious significance to the hardships of displacement, and inspire religious duty among local Muslim inhabitants to receive the displaced. However, it is important to note that the *hijra* of AD 622 was an obligatory migration that had to be taken by all of Prophet Muhammad's followers as a matter of faith, and that the Pakistani state adopted this symbolic name despite the fact that mass migration, as we have seen, was actively discouraged by it.[15]

Nichola Khan argues that the word Mohajir has several meanings. It is a highly flexible concept adopted for diverse expressions of identity and purpose, subsuming principles of Islamic statehood (propagated by Jamaat-i-Islami), of ethnicized class protest against the state (propagated by MQM), opposition to Altaf Hussain's leadership (propagated by Haqiqi) as well as a myriad of individual interests directed towards gaining legitimacy amongst peers, position in the party and within loyalties.[16]

By 1951 Karachi's population had increased to 1.137 million because of the influx of 6,00,000 refugees from India. In 1951, the Sindhi-speaking population was 8.6 per cent, the Urdu-speaking population was 50 per cent, the Muslim population was 96 per cent and the Hindu population was 2 per cent.[17] In 1958, General Mohammad Ayub Khan established military rule in Pakistan and took a number of decisions that have affected Karachi and its relationship with the rest of Pakistan. Gen. Ayub Khan decided that refugees should leave the city and the working classes, migrating into the city from other areas of Pakistan, should also be discouraged from residing in the posh localities of the city.[18] Of the approximately 7.5 million Mohajirs, near about a quarter took up residence in 'urban centres of Sindh, like – Karachi, Hyderabad, Sukkur, etc.', the 6,00,000 refugees absorbed in Karachi, more than the number of inhabitants in the 1941 census, pushed that city's population beyond that of Lahore, which also grew immediately after Partition.[19]

General Ayub government's decision to introduce Green Revolution technologies in the agricultural sector in Pakistan resulted in a mass exodus of peasants and small landowners, mostly from the Punjab, to the urban areas. Almost all of the industrialization took place in Karachi and hence people, displaced by the Green Revolution, migrated to the city in search of jobs. Thus, about 50 per cent of the city's growth during this period was due to migration.[20]

In demographic terms, the population of Karachi between 1951 and 1961 increased from 1.137 to 2.044 million. Again, between 1961 and 1971, the population increased from 2.044 to 3.606 million. Most of the increase between 1961 and 1971 was the result of migration from other parts of Pakistan.[21] This migration introduced new communities in the city, the most important of them coming from the Khyber Pakhtunkhwa (KP). They were Pashtuns or Hazarawals. Their migration was supported by the political patronage that was offered to them by the military rulers, whose leaders also belonged to the

KP. These migrants, through their hard work and contacts, came to dominate transport and building construction activities, thus replacing the local population. They also acquired an important position in the police force in Karachi and were increasingly recruited as port and industrial labour.

Thereupon, Karachi expanded rapidly. The population of Karachi stood at 54,37,984 at the census of 1981 and went on increasing at a rapid rate, mainly through migration from up country and through illegal immigration from abroad.[22] This further led to the problem of infrastructure development, as the city could not afford to amalgamate this large immigration within itself. The lower Sindh Barrage was constructed by the Government of Sindh in the 1950s; this solved the problem of water supply. But other civic amenities did not keep pace with the expansion of Karachi and there were problems of sewerage disposal, adequate transport, electricity, and above all of unauthorized settlements. Most of these problems arose from lack of foresight in planning.[23] The forces of industrial agglomeration led to the transformation of Karachi from its initial status of a small town to a metropolitan city and the centre of industry, finance and trade that it is today.[24]

Between 1951 and 1972, the population of Karachi increased by 217 per cent. Most of this increase took place in the Ayub era (1958-68). In 1958, the Kotri Barrage on the lower Indus was commissioned. As a result, the Indus delta shrank from 3,500 to 250 sq km.[25] A large number of villages, mostly of fishermen, were left without drinking water. They migrated to Karachi and started catering to the newly-developing fishing industry. In the early 1960s, the government also started giving credit and land for poultry farms. This growth was linked with the growth of the fishing industry which started to produce fish feed both for local consumption and for export. Industrialization and introduction of Green Revolution technologies were the cornerstones of General Ayub's development policies. This increased international and local trade and more than doubled Karachi's port activities. This also meant increased rural produce. During General Ayub's 'development' decade the Punjab alone produced an average surplus of Rs. 360 million per year from agriculture and most of this was invested in Karachi's economy.[26]

The other significant wave of in-migrants has been from the Punjab province, of big and small businessmen and labourers, both skilled and unskilled. The civil servants recruited prior to the 1970s were also largely from the Punjab province which accounts for their predominance in the police service for instance.[27] The creation of Bangladesh in 1971 and then the Afghan War in the late 1970s brought other waves of poor immigrants into Karachi. The Urdu-speaking Mohajirs, fleeing the crisis in East Pakistan, settled in a large poor neighbourhood, Orangi Town that was one of the three major peripheral areas initially developed in the late 1950s to resettle Karachi's poor who were occupying the city's centre. These satellite towns were developed near industrial estates so that the population living in these colonies could find employment in the nearby factories. This was the initial phase of expansion of Orangi Town, one of the largest urban poor neighbourhoods in the world.

The Biharis[28] who settled in Orangi Town in the 1970s and 1980s in significant percentages identified with the larger Mohajir ethnic politics. This link was further consolidated in the December of 1986 when there were violent ethnic riots in Karachi between the Pashtuns and Mohajirs in the area. The 1990s remain one of the most volatile periods in the city's history in terms of intra- and inter-ethnic conflict along with state-sponsored violence. From the mid-1980s onward, this conflict took on extremely violent dimensions such that Karachi, Pakistan's largest and most important commercial city, became more noted for guerrilla warfare than for its stock exchange.[29]

The Afghan War and the Iranian Revolution also had a major impact on the social, physical and political conditions in the city. About 2,00,000 refugees were added to the city's population, in addition to the 3,50,000 that had come from Bangladesh between 1972 and 1978.[30] Bangladeshis and Burmese migrants replaced the locals in the fishing industry in the 1990s and a large number of Sri Lankans and a few Filipinos became domestic servants to the richer Karachiites.

The myth of Mohajir ethnicity during the late 1980s and early 1990s was due to economic deprivation and marginalization of political power in Pakistan. During both the terms of Pakistan People's Party (PPP) rule during 1972-7 and 1988-90, Mohajir politics in urban Sindh was charged with violence and rejection of all other ethnicities. This conflict changed completely in the 1990s as instead of the ethnic factor, politics in Sindh began to be influenced by Mohajir-State confrontation.[31]

The MQM addressed this sense of 'relative deprivation' effectively, and thus became an extremely successful example of collective mobilization of ethnic loyalties.[32] The state used violent methods while dealing with the MQM and promoted divisions within it. The state also promoted Punjabis and Pashtuns to settle in Karachi against the MQM. Conflict may be defined as arising from mutually incompatible goals between two or more parties where an effective coordinating mechanism does not exist.[33]

In the 1980s, the conflict caused unaccounted number of deaths, plunged the province of Sindh into lawlessness and transformed the port city of Karachi into another Beirut.[34] In 1987, violence escalated in Karachi as those operating the transportation systems and refugees together fought for the control over the economic resources and political control of the city. The conflict acquired an ethnic colouring; a number of ethnic parties surfaced and existing ones became more powerful. Guns were used in the conflict, and the city was put under long periods of curfew.[35]

In 1992, in order to establish its credentials as a broad-based party, it changed its nomenclature from the Mohajir Qaumi Mahaz to Muttahida Qaumi Mahaz. The MQM has sought to portray itself as a party of the urban middle class fighting the reactionary feudal elements in Pakistan.[36] But this transformation is full of contradictions since by acquiring a broad-based image it would be undercutting the *raison d'être* of its existence which is ethnicity. Karachi is a deeply divided city, but also a very big city with a remarkable capacity to tolerate episodes of great violence. In 1989, the population was already 8 million, bigger than London's. By 2009, it had swelled to a megalopolis of around 18 million.[37]

In 2000, the federal Interior Ministry set up the National Aliens' Registration Authority (NARA) to collect data on international migrants. Today NARA estimates that there might be as many as 1.1 million irregular migrants from Bangladesh, and another 4,00,000 to 5,00,000 refugees or migrants from Afghanistan currently residing in Karachi.[38]

Including the population of ethnic Bengalis who are longstanding citizens of Pakistan, some commentators have claimed that there are over a million ethnic Bengalis and perhaps 2,00,000 Burmese in Karachi. However, the idea that around 10 per cent of the entire population of Karachi is made up of migrants and refugees from Bangladesh and Burma remains implausible and untested.[39]

According to the 1998 census, the population of Karachi was 11 million of which 1.2 million were 'aliens' which included migrants from Bangladesh, Burma and Iran along with refugees from Afghanistan. The growth rate had declined from 5.07 per cent between 1972-81 to 3.3 per cent between 1981-98. However, in statistical terms the number of persons added to Karachi's population per year had increased to 4,66,200, which is more than what is added to the majority of the cities on the globe.[40] According to the 1998 census, 48.52 per cent were Urdu speaking; 13.94 per cent were Punjabi speaking; 11.42 per cent were Pashto speaking; 7.22 per cent were Sindhi speaking; 4.34 per cent were Baluchi speaking and 2.11 per cent were Seraiki speaking. These figures suggest that migration from KP and the Sindh and Seraiki areas has increased considerably. Also, since there has been no major migration of Urdu speakers, their number in percentage terms has declined.[41]

Over the course of three major waves of internal migration, Pashtun and Punjabi workers, followed later by Bengali and Bihari, and Afghan refugees flooded the city, swelling its population and giving rise to multiple ethnic conflicts. In 2007, it was paradoxically Pakistan's richest city and the poorest and most violent. The state's failure to provide basic public amenities, combined with widespread unemployment,[42] led to struggles over resources, jobs, and educational opportunities, which at times exploded into violence.

The reasons for recent influx of refugees are the flood in August-September 2010, that affected near about 20 million people and the military action in the spring of 2009 against militants in Malakand region of the KP province, leading to an exodus of about 2.3 million refugees in a little over a fortnight and creating one of the largest displacement crisis in recent times. Military operations against Taliban militants in the Federally Administered Tribal Areas (FATA) bordering Afghanistan also contributed considerably to involuntary displacement, pushing the number of internally displaced persons to 2.7 million between April-July 2009, the largest internal displacement of population in the country's history until then.[43] Karachi has seen a 35-fold increase in its spatial expansion since the emergence of Pakistan. Moreover, estimates are that by the year 2015, the city may reach a population of 19.2 million with an annual growth rate of over 5 per cent.[44]

After 2006, land grabbing increased when political parties backed by the government became involved. Almost 70 per cent of the settlements in Karachi are illegal. Around 1,00,000 illegal plots change hands in the city every year. It is a Rs. 25 billion a year business. The city's boundaries have expanded at a very fast pace. The land grabbed is mainly government property. Clashes are greater in areas where there are rival parties and where land value is higher. Land grabbers join political parties.[45] The 2008 elections revealed the demographic changes occurring in Karachi. A turf war started between MQM and the Awami National Party (ANP), the emerging political force in Karachi.

The recent violence is a threat to the peace of the city. The present violence is both sectarian as well as ethnic. The growing nexus between the MQM-H (a breakaway faction of MQM-A) and the Pakistani state is another cause of concern, as both are incompatible and MQM-A is engaging in the war against everybody, be it Sindhis, Pashtuns, Punjabis, MQM-H, or the state. There are no-go areas in Karachi. Torture cells have been discovered where the MQM-A used to torture the people of opposite groups. Presently the Pashtuns have occupied the periphery of Karachi city and they are controlling the transport system, the arms trade, and the drugs trade all over Pakistan.

In the 2008 elections, the ANP for the first time won two provincial assembly seats in Karachi. This is a miniscule percentage of the 130 seats in the provincial assembly. It seems to have severely rattled the MQM, which had got used to a monopoly over the Karachi seats. It was after this that MQM denunciations of the supposed Taliban infiltration of the Pashtun community in Karachi really took off.[46]

The violence has its roots in crime because of the covert and overt support extended by the state and almost all political parties to the mafias and powerful predatory groups that have largely come to determine the highly weaponized city's urban infrastructure development. While politicians play out their games of survival in the multi-ethnic city of 17 million people, the writ of the state is nowhere to be seen. The result is that Karachi has been turned into a virtual war zone.[47]

Although the city has a history of political, ethnic and sectarian violence, the year 2011 saw horrific bloodshed that was unprecedented even by Karachi's standards. This latest violence would erupt without a warning, claim dozens of lives and would subside as abruptly and inexplicably as it had emerged. This sequence of killings was often repeated several times a week. In July alone, at least 358 people were killed in flare-ups of violence that paralyzed the city.[48] The real issues of tensions among different ethnicities of the country are regional inequality, both in economic opportunity and in the representation of different ethnic groups and provisions in government services including the armed forces and the resource allocation, not only of the government's funds, but also of the natural resources.

The uniqueness of Karachi is that due to the migration in the 1940s, 1950s and 1960s, a second generation of refugees has grown up in the city (almost 70 per cent of the population is Karachi born). These second-generation migrants see Karachi as their home; they have a more vested stake in the running of the city and feel entitled to a say in local politics and administration. And moreover, they, unlike their predecessors are educated, have broken away from their traditional clan and rural structure, and have a need to identify with urban institutions and political processes. They often feel excluded from decision-making, which they see as controlled by the elite of the city. Thus they are alienated from the mainstream of political and social life. Their attempts to rectify the situation through dialogue and political process are almost always thwarted, leading to violence and class and ethnic clashes.[49]

Impact of Ethnic Transformation

After Partition, Karachi became one of the most important centres for Pakistan's industrial and commercial growth. Until 2007, it was paradoxically Pakistan's richest city and the poorest and most violent.[50] Much of the city is divided into clusters of residential colonies and slums, some of which are ethnically homogeneous and have distinct ethnic lines. Unplanned squatter dwellings, *katchi abadi*s, have spread uncontrollably. Almost half the population lives in these unplanned settlements, which often lack electricity, sewers and running water. An estimated 3,50,000 persons still move to Karachi every year, further straining its already inadequate infrastructure.[51] Problems of accommodation are the most acute in Karachi, where the inhabitants of sprawling squatter settlements, *jhuggie*s, already live in crowded conditions without access to secure and affordable water supplies, health, education, and transportation services.[52]

However, the politics of ethnic difference linked to urbanization and rural-urban migration has led to ethnic and social heterogeneity in most urban spaces of Pakistan. In Karachi, as a microcosm of Pakistani social life, in the last three decades the nation's history unfolds with all its social and political tensions.[53] The demography of the city changed substantially. This was because of the forced migration from Afghanistan to the urban centres of Pakistan and especially Karachi. In the February 2008 elections, this demographic change assumed political contours with the ANP winning two provincial assembly seats from Karachi. Thus, for the first time in two decades Pashtuns were winning in Karachi. This was because of the fact that there are certain areas in the city where the Pashtuns are heavily concentrated. This gave them an opportunity to exert their power in the assembly elections. The erosion of control over Karachi was felt all the more because of the free run the MQM had in the city through the Musharraf years. While politicians play out their games of survival in the multi-ethnic city of 17 million people, the writ of the state is nowhere to be seen. The result is that Karachi has been turned into a virtual war zone.[54] Ira Haleem holds the view that a culture of mistrust, ethno-nationalism and sectarian hatreds, superimposed on a democratically unconsolidated polity, has encouraged fluid inter and intra-group/party alliances.[55]

There have been targeted assassinations of local leaders or supporters of various parties. There have also been increasing cases of abduction, torture and murder of people suspected of being rival political supporters or of simply belonging to a rival ethnic group. This is reminiscent of the 1990s when trussed-up bodies bearing torture marks turned up in gunny bags, sometimes with pieces of paper bearing gruesome messages of vendetta. Besides killing of political and ethnic rivals, extortion has become particularly vicious with several cases of grenade attacks on non-compliant business premises. Ominously, casualties have recently included a number of Sindh police personnel killed or wounded while intervening in armed clashes between rival groups.[56]

Land is an important issue in Karachi. There is a constant struggle to acquire and develop land through legal or illegal means. A powerful nexus between formal sector developers, politicians and bureaucrats manages not only to acquire all vacant land, but even land that has been set aside for recreational and amenity purposes. Through this nexus, developers are also able to violate bye-laws and zoning regulations, encroach upon compulsory open space and even build upon natural drainage channels and infrastructure reservations.[57]

Infrastructure in Karachi has deteriorated, including electricity and gas supply, water availability, quality of roads and transport systems and garbage collection. This has generated frequent public protests, strikes and affected commercial activity and industrial output. The law and order situation has ruined Karachi's image internationally and foreign investment and trade have plummeted, leading to flight of capital and shifting of industries/businesses to other cities in Pakistan or abroad.

As the country's main seaport and financial centre, Karachi is well connected to the global trading and financial system and is also the region's exit point for the global trade in narcotics.[58] It is Pakistan's richest and, simultaneously, it's most reprieved large city. Nowhere else in the country is per capita income higher, and Karachi alone contributes 60 per cent of the country's overall taxes and more than 40 per cent of the country's gross domestic product (GDP) – but only a fraction is reinvested in the city by the national government.[59] In this sense, the city suffers from structural violence as well as from the aggregation of individual suffering.

A parallel economy is developing in Karachi. Extortionists used to personally go and ask for *bhatta*[60] earlier. Now they send a *parchi* (chit). Sometimes a person receives multiple *parchi*s from various extortionists. Those ignoring the *parchi*s are threatened with death or kidnapping of their family. If the demands are still ignored the threats are carried out. More recently, failure to comply with *parchi* demands have resulted in hand grenades being thrown at shops. As a result of this, small businesses owned by communities that were in a minority in certain neighbourhoods have moved into areas where their ethnic population is concentrated. This is systematic ethnic cleansing and helps manipulate election results. All businesses have to contend with extortionists linked to political parties. Gangs also 'tax' drugs, gambling dens and property transactions. They give no *bhatta* to the police as they are stronger than them but used to do so six or seven years ago.[61]

The Pakistan Institute of Peace Studies (PIPS) found that ethno-political violence in Karachi claimed 636 lives in 2010, compared with 600 lives lost in the Baluchistan uprising and 2,300 deaths due to the jihadist insurgency. On current trends, Karachi's political violence is likely to become comparable, in terms of lives lost, with the war Taliban and related jihadists in the north of Pakistan.[62] Amnesty International reports that unrecorded arrests and interrogation are commonly used in Karachi to intimidate political opponents.[63]

Atul Kohli argues that ethnic conflicts depend on two variables – (a) the level of institutionalization, and (b) the quality of leadership. If the level of institutionalization is high and the institutions are developed politically then there is less possibility of any ethnic riot or ethnic conflict. Same is the case with the quality of leadership. If the leader is accommodative and accommodates the various sections of the society within the government then there is very less possibility of any ethnic riot.[64] This is exactly what happened in the case of Karachi.

Ashutosh Varshney argues that there is an integral link between the structure of civic life in a multi-ethnic society, on the one hand, and the presence or absence of ethnic violence on the other. Two interconnected arguments are there. First, inter-ethnic and intra-ethnic networks of civic engagement play very different roles in ethnic conflict. Because they build bridges and manage tensions, inter-ethnic networks are agents of peace, but if communities are organized only along intra-ethnic lines and the interconnections with other communities are very weak or non-existent, then ethnic violence is quite likely. Second, civic networks, both intra-ethnic and inter-ethnic, can also be broken down into two other types: organized and quotidian. These, in other words, can be called as associational forms of engagement and everyday forms of engagement. Both forms of engagement, if robust, promote peace; on the contrary, their absence or weakness opens up the space for ethnic violence. Vigorous associational life, if inter-ethnic, acts as a serious constraint on politicians, even when ethnic polarization is in their political interest. The more the associational networks cut across ethnic boundaries, the harder it is for politicians to polarize communities.[65]

Steve Inskeep in his book *Instant City: Life and Death in Karachi* opines that everything that makes this 'Instant City' (Karachi) vibrant can also make it violent. Its swift and disorderly growth creates room for corruption and organized crime. Ethnic groups migrate here from different places, speak different languages, and coalesce into rival political parties that battle over money, power and real estate.[66]

'Narrow, sectarian interests of religio-political leaders, an authoritarian state and a mutilated civil society, have plagued Karachi, once a vibrant and ethnically plural coastal city, into a vortex of unending violence and terror.'[67] The state of Karachi at present is like that of Hobbsean 'State of Nature', whereby everybody is at war with everybody. It is crucial to identify the different categories of violence that the city has been experiencing since the mid-1980s: authorities *vs.* the MQM, MQM-A *vs.* MQM-H, non-Mohajir *vs.* Mohajir, Haquiqi *vs.* its own rebels, criminal mafias *vs.* criminal mafias, and many more types of ethnic violence.

Karachi's agony is basically a conflictive relationship among a few powerful and highly ambitious individuals. Their use of inflammatory symbols including nationalism, religion and ethnicity, and the misuse of power by the official functionaries motivated by personal interests have not allowed any durable peace in the city. From a democratic point of view of development, the problem is not to eradicate regionalism altogether but to undercut it to manageable proportions.

The Times, London, in a lead article in November 1994, labelled Karachi as a 'City of Riches and Shattered Dreams'. It further said that Karachi had grown into a megalopolis where life moved fast and street violence had become a norm. Indeed, more than 65 per cent of Pakistan's industries and 80 per cent of its finance, banking, and business are concentrated in the city and people come to it from all over the country to find jobs and fulfill their dreams.[68]

At the end of the day, Karachi needs sustained national, regional and local initiatives based on radical decentralization and substantial democratization. Most of all, Karachiites and their fellow Pakistanis need to make a fresh beginning based on hope, tolerance, reconciliation and dynamism. Personalities – so-called strong men – should give way to enduring institutions, and differences must be resolved through negotiations and by strengthening local and accountable institutions. Kamila Shamsie sums up the situation in Karachi in the following manner:

> We all knew it would start up again – the shootings on a massive scale, the unnatural silence in the evenings, the siege mentality – but for the moment, for today, Karachi was getting back on its feet, as it had always been able to do, and that didn't just mean getting back to work, but getting back to play: friendship, chai, cricket on the street, conversation . . . in the midst of everything that was happening, Karachi had decided to turn round and wink at me. And in that wink was serious intent: yes, the city said, I am a breeding ground for monsters, but don't think that is the full measure of what I am.[69]

Conclusion

Thus, we can say that demographic concentration of all major ethnic groups leads to polarizsation and ethnic conflict. The case of Karachi is a living example. Political parties grab this opportunity and they provide patronage to ethnic mafias to attain political power which leads to state-sponsored violence. Political parties, after coming to power, pursue policies to provide benefit to their fellow ethnic groups. This kind of behaviour by political parties disappoint the people who are neutral and thereby they feel alienated.

Generally speaking, in Karachi the increase in multi-ethnic and economically marginal population and the state's inability to provide housing and other social amenities to its populace has encouraged a privatized informal sector of land grabbing and allocation, resulting in the mushrooming of unplanned squatter settlements that house almost 40 per cent of the city's population. As the size of these communities has grown in the last two decades large-scale industrial growth has also declined. Economic liberalization in the 1990s under pressure from international financial institutions like the IMF has left a deep impact on the economy of Pakistan and the lives of the working poor. The impact has primarily been on the employment sector with rising male unemployment due to privatization, retrenchment of labour in the formal sector and the lack of growth of new industries. Akbar Zaidi's important survey of Pakistan's economy has clearly shown that the impact of the Structural Adjustment Programmes (SAP) has been mixed, and the privatization of industries, the reduction in development expenditure, and the liberalization of trade and economy have only increased long-term poverty in Pakistan.

The government's stance on Karachi has been long on rhetoric and woefully devoid of substance. That has led to an entirely justifiable crisis of confidence in the government's ability and sincerity to prevail over crime and bloodshed. The state has little writ in Karachi. Whatever strategy the government had for restoring law and order in the city has clearly not worked. Karachi's present state of woe in large part is because the state either looked the other way or facilitated political parties as they formed and armed militant wings, which are in essence private militias. Instead of jointly striving to address the causes of friction and stamp out violence, all political actors in Karachi have been content with playing to the galleries in their respective constituencies. The level of mutual distrust among the main political parties in Karachi is truly astounding. However, the fact that they have remained part of coalition governments for years testifies that politics is indeed art of the impossible. All political parties should make an effort for the sake of the perpetually suffering people of Karachi to work for peace as enthusiastically as they have to arm themselves. State intervention in Karachi's politics must end. The state should think of caring for and dealing with the people instead of abandoning them to the whims of armed gangs masquerading as political groups.

Karachi is the capital of a supremely tolerant land – the land of sufi saints. Solutions which bring peace and tolerance and allow the city to grow in a smooth progression without the shocks of extreme violence and intolerance cannot be out of reach for the citizens of Karachi, and indeed for all the inhabitants of Pakistan, because for all of them the city is the gateway to life in the globalized world in the twenty-first century. It is in Karachi's destiny to become 'the glory of the East' someday, with a spirit strengthened through the retention of cultural roots and external influences as well as an embrace with the future.

Notes

1. Iftikhar H. Malik, *Pakistan: Democracy, Terror and the Building of a Nation*, London: New Holland Publishers, 2010, p. 20.
2. For an analysis of why, on the basis of a myth of common ancestry, ethnicity can take so many forms (language, race, religion, dress, diction), see Donald Horowitz, *Ethnic Groups in Conflict*, Berkeley: University of California Press, 1985, pp. 41-54. One might add that this definition, though by now widely accepted, is not without problems. If all ascriptive divisions can be the basis of ethnicity, can the landed gentry or women's groups be called ethnic? So long as we equate ascriptive identities with ethnic identities, there is no good answer to such questions. Cited in Ashutosh Varshney, 'Ethnic Conflict and Civil Society', *World Politics*, Baltimore, Maryland, vol. 53, no. 3, April 2001, pp. 362-98.
3. Ibid.
4. Stanley Tambiah, 'Ethnic Conflict in the World Today', *American Ethnologist* (Washington), vol. 16, no. 2, May 1989, p. 335.
5. Paul R. Brass, 'The Politics of Ethnicity in India', in John Hutchinson and Anthony D. Smith (eds.), *Ethnicity*, New York: Oxford University Press, 1996, p. 302.

6. Ibid., p. 303.
7. Mohammad Waseem, *Politics and State in Pakistan*, Islamabad: National Institute of Historical and Cultural Research Centre of Excellence, 2007, p. 110.
8. Charles H. Kennedy, 'Policies of Ethnic Preference in Pakistan', *Asian Survey* (Berkeley), vol. 24, no. 6, June 1984, pp. 688-703.
9. Tai Yong Tan and Gyanesh Kudaisya, *The Aftermath of Partition in South Asia*, London: Routledge, 2000, p. 181.
10. Ibid.
11. Kennedy, 'Policies of Ethnic Preference in Pakistan', pp. 688-703.
12. Maneck B. Pithawalla, *An Introduction to Karachi: Its Environs and Hinterland*, Karachi: The Times Press, 1950, p. 1.
13. Hamida Khuhro, 'The Capital of Pakistan', in Hamida Khuhro and Anwer Mooraj (eds.), *Karachi: Megacity of Our Times*, Karachi: Oxford University Press, 2010, p. 85.
14. Population Census Organisation; Government of Pakistan, Population Census Reports, 1951. Cited in Arif Hasan, *Understanding Karachi: Planning and Reform for the Future*, Karachi: City Press, 1999, p. 24.
15. Vazira Fazila-Yacoobali Zamindar, *The Long Partition and the Making of Modern South Asia: Refugees, Boundaries, Histories*, New Delhi: Viking Publishers, 2012, p. 45.
16. Nichola Khan, *Muhajir Militancy in Pakistan: Violence and Transformation in the Karachi Conflict*, London: Routledge, 2010, p. 143.
17. Oscar Verkaaik, 'Muhajir Politics: Ethnicity, Islam and the Muhajir Qaumi Movement' in Ravi Kalia (ed.), *Pakistan: From the Rhetoric of Democracy to the Rise of Militancy*, New Delhi: Routledge, 2011, p. 51.
18. Hasan, *Understanding Karachi: Planning and Reform for the Future*, p. 24.
19. P.M. Townroe, 'The Case for a National Urban Growth Strategy for Pakistan', Institute of Urban and Regional Development, University of California (Berkley), Working Paper, no. 276, June 1977, p. 12. Cited in Samuel S. Lieberman, 'Demographic Perspectives on Pakistan's Development', *Population and Development Review*, New York, vol. 8, no. 1, March 1982, p. 93.
20. H. Meyerink and R. Vekemans, 'Class Structure in a Basti: The Relation between Resistance on the Urban District Level and Class Struggle', in Johan Willem Schoorl, J.J. van der Linden and K.S. Yap, *Between Basti Dwellers and Bureaucrats: Lessons in Squatter Settlement Upgrading in Karachi*, Oxford: Pergamon Press, 1983, p. 86.
21. Hasan, *Understanding Karachi: Planning and Reform for the Future*, p. 153.
22. Khuhro, 'The Capital of Pakistan', p. 98.

23. Ibid.
24. Shahida Wizarat, 'An Economic Perspective', in Khuhro and Mooraj, eds., *Karachi: Megacity of Our Times,* p. 132.
25. Hasan, *Understanding Karachi: Planning and Reform for the Future,* pp. 26-7.
26. H. Meyerink, 'Karachi's Growth in the Historical Perspective', in Johan Willem Schoorl, J.J. van der Linden and K.S. Yap, *Between Basti Dwellers and Bureaucrats: Lessons in Squatter Settlement Upgrading in Karachi,* Oxford: Pergamon Press, 1983, p. 156.
27. The provincial quota now limits the recruitment of non-Sindhis to civil posts in urban sindh (i.e. Karachi, Hyderabad, and Sukkur) to 2.5 per cent.
28. Biharis are the people who came to live in Pakistan after the separation of its eastern wing in 1971. They mostly live in the Orangi Town area of the city. They migrated to Pakistan's eastern wing during the partition of the subcontinent from the present Indian state of Bihar, Jharkhand and Odisha.
29. Alyssa Ayres, *Speaking Like a State: Language and Nationalism in Pakistan,* New Delhi: Cambridge University Press, 2009, pp. 48-9.
30. Arif Hasan, 'The Growth of a Metropolis', in Khuhro and Mooraj (eds.), *Karachi: Megacity of Our Times,* p. 159.
31. Arshi Saleem Hashmi, 'Conflict Transformation from Ethnic Movement to Terrorist Movement: Case Studies of Tamils in Sri Lanka and Muhajirs in Pakistan', Policy paper published by *Regional Centre for Strategic Studies* (Colombo), Policy Studies 45, 2008, pp. 26-7.
32. Farhat Haq, 'Rise of the MQM in Pakistan's Politics of Ethnic Mobilization', *Asian Survey* (Berkeley), vol. 35, no. 11, November 1995, p. 993.
33. Joseph Montville, 'Transnationalism and the Role of Track-Two Diplomacy', in W. Scott Thompson and Kenneth M. Jensen (eds.), *Approaches to Peace: An Intellectual Map,* Washington, D.C.: United States Institute of Peace Press, 1992, p. 262.
34. Beirut is amongst the world's most dangerous cities as it has very high rate of deaths during conflict and the situation in the 1980s in Karachi was quite similar to that of Beirut. URL: http://globalgeopolitics.net/wordpress/2011/07/12/karachi-beirut-of-south-asia/ (accessed on 25 April 2012).
35. Arif Hasan, 'Karachi and the Nature of Urban Violence', *The Urban Age* (London), vol. 1, no. 4, September 1991, p. 6.

36. Teesta Ghosh,'Ethnic Conflict in Sindh and its Impact on Pakistan', in Rajat Ganguly and Ian Maccduff, eds., *Ethnic Conflict and Secessionism in South and Southeast Asia: Causes, Dynamics, Solutions,* New Delhi: Sage, 2003, pp. 110-15.
37. Anatol Lieven, *Pakistan: A Hard Country,* London: Allen Lane, 2011, p. 303.
38. The NARA data are assumed to derive from a survey conducted by the interior ministry. The full results of this survey, or indeed its methodology have not been made public. It is not clear whether this survey was based on statistical sampling, and it is more likely to be based on informed guesswork and extrapolation. There are strong grounds for suspecting that the results of this survey, particularly those pertaining to migrants from Bangladesh, might be problematic. Moreover, there are no other known surveys of international migrants – regular or irregular – that can help to verify, corroborate or indeed, query, the figures presented by NARA. Cited in Marcello Balbo,ed., *International Migrants and the City,* Venice: UN-Habitat Publications, 2005, p. 155.
39. Haris Gazdar,'A Review of the Migration Issues in Pakistan', paper presented at the 'Regional Conference on Migration, Development and Pro-Poor Policy Choices in Asia', organized by the Refugee and Migratory Movements Research Unit, Bangladesh, and the Department for International Development, UK, at Dhaka, Bangladesh, 22-4 June 2003.
40. Hasan,'The Growth of a Metropolis,' p. 163.
41. Ibid.
42. The 1998 census put Karachi's unemployment rate at 17.5 per cent, although experts estimate that nearly 30 per cent of the male workforce may be unemployed.
43. Najam U Din, 'Internal Displacement in Pakistan: Contemporary Challenges', Human Rights Commission of Pakistan, October 2010, p. 5.
44. World Business Council for Sustainable Development.URL: http:// www.wbcsd.org/plugins/DocSearch/ details.as p? type=DocDet& ObjectId=Mtg1,2005-10-11 (accessed on 26 November 2011).
45. 'Report of a Human Rights Commission of Pakistan Fact-Finding Mission', Human Rights Commission of Pakistan, p. 9. URL: http:// www.hrcp-web.org/pdf/final%20Karachi%20FF%20report.pdf (accessed on 25 May 2012).
46. Ibid., p. 321.

47. Anita Joshua, 'Pakistan's Commercial Capital on the Boil', *The Hindu* (New Delhi), 19 August 2011.
48. 'Report of a Human Rights Commission of Pakistan Fact-Finding Mission', p. 1.
49. Hasan, 'Karachi and the Nature of Urban Violence', p. 4.
50. International Crisis Group, 'Pakistan: Karachi's Madrasas and Violent Extremism', *Asia Report,* no. 130, 29 March 2007, p. 3.
51. Ibid.
52. I. Hussain, M. Afzal and S.A.A.B. Rizvi, *Social Characteristics of the People of Karachi* (Karachi: Pakistan Institute of Development Economics, Monographs in the Economics of Development, No.14, 1965. Cited in Samual S. Liberman, 'Demographic Perspectives on Pakistan's Development', *Population and Development Review*, New York, vol. 8, no. 1, March 1982, p. 82.
53. In late twentieth century, Karachi remained the industrial, commercial and trade-centre of Pakistan along with its major port. It housed approximately 8 per cent of its overall population and 24 per cent of its urban population. On the one hand, spatially the city today is segregated into privileged neighbourhoods with private security arrangements and independently managed social services. On the other hand, the phenomenal growth has resulted in the mal-distribution of civic resources to the poorest of its population.
54. Joshua, 'Pakistan's Commercial Capital on the Boil'.
55. Ira Haleem, 'Ethnic and Sectarian Violence and the Propensity towards Praetorianism in Pakistan', *Third World Quarterly* (London), vol. 24, no. 3, June 2003, pp. 463-77.
56. Haris Gazdar, 'Karachi Battles', *Economic and Political Weekly* (Mumbai), vol. 46, no. 38, 17-24 September 2011, p. 20.
57. Hasan, *Understanding Karachi: Planning and Reform for the Future*, pp. 51-2.
58. Peter Gizewski and Homer-Dixon Thomas, 'Urban Growth and Violence: Will the Future Resemble the Past?', Occasional paper for the project on *Environment, Population and Security,* American Association for the Advancement of Science (Washington D.C.), 2005, p. 16. Cited in Daniel Esser, 'The City as Arena, Hub and Prey Patterns of Violence in Kabul and Karachi', *Enviornment and Urbanisation* (London), vol. 16, no. 31, 2004, p. 35.
59. Navid Kermani, *Schoner neuer Orient. Berichte von Stadten und Kriegen*, Munich: C.H. Beck, 2003. Cited in ibid.

60. *Bhatta* means 'extortion money'. Traders in Karachi have to give *bhatta* to the ethnic gang mafias, to continue their trading activities unabated.
61. 'Report of a Human Rights Commission of Pakistan Fact-Finding Mission', p. 31.
62. Gazdar, 'Karachi Battles', p. 19.
63. 'Pakistan: Human Rights Crisis in Karachi', *Amnesty International Report*, February 1996. URL: http:// www.amnesty.org/en/library/asset/ASA33/001/1996/en/9ae57e3d-eb13-11dd-98d3-79fb64d46c94/asa330 011996en.pdf (accessed on 8 June 2012).
64. Atul Kohli, 'Can Democracies Accommodate Ethnic Nationalism? Rise and Decline of Self-Determination Movements in India', *The Journal of Asian Studies* (Ann Arbor, Michigan), vol. 56, no. 2, May 1997, pp. 325-44.
65. Varshney, 'Ethnic Conflict and Civil Society: India and Beyond', pp. 362-3.
66. Steve Inskeep, *Instant City: Life and Death in Karachi,* New Delhi: Penguin Books, 2011, pp. 11-12.
67. Iftikhar H. Malik, 'What is Wrong in Karachi?', *Economic and Political Weekly* (Mumbai), vol. 33, nos. 33/4, 15-28 August 1998, p. 2219.
68. Mehtab S. Karim, 'Changing Demographic, Social, and Economic Conditions in Karachi City, 1959-94: A Preliminary Analysis', *The Pakistan Development Review* (Islamabad), vol. 34, no. 4, part III, Winter 1995, p. 1093.
69. Kamila Shamsie, *Kartography*, London: Bloomsbury Publishing, 2003, p. 259.

CHAPTER 5

Environmental Movements in Pakistan

A Case Study of Mangla Dam in Mirpur

Puyesh Kant Sharma

Introduction

THE DEVELOPMENT of environmental issues and activities in Pakistan has caught the concerns of civil society, intelligentsia, policy makers and people at large. It has given rise to the debate of balancing economic growth, the beneficiaries of growth and ecological sustainability in Pakistan. The lack of the management of e-waste and building of big dams for power generation that result in migration, violation of the rights of the indigenous people, degradation of their health and disturbance in the ecosystem shows the apathetic nature of the state towards the local people and ecology. The growing consciousness with regard to environmental deterioration has given rise to environmental movements in Pakistan. However, the state apparatus has applied the 'legitimate' violence clause to suppress the movement of the masses, especially the anti-Mangla Dam movement in Mirpur. Here in the name of development, the rights of indigenous people are being violated, their culture is being suppressed, their economy shattered and they are politically alienated. This arises questions that need answers. These questions are:

- What are the patterns of development?
- Development for whom?
- Where is sustainability?
- Why are the indigenous people being suppressed?
- If so, has this raised the basic issues of livelihood, social justice and equity?

Looking at such a state of affairs, the state along with civil society groups has tried to manage these concerns. Here again the dual policies on the part of government of Pakistan has given rise to the notion of nationalism and identity politics, especially after the policy of the government of Pakistan over Mangla Dam in Mirpur and Kalabagh Dam in Sindh. Besides, ecological imbalance and mass rehabilitation as a result of the construction of dams, has created concerns about environmental and human security in Pakistan. In such a state of affairs, it is the environmental movements which are raising mass consciousness and reasonable concerns of people and policy makers towards sustainable economics, politics and ecology of Pakistan.

State of Environment in Pakistan

No doubt, Pakistan has a diverse landscape, hosts large deserts, gushing rivers, and a number of the highest peaks in the world. But its environment is marred by many issues such as poor solid waste management, degradation of forests, scarcity of water, excessive use of pesticides for agriculture, poor environmental standards in industries, and weak governance structures.[1] Environmental laws enacted are not enforced properly to help stop the disasters.

Pakistan is an agriculture-based country; experts consider climate change a great threat. Having such vulnerabilities, it is not adequately concerned about crop failure and loss of livestock that will lead to food insecurity and serious conflicts over resources. Droughts, floods, scarcity of water resources, health risks, meager energy resources, socio-economic and political instability can be disastrous to the people of Pakistan. The flood that occurred in July 2010 and again in 2011 is also thought to be influenced by climate change, increased temperatures and rapid glacial melt. All these environmental concerns need serious attention on the part of civil society, intelligentsia, policy makers and people.

Legislations as Part of Environmental Movements

It was in the 1980s that the environmental movement in Pakistan initiated. The enactment of the Pakistan Environmental Protection Ordinance in 1983, followed by the formation of the Pakistan Environmental Protection Council (PEPC) in 1984, an apex body for setting up environmental policies in the country, are the various steps taken by the government. However, no major action in terms of environmental policies or practices was carried out until 1992, when the government endorsed the National Conservation Strategy (NCS) as an environmental policy at the sectoral level.[2] The then prime minister of Pakistan Mian Nawaz Sharif presented the NCS at the Rio Earth Summit in 1992. This also proved to be the starting point of the revolution of Information and Communication Technologies (ICTs) in the country, when the United Nations awarded a grant to Pakistan via the International Union for Conservation of Nature (IUCN) for the implementation of its much-acclaimed Sustainable Development Networking Programme. Even though the destruction of the environment continued at a rapid pace, yet significant steps were taken towards institutional development and policy formulation to safeguard the environment in the country. In this context, the important milestones include the Pakistan Environmental Protection Act in 1997, the establishment of the Federal and Provincial Environmental Protection Agencies (EPAs), Environmental Protection Authority (EPA), the approval of National Environmental Quality Standards (NEQS), the initiation of the Provincial Conservation Strategies, and acceptance of local communities/NGOs as partners in environmental management.

Pakistan Environmental Protection Act, 1997

The Pakistan Environmental Protection Act, 1997 (PEPA, 1997) provides for the protection, conservation, rehabilitation and improvement of the environment, for the prevention and control of pollution for sustainable development. It focuses on the implementation of policies, delegation and devolution of power to government agencies, enforcement of National Environmental Quality Standards, introduction of Environment Impact Assessment (EIA), regulatory regimes for hazardous and waste substances and providing appellant forum for environmental cases.

Under the act following rules were drafted and notified:

- National Environmental Quality Standards Regulations, 2000
- Pakistan Environmental Protection Agency and Environmental Impact Assessment Regulations, 2000

- Revised National Environmental Quality Standards, 2000
- Provincial Sustainable Development Fund (Procedure) Rules, 2001
- Environmental Sample Rules, 2001
- Pakistan Biosafety Rules, 2005
- National Biosafety Guidelines, 2005

Implementing Agencies of PEPA

PEPA, 1997 is responsible for the implementation of the project. Other implementing agencies include:

- Baluchistan Environmental Protection Agency
- North West Frontier Province Environmental Protection Agency
- Punjab Environmental Protection Agency
- Sindh Environmental Protection Agency

Pakistan is a member of the following chemicals and waste-related international conventions:

- Basel Convention on the Control of Transboundary Movements of Hazardous Wastes and their Disposal.
- Rotterdam Convention on the Prior Informed Consent Procedure for Certain Hazardous Chemicals and Pesticides in International Trade.
- Stockholm Convention on Persistent Organic Pollutants.
- Vienna Convention for the Protection of the Ozone Layer and Montreal Protocol on Substances that Deplete the Ozone Layer.

Environmental Impact Assessment (EIA) in Pakistan

EIA in a country like Pakistan is a hard and challenging task particularly when the environmental institutions are weak and the awareness level is low. It is quite encouraging that now the EIA process has started to begin in the country in an organized manner. However, there is greater need for improvement and overcoming the practical constraints. There are limited capacities and capabilities with many agencies responsible for protecting environment in relation to the evaluation of the Initial Environmental Examination (IEE) or EIA. There are no training programmes for persons responsible for the evaluation of IEE/EIA reports. The key challenges of EIA process management and practice are to make the system more effective, more practical especially in dealing with strategic environmental assessment, more efficient and transparent, and more accountable. With respect to natural environment, there are also many challenges, which are encountered during assessment of environmental impacts of activities of proposed projects in various sectors. Some of them are project specific and some are general. The three major challenges are:

- Protecting human and environmental health from contamination of environment
- Conservation of biodiversity
- Safeguarding the productivity of natural resources.

Even most government departments are not aware of the legal requirement that development projects need to go through an IEE or EIA process. The result is that government departments, such as development authorities support the projects without checking for compliance with the EIA regulations. Particularly projects approved at Departmental Development Working Party (DDWP) level within the budgetary limit of € 0.5 million, which are not submitted to the Planning and Development Divisions (P&Ds). Normally, a representative from that particular section of P&Ds attends the meeting of DDWP who is not or least concerned about the environmental impact of the projects.

But it is of upmost importance to understand that the increasing population and improper management of natural resources has been always a threat to the environment of Pakistan. Like all other developing countries Pakistan has always strived hard for economic growth, controlling population growth and fulfilling the ever-increasing energy demands rather than having concerns about the output of such processes in the form of environmental hazards. As a result, 'green' concerns have never been up on the agenda. Due to focus on economic growth and reducing the poverty rate with limited resources, the country's environmental record is quite poor. Although Pakistan was among the first countries to introduce environmental laws in the 1980s yet it has not been able to back up its commitment to environmental protection. There are some serious steps taken at the government and industrial levels to meet the requirements of the ever changing needs of the environment in the local and global contexts. But it is clear that the government needs to take a step forward and lay greater emphasis on environmental issues facing the country.

Movement to Manage E-waste

Because of widespread poverty and sharp inequality, Pakistan is at the receiving end of the e-waste divide. Besides, e-waste management has been emerging as one of the major hazards to the health of both the environment and the people. If e-wastes are left untreated and lie around in landfills or dumps, they leach into the surrounding soil, water and the atmosphere, thereby adversely affecting human health and ecology. Many elements of e-waste are hazardous such as circuit boards, cathode ray tubes, connectors and other elements that are essential for most electronic goods. These goods contain poisonous substances such as lead, tin, mercury, cadmium and barium. Old electronics are often dumped into municipal waste and then burnt, releasing toxic and carcinogenic substances into the air, which may stunt brain development, disrupt hormone functions or affect reproduction.[3] Pakistan faces the problem mainly on two fronts: on the one hand, the country is used as the dumping ground for over 50,000 tonnes of e-waste by developed countries and, on the other, it generates thousands of tons of local e-waste every year.

Pakistan is a signatory to the Basel Convention and ratified it on 24 July 1994. This convention monitors the movement of toxic wastes. However, the convention becomes flexible when the goods are to be used for the purpose they were designed for. As a result, the relevant regulating agencies in Pakistan allow the import of used computers, as these can be reused. The prices of used computers are low in comparison to new ones, thus creating an increase in demand for old computers. However, such equipments exploit more energy and people are unaware of both the environmental and health problems which can arise when these are disposed of irresponsibly.

The major dumping ground for e-waste from all around the world is Karachi. Although the dumping of waste is prohibited under the EPA Act of 1997, no serious action is taken. Most of the scrap is dumped in the town of Surjani. In the district of Lyari, livelihoods are eked out by hundreds of workers including women and teenage children who dismantle the electronic scrap and extract valuable components such as copper. It may appear to be a convenient way of making a living from trash, but the workers have no idea of the hazards they are exposed to. They usually burn the plastics without proper safety measures or use furnaces that have serious health consequences. The workers, mostly women and children, are exposed to all sorts of toxins. Chemicals such as beryllium, found in computer motherboards, and cadmium, used in chip resistors and semiconductors, are poisonous and could lead to cancer. Chromium in floppy disks, lead in batteries and computer monitors, and mercury in alkaline batteries pose severe health risks. The waste generated by this industry is dumped in the Lyari River, and eventually finds its way into the Arabian Sea, where it contaminates the marine ecosystem. Some of the waste is dumped in landfills where it contaminates the soil. Such landfill sites are also not properly administered.

In the Shershah area, unusable parts and machines are brought to enterprising recycling initiatives which are mostly from the informal sector, where occupational safety laws, safety measures and pre-requisites such as properly ventilated working areas are rarely in place. The workers, mostly women and children, are exposed to all sorts of toxins. So far no strategy has been devised to tackle e-waste in Pakistan, nor are there provisions to regulate e-waste disposal in the national Informational Technology Policy and Action Plan of 2000. At the South Asian Association for Regional Cooperation (SAARC) level there is a ban on hazardous waste and radioactive waste in its environmental strategic development goals but unfortunately e-waste is not included in it. In this background it is important to look into the role of civil society in the management of e-waste in Pakistan in general and Karachi in particular.

Civil Society Initiatives

In such a state of affairs, Mobilink, a leading mobile phone operator, has started the Mobilink Handset Recycling Program, in collaboration with the Pakistan Association of the Deaf (PAD) and the Disabled Welfare Association (DWA).[4] It aims at sharing the benefits of mobile communication with the hearing impaired and the disabled, as well as minimizing the environmental impact of e-waste through recycling. Old and damaged mobile phones, batteries, chargers and accessories are donated by simply dropping them in the recycling bins that have been specifically placed for this purpose at select Mobilink Centres across Pakistan. The company is a leading multinational specializing in GSM products and after-sales services and maintains high environmental and social standards. The donated mobile phones found to be unusable are disposed of in proper manner by Waste Busters, an internationally recognized and fully integrated waste management organization.

But concerns about e-waste so far have gained little attention from the government and NGOs. Till now no scientific study has been made to assess the impact of e-waste processing on environment. No reliable data is available on the volume of used electronic components imported and the fraction of it recycled or dumped as solid waste. Alongside there is a dire need to determine the detrimental impact of e-waste processing on public health. Fast-tracking measures and a national strategy to avoid transforming the cities of Karachi and Lahore into dumping yards is the need of the hour in Pakistan.

In this way, e-waste is an issue which clearly must be addressed immediately before it becomes even more of a problem. Strategies must be evolved to reduce the generation of e-waste and to prevent the legal or illegal import of such waste. It is trying to develop feasible and safe ways of dealing with it. Otherwise the unregulated accumulation of e-waste may well lead to health disasters for all living beings.

Controversy over Kalabagh Dam in Sindh: A Biodiversity Deficit

The Kalabagh dam project is controversial for many reasons. A key reason has to do with the decision-making process. This process is highly centralized, politically coercive – the belated decision for consensus notwithstanding – and technically flawed. The project comes at an important confluence of events. It reflects a crisis of governance, where decision-makers are at odds with an increasingly vocal society. Also, the global and regional context for assessing large dams like Kalabagh is changing, with conventionally described irrigation, flood control and energy benefits being viewed through the prism of sustainable development. The issues related with the construction of Kalabagh dam are water availability; food and energy; environmental impacts; community displacement and rehabilitation and; the technical and financial feasibility of Kalabagh Dam.

In the Sindh province of Pakistan, Kalabagh Dam could trigger irreversible degradation of the Indus River ecosystem. The global and regional context for assessing large dams like Kalabagh is changing, with conventionally described irrigation, flood control and energy benefits. It also analyses the prospects of sustainable development in Pakistan. The present level of silt discharge, estimated at 100 million tonnes per year, is a four-fold reduction from the original level before the rivers were dammed in the Indus River ecosystem. The combination of salt-water intrusion, and reduced silt and nutrient flows has changed the geomorphology of the delta considerably. The area of active growth of the delta has reduced from an original estimate of 2,600 sq. km (growing at 34 m. per year) to about 260 sq. km.[5] Also the delta is being changed by strong wave erosion, an increasing dominance of sand at the delta front and an increase in wind-blown sand deposits as a result of losses in vegetation. The consequent ravages to the ecosystem have been exceptionally severe, in particular to the mangroves which are its mainstay. They sustained the fisheries, act as natural barriers against sea, keep bank erosion in check and are a source of fuel wood, timber, fodder and forest products, a refuge for wildlife and a potential source of tourism. Without mangroves and the nutrients they recycle and the protection they provide, other components of the ecosystem would not survive.

The direct and indirect benefits of mangroves are enormous. In 1988, Pakistan earned Rs.2.24 billion from fish exports, of which shrimps and prawns constituted 72 per cent. The collective imputed income from fuel wood and forest products was another Rs.100 million. These are broad orders of magnitude, which are threatened by mangrove degradation. Even where numbers are absent, the functions are, in themselves, indicative. For instance, substituting natural with physical barriers (dykes, walls, and dredgers) would entail enormously high capital and maintenance costs. In addition, the wildlife and tourism potential of the mangrove swamps has not been exploited yet and is, potentially, an additional source of income.

A community of about 1,00,000 people resides in coastal villages in the northern side of the Indus delta. The mangroves are a vital source of livelihood for them, both directly (fuel, fodder, grazing) and indirectly (fish, amenity values). The prevailing view is that being under privileged such communities are prone to degrade their environment. However, it is difficult to fathom why poor communities should endanger the very basis of their existence. The more likely explanation is that community practices have not changed, but they appear unsustainable because the resource base has begun to degrade. Communities are more often the victims than the agents of such degradation. The real culprits are water diversion, biological and chemical water contamination and large-scale commercial practices, compounded both by institutional ignorance and complicity in such practices.

Social Mobility, Community Displacement and Rehabilitation

The construction of big dams has given rise to major problems like resettlement, rehabilitation and compensation in land acquisition. With regard to each of these issues, the initial attitude of the Pakistani state towards affected communities was one of dismissal and neglect. However, as more large dams were built (Tarbela, Mangla, Ghazi-Barotha, Chotiari), rising community disaffection coupled with donor pressure ostensibly elicited a measure of response. The formal expression of such response is donor-inspired resettlement action plans, operational guidelines on involuntary resettlement, environmental impact assessments and environmental monitoring systems. With respect to each of these issues, the attitude towards affected communities was one of dismissal and neglect. Regarding Kalabagh Dam project, Shaheen Rafi Khan has highlighted the serious problems because of the following reasons:

- Its viability is premised on water availability figures that are highly questionable.
- The land constraint precludes substantive increases in cultivable area, additional water notwithstanding.
- Crop yield increases based on additional water do not account for the aggravated water logging and salinity that would result; furthermore, higher doses of water are associated with high input use, which degrades both soil, and water quality. Using existing water more efficiently is clearly a better option.
- Hydel energy is not unequivocally cheaper, given the growing propensity to factor in displacement and environmental costs. Also, borrowing costs are likely to be higher as donors have indicated a clear preference for thermal power projects.

- Kalabagh would further exacerbate ecosystem degradation, adding to mangrove and species loss and impoverishing communities which depend on the ecosystem's resources. Also, as an instrument of flood control Kalabagh is poorly supported by historical evidence.

In view of these facts, the option of implementing a sedimentation management project on Tarbela appears a clear winner on all grounds – financial, economic, social and environmental. As a result there is a controversy with regard to the construction of the Kalabagh Dam.

Case Study of Mangla Dam in Mirpur

History of the Dam

Mangla Dam was built on Jhelum River in Mirpur district of 'Azad' Jammu and Kashmir (AJK) after the Indus Water Treaty between India and Pakistan in 1960. The five main rivers which are the lifeline for Indian and Pakistani agriculture and industry originate from Jammu & Kashmir. Pakistan accused India of shortened water supply and claimed that this has ruined the aggregated cultivable land in Pakistan which poses serious threat of famine. The World Bank mediated the Indus Water Treaty to resolve the dispute. The treaty confirmed the Indian authority over the three rivers with the condition that the Indian government will not cut the water supply to Pakistan. Against this background the then Government of Pakistan, headed by General Ayub Khan decided to build the Mangla Dam. This could be good news for Pakistan. However, for AJK in general and for Mirpur district in particular the news was disastrous and they stood against it.

Opposition to the Construction of Mangla Dam

In the beginning, the people of Mirpur who had not yet recovered from the trauma of Partition could not believe that Pakistani government would carry out any plan which will submerge the entire city of Mirpur and its surrounding villages. But, when they became aware of what exactly was going to happen, they rose up in revolt. They formed the Anti-Mangla Dam Movement (AMDM). Kashmiris of all political views, sects, professions, ages and gender opposed the dam and the local political leadership of AJK stood with the people. But the movement was crushed through military might; the top leadership of AJK government is said to have been given an attractive compensation package along with resettlement and development of the displaced Mirpuris.

Promises by the Government of Pakistan

The Government of Pakistan promised new colonies, appropriate compensation, relocation in a new Mirpur inside Pakistan, visas and vouchers for England, cheap electricity and water, new roads and bridges and loyalty to the government of AJK. After such promises the water was released in 1967. The entire Old Mirpur City, 65,000 acres of surrounding land and 260 villages drowned before the tearful eyes of thousands of Mirpuris.

Reality of the Promises

None of the promises made by the Pakistan state were met in letter or spirit.

- The few colonies which were eventually built lacked most of the basic amenities such as water and electricity.
- Hundreds of families went to live inside Pakistan only to discover that they were deceived and cheated. The fertile land promised to them was nowhere seen. Instead there was barren saline land around them. Even for this they had to fight with local landlords and officialdom to gain property rights. So, many of them returned to Mirpur.
- Not even a single Kashmiri came to Britain on the promised voucher or visa. Majority of them came through their personal efforts and contacts with the Kashmiris in Britain who had settled there long ago.
- Hundreds of families are waiting till this day for compensation.
- The electricity tariff in AJK today is Rs. 4.25 a unit compared to Rs. 2.85 a unit in Pakistan.
- A road linking New Mirpur to other parts of Mirpur and Kotli district was built. It is a road without which the movement of

Pakistani army in AJK is virtually impossible. The bridge, which links Dadyaal, one of the seriously affected areas, with Rawalpindi and Islamabad was built only after the people in Dadyaal rose up in rebellion against the AJK government and Pakistani authorities.

- New Mirpur was built but its current prosperity and development owes a lot to the overseas Kashmiris' remittances and investments.

Consequences of the Mangla Dam

As far as Pakistan is concerned Mangla Dam is a vital asset which brings many benefits, second only to the mighty Tarbela as a source of hydroelectric power. It also serves as the principal water storage reservoir for the entire canal system of West Punjab. Thus, Mangla Dam is critical to the success of the Pakistani economy as a whole. However, despite the great benefits in terms of cheap electricity, year-round irrigation and security from flooding which Mangla has brought to everyone in Pakistan proper, those unfortunate enough to live immediately upstream of the dam have had to, as in so many other similar projects elsewhere, bear the brunt of its environmental costs. It is the Mirpuris who have had to witness the disappearance of much of their fertile agricultural land, as well as the district's two market towns, Mirpur and Chaomukh, beneath the waters of the lake. They too have to cope with the intensely disruptive impact of the rising waters on the local infrastructure and particularly on transport and communications. Infrastructural damage is, of course, an inevitable consequence of all such projects. Culturally, the mosques, playgrounds, graveyards, etc., that were eroded have given rise to severe social and mental pressure on an already excluded and traumatized community which has been living under the threat of war for over half a century and has not yet fully recovered from the forced division of state in 1947. Environmentally, in addition to the damage which the resettlement will cause to the surrounding areas, the water of the extended reservoirs of the dam will expand right under the hundreds of homes increasing the risk of children and cattle drowning, pesticide poisoning and snake bites. Although no official record is available common estimates show that an average of 20 children are drowned in the reservoir every year in the Mirpur district.

Rise of Kashmiri Nationalism

So it is that even though the boundary between AJK and Pakistan is, in this region, largely artificial in cultural terms – for there are few, if any, linguistic or cultural differences between those who live on either side of the river Jhelum – Mirpuris now feel themselves to be very different from other Potohari Punjabis. They regularly assert that they are Kashmiris, and by that token not Pakistani. It is not hard to see that the sense of Kashmiri nationalism has emerged so swiftly and so vigorously in Mirpur. Given their very reasonable view that Pakistan has not only overlooked their interests, but has unashamedly exploited both their environmental resources and their hard-earned financial assets, their self-definition as Kashmiris, and not as Pakistanis, provides Mirpuris with a powerful means of both expressing and legitimizing their grievances. Hence there is a great deal of enthusiastic support both within the district itself and even more so amongst the Mirpuri diaspora for the prospect of a Kashmir which is truly *azad* (free). 'Kashmir Zindabad! Pakistan Murdabad!'[6] they cry with great enthusiasm.

Yet, however, genuine these feelings of Kashmiri nationalism may be, they must also be put in context. In the first place they are reinforced by some yet more parochial considerations, not least because the present administration in distant Muzaffarabad which can be reached much more quickly by way of Islamabad and Murree than along the long winding road through the hills, is not only controlled by non-Mirpuris, but by people who ultimately favour Kashmir's incorporation into Pakistan. So it was that when Sardar Qayyum, an integrationist Poonchi Sudhan who was subsequently to become the prime minister of AJK, sought to speak at an election rally in Dadyaal in 1985, he faced hostile demonstrations. Only when protected by a substantial military presence could he be escorted safely out of town. Such tensions remain to this day. As a result of this, there is a rising sense of Kashmiri nationalism in Mirpur.

Further Extension of the Dam

A feasibility report prepared by the Water and Power Development Authority (WAPDA) claims that due to sedimentation the water storage capacity of the dam has declined from the original 5.88 million acre feet (maf) to 4.72 maf. A 50-ft rise in the dam has been estimated to increase the storage capacity to 8.01 maf. This will also generate 1,000 gigawatt hour additional electricity, which is 18 per cent of the total output. General Pervez Musharraf had already promised the additional 3 maf of water to the landlords in Sindh province of Pakistan. All these factors further raised the protests of the people of Mirpur through collective agitation and presentations.

Movement against the Extension

Widespread opposition to the dam extension expressed through the AMDEC is based primarily on the following grounds:

- The rise in silt level is a result of WAPDA's failure to clean the dam every year, which was part of the maintenance plan and appropriate machinery that was provided to carry out this task at the time of dam construction. WAPDA has not cleaned the dam even once over the past 37 years. Therefore, anti-extension campaigners say 'clean the dam and do not cleanse Kashmiris'.
- The rise in silt level is also a result of deforestation in AJK by the Pakistani authorities through their puppets in AJK. A land with 40 per cent forests has become nearly barren due to collaboration between Pakistan and AJK authorities who are once again collaborating to wipe out another large chunk of the Mirpur district and throw over 70,000 people out of their homes.
- Land is already scarce in Mirpur. Even if the Government of Pakistan delivers its promises of resettling displaced people in the nearby land, what will happen to the surplus population of the district in the near future?
- While the dam is built on Kashmiri land all the official Pakistani documents show it to be in Pakistan.

However, the arguments and demands put forward by the AMDEC have fallen on deaf ears. Instead General Pervez Musharraf decided to come to Mirpur and force the extension project on the people. Eleven people including the spokesperson of the campaign, Mohammed Arif are still in prison. The protests are spreading out of AJK into Britain, Europe and USA where committees are being formed to make the world aware of the anti-extension campaign and expose the suppressive practices of the Pakistani government. The question every Kashmiri asks today is:

- Is this merely an issue of water and power needs of Pakistan or Pakistani rulers have made some new deals on the Kashmir and this is just a camouflage?
- Why do not they build Kalabagh Dam in Pakistan that has been shelved for over four decades?

These views have caused a lot of resentment among the people in Mirpur. They have been deprived of their ancestral land, their cultural roots have been affected, their economy has been shattered and their right to live with dignity is being challenged.

Dual Stand of the Government of Pakistan

In the article 'Mangla Dam: Get Out',[7] Shabir Chowdhary argued that planning for Mangla and Kalabagh dams were made around the same time. One dam has lived its natural life and paid back the money spent on it within ten years of its completion; the planning for the other dam is still on the shelves gathering dust.

During President Musharraf's visit to Mirpur there were protests. The protesters were telling those who were there to start the new project to 'get out' of their homeland. They knew plans had been finalized to get them out of their homes and to drown their city once again.

The protesters were shouting 'get out', the planners of the new project at Mangla Dam wanted the Mirpuris to get out of their homes without any fuss because it was in the national interest of Pakistan, and moreover in the interest of *jagirdar*s and industrialists of Punjab. What remains to be seen is who will get out – the authorities have successfully laid down foundations for the new project, but they have also laid down foundations for a movement which could have far-reaching consequences for Pakistan and the people of AJK.

Conclusion

This article has attempted to provide a logical and coherent link between the environmental issues arising out of economic development and policy implementation on one side and strengthening political movements and environmental activism on the other. The devastation because of recent floods in Pakistan, the issue of managing e-waste, the controversy over Kalabagh Dam and the strong resentment against Mangla Dam has given rise to environmental consciousness in Pakistan. People in AJK in general and Mirpur in particular have a sense of insecurity created by the construction of dams. This insecurity has brought a sense of alienation among the people in AJK against Pakistan. Their basic aspirations, needs, right to livelihood and life of dignity have been badly affected. However the case study of Mangla Dam raises many issues which the developing countries as a whole need to address. These are the concerns of development pattern arising out of growth trajectory and exploiting the resource base for economic growth has brought into focus issues of sustainable development, human security and eco-migration. Besides, other issues like the challenge for having secured dams in earthquake zones like South Asia, ability of dams to enhance earthquakes, producing methane gas for global warming and destroying natural ecological balance of the region are the vital parameters to be considered for the economic growth and development of society.

Notes

1. Shahzad Ahmad and Marriyam Rehman, 'Pakistan Report Year 2010 ICTs and Environmental Sustainability' (Report), p. 1. Cited in URL: http://www.giswatch.org/country_report/2010_icts_andenvironmentalsust ain ability/pakistan (accessed on 20 March 2011).
2. Ibid., p. 2.
3. Sabiha Alam, 'Environmental Governance in South Asia', in Abdul-rahim P. Vijapur and Rashmi Doraiswamy, eds., *Globalization and the Third World,* New Delhi: Manak Publications, 2009, pp.145–9.
4. Ahmad and Rehman, 'Report Year 2010 ICTs and Environmental Sustainability', p. 3.
5. Shaheen Rafi Khan, 'Report on the Kalabagh Controversy', CCCSP/SDPI, pp. 1–3. Cited in URL: http:// www.sanalist.org/kalabagh/a-14.htm (accessed on 21 March 2011).
6. Ballard Roger, 'Kashmir Crises: View from Mirpur', *Economic and Political Weekly,* vol. 26, no. 9/10, 2–9 March 1991, Mumbai, p. 516.

7. Shabir Choudhary, 'Mangla Dam- Get Out' (Report) URL: hptt://www.kashmiri.info/index2.php?option=com-content&do_pdf=1&id=907.(accessed on 20 March 2011).

References

Ahmad, Shahzad and Marriyam Rehman, 'Pakistan Report Year 2010 ICTs and Environmental Sustainability' (Report) 2010. URL:http://www.giswatch.org/country_report/2010_icts_andenvironmental sust ainability/pakistan (accessed on 20 March 2011).

Ballard, Roger, 'Kashmir Crises: View from Mirpur', *Economic and Political Weekly* (Mumbai), vol. 26, nos. 9/10, 2-9 March 1991, pp. 513-17.

Dobson, Andrew and Robyn Eckersley, *Political Theory and Ecological Challenge*, New York: Cambridge University Press, 2006.

Hassan, Parvez, 'Pakistani Environmental Laws' (Interview). URL: http://www.pace.edu/school-of-law/sites/pace.edu.school-of-law/files/IJIEA/jciHassanInterview2_jci_2%20jl_13-10_cropped.pdf

Homer-Dixon, Thomas F., *Environment, Scarcity and Violence*, New Jersey: Princeton University Press, 1999.

Mclean, Iain and Alistair McMillan, *Concise Dictionary of Politics,* Indian Edition, New Delhi: Oxford University Press, 2008.

McVean, D.N. and V.C. Robertson, 'An Ecological Survey of Land Use and Soil Erosion, in the West Pakistan and Azad Kashmir Catchment of the River Jhelum', *Journal of Applied Ecology,* vol. 6, no. 1, April 1969, pp. 77-109.

Ministry of Environment, 'Report on Local Government and Rural Development: Environmental Challenges and Responses of Pakistan'. URL: http://unpan1.un.org/intradoc/groups/public/documents/apcity/unpan004673.pdf

P. Vijapur, Abdulrahim and Rashmi Doraiswamy, eds., *Globaliz-ation and the Third World*, New Delhi: Manak Publications, 2009.

Stephans, Piers H.G. with John Barry and Andrew Dobson, *Contemporary Environmental Politics*, New Delhi: Routledge, 2007.

EDUCATION, MEDIA AND POPULAR CULTURE

CHAPTER 6

Language Controversy and Education in Pakistan

Azad Ahmad Khan

Introduction

LANGUAGE IS NATURALLY connected with the people's day-to-day life, their culture, society and their interaction with other people. It also has the compelling symbolic importance as it helps in looking at the outside world the way an individual wants to see.[1] People tend to think, interact and associate first with their own language. Although language is a powerful marker of social identity and prestige, no language is superior or inferior to others but there is a tendency in South Asia to give the language of the ruling class or powerful groups undue importance thereby acknowledging its predominance.[2] However, in a diverse country, dominance of a particular language acts as an important political force to have control over the country's otherwise linguistic minority by having undue advantage over socio-political as well as economic resources of the country.[3] It is marked by cultural and social fragmentation within the society. However, in the changing global scenario, language barriers are barriers to progress, development and upliftment of the society as a whole.

At the time of Mughal Empire, Arabic and Persian, languages of the rulers, were imposed as the official languages and even the native Hindu people had to learn them to get into administrative posts. Other languages were discredited in order to have political control over the subjects.[4] Though Mughals chose Persian as the official language of the state but it is also true that Hindvi was appreciated as a regional language which got semi-official status.[5] When the British came to India they promoted English for their own reasons as to breed a class of elite Indian people to help them in administering the British Indian Empire. Missionary schools were given official patronage and a policy of discrediting the existing languages like Persian and Arabic was followed and the subsequent promotion of Hindustani was taken up.[6] The Hindi language advocates such as the Arya Samaj, Arya Sanskrit, Arya Bhasha and Arya Lipi alienated Muslims and Sikhs in the north over the language issue. But they could not do so among their co-religionists in south India where anti-Brahmanical and pro-Dravidian movements were going on.[7] The Urdu-Hindi controversy of the nineteenth and twentieth-century British India was actually a part of the power struggle between the Hindu and Muslim Salariat class.[8]

Pakistan inherited an under-developed educational infrastructure from the British. After the creation of the country, it was aimed to replace the existing colonial educational system with that kind of education which would cater to the real needs and advancement of the Pakistani nation.[9] There are three streams of education in Pakistan: English medium, the Vernacular medium and the *madrasa* institutions. These schools cater respectively to the rich and the powerful, the ordinary middle class families, and the deprived, poor and marginalized sections of the society.[10] Urdu was chosen as the national language by Mohammad Ali Jinnah, the founder of Pakistan, and was made the official language of the country. It quickly dominated the Pakistani political scene and was made compulsory in all the educational institutions as part of a strategy to promote the so-called 'national unity' or integration. It was promoted subsequently by undermining the indigenous languages and cultures of the people belonging to non-Urdu speakers such as Bengali, Punjabi, Sindhi, Pashto, Baluchi, Siraiki and so on (Table 6.1).

Pakistan is a multi-lingual and multi-cultural society. According to the 1998 census[11] Punjabi is the dominant language of Pakistan followed by Pashto, Sindhi and Siraiki. Urdu is the official and national language of the country and is spoken by not more than 7.57 per cent of the population. It was not the sole language of the region which today comprises Pakistan until British India was divided into India and Pakistan and the Urdu-speaking immigrants from northern India moved to Pakistan. From then onwards Urdu came to be used in all the domains of power in the present state of Pakistan.

TABLE 6.1: LANGUAGES SPOKEN IN PAKISTAN (IN PERCENTAGE)

Census	*1951*	*1961*	*1981*	*1998*	*Change between 1981 and 1998 Census*
Punjabi	28.55	29.02	48.17	44.15	- 4.02
Sindhi	8.47	8.51	11.77	14.10	+ 2.33
Pashto	3.48	3.70	13.14	15.42	+2.28
Siraiki	-	-	09.03	10.53	+0.70
Urdu	2.37	2.65	07.60	07.57	- 0.03
Balochi	1.29	1.09	03.02	03.57	+ 0.55
Others	-	-	02.81	04.66	+1.85

Sources: Census of Pakistan (1998), Government of Pakistan; 'Population by Mother Tongue', Islamabad: Population Census Organisation, 1998; Tariq Rahman, *Language and Politics in Pakistan*, New Delhi: Orient Longman, 2007, p. XX and Aftab A. Kazi, *Ethnicity and Education in Nation Building in Pakistan*, Lahore:Vanguard, 1994, p. 72.

Language and the Demand for Separate Muslim Homeland

The British in colonial India were not concerned with mass education. They founded various schools and colleges in colonial India to train its officers in the local languages so that they could function in their administrative roles more efficiently. They also recruited and trained the local people later to serve in British administration to carry on their economic and political interests. They started giving official patronage to Hindustani language by replacing the erstwhile Persian language which led to suspicion in the minds of Muslim masses.

Language Issue at the Time of Partition

In 1837, English was declared as the official language and the medium of instruction in British India. This was to help spread Western education.[12] Though British made English the official language of the administration, local languages were also used for the purposes of administration wherever it was necessary and for that they allowed colonial administrative officers to be trained in various local languages. This was for the smooth conduct of the administration of the colonial landscape. As an after-effect of the First War of Independence in 1857, the British started giving official patronage to Hinustani language in place of Persian to keep Muslim elites at bay. At the mass level the official patronage of Hindi/Hindustani affected the importance of Urdu which is largely influenced by classical Persian language and script. Like Persian, Urdu was also identified as the language associated with the Muslim aristocracy and masses.

Urdu-Hindi Controversy

In the minds of the majority of the people (Hindu community) in colonial India, Urdu language was seen as a foreign imposition. For the people, it was a strange script with unknown words which was brought by the outsiders.[13] As Hindi became a powerful socio-political force, Urdu speakers felt themselves under attack. Urdu then became a language in need of being defended. Muslims in British India were fearful of their language being attacked by the Hindus. They were so apprehensive that they started projecting the protection of Urdu as the protection of Muslim interests. Urdu was not only projected as the language of Muslims in British India but as the language of entire South Asian Islam. Now people started associating Urdu with Islam and Hindi with Hinduism. Those Muslims who were opposed to Urdu were labelled as anti-Pakistanis in the later days of the demand for Pakistan. Maulana Ashraf Ali Thanvi, an Islamic scholar of Deobandi School said: 'In the present circumstances, therefore, protection of the Urdu language is protection of our religion. Thus this protection is a religious obligation of every Muslim according to his capacity.'[14]

Urdu and Hindi were the main languages which mobilized both the Hindus and the Muslims respectively and created new politicized identities in British India. Hindi, being Sanskritic in vocabulary and script, as a linguistic symbol ignored the Muslim part of the composite Indian culture and emphasized the Hindu as one. This aspect of Hindi alienated the Muslims.[15] Symbols of these two languages were being used to mobilize people politically which ultimately resulted in the creation of Pakistan out of British India.[16]

Hindi-Urdu controversy was basically related to politics in British India. Hindus started associating with Hindi as Muslims with Urdu. Muslim elites of British India, keeping their earlier Mughal stature in mind, wanted to have political dominance and power which was not possible if Hindi was made the official language. At the same time Hindus considered Muslims as conquerors who came to India from outside and ruled them despite being in the minority.

Pakistan inherited inequitable state institutions of administration and education facilities at the time of its inception. Those institutes which came in Pakistan's fold were using English as their language. The elite government colleges, the civil services, the courts and the country's top leadership conducted their businesses in English. The language controversy which was earlier between Urdu-Hindi in British India now converted into Urdu-Bengali and after the dismemberment of Pakistan between English, Urdu and vernaculars. The current make-up of Pakistan's education sector is fundamentally derived from the erstwhile British colonial system. Elitist English-language schools such as military cadet and Christian mission schools as well as private schools cater to the privileged classes, and the vernacular, Urdu and provincial-language public schools, including *madrasas*, catering to the poorer classes of the society. The present state of English is the same as was at the time of its creation.[17]

Education in Pakistan

Education in Pakistan falls within the jurisdiction of the provincial governments.[18] There are basically three types of educational institutions running in Pakistan: public and non-elite private schools, elite schools and religious seminaries or *madrasas*. Approximately 73 per cent of the school-going children are enrolled in public schools; about 26 per cent are in private schools and around 1 per cent attend *madrasas*.[19]

According to 1998 census[20] of Pakistan, a literate person is one who is able to read a newspaper and write a simple letter in any language. Education is on the concurrent list of subjects under the constitution of Pakistan and is therefore jointly administered by both federal and the provincial governments. The important point where the provincial governments are against the federal government is the retention of curriculum and finance by the federal government.[21] The entire history of educational policy making in Pakistan is one of grief, broken promises, and lofty claims. Each successive government accuses the previous government of not being serious and committed to the educational cause of the nation.[22] However, despite all the immense assurances given by each of the successive regimes, the educational system of Pakistan has remained largely underdeveloped both in quantitative as well as qualitative terms.

According to the official data from the Ministry of Education, Government of Pakistan, the state allocated 2.5 per cent of the GDP during 2006-7, 2.47 per cent in 2007-8, 2.1 per cent in 2008-9 and 2 per cent in 2009-10 which shows a persistent declining trend.

The education system of Pakistan is polarized according to the socio-economic classes. It seems that major vernacular-medium schools (Punjabi, Sindhi, Siraiki, Baluchi and Pashto) and Urdu-medium government schools are meant for the working classes and the lower middle classes. The English-medium schools are meant for the middle and upper classes.[23] There is a widespread consensus that education plays a critical role in promoting the cultural, social, economic and political development of a country.[24] After the creation of Pakistan, the first meeting on education was held in Karachi from 27 November to 1 December 1947. Among the various things they decided was to include Islamic Studies in the curriculum; declare that the syllabi would be in conformity with Islam; and make Urdu compulsory for all. Urdu was projected as a symbol of unity for the new ruling elite of Pakistan.[25]

The existing picture in Pakistan presents a very grim situation of education. It has been a critical area of neglect. Historically, Pakistan has given a low priority to education. The major problem in addition to all the problems of inadequate funding, lack of resources, lack of good staff, lies in the medium of instruction in schools and colleges. Right since the inception of the country, there has been no consensus among the major political actors as well as the local people over the issue of uniform medium of instruction. There is a wide disagreement between the indigenous language of the people, Urdu and the English language as the medium of instruction in educational institutes. Sometimes vernacular language people sympathize with their indigenous language but at the same time they uphold Urdu whereas English-medium schools remain more or less untouched. Due to all these dilemmas there is a huge language controversy *vis-à-vis* education in all the major languages like Urdu-English, Urdu-Sindhi, Pashto, Punjabi-Urdu, Siraiki-Punjabi-Urdu, Baluchi and so on.

Medium of Instruction in Pakistan's Education System

After the creation of Pakistan in 1947, the official policy of the country has been to promote Urdu as the national language and a symbol of national identity and integration.[26] As mentioned earlier, the first meeting on education which was held in Karachi called for promoting and using provincial languages as the medium of instruction in primary level education, along with Urdu at the secondary level and recognizing English at the university or college level.[27]

The Commission on National Education, 1959 or the Sharif Commission as it was popularly known stated that language acts as a link between the past and the present. It is also a part of the concept of nationhood, enabling people at large to think and feel culturally attached and act as a unified group.[28] It was assumed that Urdu by right should be the national language of Pakistan. Accordingly national education and language policies were designed to shape the country by assuming that promoting Urdu as the national language is a powerful source for developing a sense of nationhood which would in the long run help fuse people into one homogenous unit.[29] It laid the foundational structure of the educational system in Pakistan which in essence remains intact, despite ideological shifts during the subsequent periods.

Fazlur Rahman, Member of the Constituent Assembly and the Education Minister, in his address to the All Pakistan Educational Conference in November 1947, proposed for the mother tongue to be used as the medium of instruction in the primary level education.[30] The conference proposed to adopt the Soviet formula of dual language policy in Pakistan. It called for giving to all the provincial languages maximum scope for growth and at the same time promote Urdu for inter-provincial communication, thereby making it the *lingua-franca* of Pakistan.

There is wide discrepancy over the medium of instruction in schools. Most of the time students coming from diverse language backgrounds such as native speakers, Urdu-speaking students and English-speaking elites tend to have dissimilar preferences as well as approach towards education. Common people find it very difficult to get into such schools where the medium of instruction is not their own language but a language which they do not understand.

Language Controversy and Education

In order to extensively promote Urdu as the national language of the country, the National Language Authority (NLA),[31] an autonomous regulatory organization was established on 4 October 1979 in Islamabad to standardize and promote Urdu language. It follows the Persian pattern and has been emphasizing, promoting and facilitating Urdu as an official and the major medium of instruction in all the educational institutes. Its objective is to establish cordial communication links between federal and the provincial governments. It looks after the translation of major legal, scientific and educational contents in Urdu. Since its inception the NLA has not been very successful in spreading the Urdu language among the non-Urdu speakers as the percentage of Urdu speakers has not increased. The number of Urdu speakers which was around 4 per cent at the time of the creation of the country in 1947 is today not more than 7.6 per cent of the total population. Even the 3 percentage increase in number came after the dismemberment of the country which shows that despite of all the efforts on the part of the establishment, the language is not being accepted by the majority of the people.

The website of NLA[32] opens with Jinnah's message to the country which was given on 21 March 1948 in Dhaka where he said that Urdu and only Urdu will be the national language of Pakistan and no other language. The NLA gives much emphasis to this statement and takes it as a guiding principle for the organization.

According to the Pakistan Social and Living Standards Measurement (PSLM)[33] Survey 2008-9, the overall literacy rate (age 10 years and above) is 57 per cent compared to 56 per cent for 2007-8 which is still below the set target. The very first meeting of the Advisory Board of Education for Pakistan in Karachi from 7 to 9 June 1948 called for government's policy to teach children in the mother tongue, switch over to Urdu after 5 to 6 years of schooling and then to be taught in English at the higher levels.[34] The language controversy with regard to medium of instruction and education involves all the major languages of the country like Urdu, English, Punjabi, Sindhi, Siraiki, Baluchi, Brahui and Pashto. Supporters of each language demand that their language be given due importance and official status and in the educational institutes of their area, the medium of instruction should be their own native language. Some of them are even demanding a separate province of their own like the Siraiki people who have gone an extra mile by demanding a separate Siraiki province of their own.

Urdu-English Controversy

In Pakistan, English language is seen as the torch bearer of Western liberal values and Urdu as an Islamic and Pakistani-nationalist language.[35] The role of English in the country still remains controversial. Although Urdu is the national language of the country, English is being promoted and used in all the official documents. It continues to be the official language and is the only means of communication between two provinces.[36] It also acts as a *lingua-franca* among the people of different provinces. It is taught as a subject and is the medium of instruction in all the elitist schools in Pakistan and is commonly called as the second language of the country.[37] It serves to maintain and preserve the present power structure, which is simultaneously disempowering most of the people.[38] Earlier it was resisted as the language which was against Muslim identity and therefore was suspected but now it is being resisted on socio-economic and political grounds.[39] Right since the time of General Muhammad Ayub Khan, former president of the country, English is being promoted even at the cost of Urdu and all Pakistani native languages. When General Zia ul-Haq came to power he made Urdu the official language but even then English remained untouched and was promoted in the elitist schools.[40] Elites in Pakistan consider English as a status symbol and in order to preserve their privileges they continue to use English in their day-to-day life.

Urdu and the Vernacular Languages

In Pakistan, indigenous languages are given only symbolic importance. Although these languages are not minority languages they continue to be dominated politically, socially and culturally by Urdu and English which enjoy 'high status' and are reserved for public and official use.[41] The main regional languages – Punjabi, Baluchi, Sindhi and Pashto, though rich in literature, rely heavily on the oral tradition and moreover lack a unitary system of speech.[42] Those students who come from and speak Baluch, Pashto, Punjabi, Sindhi, Siraiki, Brahui as well as other minor languages know neither Urdu nor English. They are lagging behind economically, socially as well as politically compared to those who understand Urdu or English. The common masses who are educated in their native languages have to first master Urdu or English as to be able to compete with the students of English-medium elitists institutions in the educational as well as in the job markets.[43] This is increasing the gap between the rich and the poor day by day. All these have polarized the Urdu, English and vernacular medium educated students. They possess a different world-view altogether.

Language Movements and Riots

There have been various language movements and riots in Pakistan. The major among them are Bengali language movement, Sindh language riots, Punjabi, Pakhtuns, Siraiki, Balochi language movements and so on. According to the Human Rights Commission of Pakistan (HRCP), there has been ethnic resistance against the Urdu language being made and imposed as the national language of Pakistan. The HRCP considers adoption of mother tongue as the most effective means of instruction at the elementary level of education.[44]

Bengali Language Movement: In 1948 and 1952, a number of urban Bengalis, mostly students, intellectuals and educated people, demanded that Bengali language should be made the national language of Pakistan and be used in public domain too.[45] This movement basically came as a reaction to West Pakistan's decision of imposing Urdu as the national language of the country.[46] Language was the major symbol of ethnicity for Bengalis and Sindhis, while it was important, though not the sole symbol, for the Mohajirs. Bengalis' language-based ethnicity was so strong against the unequal nature of the West Pakistan that it resulted into the dismemberment of the country and the creation of a new state of Bangladesh.

Sindhi Language Movement: Sindh is the worst affected province of Pakistan due to the language controversy. The tension between the supporters of Urdu and Sindhi led to language riots in Sindh in 1971 and 1972. Conflicts between Sindhi-Mohajir and Mohajir-Pakhtuns are very common in Sindh.[47] Urdu was opposed by the Sindhi speakers which led to the language crisis in Sindh. The declaration of Sindhi as the official language by the provincial government in 1972 invited stiff language conflict between Sindhis and the Mohajirs. From Partition onwards the sons of the soil (Sindhi speakers) became less in number due to the growing number of the non-Sindhi population. Moreover in the urban areas the 'Sindhi speakers' became a minority. There were riots in 1972-3 in Karachi between Sindhi speakers and Urdu speakers over the issue of quota system in jobs as well as in the education sector. There were many riots in urban Sindh due to the ethnic polarization of Sindhi speakers, Pashto speakers, Urdu speakers and Punjabi speakers in the 1980s, 1990s and in the present decade as well.

The clash between Urdu-speaking Mohajirs and the Sindhi speakers are really a dimension of the struggle for power. As in the case of Sindh, Sindhis started demanding that their language alone be made the official language of the province as well as the exclusive medium of instruction in schools and colleges along with English. At the same time they emphasized that Urdu should not be given any space, therefore inviting the Sindhi-Urdu controversy or we can say Sindhi-Mohajir conflict, where Mohajir too started calling themselves a different ethnic group of their own.

Baluchistan: Baluchistan is a multi-lingual province. Balochi, Brahui and Pashto are reasonably well spoken in Baluchistan. There have been various language movements on the part of Baluchi people to preserve and protect the Baloch identity.[48] Baluchistan adopted Urdu as the official language for temporarily setting aside the choice between Balochi, Brahui and Pashto, mainly to address the problem of education, employment, social status and so on.[49] Although Balochi and Brahui are the prevalent languages of the province, Urdu is the administrative language for all practical purposes. Due to the huge migration of Pakhtuns to the north of Baluchistan, it has caused apprehension between the native Balochi speakers and the Pashto speakers.

Khyber Pakhtunkhwa: There are Pashto language movements which call for advocating the cause of greater Pakhtunistan through the use of Pashto identity. They give primacy to their Pakhtun identity more than to Pakistani or Muslim identity. They are against the imposition of Urdu language as the medium of instruction in their schools at the cost of subjugation of Pashto language. There have also been secessionist movements by the Pakhtuns but the National Awami Party (NAP), a Pakhtun nationalist party, accepted Urdu as the official language of Khyber Pakhtunkhwa. However, Pashto remains an identity marker and part of Pakhtun nationalism.[50]

Punjabi: There was a Punjabi language movement which was known as Punjabiyat. It emphasized distinctiveness on ethnic, cultural and political grounds to gain greater political power. Their main aim was to 'restore' Punjabiyat to its rightful place in the nation.[51] According to Sabiha Mansoor, majority of the Punjabi students (59 per cent) display negative attitude to Punjabi language. They do not approve of studying in Punjabi. Today Punjabi families prefer giving education to their children in English and Urdu only. Elites of Punjab have started supporting Urdu and English and they themselves have marginalized Punjabi. Ruling elites in Punjab have themselves been opposed to Punjabi language being used even in the primary schools in Punjab. They regard Punjabi as an unimportant language and do not consider it a language which would help them in getting administrative positions, and are therefore promoting Urdu and English instead of Punjabi.[52] On the contrary activists of the Punjabi movement want Punjabi to be used for educational, administrative and judicial purposes in the province of Punjab.[53] The perception is that it is being given very little patronage both by the centre as well as the province despite the fact that both the state apparatus (federal and provincial) of the government are dominated by Punjabis.

Siraiki: Siraiki movement is a weak, middle-class phenomenon. The movement is largely concentrated in the southern part of Punjab and the people of this part blame both the federal as well as provincial governments of imposing Urdu as a dominating language while simultaneously destroying and discrediting the Siraiki language. It is against the domination of Urdu as well as Punjabi. It calls for quotas in employment and admission to educational institutions on the basis of separate Siraiki identity.

Consequences of the Language Controversy

In an irony, more the state has tried to centralize and unite everyone under one slogan, one religion, one nation, one set of values and beliefs, the greater is the tendency to be divided, to differ, to disunite, to assert ethnic or sectarian differences.[54] After decolonization, the newly-independent states declared a new single national language and promoted it vigorously to effect their national usage in order to promote national unity.[55] Pakistan is one among those countries which followed this pattern vehemently. This has created many problems in the sphere of education in Pakistan. There is a mismatch between education and economic opportunities in the country. The system is not able to provide good quality and uniform education to its citizens. The politics of language in Pakistan complicates the situation and it most often is related to the capture of political as well as economic power. The implications of this language policy are reflected on the education sector where Urdu is being promoted while rich native languages are being abandoned. The national education system in Pakistan with its emphasis on Urdu as the medium of instruction has badly affected school education.

The question of medium of instruction is a complex issue in the educational system of Pakistan as even at the level of primary education Urdu and English are being promoted at the cost of other native languages. At the secondary level and when they go for higher education too they find the medium of instruction in English only. Another problem is that Urdu is being made an all prevailing entity over other languages in Pakistan. The primary school children can read Urdu but cannot understand English. The matriculates know a little English but not enough to converse in it. Right since the creation of the country, the imposition of Urdu language over other provincial languages has proved to be a more disintegrating than an integrating policy. In an effort to promote Urdu language in educational institutions, the government has done many injustices to the native languages. The feeling of alienation and marginalization has gone deep into the minds and hearts of the people where they see that access to better opportunities is unequal rather than missing.

In Pakistan, language is seen by the people as the strongest symbol of group solidarity and cultural identity. There have been increasing demands for cultural autonomy as well as the use of native languages in the schools as well as in the official spheres of the provinces. These demands emanate from those people who are resentful towards the government's policy of discriminating the rich native languages of Pakistan. People criticize the educational policies aimed at promoting English as the *lingua-franca*. The policies are also being criticized for not being serious about the indigenous languages of the country.[56]

The promotion of a particular language in schools as well as a different national language is not a bad idea as far as any post-colonial state like Pakistan is concerned. But this promotion should not be at the cost of other rich native languages. If the local language and cultural identity are suppressed or destroyed a plural culture can never be developed. This is because people identify themselves more with their mother-tongue or native language or identity rather than with the national language or identity. The diversity of the country is being threatened. The rigid language policy of the state led to the dismemberment of the country in 1971 as the state establishment refused to give due place to Bengali language in the national life of Pakistan.

The common people who neither understand Urdu nor English feel exploited at the workplace or are in the schools which are relatively underdeveloped. They are not able to compete with students coming from English-medium schools as they are at the lowest rung of the Pakistani social structure. Due to compulsion, now the common people have started giving preference both to Urdu as well as to English in comparison to their native or local languages as the medium of instruction in educational institutions. Although they are attached to their native languages, they prefer to ignore it on the professional front due to lack of opportunities.

People argue that if Pakistan is to survive as a nation state, it must adopt Urdu as a national language of the country. It will help promote among the people a sense of common national consciousness which will help in uniting the various different ethnic and linguistic groups in Pakistan.[57] Although the state has been trying to promote Urdu language right from day one, it has not been able to create the kind of consciousness among the common people where they wholeheartedly accept the predominance of Urdu which is being imposed from the top. The desire to learn English among school students of all ages is very high. It is also because most of the people in Pakistan know that it is only through learning the English language in addition to Urdu that they will be able to move forward, socially, educationally as well as economically.

The newly-created state of Pakistan declared a single national language and promoted it vigorously to effect its national usage in order to promote national unity.[58] However, it is not always essential to have a national language to promote national unity, as we see in the case of India where there are more than 22 different languages but the country has managed to protect and promote national unity.

Indigenous people who know only provincial language, find it very difficult to get into good educational institutes, have limited job opportunities, unequal social status and lack a good and respectable life. They have no option besides learning Urdu. And after learning

Urdu, the problem is that the people who know Urdu and English are not ready to assimilate the people who do not understand English and know only the provincial language.

Urdu-Medium Public Schools

In Pakistan, the most easily accessible schools are Urdu-medium public schools. These schools are the largest in number along with some provincial language schools. The medium of instruction in these public schools is predominantly Urdu. Such schools lack the capacity to develop a minimum level of proficiency in the English language, which is necessary for most white-collar jobs.[59] Indigenous language medium schools, if at all, are only up to primary classes and after that these students have to switch over to Urdu-medium schools. But the quality of these Urdu-medium public schools is very sub-standard. They lack basic infrastructure, space as well as other required facilities.

Lack of basic facilities such as electricity, drinking water and toilets are deterrents to school attendance in such Urdu-medium public schools.[60] Teachers are given less salary compared to elite English-medium schools, although it is a fact that these teachers also lack proper understanding of their respective subjects. Only the middle class and lower middle class students attend these schools.

Elite English-Medium Schools

Language controversy is benefitting the private English-medium schools which are mushrooming very fast in Pakistan. They charge more fees compared to ordinary Urdu-medium schools. These English-medium schools are given higher financial grants-in-aid even by the state-controlled bodies compared to ordinary Urdu-medium public schools. The latter in fact find it very difficult even to get state or government assistance. The elite schools cater mostly to the government and military personnel's children and are largely untouched by the government regulating authority on excellence grounds. These schools can be afforded only by the rich or powerful.

These elitist schools follow higher educational standards but at the same time many ordinary profit-motive English-medium private schools are exploiting the students in the name of English. As these students study in elite or private English schools, they tend to associate less with the ordinary people and possess a different world view altogether compared to those in Urdu-medium schools. Students of the elite schools are highly dismissive of their Urdu and vernacular medium counterparts.

Non-Elite Private Schools

The language controversy in education is benefitting private schools of a different kind. These private schools are non-elitist in many aspects; apart from English they teach mathematics and science in English and rest of the subjects in Urdu. These non-elite private schools cover almost 1/3 of the total primary school-age enrollment. The demand for private schools in Pakistan is related more to better quality learning opportunities in contrast to the widely held perception that these private schools are exploiting the low income and mostly illiterate people who are not able to assess their children's performance.[61] These schools give English just a symbolic importance and not more than that. Students coming from middle and lower middle class attend these schools in large numbers.

Most of the educational institutes in the private sector in Pakistan follow English as the medium of instruction. English has always been the language of the elite which is now seen as the passport to social, educational, economic as well as political upliftment. The middle and upper middle class in Pakistan support English because they believe that it will equip them with better means for entering the elite class. According to Sabiha Mansoor more Punjabi and Urdu-speaking students want to study English both as a compulsory subject and as the medium of instruction. In fact, more students want to study English than Urdu.[62] The rich and powerful go to English-medium schools as well as private universities; the lower middle and working class go to Urdu-medium schools and public universities; the very poor and rural youth go to *madrasas*.[63]

Conclusion

Education in Pakistan is generally offered with Urdu and English as the medium of instruction. The imposition of one language over others has proved to be counter-productive for the state of Pakistan. Language had been an important point of discontentment, the Bengali language movement in East Pakistan leading ultimately to the dismemberment of the country and the formation of Bangladesh. There have also been various conflicts as well as language riots in Pakistan. The people in regions where neither Urdu nor English is understood feel exploited and these areas are underdeveloped compared to others. The students here are not able to compete with students coming from English-medium schools.

The language issue is very complicated in the case of Pakistan. The common people give preference both to Urdu as well as English in comparison to their native or local languages as the medium of instruction in educational institutes. This is because it gives them better opportunities in the job market as well as enhances the social status of the people. It helps them in taking admission in higher educational institutes. It also acts as a *lingua-franca* among the people of different provinces. Even Urdu-speaking students now want to study English. It helps them in availing good opportunities not only within the country but outside too.

Today Pakistan invests only in those sectors where there is a greater possibility of quick return than education, which is considered as investment in human capital and takes time to give output. The country has very meagre resources compared to the increasing demands and the largest share of the budget is given to the military as opposed to the education sector. The reform process can begin by giving due importance to native as well as Urdu and English language medium schools.

Qurratulain Hyder, in her landmark novel *River of Fire* has commented on the state of Pakistan's language issue: 'In the demand for Pakistan, Urdu was most thoughtlessly declared to be the language of a "separate Muslim nation", so it is also paying the price for the creation of the "homeland".'[64]

Notes

1. Naz Rasool, 'Language and Communicative Competence in the Twenty-First Century: Examining the Role of Education', in Sabiha Mansoor, Shaheen Meraj and Aliya Tahir, eds., *Language Policy, Planning and Practice: A South Asian Perspective*, Karachi: Oxford University Press for Aga Khan University, 2004, p. 4.

2. Tariq Rahman, *Unpleasant Essays: Education and Politics in Pakistan*, Lahore: Vanguard, 2000, pp. 41-9.
3. Rasool, 'Language and Communicative Competence in the Twenty-First Century: Examining the Role of Education', p. 5.
4. Aftab A. Kazi, *Ethnicity and Education in Nation-Building in Pakistan*, Lahore: Vanguard, 1994, p. 56.
5. Alyssa Ayres, *Speaking Like a State: Language and Nationalism in Pakistan*, New Delhi: Cambridge University Press, 2009, p. 152.
6. Kazi, *Ethnicity and Education in Nation-Building in Pakistan*, p. 56.
7. Ayres, *Speaking Like a State: Language and Nationalism in Pakistan*, p. 162.
8. Tariq Rahman, 'Language and Ideology', *Economic and Political Weekly* (Mumbai), vol. 37, nos. 44/5, 2-15 November 2002, pp. 4556-60.
9. Sajid Ali and Mohammad Babur, 'Educational Governance in Pakistan: A Historical Policy Perspective', in Jan-e-Alam Khaki and Qamar Safdar (eds.), *Educational Leadership in Pakistan: Ideals and Realties*, Karachi: Oxford University Press, 2010, p. 3.
10. Tariq Rahman, *Denizens of the Alien World: A Study of Education, Inequality and Polarization in Pakistan*, Karachi: Oxford University Press, 2004, p. 20.
11. Government of Pakistan, 'Census of Pakistan 1998: Population by Mother Tongue', URL: http://www.census.gov.pk/MotherTongue.htm (accessed on 25 August 2011).
12. Munir Ahmad, 'Education' in Rafi Raza, ed., *Pakistan in Perspective 1947-1997*, Karachi: Oxford University Press, 2001, p. 240.
13. Ayres, *Speaking Like a State: Language and Nationalism in Pakistan*, p. 22.
14. Cited in Tariq Rahman, *Language and Politics in Pakistan*, New Delhi: Orient Longman, 2007, p. 75.
15. Ibid., p. 78.
16. Ibid, pp. 250-1.
17. Ayres, *Speaking Like a State: Language and Nationalism in Pakistan*, p. 36.
18. Government of Pakistan, Federal Bureau of Statistics, 'Pakistan Social and Living Standards Measurement Survey 2010-11' (Islamabad, September 2011), URL: http://www.statpak.gov.pk/fbs/sites/default/files/pslm/publications/pslm_prov2010-11/education.pdf (accessed on 10 September 2011).
19. Cited in C. Christine Fair, *The Madrassah Challenge: Militancy and Religious Education in Pakistan,* Lahore: Vanguard, 2009, p. 30.
20. Government of Pakistan, 'Census of Pakistan 1998: Population by Mother Tongue'.

21. M. Ayaz Naseem, *Education and Gendered Citizenship in Pakistan,* New York: Palgrave Macmillan, 2010, p. 37.
22. Ibid., p. 35.
23. Rahman, *Denizens of the Alien World: A Study of Education Inequality and Polarization in Pakistan*, p. 24.
24. Cited in Nasir Jalil, 'Education in Pakistan: Past Dilemmas and Future Prospects', in J. Henry Korson, ed., *Contemporary Problems of Pakistan*, Boulder: Westview Press, 1993, p. 65.
25. Rahman, *Denizens of the Alien World: A Study of Education Inequality and Polarization in Pakistan*, pp. 7-8.
26. Sabiha Mansoor, 'The Medium of Instruction Dilemma: Implications for Language Planning in Higher Education', in Mansoor et al., *Language Policy, Planning and Practice: A South Asian Perspective*, p. 57.
27. Ahmad, 'Education', p. 243.
28. Rubina Saigol, 'Glories of the Past, Aspirations for the Future: Time as a Dimension of National Education in Pakistan', in Krishna Kumar and Joachim, eds., *Education and Social Change in South Asia,* New Delhi: Orient Longman, 2007, p. 291.
29. Ayres, *Speaking Like a State: Language and Nationalism in Pakistan*, p. 189.
30. Fazlur Rahman, *New Education in the Making in Pakistan: Its Ideology and Basic Problems*, London: Caisell and Company, 1953, p. 17.
31. Government of Pakistan, 'National Language Authority', URL: www.nla.gov.pk/index.php (accessed on 17 September 2011).
32. Ibid.
33. Government of Pakistan, Federal Bureau of Statistics, 'Pakistan Social and Living Standards Measurement Survey 2008-09' (Islamabad, 2009), URL: http://www.statpak.gov.pk/fbs/content/pakistan-social-and-living-standards-measurement-survey-pslm-2008-09-national-provincial (accessed on 10 September 2011).
34. Rahman, *Denizens of the Alien World: A Study of Education Inequality and Polarization in Pakistan*, p. 10.
35. Rahman, 'Language and Ideology', pp. 4556-60.
36. Liaquat Ali Khan Niazi, *Development of an Exemplary Educational System for Pakistan: In the Light of the Teachings of the Holy Prophet (PBUH),* Lahore: Sang-e-Meel Publications, 2002, p. 193.
37. Tariq Rahman, 'English Teaching Institutions in Pakistan', in Mansoor et al., *Language Policy Planning and Practice: A South Asian Perspective*, p. 27.
38. Ibid., p. 50.

39. Ibid., p. 44.
40. Rahman, *Language and Politics in Pakistan*, pp. 233-40.
41. Rahman, *Denizens of the Alien World: A Study of Education Inequality and Polarization in Pakistan*, p. 148.
42. Sabiha Mansoor, *Punjabi, Urdu, English in Pakistan: A Sociolinguistic Study*, Lahore: Vanguard, 1993, p. 6.
43. Rahman, *Denizens of the Alien World: A Study of Education Inequality and Polarization in Pakistan*, p. 148.
44. Human Rights Commission of Pakistan (HRCP), 'State of Human Rights in 2010', Lahore: HRCP, April 2011, URL: www.hrcp-web.org/publications/AR2010.pdf (accessed on 28 August 2011).
45. Tariq Rahman, 'West Pakistan Perceptions of the Bengali Language Movement with special reference to the Quaid-i-Azam', URL: http://www.tariqrahman.net/language/West%20Pakistan%20 Perceptions%20of% 20the% 20Bengali%20Language.htm (accessed on 1 September 2011).
46. Ibid.
47. Tariq Rahman, 'Language and Ethnicity in Pakistan', *Asian Survey*, Berkeley, vol. 37, no. 9, September 1997, pp. 833-5.
48. Ibid.
49. Rahman, *Language and Politics in Pakistan*, pp. 164-5.
50. Rahman, 'Language and Ethnicity in Pakistan', pp. 837-8.
51. Ayres, *Speaking Like a State: Language and Nationalism in Pakistan*, p. 190.
52. Rahman, 'Language and Ethnicity in Pakistan', pp. 833-6.
53. Rahman, *Language and Politics in Pakistan*, pp. 207-9.
54. Saigol, *Knowledge and Identity: Articulation of Gender in Educational Discourse in Pakistan*, p. 9.
55. Ayres, *Speaking Like a State: Language and Nationalism in Pakistan*, p. 150.
56. Zobaida Jalal Khan, 'Language Policy in Pakistan', in Mansoor et al., *Language Policy, Planning and Practice: A South Asian Perspective*, p. 23.
57. Naseem Jaffer Quddus, *Problems of Education in Pakistan,* Karachi: Royal Book Company, 1990, p. 216.
58. Ayres, *Speaking Like a State: Language and Nationalism in Pakistan*, p. 150.
59. Shanza Khan and Moeed Yusuf, 'Education as Strategic Imperative', in Maleeha Lodhi, ed., *Pakistan: Beyond the 'Crisis State'*, New Delhi: Rupa, 2011, p. 258.
60. Ibid., p. 254.

61. Fair, *The Madrassah Challenge: Militancy and Religious Education in Pakistan*, p. 18.
62. Mansoor, *Punjabi, Urdu, English in Pakistan: A Sociolinguistic Study*, pp. 141–4.
63. Rahman, *Denizens of the Alien World: A Study of Education Inequality and Polarization in Pakistan*, p. 148.
64. Cited in Ayres, *Speaking Like a State: Language and Nationalism in Pakistan*, p. 31.

CHAPTER 7

Construction of History in Pakistani Textbooks

Zarine Khan

Ernest Renan has famously said that 'Getting its history wrong is part of being a nation'.[1] History taught in schools of Pakistan is full of errors that have been pointed out in earlier works by Pakistani scholars.[2] The aim of this article is not to do the same. Nations are not as old as history and in the case of Pakistan, nation is clearly a constructed category. But it is in the nature of the nation state to claim itself as 'old', 'pre-modern', 'pre-historic' and construct a linear narrative from past till present that justifies its existence and order. Pakistan is no exception, rather being a modern state born in 1947; the challenge of constructing this past becomes more difficult and may become painful if it has to share its past with the neighbour that threatens its existence and remains hostile towards it (the hostilities are obviously reciprocated). An important key in understanding Pakistan is to see how Pakistan sees itself, i.e. how it has constructed its history in order to achieve its objective of nation-building.

History plays an important role in legitimizing invented traditions and frequently becomes the 'actual symbol of struggle'.[3] History (the 'glorious [*sic*] past of the Muslim rule') did become an 'actual symbol of struggle' in the movement for Pakistan to mobilize masses (as also it did in the case of the Indian National Movement). History found today in the textbooks of Pakistan (as would be the case with any other nation) is not what 'became the part of the fund of knowledge or the ideology of nation'[4] but what has been 'selected, written, pictured, popularized by those whose function it is to do so'.[5]

The historian has to be 'necessarily selective'[6] with the facts. He evaluates and selects them. This evaluation depends for whom and by whom the history is being written. When states write histories, it is with the view to promote the state's project of nation-building.

Pakistan's project of nation-building received a setback with the secession of East Pakistan in 1971 and post-1977 under General Zia, when a new education policy was adopted. Obviously the aim of the policy was to promote nationalism and make law abiding citizens. It was important for the state to legitimize the two-nation theory as with the secession of East Pakistan the theory was under attack and has remained to be so. The following line from Pakistan Studies textbook for BA/MA-level puts the situation in perspective for its students as 'The separation of East Pakistan was a great blow to the ideology of Pakistan and the Prime Minister of India Indira Gandhi claimed that the two-nation theory had been drowned in the Bay of Bengal as a result of creation of Bangladesh.'[7]

It is with respect to this present, where Pakistan is being said to be having an identity crisis and aspersions are cast on the basis of its legitimization, that the state is writing its history. This makes research on it an important exercise.

Ancient Past

It is through history writing that a nation constructs a linear narrative stretching right from antiquity to present. History is all about remembering and it is the nation that decides which parts one should remember and how. Pakistani textbooks when reinforcing the ancient past use 'race' and 'culture' as synonyms and thus obviously blur the line between a race and a nation. The textbooks imply that area that is now Pakistan has always had a distinct civilization from the rest of the subcontinent. The Indus Valley Civilization is claimed as a 'distinctive pre-historic civilization' from that of the civilization that existed on the plains of 'Ganga and Jamna' and that this distinction has always existed and maintained itself till present.

The National Board of Pakistan Studies textbook for classes XI –XII in its section on 'Pakistan: With Reference to Ancient Civilization'[8] summarizes three 'findings' that are:

1. The area that now forms Pakistan had a distinct cultural identity, even in the remotest past.

2. History shows that the territory of Pakistan was culturally linked with the Middle East and not with the Ganges Valley (now part of India).
3. The people of Pakistan have closer ethnic affinity with the racial groups settled in the Middle East.[9]

The national history is suitably tailored to include all the provinces of Pakistan and link them to the remotest past. By rooting them in antiquity it makes a strong case for their existence.

The discourse even at this stage is set in the tone of 'us' and 'them'. It promotes the idea that the two civilizations that existed at the sites of Pakistan and India were different and remain to be so even today. The difference in 'culture'/'civilization' is emphasized and rooted in antiquity to make a strong case to perpetuate it. Clearly this was not a factor in building national consciousness and an invention later to suit the present requirements of the state.

History is the study of the past through the present. Pakistan has established itself as an Islamic Republic and is an important part of the Islamic states' organizations and actively pursues a policy of friendship towards most of them, especially Saudi Arabia. This urge to identify with the races of Middle East can be interpreted in that light. Also, Middle East is the birth place of Islam and Pakistan, as we shall further see that the state of Pakistan is currently running its project of nation-building by inculcating a strong Islamic identity amongst its citizens.

Islam as Past

Islam is an important pillar of the present project of nation-building in Pakistan. The textbooks at certain junctures almost become textbooks of Islamic Studies rather than Pakistan Studies. The present state of Pakistan has built its historical discourse so as to identify itself with the entrance of Islam in the subcontinent and even goes a step further to identify itself with the history (mythic) of Islam that establishes its connection with the very first man to walk on earth.

Pakistan claims itself to be an ideological state and it traces its ideology right to the advent of Islam and its history. It has constructed its history deliberately in a manner that being obedient to the state or subscribing to its ideology somehow makes you a good follower of Islam or vice versa.

The first page of Pakistan Studies textbook for classes IX–X quotes the following verse from Quran, 'Have we not shown the two clear paths of right and wrong to man?' (90: 10)[10] and then follows it with these lines

A Muslim individual and a Muslim community are bound to follow the path of Allah. . . . When a community of Muslims joins hands to march in unison on the way of Allah it is called a community of the faithful (Mo'mineen) or the Muslim nation or the Muslim Ummah.[11]

This discourse is build up to finally suggest that Pakistan is a manifestation of basic tenets of Islam, i.e. *Tauheed* (Sovereignty of Allah) and *Risalat* (Finality of Prophethood of Prophet Muhammad) and this makes Pakistan 'a state based on clearly stipulated objective principles; these principles are equally binding upon all citizens from the head of the state to the commonest of citizens'.[12] The project of nation-building is to convince its citizens that the state of Pakistan derives power and legitimacy from religion making its authority absolute. Islam is used to sanction and validate state and serve its functions first and foremost.

Pakistan has (like any other nation does in its own way) invented concepts. The concept invented here is equating the past of Islam as the past of Pakistan. Jinnah is quoted to have said that, 'Pakistan came into existence the day the first Indian national embraced Islam'.[13]

From here onwards the history of Pakistan is a careful narrative of Muslim conquests in the region and establishment of the Muslim rule and the spread of Islam in the region. Anything that has to do with Islam in the subcontinent is portrayed to have links with the idea of Pakistan.

Pakistan identifies itself with the Muslim empires of the subcontinent and it remembers it as a rule of Muslims over Hindus. The homogenization of the two identities is difficult to miss in the textbooks. The Pakistan state also identifies itself with the various Sufi movements that lead to the spread of Islam in the subcontinent and chronologically presents them to the students, sometimes as movement for propagation of Islam and sometimes as Islamic revivalist movements.

Ideology of Pakistan and Two-Nation Theory

It was under General Zia's regime that a chapter 'Ideology of Pakistan'[14] became mandatory for all Pakistan Studies textbooks. In almost every textbook it is the first chapter. The 'Ideology of Pakistan' is explained to be based on the two-nation Theory, i.e. the Hindus and Muslims form two separate nations of the subcontinent. This theory is linked to Islam and presented to the students in textbooks as 'Muslims believe that the people of the world are divided into two major communities or millats on the basis of faith. Followers of Islamic creed are a separate and distinct nation from the rest of the mankind.'[15]

The Pakistan Studies textbook for BA/MA level first explains the basis of Pakistan ideology as:

> Pakistan ideology is based on the ideals of the Islamic system. It was a reaction to the Hindu and British exploitation of the Muslims of the sub-continent. It was a revolt against the prevailing system of India where the Hindu Nationalism was being imposed on the Muslims and their culture. It contained a strategy to save the Muslim culture from total elimination.[16]

The narration is built such that it makes the student believe that formation of an Islamic state is the only way to safeguard the interests of Muslims. The contradictions and gross generalizations cannot be ignored in the above excerpts from the textbook. First, the South Asian Muslims are thought as a homogenous entity. Second they are assumed to differ from the Hindus of the subcontinent in every respect. Third, creation of a modern nation-state was the only option to protect 'Muslim culture'. Fourth, what is this Muslim culture remains ambiguous. Fifth, how is the philosophy of Islam in contradiction with the concept of unified India? There are many other points that can be raised but through just these five points we can see the problem with the text that is being taught to students.

Creation of Pakistan as a separate state was not in the minds of the proponents of Muslim League till very late in the movement. The demand was for an autonomous federating unit under the federation of India. It can be argued that the 'Ideology of Pakistan' that is now being taught was not present at that time. The phrase 'Ideology of Pakistan' is of recent origin. It emerged on the scene only in the 1970s. The invention of this phrase can be interpreted in the light of the project of nation-building by the Pakistani state. The phrase is novel but attempt is made to root it as far in the past as possible.

With the creation of Bangladesh, the fallacy of the two-nation theory was exposed. This issue too has been dealt with in the textbooks. Obviously the textbooks reject this claim, however what is interesting is that at least they have made an effort into address the uncomfortable questions raised by the creation of Bangladesh. The Pakistan Studies textbook for secondary classes published by the central board explains in the context of creation of Bangladesh the following implications of the two-nation theory. The textbook notes, 'Bond of national unity does not imply that all Muslims of the world should be united under one sovereign state'.[17] The textbook also says that

> the union of the North Eastern and North Western Muslim areas into one state was a matter of expediency or choice. This was not a prerequisite of the Two Nation Theory or the Pakistan ideology. . . . Bangladesh did not forsake Indian hegemony as many people in Pakistan predicted it would. It did not forsake her Islamic identity. . . .[18]

and since it maintained its 'brotherly ties' with Pakistan it is 'unfair to interpret the separation of East Pakistan as a death blow to the Two Nation Theory'.[19]

Urdu

The symbolic significance of Urdu language played an important role in the movement lead by Muslim League that culminated with the creation of Pakistan than the actual use of the language. The newly-formed Pakistani state proclaimed Urdu as its national language. The state pursues its hegemonic agenda where supremacy of one social group, Punjabis followed by Mohajirs in case of Pakistan, dominates the state machinery and continues with the hegemony of ideas through education, particularly history. The textbook of Pakistan Studies for secondary classes in a chapter titled 'Culture of Pakistan' informs students that 'Urdu is our national language; Urdu has played an important role in the articulation of Muslim culture in South East Asia. It has been rightly said that Urdu has been a symbol, an issue, and a weapon in our struggle for independence.'[20]

Under a separate heading 'Importance of National Language *vis-à-vis* National Unity' the textbook says that

> In Pakistan, Urdu has an apparent disadvantage of not being the spoken mother-tongue of any of the major ethnic groups in the country. This disadvantage proved an advantage in disguise. Urdu became acceptable for all and was able to establish itself as everybody's language as well as a symbol of national unity only because it was nobody's language.[21]

It is interesting to study here the excerpt from the chapter titled 'Population of Pakistan' from the same textbook. It says

> Urdu is our national language and it is said that Urdu is understood throughout Pakistan, but the ratio of Urdu speaking population, according to the survey conducted by the Population Census Organization, is extremely low, i.e. 7.6%. This is much lower than our literacy rate (i.e. 45%).[22]

It even provides a detailed table titled 'Division of Households by Languages Spoken' that gives the percentage of people speaking different languages in Pakistan. It gives the data in this order: Urdu – 7.6 per cent, Punjabi – 48.2 per cent, Pashto – 13.2 per cent, Sindhi – 11.8 per cent, Balochi – 3.0 per cent, Siraiki – 9.8 per cent.

By giving these details to the student the author has already questioned the basis of Urdu being given the status of national language. However, how much time is spent in the classroom in discussing this data and the comment is an important factor too that would shape the knowledge of the student.

Urdu has also been presented to the student as a bond between the Hindu and the Muslim. The textbook for intermediate classes in an introductory note to Urdu language explains:

> Urdu is the product of the centuries of cultural interaction between the Hindu and the Muslim communities of India, and was identified to be the symbol of Hindu-Muslim unity, but on a particular juncture of history the Hindus totally alienated themselves from it. With this, cracks started appearing in the body of the magnificent Indian culture built on the basis of Hindu-Muslim unity. In this way the process that started with meager linguistic differences ended up in a total separation of the two nations.[23]

It is useful to note here that the author accepts that there existed a 'magnificent Indian culture' although the blame for destroying it is squarely put on Hindus rejecting Urdu. This is an oversimplification and we need not go into the merits and demerits of this statement. What we note here is that the entire theme of the book has been based on the notion that there have always been a separate 'Muslim culture' and a 'Hindu culture' [*sic*] and to write at this point of a common 'Indian culture' is a deviation (a positive one). However, we cannot read much into it, as the 'magnificent Indian culture' that the author talks about cannot be proven to not be the one of the elites of north India.

After the introduction the book has an entire section titled 'Why only Urdu should be the National Language of Pakistan'[24] citing reasons for it being a *lingua-franca* to being more closer to 'other languages' of the Muslim world'.[25]

The urge of Pakistani state to identify itself more with West Asian Islamic countries is projected here as well.

Selection of Events, Arrangement and Pacing

Here I look at the selection of facts, their arrangement and pacing in Pakistani textbooks. By arrangement I mean, the chain or linear narrative that the historian constructs trying to establish link between events and presenting to the student in a linear fashion. By pacing I mean, 'rapid movement from event to event, with a few points thrown in by way of explaining the direction that the events took'.[26]

Pakistani freedom movement is the recurrent theme in every textbook. Pakistani historians (like the Indian historians) have neatly located a beginning to the freedom struggle in 1857 that culminated in 1947. Post-1947 is another section of Pakistani history that deals with the formation of a new nation, the problems it faced, formation of various constitutions and dismemberment of East Pakistan and the process of Islamization.

For the purpose of this study we need not look into every event. We shall look into 1857 and 1947.

In Punjab Board's social studies textbook for class VIII, 1857 is presented to the student as 'War of Independence'. It says:

> . . . 1857 has to be viewed as the last ditch battle on the part of the Muslims and also other nations of the sub-continent, for the preservation of liberty. . . . At the end of the War, the entire blame of the uprising was put on the Muslims and Hindus assured the British of their loyalty and continued faithfulness. As a result of Hindu-British collusion, Muslims were subjected to great hardships. . . . They could not be cowed down by the atrocities committed on them by the British and the Hindus. Rather, they continued their struggle more vigorously, which culminated in the creation of Pakistan in August 1947.[27]

The continuity between 1857 and 1947 is deliberate and at best can be described as false. It is not uncommon for states to actually invent continuity, either by semi-fiction or forgery. 1947 is taught through two lenses. One is that of the ordinary Muslim who was massacred by the Sikhs and Hindus during Partition and the other is the perspective of the state – the problems it had to face immediately after Partition. The Pakistan Studies textbook for BA/MA level inform the student that:

> The Hindus and Sikhs had chalked out a systematic programme for the massacre of Muslim refugees migrating to Pakistan. . . . The state troops were employed in the massacre of Muslims with Hindus and Sikhs who were allowed to kill and mutilate Muslim men, women and children. . . . A Sikh mob paraded a number of Muslim women naked through the streets of Amritsar, raped them on the roads and then cut some of them to pieces with Kirpans and burnt the other alive. In this way the revenge for the partition of India was taken from the Muslims. . . . The trains reached Pakistan with large number of dead bodies and wounded persons to tell the tales of terrible atrocities committed by Hindus and Sikhs.[28]

The narration can best be described as one sided. One may debate the nature and authenticity of details that the author has provided in some instances, but the larger picture that emerges is of a helpless Muslim/Pakistani who is betrayed by the Hindu and Sikh of India. The narration does not mention any violence that was either perpetrated or retaliated by Muslims/Pakistanis.

From the perspective of the state the book gives a long detail of the problem the newly formed Pakistani state had to face and the injustices done during Partition to the state.

> Pakistan came into existence under the most appalling conditions. The Government of Pakistan could not get enough time to set up workable administrative machinery because of the great difficulties created by the Congress. The Indian government adopted delaying tactics in transferring the government servants and official record which aggravated the situation. . . . The Government officials began working with zeal and zest and sentiments of sacrifice. There was no office equipment, no furniture, no official record and no stationary to pull the official routine. The Government officials, full with national sentiments, did not care for the inadequacies and set to face the challenge under the dynamic leadership of the Quaid-i-Azam.[29]

The students are taught about the inequalities in the division of assets, military and financial. Accession of the princely states of Junagarh, Kashmir and Hyderabad is another issue. Rehabilitation of refugees and canal water dispute is another theme that completes the section or chapter on 'Initial Problems' of Pakistan in different textbooks.

The formation of Pakistani state and the problems it faced form an important part of Pakistan's becoming. It is evident from the above excerpt that state machinery is glorified and the state is portrayed as the one that took great pains and sacrifices for the cause of its people. Indian state is established as a threat to the survival of Pakistan from the very beginning that created every possible problem during Partition.

Portrayal of 1857 and 1947 can be identified as a major source of grievance that can be said to be the underlying sub-theme in the Pakistan Studies textbooks. The Muslim is betrayed from 1857 by the collusion of Hindu and British, taken advantage of, and pushed to the margins of society. He organizes himself around Muslim League that is time and again betrayed by the Congress. Jinnah, an icon of 'Hindu-Muslim' unity, becomes a staunch believer of the Two-Nation theory, and finally creation of Pakistan marks the beginning of self-rule by Muslims once again. This narration makes India (Hindus) a perpetual threat that cannot be trusted.

Personalities

National heroes are an important part of nationalist histories. Images of national heroes and their stories play an important role in helping people identify with the concept. They become icons of struggle. Their portrayal is such that they are conceived as forthright, just and above all nationalist who made great sacrifices for their countrymen. This is more so in the case of history written for school children. To fit these descriptions history is often reinterpreted and leaders are cast in neat pigeon holes. It has long been a charge that Pakistani textbooks have converted Jinnah into a religious man from a secular leader. It is also interesting to note how Indian leaders are portrayed in Pakistani textbooks. Gandhi finds mention in all the texts. Nehru is absent barring a one line or so of mention in a few of the textbooks. It is Gandhi *vs* Jinnah, the fathers of two rival nations. Also, Sir Syed Ahmad Khan and Iqbal find elaborate mention in all Pakistani textbooks – Sir

Syed Ahmad Khan for first using the words 'Two Nations' to describe Hindus and Muslims as separate nations and Iqbal for propounding the two-nation theory. I will focus on portrayal of Jinnah and Gandhi in Pakistani textbooks.

Jinnah

Jinnah is referred to as 'Quaid-e-Azam Mohammad Ali Jinnah (RA)' in Pakistan Studies textbook published by the central board for intermediate and secondary classes. The abbreviation 'RA' in brackets is for the Arabic word 'Radiallahu Anhu' that is usually used after the names of the companions of Prophet Muhammad and after the names of caliphs of the Islamic world to praise them. By using it after the name of Jinnah, the state has created the image of a pious leader who can be compared to the ones who lead the Muslims after the death of Prophet. In a way he acquires a status of the one chosen by the divine to fulfil the destiny of the 'Muslims of Indian subcontinent' [*sic*]. The same textbooks use the same abbreviation after the names of Sir Syed Ahmad Khan and Iqbal. This can be interpreted as another step in the process of Islamization being carried on in the country and its education. Jinnah was a secularist and the following is famously quoted from one of his speeches to prove the point 'You are free; you are free to go to your temples, you are free to go to your mosques or to any other place of worship in this state of Pakistan. You may belong to any religion or caste or creed- that has nothing to do with the business of the state.'[30]

The textbook for the intermediate classes says:

> The Muslim masses had reposed trust in the Muslim League mainly because the party was committed to establishing a state based on the principles of Islam. But unfortunately, a strong group of the members of the Constituent Assembly had secular tendencies and they made no secret of it. The Quaid-e-Azam (RA) repeated it time and again that the future constitution of Pakistan shall be formed on the basis of the principles laid down in the Holy Quran and the Sunnah.[31]

The image of Jinnah as a pious leader is more consistent with the project of nation-building based on Islamization. The textbooks do not mention Jinnah's public life before his return to India to reorganize the Muslim League. The books emphasize on his departure from the

Congress, referring to its Hindu character and composition. Jinnah is portrayed as the protagonist of Hindu-Muslim unity but deceived by the Congress that alienated the Muslims.

Gandhi

It is interesting to study how Gandhi is portrayed in the Pakistani textbooks. 'Gandhi' becomes 'Mr. Gandhi' in the textbook for BA/MA level when the author informs the students about Gandhi's decision to go on hunger strike if the cash that was to be transferred to Pakistan is withheld by the Indian state immediately after Partition. The textbook for intermediate classes published by the central board calls him 'Gandhiji'.

It says 'Gandhiji brought forward a programme of non-cooperation with the government, which was to be executed in four stages. . . . Gandhiji was elected leader of the Non-Cooperation Movement.'[32]

The same textbook later decides to call 'Gandhiji' as 'Mahatma Gandhi'.

> India's great leader Mahatma Gandhi use to say that the establishment of Ram Rajjiya (rule of God) was his cherished dream, asked what he really meant by Ram Rajjiya he said that it would be modeled exactly on the pattern set by Hazrat Omer (RA) and Hazrat Abu Bakr (RA).[33]

The textbook for class VIII published by the Punjab Board says 'Mr. Gandhi was a shrewd politician'.[34]

The personality of Gandhi can best said to be in a state of flux in Pakistan. Different books present him differently – some as the sole cause of mobilization of Hindus against Muslims and some as an impartial party who wanted to implement self rule. This impartiality is somehow subdued in the texts and has a good chance of getting ignored by the surrounding themes that present Congress as a totally Hindu organization and Gandhi being a part of it.

Conclusion

Construction of the 'other' is an important part of defining the self which is important in the construction of nationalist histories. In this case, it is the 'Hindu', 'Sikh', 'Hindu Congress', 'Hindu India', 'Bharat' or simply India that is the other.

The two countries are taught as homogeneous entities, one 'Hindu India' vs 'Muslim Pakistan'.

The state of Pakistan embarked upon a process of Islamization under the Zia regime and with that the identities of the 'Muslim Pakistan' and 'Hindu India' became more rigid. As the narrative enters the modern period the 'other' is defined more sharply and distinctively. Muslims and Hindus are portrayed as homogeneous communities. There are examples where more than one side of the story is being taught to the students. Jamaat-i-Islami was opposed to the idea of Partition now finds mention in the textbooks. Different divisions that occurred between the Muslim Ulema also find mention. This can be seen as a beginning of acceptance of realities from different perspectives. Portrayal of Mahatma Gandhi in Pakistan Studies textbook is another encouraging development. This article makes a strong case for further research in identifying the themes that can help in transforming the conflict between India and Pakistan.

Notes

1. Ernest Renan, 'Qu'est que c'est une nation?', pp. 7–8. Quoted by E.J. Hobsbawm in *Nations and Nationalism Since 1780: Programme, Myth, Reality*, p. 12.
2. There have been many articles written on the subject but the most comprehensive work has been done by K.K Aziz in *The Murder of History*, in which he has analysed and pointed out errors in 66 textbooks taught all over Pakistan.
3. Eric Hobsbawm, 'Introduction: Inventing Traditions', in Eric Hobsbawm and Terence Ranger, eds., *Invention of Tradition*, p. 12.
4. Ibid., p. 13.
5. Ibid.
6. E.H. Carr, 'The Historian and his facts', *What is History*, p. 6.
7. M. Ikram Rabbani, *Comprehensive Book of Pakistan Studies*, p. 289.
8. Abdul Qadir Khan, *Pakistan Studies for Intermediate Classes*, pp. 114–15.
9. Ibid.
10. Abdul Qadir Khan, *Pakistan Studies for Secondary Classes*, p. 1.
11. Ibid.
12. Ibid., p. 2.
13. M. Ikram Rabbani, *Comprehensive Book of Pakistan Studies*, p. 15.
14. The term 'ideology of Pakistan' entered the educational discourse at the insistence of the Zia regime. Pakistan Studies as a subject was

introduced replacing social studies and it was mandatory to teach students about the ideology of Pakistan. In all the Pakistan Studies books the first chapter is the 'Ideological Basis of Pakistan'.

15. Abdul Qadir Khan, *Pakistan Studies for Secondary Classes*, p. 3.
16. M. Ikram Rabbani, *Comprehensive Book of Pakistan studies*, p. 2.
17. Abdul Qadir Khan, *Pakistan Studies for Secondary Classes*, pp. 62–4.
18. Ibid.
19. Ibid., p. 159.
20. Ibid., pp. 162–3.
21. Ibid., pp. 146–7.
22. Ibid., p. 57.
23. Abdul Qadir Khan, *Pakistan Studies for Intermediate Classes*, pp. 131–2.
24. Ibid.
25. Ibid.
26. Krishna Kumar, *Prejudice and Pride*, p. 73.
27. Social Studies class VIII, Punjab Board, pp. 71–2.
28. M. Ikram Rabbani, *Comprehensive Book of Pakistan studies*, pp. 148–9.
29. Ibid., pp. 146–7.
30. Jamiluddin Ahmed, *Speeches and Writings of Mr. Jinnah.*
31. Abdul Qadir Khan, *Pakistan Studies for Intermediate Classes*, p. 69.
32. Ibid., p. 13.
33. Ibid., p. 106.
34. Social Studies class VIII, Punjab Board, p. 81.

References

(*indicates primary source)

Ahmed, Jamiluddin, *Speeches and Writings of Mr. Jinnah*, Lahore: Government of Pakistan, 1964.

Aziz, K.K., *The Murder of History: A Critique of History Textbooks Used in Pakistan*, Lahore: Vanguard, 1993.

Carr, E.H., *What is History*, London; MacMillan, 1961, p. 6.

Hobsbawm, E.J., *Nations and Nationalism since 1780: Programme, Myth, Reality*, Cambridge: Cambridge University Press, 1990, p. 12.

Hobsbawm, E.J., ed., *The Invention of Tradition*, Cambridge: Cambridge University Press, 1983.

*Khan, Abdul Qadir, *Pakistan Studies for Intermediate Classes*, Islamabad: National Book Foundation, 2009.

*———, *Pakistan Studies for Secondary Classes*, Islamabad: National Book Foundation, 2009.

Kumar, Krishna, *Prejudice and Pride*, New Delhi: Penguin Books, 2001, p. 73.

★ *Pakistan Studies*, class IX–X, Lahore: Punjab Textbook Board, 2009.

★ Rabbani, M. Ikram, *Comprehensive Pakistan Studies*, Lahore: Caravan Book House, 2008.

★ *Social Studies*, class VIII, Lahore: Punjab Textbook Board, 2009.

CHAPTER 8

Media Agenda Setting in Pakistan

Prospects for Socio-Political Transformation

Dheeraj Kumar

> The media doesn't tell us what to think; it tells us what to think about.
>
> Bernard C. Cohen (1963)

TODAY, PAKISTAN IS witnessing the process of liberalization and democratization in tune with the general process of the world. Now there are several issues such as social transformation, human rights, environmental issues, media autonomy and feminist issues emerging in Pakistan. We are seeing a new liberal class formation, so the agenda of the public is changing simultaneously. Pakistani media has been playing an important role in the political transitions since the judiciary crisis. In these circumstances it is very essential to explore the role of media agenda setting in Pakistan. It is the media that can convert the public issues into discussion, formulating its own agenda.

The aim of this article is to identify the attribute salience via print media in Pakistan. This analytical study also explores the challenges and prospects for print media agenda in the context of socio-political changes that are taking place in Pakistan.

This study has adopted the analytical method to identify the loopholes of Media Agenda Setting in Pakistan which is based on secondary data (content analysis as well as survey research) taken from a previous study done by Saqib Riaz. Content analysis and audience survey is based on two daily newspapers, the *Jang* (the largest circulated

Urdu newspaper in the country) and the *Dawn* (the largest circulated English newspaper in the country).

In the conclusion the study finds that there is a growth in mass media which provides social and psychological gratification to the people of the country. The role of media agenda setting is very important in Pakistan for liberalization and democratization. Media organizations should understand that media agenda will finally become the public agenda which can affect the public and societal interest. In this context objective, cautious and balanced reporting should be mandatory for the media houses. Pakistani government, media organizations and media regulatory authorities need to take special care in the formulation of media agenda for the socio-political need and development of the country.

Introduction

Every day important events and issues are taking place in the world. The media is reporting daily to inform us about the latest actions and changes in the world beyond our reach. As a result, most of the public perceptions about the world are recycled versions of the reality, which is created by the mass media. The concept of agenda setting is based upon the ability of the mass media that carry the issue on their own agenda and then transfer it to the public agenda. Journalists and editors decide which issue is to be covered and which is to be ignored.

Pakistan, which was recognized as a home of al-Qaeda, armed with nuclear weapons and infected with radical Islamists, is now welcoming the wave of liberalization and democratization.[1] Following the judiciary crisis (the dismissal of the Chief Justice of the Supreme Court, Justice Iftikhar Muhammad Chaudhry and the lawyers' protest movement) we saw the new face of the Pakistani people as well as Pakistani media. Pakistan has been ruled by the military more than the civilian from its origin. The rulers have used legal and constitutional powers to prevent the mass media from engaging in public debate and criticism. Pakistani mass media has faced threats, violence and economic pressure. But one good thing that happened during the General Musharraf regime was that Pakistan moved from one state-controlled TV channel to over 50 private TV channels. Now the Government of Pakistan is promising maximum freedom for the mass media.

Pakistan is experiencing rapid growth in the mass media sector which is not only compulsory for democracy but also needed for stability of the government and economy. Since 2007, the issues which have been highlighted by the media are terrorism, Indo-Pak relations, energy crisis, food crisis, the dismissal of the Chief Justice of the Supreme Court, Justice Iftikhar Muhammad Chaudhry, the issue of Lal Masjid, the declaration of emergency, the assassination of PPP leader Benazir Bhutto and the end of Osama-bin-Laden.[2]

Pakistani media has been more informative than ever before. At present the main issues are health, education, sanitation, unemployment, increasing prices of essential commodities, oil price rise, electricity load shedding, floods, declining agricultural production and war and terrorism.[3] So the agenda setting role of the media is very important for making Pakistan a welfare state and for establishing a real democracy in the nation. Then the agenda setting role of Pakistani media becomes very crucial to create genuine public enlightenment about real life issues.

Objectives

The aim of the study is to identify the attribute salience via print media in Pakistan. This analytical study also explores the challenges and prospects for print media agenda in the context of socio-political changes that are taking place in Pakistan.

Methodology

The methodology used in this article is a critical analysis of the role of media agenda setting in Pakistan. Secondary data is used to understand the loopholes of agenda setting. The secondary data (content analysis as well as survey research) is adopted from a previous study carried out by Saqib Riaz. Content analysis of two daily newspapers, the *Jang* and the *Dawn* had been taken up by the researcher. The variables of the content analysis are frequency, length and slant of the news story. An audience survey, based on 300 regular newspaper readers in which 150 were the readers of the *Jang* while 150 were the readers of the *Dawn*, was also considered for this study.

Agenda Setting Role of Media

Today mass media is an important source of information about world affairs. If we see the content presented by the mass media critically we find that mass media organizations are interested in some specific events than the others. Some issues are imposed by the gate-keepers such as reporters and editors and some are imposed by their owners for their financial and economic interests. Surviving and profit making factors play an essential role in choosing the stories to be aided/written about, to be rejected and that are to be interpreted and manipulated in desired ways.[4]

According to the agenda-setting theory, because of the fact of paying attention to some issues and neglecting and ignoring some others, the mass media will have an effect on public opinion. People will be inclined to know about those issues and things, which are highlighted by the mass media and they adopt the order of priority assigned to different issues. We can see only reflections of reality (not reality itself) in the news media. Yet, those reflections provide the basis for our pictures.[5]

Agenda Setting Theory is one of the most relevant media theories in the current scenario. In the words of McCombs, in a typical daily newspaper, over 75 per cent of the potential news of the day is rejected and never transmitted to the audience. This is the role of the media as a gatekeeper. But the issues do not receive equal treatment when presented to the audience. Some issues are published in greater length but others receive only shorter attention.[6]

Agenda Setting claims that audiences identify their agenda with those of mass media. The theory argues that the news media have a large influence on audiences by their choice of what stories to consider newsworthy and how much prominence and space to give them.[7] In fact, Agenda Setting describes the transmission of these salience as one of the most important aspects of mass communication. The theory of Agenda Setting is opening new dimensions in mass media research. A comparison has been made between the media agenda and the public agenda in most of the researches.[8]

The Agenda Setting Theory came in to existence in the background of dissatisfaction of the magic bullet theory.[9] The Agenda Setting Theory argues that the media agenda is the set of issues addressed by media sources and the public agenda are issues the public regard as significant.[10] McCombs and Shaw conducted the first test of Lippmann's theory during the 1968 presidential election of the USA, in Chapel Hill, North Carolina.[9] At that time, the existing theory was that the mass media had only limited effect on the public. Earlier studies conducted by some scholars stated that exposure to campaign information had little influence on the public's voting behaviours.[11] The theory explains the correlation between the rate at which news media cover a story and the amount that people think that this story is essential. The theory became relevant when this correlation occurred repetitively.[9] Subsequent research on Agenda Setting Theory provided evidence for the cause-and-effect chain of influence being debated by critics in the field.

The Agenda Setting function has multiple mechanism such as media agenda are issues discussed in the mass medium, public agenda are issues discussed among the public, policy agenda are issues that policy makers consider significant whereas corporate agenda are issues that huge corporations consider important. These agendas are interconnected with each other.

The idea of measuring Agenda Setting effects can be regard as three different levels of public agendas. The first public agenda is intrapersonal or self public agenda. Then comes interpersonal public agenda when people talk about certain issues with their family members and friends. The third public agenda is about the apparent community or public agenda. It appears when people explain what others in the society consider as most important issues.[12]

We consider on the basis of wide-ranging research that to a great extent the media set the agenda of the public. Then the question emerges in our mind that who sets the media agenda? A number of factors inside and outside media organizations play an important role in setting the media agenda by influencing the media content. Mass media content is influenced by media workers' socialization and attitudes. Professional training, personal and political attitudes and affiliations of media workers lead them to produce a social reality. Media content is also influenced by media routines in which media workers and their organizations perform their work. News media content is influenced by the ideology of those who are in power in the society and they follow an ideology regularly with those motives and interests, which helps ensure that society will continue in its present form. Social institutions, pressure groups and other forces also influence media content. This approach suggests that economic and cultural factors and audience members determine content.[13]

The earlier research studies considered media as a channel, like a nonaligned transmitter which flows information and links senders to receivers. But modern studies rejected the passive role of mass media. Modern researchers believe in the active role of media and they consider that media content is necessarily manipulated when events are relocated and reproduced into news.[14] In these theoretical contexts the study identifies the loopholes of Media Agenda Setting in Pakistan. This analytical study also explores the challenges and prospects of Pakistani media agenda setting in the context of socio-political changes that are taking place in the country.

Agenda Setting Role of Media in Pakistan

Pakistani media agenda is going through a transformation because of new FM radio stations, and privately owned TV and print media. The increasing number of private radio and television channels in the last few years has ended the domination of the state-owned TV. Now media have become pluralistic and TV news channels are significantly influencing the elite and the middle class in Pakistan. The users now have more control over the communication process. The private channels prefer to go by the newsworthiness of events. Private TV channels and the cable TV have brought the world closer to the domestic viewers and now they are connecting themselves with the rest of the world.[15]

The population of about 160 million with diverse ethnic groups and languages affects Pakistan's media and there's a gap between Urdu and English media. Urdu newspapers are widely read in rural regions while the English media is more liberal and professional compared to the Urdu media because of its urban and elite-centric status.[16] Poor literacy rates, urban orientation of the press, and the high price of newspapers are the factors responsible for the low circulation rate. The circulation of newspapers per capita in Pakistan is among the lowest in the world.[17]

Language is also a divide between the audiences and the Pakistani media has to present news in very sensible manner and consider it as a communication challenge. Now the scenario is changing simultaneously and the newly-growing liberal middle class has started impacting the political process.[18]

At present distortion of Pakistani media is continuing because of propaganda, pressure, bribery and other reasons.[19] Poor literacy, urban orientation of the press, and the high price of newspapers are factors for the under-development of print media in Pakistan. Religious people and lower middle class are criticizing some of the private TV channels for their Western orientation in their contents and 'immoral' entertainment programmes. In this regard, Waseem says, 'this concession to religious elements tantamounts to recognizing their social power base'.[15] Beside these barricades, we can now easily perceive a shift from centralized broadcasting to an open competition broadcast system, which enables the power of selective exposure for the audiences. Now the government of the Pakistan People's Party has promised maximum freedom of the press.

A survey done by the Pakistan Institute of Peace Studies (PIPS) found that radicalization is affecting the mass media agenda in Pakistan.[20] But Pakistani people are keen to accept democracy as the best system of governance. People need timely and credible information which is necessary for decision-making and making the government accountable. In this context media is playing a significant role in unfettering the Pakistani society and transform it from being conservative to moderate.

Pakistan has faced political crisis for a long time. The country is neither a democratic state nor an authoritarian regime.[21] However, one good thing that has happened in Pakistan is that the mass media has emerged as an important pillar for promoting democracy. Private TV channels and print media repeatedly criticize the government for the deteriorating law and order situation, playing with the spirit of the constitution, infringing democratic values, inflation, unemployment and poverty. This changing phenomenon has changed the perception and behaviour patterns of the Pakistani people.

If we critically examine the role of media agenda setting in Pakistan, we find a strong relationship between the media and the public agenda on the issues of the study except those related to personal sufferings. In the content analysis of the two daily newspapers, *Jang* and *Dawn*, the issue of judiciary crisis got the maximum coverage in *Jang*, while the issue of terrorism got the maximum coverage in the *Dawn* (as shown in Figs. 8.1 and 8.2).[22]

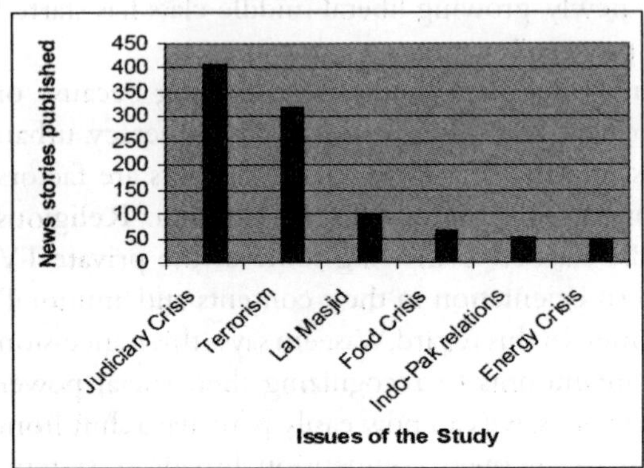

Source: Saqib Riaz (2008: 101-2).

FIG. 8.1: FREQUENCY OF THE NEWS STORIES PUBLISHED IN DAILY *JANG*

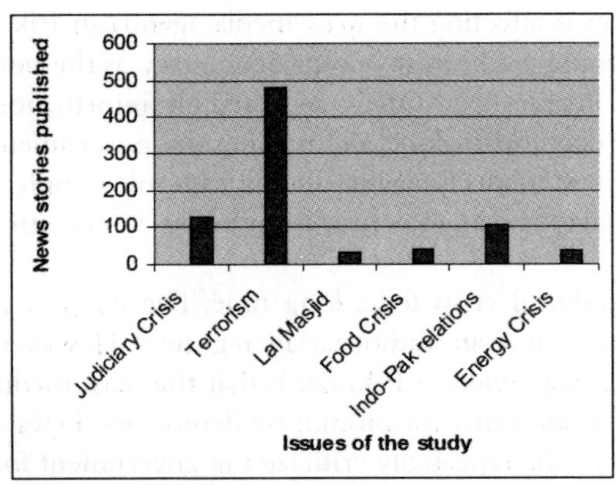

FIG. 8.2: FREQUENCY OF THE NEWS STORIES PUBLISHED IN DAILY *DAWN*

Similarly in case of length (space), the issue of judiciary crisis acquired the largest portion in the daily *Jang*, while the issue of terrorism acquired the largest portion in *Dawn* (as shown in Figs. 8.3 and 8.4).[23]

On the other hand, audience survey finds that the readers of the daily *Dawn* stated that the issue of terrorism is the most important issue among the list of the issues given to them while the readers of the

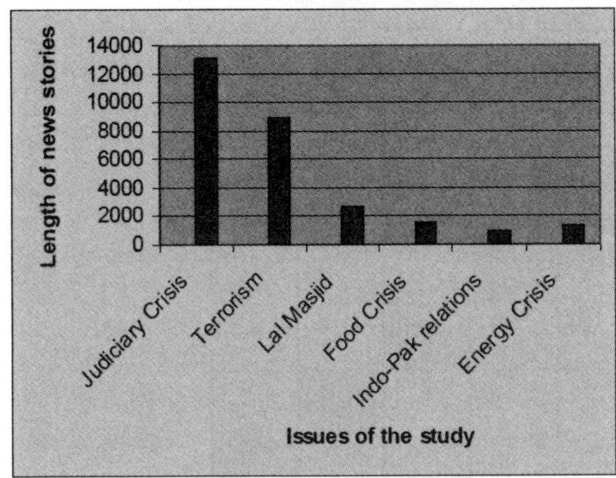

Source: Saqib Riaz (2008:104)

FIG. 8.3: LENGTH OF NEWS STORIES PUBLISHED IN DAILY *JANG* IN CENTIMETERS PER COLOUMN.

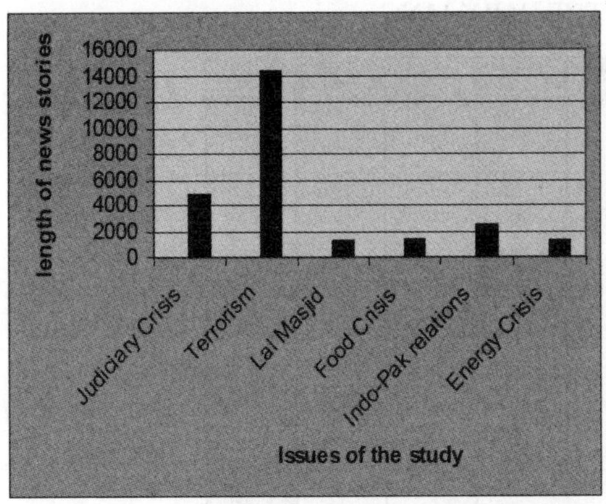

FIG. 8.4: LENGTH OF NEWS STORIES PUBLISHED IN DAILY *DAWN* IN CENTIMETERS PER COLOUMN

daily *Jang* stated the issue of the judiciary crisis as the most important issue[24] (as shown in Tables 8.1 and Table 8.2).[24]

Data shows a strong correlation between the public and the media agenda. In this context we can say that the media is able to set the

TABLE 8.1: RANKING ORDER OF THE PUBLIC AGENDA OF THE READERS OF THE DAILY *DAWN*

Issues	1st	2nd	3rd	4th	5th	6th
Terrorism	64%	11%	9%	7%	5%	4%
Judiciary Crisis	11%	64%	10%	7%	5%	3%
Food Crisis	7%	9%	51%	10%	11%	12%
Energy Crisis	6%	13%	9%	61%	6%	5%
Indo Pak Relations	0%	5%	9%	11%	58%	17%
Lal Masjid	3%	5%	7%	9%	13%	63%

Source: Saqib Riaz (2008: 126).

TABLE 8.2: RANKING ORDER OF THE PUBLIC AGENDA OF THE READERS OF THE DAILY *JANG*

Issues	1st	2nd	3rd	4th	5th	6th
Judiciary Crisis	63 %	13 %	9%	7%	7%	1%
Terroris m	15 %	59 %	12 %	9%	5%	0%
Food Crisis	7%	11 %	56 %	9%	10 %	7%
Energy Crisis	10 %	9%	11 %	58 %	7%	5%
Lal Masjid	5%	6%	8%	9%	63 %	9%
Indo Pak Relations	2%	3%	6%	7%	11 %	71 %

Source: Saqib Riaz (2008: 126).

importance of certain issues in the public mind. Then it can be stated that there is a need of formulation of the media agenda according to the socio-political needs of Pakistan.

The slant of the news stories published about the issues of the study was measured in terms of favourable, unfavourable and neutral. In case of *Jang*, 1,592 out of 5,261 stories are favourable to Government of Pakistan and the US; 2,849 out of 5,261 stories were unfavourable for the Government of Pakistan and the US and 820 out of 5,261 stories were neutral toward Government of Pakistan and the US. On the other hand, in case of *Dawn* 3,058 out of 7,023 stories are favourable for the Government of Pakistan and the US, 2,603 out of 7,023 stories are unfavourable for the Government of Pakistan and the US and 1,363 out of 7,023 stories are neutral towards Government of Pakistan and the US. Data show that the Pakistani media publishes some stories favourable to government and some are unfavourable. Here we reached to the conclusion that Pakistani media has to focus on balanced news stories.[25]

Mostly media contents are related to the political issues and the government. There are evidences that journalists are making value statements about issues and policies. Media give significance to some people or group by portraying them repeatedly and marginalizing others by ignoring them. Majority of news stories in print and electronic media incorporate violence and criminal acts. The major TV news channels are concerned with politicians, political candidates, ministers, leading federal and provincial officials, government conflicts and disagreements, government decisions, ceremonies, proposals, violent protests, criminal acts, scandals, disasters and investigations. The channels mostly broadcast news related to murder, fraud, drug and terrorism, which is harmful for the society. A few are related to strikes, protests, victims and rioters. The national media of Pakistan has to give proper coverage to the real issues of the Pakistani society.[26]

Sources of information play a vital role in the agenda setting of the public. The audience survey revealed that the electronic media is the most important source of information after the print media. Rapid growth of the electronic media has increased their level of penetration among the public.[27] The news stories broadcast by the electronic media maintaining balance about Pakistani political affairs. The role of the Pakistan Electronic Media Regulatory Authority (PEMRA) has become very important in order to provide suitable atmosphere for the electronic media in Pakistan but for this the present PEMRA laws and Code of Conduct have insufficient fundamental democratic features. So the PEMRA has to liberalize its rules in order to provide autonomy to the electronic media.[28]

In Third World countries like Pakistan, media agenda setting has great prospects of implementation. The media not only articulate people's demands but also develop public opinion. So the agenda should not be biased and subjective and not so far away from the people's socio-political needs.

Challenges and Prospects for Pakistani Media

In Pakistan, lack of maturity and professionalism are the obstacles for objective and independent media.[29] Boom in the media sector demands good media scholars to join and make Pakistan, a liberal and democratic state. Then the role of reporters and editors is very essential because they are directly affecting the media agenda setting process. Most Pakistani journalists are not trained to understand, probe and evaluate the complex issues related to politics, conflict and radicalism due to their insufficient academics, personal biases and non-proficiency. So the media organizations are not able to focus on delivery of the news contents which are concerned with the public and societal interest.[30] State institutions and local brokers are always eager to enjoy favourable publicity so they are manipulating the media agenda with the help of media owners.

The bad educational system in the country is also a big challenge for the future of the media in Pakistan. Most of the Pakistani journalists are the products of General Zia-ul-Haq's education policy. Pakistani media professionals have been psychologically and socio-culturally associated with tradition and religion.[31] However, the scenario is changing and media education is gaining grounds. The standard of existing media education in Pakistan is improving. The education of journalists has brought considerable change in the content presentation and sociology of the media in the country.[32] So it is essential that the Pakistani educational system give proper consideration to media education. Media organizations have to revise the recruitment process of journalists so that the qualified and capable media scholars join the media and neo-liberal representation takes place.

Pakistani journalists are working in an environment which subjects them to diverse internal and external pressures and constraints. Organizations have been struggling hard to achieve mass media liberties. In these circumstances accuracy of reporting is directly affected. More than 45 journalists have been killed in Pakistan in the last 10 years. Pakistani media have to be very aware of the radical elements which are influencing the whole system including media. Journalists operating in the Taliban-controlled areas such as the Federally Administered Tribal Areas (FATA), Swat, North West Frontier Province (NWFP) are discouraged from expressing their viewpoints.[33] In this context there is a great need that the government of Pakistan provide full assurance to the journalists to work in secure ways. The Pakistani government has to take into account that there is a need to focus more on the improved security conditions for journalists through risk-awareness training and conflict-sensitive journalism.[34]

Government advertisements focus on the self-sufficiency of the press, and always control media contents. Three major media groups the *Jang*, the *Dawn* and the *Nawa-i-Waqt* exist in Pakistan, which to some extent also have political affiliations. This force has significantly affected the 'watchdog role of media' in the country. State-run TV and radio channels operate as a propaganda tool of the government.[35]

Media in Pakistan is highly influenced by the ownership structure. The marketing managers of the media groups decide the space and coverage of issues. Owners also exercise influence on space and exposure for the news reports, especially on the editorial policy and administrative matters. News stories are drafted in accordance with their political and commercial interests. Media owners have managed to target and take over professional editors. By doing so, the space for unbiased and balanced journalism has ceased to exist. Then negligible space is left is for the coverage of social issues, along with human rights issues and these issues are not on the agenda of most of the Pakistani media.[36]

In terms of prospects for the liberal Pakistani media, the door is open for private regional and national TV channels. Private satellite TV channels are increasing the competition for the state-run TV channel (PTV). The number of FM stations is increasing in the country. In this context the young qualified media personnel join and replace the non-qualified media workers. The education of journalists has brought extensive change in the content presentation and sociology of the mass media in the country. So the government should take steps to promote mass communication as an important subject in educational institutions and regulate mass media in a well-organized manner.

Conclusion

There is a growth in mass media which provides social and psychological gratification to the people of the country. The role of media agenda setting is very important in Pakistan for its liberalization and democratization. Media organizations should keep the theory of Agenda Setting in their mind while formulating the agenda of their own media houses. They should understand that media agenda will finally become the public agenda which can affect the public and societal interest. Pakistani mass media organizations and the Government of Pakistan have to take all necessary steps in the interest of democratic enrichment of the country. Media organizations and media regulatory authorities must take special care in formulations of the media agenda for the socio-political needs of the society and the country.

The controversial issues need special care at the time of coverage and broadcasting. Even a little negligence can be dangerous for the masses. Sensitive issues need cautious and balanced reporting from the media organizations. Some of the media organizations do not bother about factual and objective reporting due to their vested economic and survival interests. Objective and balanced reporting should be mandatory for media houses.

Notes

1. International Media Support (IMS), 'Report on the Media in Pakistan: Between Radicalization and Democratization in an Unfolding Conflict, 2009', Available on the internet at www.i-m-s.dk/files/publications/1491%20Pakistan.final.web.pdf (accessed on 10 September 2011).
2. Saqib Riaz, 'The Relationship between the Public and Print Media Agendas on National Issues in Pakistan', thesis submitted to the Allama Iqbal Open University, Islamabad, Pakistan, October 2008, p. 5, Available on the Internet at prr.hec.gov.pk/Thesis/27S.pdf
3. Wassan Aijaz Ali, 'Role/State of Electronic Media in Pakistani Society: A Sociological Analysis', Draft Paper presented at the International Conference on the Roles of the Humanities and Social Sciences in Engineering, Perlis, Malaysia, 5-6 December 2008, p. 47, Available on the Internet at http://dspace.unimap.edu.my/dspace/bitstream/123456789/5835/1/ROLE%20%20STATE%20OF%20ELECTRONIC%20MEDIA%20IN%20PAKISTANI%20SOCIETY%3b%20%20A%20SOCIOLOGICAL%20ANALYSIS.pdf
4. Riaz, n. 2, p. 20.
5. W. Lippmann, *Public Opinion,* New York: Macmillan, 1922.

6. Maxwell McCombs and Amy Reynolds, *News Influence on Our Pictures of the World, in Media Effects'*, 2nd edn., UK: Lawerence Erlbaum Publishers, 2002), pp. 1-18, available on the Internet at http://poq.oxfordjournals.org/content/36/2/176.full.pdf+html
7. Brian S. Brooks et al., *News Reporting and Writing*, 7th edn., Bedford/Missouri Group, 2002, p. 27.
8. Riaz, n. 2, p. 41.
9. M.E. McCombs and D.L. Shaw, 'The Agenda-Setting Function of News media/Mass Media', *Public Opinion Quarterly*, vol. 36 (1972), pp. 176-87 (available at http://poq.oxfordjournals.org/content/36/2/176.Abstract).
10. K. Miller, *Communications Theories: Perspectives, Processes and Contexts*, 2nd edn., Boston, MA: McGraw-Hill, 2005.
11. B. Berelson, P.F. Lazarsfeld and W.N. McPhee, *Voting: A Study of Opinion Formation in a Presidential Campaign,* Chicago: University of Chicago Press, 1954, pp. xiii, 395.
12. J. McLeod, L. Becker and J.E. Byrnes, *Another Look at the Agenda Setting Function of the Press. Communication Research,* Mahwah: Lawrence Erlbaum Associates, 1974, pp. 131-65.
13. P.J. Shoemaker and S.D. Reese, *Mediating the Message: Theories of Influences on Media Content,* 2nd edn., New York: Longman, 1996.
14. Ibid.
15. M. Waseem, 'The Electronic Media Explosion', *Dawn*, 5 November 2006, available on the Internet at http://www.asiamedia.ucla.edu/article
16. Report of International Media Support, n.1, p.14.
17. Pakistan Press Foundation, 'Report on Journalism in Pakistan: An Overview', 2006, available on the Internet at http://pakpressfoundation.wordpress.com/2006/05/05/pakistan-pressfoundation/ (accessed on 17 September 2011).
18. PEACE BRIEF, United States Institute of Peace, 'Covering and Countering Extremism in Pakistan's Developing Media, 2011', available on the Internet at http://www.usip.org/files/resources/Covering_and_Countering_Extremism_in_Pakistan%E2%80%99s_Developing_Media.pdf (accessed on 15 September 2011).
19. Report of International Media Support, n. 1, p. 30.
20. Report of Pakistan Institute of Peace Study (PIPS), 2010, available on the Internet at http://san-ips.com/download.php?f=77.pdf
21. Report of International Media Support, n. 1, p. 10.
22. Riaz, n. 2, pp. 101-2.

23. Ibid., p. 104.
24. Ibid., p. 126.
25. Ibid., p. 105.
26. Saqib Riaz, 'Agenda Setting Role of Mass media', *Global Media*, vol. I, Issue II, Islamabad: Allama Iqbal Open University, 2008, pp. 187-202, www.aiou.edu.pk/gmj/artical1(b).asp
27. Riaz, n. 2, p. 130.
28. Report of International Media Support, n. 1, p. 18.
29. Marco Mezzera and Safdar Sial, *Media and Governance in Pakistan: A Controversial yet Essential Relationship*, IFP Democratization and Transitional Justice Cluster, p. 18.
30. Report of International Media Support, n. 1, p. 34.
31. Mezzera and Sial, n. 29, p. 41.
32. Syed Abdul Siraj, 'Critical Analysis of Press Freedom in Pakistan', *Journal of Media and Communication Studies*, vol. 1, no. 3 (September 2009), pp. 43-7.
33. Report of International Media Support, n. 1, p. 6.
34. Ibid., n. 1, pp. 39-40.
35. Ibid., p. 14.
36. Mezzera and Sial, n. 29, p. 18.

CHAPTER 9

Pakistani Women Poets and the Dynamics of Religion, Politics and Society

A Comparative Study of Kishwar Naheed and Zehra Nigah

Urvashi Sabu

My voice is the voice of my city
My voice is the voice of my age
My voice will influence generations.
What do you think it is,
That you call my voice a clamour?
. . . How can you think
The coming storm a mere illusion?

'Speech No. Twenty Seven', Kishwar Naheed[1]

IT HAS RARELY BEEN easy to be a woman and a writer. Most often, women do not have a language of their own nor do they have the economic independence and the confidence to write freely. They do not even have a right to their own body and the support of inspiring traditions. At some point of time, it thus becomes imperative that they refuse to remain victims and choose to educate and define themselves as thinking individuals in their own right.

'To be born a woman in Latin America (or in any Third World country)', writes Isabel Allende in the foreword to *Other Fires*[2] 'is to have a destiny of servitude or at best, a second class citizenship. It requires very strong spirit, great lucidity and a good star to overcome the luck of the draw that society has reserved for us'. Such is the lot of women writers across the world and Pakistani women poets in particular.

Women, even in today's Pakistan, are at crossroads. They make invaluable contributions to all spheres of life, from the political to the literary, and yet continue to be disadvantaged and underprivileged in terms of social status, literacy, health, freedom of expression and overall development. They have to mediate between multiple identities, struggles and conflicts in a society that is becoming increasingly less tolerant and dominated by extremism. Fawzia Afzal Khan, noted Pakistani writer, when asked in an interview about what causes women to write, answered, 'It is a combination of male prejudice from within their societies against which women creatively militate and also western ignorance and prejudice against Islam in general and Muslim women in particular'.[3]

In order to place the argument in a perspective it would be pertinent to make a reference to the linguistic scenario in Pakistan. After Partition, Urdu was adopted as the national language of Pakistan in which a substantial body of literary texts was written. The richness of this linguistic and literary phenomenon, however, presents an astounding anomaly. As Rukhsana Ahmed points out in her Introduction to *We Sinful Women*,

> For a long time Urdu poetry has been dominated by male writers whose reputations, established and confirmed by male critics, have remained colossal in comparison with those of women poets. The bulk of Urdu poetry still tends to be love poetry bound in the old idioms and conceits. The self-appointed arbiters of taste and aesthetics are still men. They define the literary canon, build or wreck reputations and by largely ignoring women's writing, marginalise it.[4]

However, since its inception, particularly in the last fifty years, women poets from Pakistan have emerged as a potent influence on the literary scene. In order to convey real contemporary issues, they have abandoned the more conventional forms of poetry such as the *ghazal* with its charming and stylized images and traditional portrayals of women. They are exploring the possibilities of extending the language to include and express their unique experiences, rejecting the stilted formal diction popular with earlier Urdu poets. In their use of the *nazm* as the preferred style of writing, they not only refuse to conform to the notion of the ideal woman, but set out to defy it and create a new identity. They are now neither hesitant, docile, timid, defeatist or fatalist in their themes; nor are they content to be subdued to a whisper or ignored as insignificant any more. Fearlessly, without faltering, they have begun voicing their truths, exploring new vistas, exposing the exploitative rituals of patriarchy. In their poetry they reveal a new vision, a hitherto undiscussed, uncannonical version of reality as they perceive it. According to Christina Oesterheld,

> It is in poetry that the female voice is differentiated most from its male counterpart, because of the greater depth of subject matter, increasingly dealing with female issues, although there is no lack of universal topics. . . . Although a few women poets may sometimes have a preference for classical diction and closely follow traditional conventions, many more consciously refuse to accept the male poetic legacy which gives enormous importance to form and conveys, by means of a stilted language, an idealized message no longer apt to reflect social reality.[5]

Women poets from Pakistan have been expressing themselves on a variety of themes, not just the conventional ones of life, death, love, family, marriage and religion but deeper introspective and public questions related to the volatile nature of politics in Pakistan, its conflicting dialectics, and rage against a discriminatory political dispensation. Ideas of home and belonging, notions of personal freedom, social roles and the divide between public and private spheres have engrossed their attention. They have been passionate about the issues of identity and the stark experience of confinement and bondage. They have found a voice, not just in talking about man, but the entire world surrounding their inner and outer selves.

The socio-political conditions in post-Partition Pakistan have been oddly and perversely conducive to the writing of poetry by women. Although the overarching hold and reach of religion in the socio-political fabric of the state, and the repressive nature of political regimes in the 1970s and 1980s have spurred women to use poetry as an instrument of denunciation and political struggle; there are other voices too, equally prolific and profound, that bypass aggressive political agendas for a more personal, individualistic apprehension of the female psyche, thereby creating a multi-hued fabric of women's poetry in Pakistan. Women poets in Pakistan today are no longer content with having their work seen as trivial, limited or unimportant if it deals openly with their experiences as women. Thus, their conscious engagement with their socio-political context and their deeper explorations of issues of gender and psychology make them a perfect subject for critical study.

This article attempts a critical and comparative analysis of two of the foremost women poets of Pakistan, Kishwar Naheed and Zehra Nigah, based on interviews with both and a close study of their poems.

I met Kishwar Naheed fortuitously in the MMAJ Academy of International Studies, Jamia Millia Islamia, New Delhi at an international seminar on 'The State of Pakistan' in February 2011. She graciously agreed to meet me for an interaction at the residence of Professor Shamim Hanifi of Jamia Millia Islamia. In an interview that lasted for the better part of two hours, she spoke candidly about her personal life, her experiences of suppression, the inspirations for her poetry, her choice of subjects, the state of Pakistan and her stature as a government official, thinker, writer and activist.

Born in 1940 in Bulandshahr in Uttar Pradesh, India, Kishwar acquired an M.A. in Economics from the Punjab University, Lahore. She began writing poetry at a very early age, but had to suffer the ridicule of her family, especially her father who, as she confessed during our interaction, did not believe that the couplets she had recited at a *mushaira* were actually written by her. Angrily, he asked her to return the couplets to the one she had borrowed them from. Faced with opposition and the allegation of ruining the honour of the family, she wrote in secret. The same situation continued even after her marriage, when her poet-husband accused her of 'washing her dirty linen in public' and maligning his reputation in society. Perhaps it was this willful suppression that motivated her to rebel; to rise above the limitations of her gender and carve a niche for herself as an individual and a unique, fearless woman. She held a powerful position above her peers as the editor of a prestigious monthly, *Mah-e-Nau*, a government publication which acquired a reputation for editorial independence and literary quality. As editor, she was charged with various offences on at least 30 different occasions. One of these was a charge of obscenity brought against her after she published an abridged translation of Simone De Beauvoir's *The Second Sex*. I asked her why she chose this text for translation and she replied, 'So far, most books on women were written by men. Simone was the first woman to write on the subject of women.' The book sold 5,000 copies in the open market before finally being banned on the grounds of obscenity and pornography.

Kishwar finally won the court case and was successful in having her post as an officer reinstated which had been stripped as a punishment.

'If there is any woman', says Rukhsana Ahmed, 'who poses a serious threat to men through her work, her lifestyle, her manner and through serious verbal challenge, it is Kishwar Naheed. She does this with a professional dedication which either endears or enrages, there are no half measures. . . . She is above many strictures that other women in Pakistan have to observe, and those which remain, she flouts with a relish.'[6]

Kishwar's poetry has thrived on the persecution she was subjected to as a civil servant. Undaunted by threats of persecution and violent repercussions, she opined during the interview that the bullet which was meant for her would one day come to her, but until then she would fearlessly continue writing and living by her convictions. During our interaction, she reminisced how the Superintendent of Police who came to arrest her on grounds of publishing pornography after her translation of Beauvior actually requested her to go away to another place so that he wouldn't have to arrest her. It was the period of the Martial Law in the 1980s, and true to her nature, Kishwar refused to flee. She was respectfully taken to jail, made to stay for 24 hours and courteously released. As she acknowledged during our meeting, 'We have supporters of our ideology too. If we didn't, we couldn't have survived.'

Kishwar is one of the most prolific poets of her generation. She began with writing about women and her early poetry evinces a strong streak of cynicism, perhaps because her early marriage to classmate and poet Yusuf Kamraan was unconventional and not the fairy-tale ending that the youthful poets had expected it to be. For example, her poem 'How Crazy are Those Who Love You So Much':

With words of chastity he adorned my hands,
Chained my feet like prisoners,
And called it modesty.
How sweet and pleasant it sounds,
Like a diamond,
Like the gleam of a knife! . . .
How lovingly and hopefully built,
this home full of ideals and dreams!
It's been tested with screams,
making sure that if a sound

dare penetrate some crevice
it will turn to foam, exhausted,
and nothing will get through.[7]

It is clear that many of the sentiments expressed in the poem come from a direct engagement with the *purdah* imposed on her as the result of marriage into a conservative family.

Poems like 'The Night Cometh' reveal her bitter awareness of the fact that power relationships between men and women are uneven, almost always inclining in favour of men.

Two beds
In one room, beneath one roof,
Here a flowing river of sleep,
There a dreamless desert bleak;
One, lapped by gentle breeze,
The other, by burning winds besieged.
. . . Two beds –
No shore betwixt,
No desert wide,
Yet a long and deep divide![8]

Her early poetry also speaks of her grappling and coming to terms with changes in her life. 'Kishwar Naheed' is one such poem:

You thirty eight years of age,
In your cheeks and hair,
In descending autumn,
And in the storm of weakening emotions
Like unripe fallen fruits
All relationships
Like the bright countenance of life
Have loosened.
Kishwar Naheed!
You are like the closed mouth shell
In the sea of life, . . .
The desire to see you silent is overflowing from the graves.
But you speak!
Because to hear is prohibited here
The emotions which had terrified me,
Now in expressing them
I am looking at others trembling with fear.[9]

In an interview to Asif Farrukhi, Kishwar said,

I alternated between monologue and self torture. My children were growing up, life was moving on, and my sorrows and pains had reached their pinnacle. The CIDs were constantly following and watching me and because of this a number of close friends decided to break all ties with me. So many painful truths were gathered around me that I could not help giving expression to them.[10]

Another poem, 'Anti-Clockwise' deepens into defiance of social repressions:

Even if my eyes become the soles of your feet
Even so, the fear will not leave you
That though I cannot see
I can feel bodies and sentences
Like a fragrance.
Even if for my own safety,
I rub my nose in the dirt till it becomes invisible
Even so, this fear will not leave you
That though I cannot smell
I can still say something
Even if my lips, singing praises of your godliness
Become dry and soulless
Even so, this fear will not leave you
That though I cannot speak
I can still walk.
Even after you have tied the chains of domesticity,
shame and modesty around my feet
. . . this fear will not leave you
that even though I cannot walk
I can still think.[11]

In this poem, Kishwar challenges man, God and Islam to restrict her movement. The poem ponders over the numerous insidious ways in which she has been controlled and confined by her 'beloved' and proceeds to subvert them openly. The lover fears his beloved's powers because he has no control over them. Even though he can confine her physically, her mind and thoughts are still her own. They will not be chained by domesticity or familial expectations. Thus, every obstacle that the beloved throws in her path, she converts into an act of power. 'Anti-clockwise', as Anita Anantharam says 'is all the more powerful not only because of its resistance to hegemonic socio-political structures, but also because, it grants power to women's voices within those very subjugating structures of Islam or Pakistani modernity'.[12]

Over the years, Kishwar's writing has become more political, developing partly because of her determination to expand her work and partly in response to the political climate in Pakistan which became increasingly intolerant towards women during the military regime of Gen. Zia-ul-Haq (1977-88). The Islamization policy which was initiated in small measures by Zulfikar Ali Bhutto in the 1970s was carried forward with alarming persistence and speed by Gen. Zia. He banned women from participating in or being spectators of sports, and promoted *Purdah*. A nation-wide campaign called *Chadur and Chardiwari* was launched to enforce the seclusion of women. This was followed by an anti-pornography campaign which reduced the participation of women in television and entertainment. A serious attempt was made to deny educational opportunities to young girls and women. The first real inkling of the problem came with the promulgation of the *hudood* ordinances[13] on 10 February 1979. These dealt with drunkenness, theft, bearing false witness (*qazf*) and *zina* which included adultery and rape (*zina-bil-zabr*). Rape required the same testimony as adultery, i.e. four male Muslims of good repute who testify to have seen the act of penetration. This made prosecution for rape impossible under this law. The enforcement of these ordinances resulted in large-scale exploitation of women, many of whom were interred in jails as they were unable to prove their innocence before the Sharia courts. While the *hudood* ordinances would have serious repercussions for women in Pakistan, this decade in Pakistan's political history would mark the beginning of women's direct participation and collective protest against the state's injunction of *hadd* as it controlled and pertained to women's bodies and sexualities. The government's regulation of such disparaging laws resulted in a gradual but visible diminishing of women's powers in matters of economic, legal and educational representation. Thus, the women's issue was used by Gen. Zia to control society in a much more repressive grip. Kishwar was amongst the few women who came together in September 1981 in Karachi to oppose the *hudood* ordinances on the grounds that they were blatantly prejudiced against women. It was during this period, as she narrated during our interaction, that she wrote her scathingly defiant poem 'We Sinful Women' after a protest in which the slogan shouting protestors were beaten up by the police and not allowed to continue their peaceful march. This poem is ironical, fearless and defiant:

It is we sinful women
who are not awed by the grandeur of those who wear gowns
who don't sell our lives
who don't bow our heads
who don't fold our hands together . . .
Who find stories of persecution piled on each threshold
who find the tongues which could speak have been severed.

A note of determination, of breaking free from suppression infuses the last few lines of the poem.

. . . Now, even if the night gives chase
these eyes shall not be put out.
for the wall which has been razed
don't insist now on raising it again.[14]

The experience of being a woman living in the oppressive socio-political conditions of Pakistan is a recurrent theme in Kishwar's poetry. In many of them, the distinction between the private and the public is blurred as she refuses to segregate her personal from her collective experience. 'Can you call it a personal experience when a prisoner is being flogged and a microphone is placed before him to relay his screams to the crowd gathered outside the jail, and when I too am part of the crowd'.[15] This situation is reflected in a number of poems. For example, 'Charge Sheet 1990':

The lock on my door has been loosened
But the door remains closed.
The cloth over my eyes has been removed
But I still cannot see anything
The seals around my lips have been broken
But I have lost the gift of speech.
I am free or in bondage
I am happy or grieving
I have a chaadar over my head and my body is naked
I wear a crown on my head and fetters on my feet.
From adultery to a half-witness
All abuses are meant for me

And for me this award
That I am the first woman to enter the city
And be crowned . . .
From adultery to half-witness
My charge sheet is pretty long!

This theme became increasingly important for Kishwar as she became actively involved in working with women at the grassroots level.

Kishwar's angst and anger at the curtailment of the freedom of expression, the exploitation of women under the pretext of social mores and religion and the intellectual strangulation that is endemic to any oppressive dictatorial regime is also visible in other poems such as 'Nightmare': 'Every morning, I am slaughtered at my office desk/ for telling lies';[16] 'Who am I': 'I am the one you needed to bury alive/ to feel fearless as the wind again/For you never knew/that stones can never suppress a voice;'[17] 'Talking to Myself': 'Punish me/for I have written the significance of the dream/ in my own blood/. . . for I have . . . demonstrated the power of the pen to the mind/. . . for I have freed womanhood from the insanity of the deluded night. . . .'[18] 'The Grass is Really Like Me': 'The grass is really like me/As soon as it can raise its head/the lawnmower,/obsessed with flattening it into velvet,/mows it down again./How you strive and endeavour/ to level down woman too!/But neither the earth's nor the woman's/ desire to manifest life dies.'[19]

Kishwar's strategic use of metaphors thus becomes a necessity for translating her political visions. Her bold themes and no-holds barred expression often barely conceal the rough edges of her poems. Their texture is tense and brittle. They have an openness which makes them a kaleidoscope of possibilities, yet they are firmly embedded in her experiences as a woman and a crusader against injustice. In her role as a politically conscious active feminist, Kishwar Naheed is a highly respected and much loved public figure. In her life, as in her work she personifies the spirit of challenge and opposition to the male-imposed strictures and male-dominated conventions of Pakistani society. As Asif Farrukhi says:

Kishwar has contributed to the slaying of what Virginia Woolf calls 'the angel in the house', the stereotype of the quiescent, young woman acceptable to the conventional male audience. She has thus contributed to liberating the space in which other later women poets have found their personal voice.[20]

Warm, unassuming, and gracious, Zehra Nigah epitomizes the essence of tolerance and fortitude. I met Zehra for the first time at a poetry recital at Ghalib Academy, Delhi, in early 2011. When she began reciting her poems, I, like the rest of the audience, was captivated by her eloquence and sophisticated style of presentation. She visited India again a few months later to attend the centenary celebrations of Faiz Ahmed Faiz, in her own words, 'a mentor and friend'; and I had the good fortune of meeting her a second time; this time for a close interaction at the elegant residence of her nephew. I was bemused when she began the *tete-a-tete* with characteristic self deprecatory humour and humility, saying she wasn't a worthy subject for a Ph.D and had counseled numerous aspiring scholars not to undertake such a project as there really was nothing of consequence that could be said of her or her works. Over a period of two hours, she talked eloquently about her life, her family, her works and the inspirations for her poetry.

Born in 1935 to progressive and forward thinking parents, Zehra Nigah became one of the first two poets (the other being Kishwar Naheed) to have achieved prominence in the 1950s in a predominantly male realm at that time. She participated in her first *mushaira* at the behest of her school teacher when she was in class IX. After the success of this first public recital, she began to be invited regularly to *mushaira*s all over Pakistan, achieving acclaim not only for the beauty and elegance of her verse, but also for her spell-binding musical renditions of her poems. As she recounted during our interaction,

> I was fortunate enough to be accorded affection and respect by the established senior poets of my time. The general opinion about poets in those days was that they lived unconventionally and misbehaved, but I cannot recount any instance of misconduct towards me by the senior poets. My family, especially my father was extremely supportive of my writing and encouraged me not only to write, but also to participate in *mushaira*s.

Zehra's husband, a civil servant with the International Monetary Fund (IMF), also encouraged her literary talent. After marriage, she chose to concentrate on her domestic responsibilities, nurturing her two sons and being a full-time home maker. It was only when her sons grew up that encouraged and supported by her husband and family, she began writing again, this time in her changed avatar as 'a complete woman'.

I infer that the gentle tone of her poems, her non-belligerent attitude to writing is a consequence of this social background, the grooming of tolerance that she received as a child and the supportive family structures into which she was born and subsequently married. Yet, for all their beauty and tenderness, her poems are also suffused with wistfulness. They convey subtly the pathos of her resignation, her acknowledgement of the power of the forces to which women must submit. That she voluntarily chose her path, (as she says) is undoubtedly true, but there is also a deeper underlying fact: she accepted her lack of choices with grace and dignity, allowing her regrets to emerge in the symbolic images of her poetry. According to Anita Anantharam, 'Poetry facilitates intimate self expression as it allows the author to explore sensitive issues like identity, kinship and marriage through the protective blankets of metaphor, symbolism and literary convention'.[21] For example, 'Compromise':

Warm and tendersoft, this *chadar*
of compromise has taken me years to knit.
No flowers of truth embellish it
not a single false stitch betrays it.
It will do to cover my body though
and it will bring comfort too,
if not joy, nor sadness to you.[22]

Her reminiscences of a playful, happy childhood are speckled with references to the power of insidious forces. In 'The Moonflower Tree', she writes,

. . . I remembered last night,
the tree in a corner of my garden,
studded with flowers of moonlight.
I would play beneath its shade,
. . . swing on the boughs,
. . . touch the flowers and run.
Into its trunk had been sunk
scores of nails.
Many a time I had been warned
not to touch those nails.
The tree, they said,
was haunted.

. . . Should anyone pull out those pins,
it would release the genie within.
. . . within the confines of this body and soul
dwells such a moon silvered tree
. . . I dearly love
the shade of this, my tree.
And in its trunk until this day
lives bewitched that same genie.
Even now I live in dread
if ever I should touch those nails
that ogre might escape
. . . my home he would surely burn!
Would it really into ashes turn?[23]

The nostalgia of childhood friendships finds expression in 'My Playmate':

. . . A dark, sad girl
her body wrapped in a white veil,
. . . my playmate of many years, she's known me for ages
. . . a thousand storms the rose of our friendship had weathered
yet still its fragrance blooms in our hearts
. . . though a thousand darknesses cast their sinister nets around us
steadfast this blame of human love blazes.[24]

Zehra Nigah's poetry is intensely personal rather than publically political. She admitted during our interaction that she writes 'straight from the heart', more with emotion and feeling rather than with any consciously subversive political agenda. She is fully conversant with and concerned about the political scenario of Pakistan since its inception to the present day but chooses to stress on its emotional impact on individuals, especially women. Her poem, 'Hudood Ordinance' is suffused with sadness, a resignation and irony that are devoid of propagandist activism. The subtitle of the poem 'To the girls suffering imprisonment under the Hudood Ordinances' is in itself expressive:

In this tiny cell
I am both fettered and free
there's a tiny window
almost as high as the ceiling
A handful of rays
beam through the window
they form a kind of path

for me to tread on
so I can go home.
Even now my father brings me
bangles and combs from the city.
Apa leaves my share of *rotis*
. . . my brothers still go
to the mosque to study
all God's commandments-
. . . Ma, crazed by her grief for me,
. . . spends her time picking pebbles
or . . . talking to the birds
she says when these birds
understand what she is telling them
they will pick pebbles in their beaks
. . . and such a storm shall rage
that every judge and every pulpit
will shatter into smithereens.
But I am not the *Khan-e-kaaba*
who will come to save me?[25]

As Anita Weiss emphasizes,

Laws enforced during Zia-ul-Haq's Islamization programme exacerbated prevailing culturally sanctioned violence. . . . Due to the tendency to censure the victims of domestic abuse, women are often reluctant to discuss violent act of abuse. Indeed in Pakistan, a woman who claims to be a victim of rape but is unable to prove it can be charged with adultery (*Zina)* and imprisoned . . . violence against women within their homes is an extension of the subordination of women in larger society, re-enforced by religious beliefs, cultural norms, traditional practices and actual laws. It is likely exacerbated by the social expectations held by men that they exert control over the actions of 'their women'. The cultural structure of the family not only places women in a subordinate role but also fosters gender-based violence and coercion.[26]

Zehra's poems convey her empathy for women and underscore the emotional tribulations and psychological suppressions that women face in a discriminatory and restrictive socio-political-religious scenario. For example, 'My Crime: A Promise':

My child I told you a story thousands of times
. . . I promised you something

that promise which is the destiny of human beings
of protection, of honour of esteem.
My child
the tired and exhausted girl in the story
was not a princess, it was me
the enchanted palace
which burnt to a desert in an instant was my home
Where only the needles in the eyes remained
those dreams were mine
and all those who besieged me
were not outsiders, they were my own kin.[27]

At the same time there is a profound understanding that the lot of women, irrespective of their country or religion is the same, as seen in her poem 'The Girl by the Lamp Post', a poignant evocation of her chance encounter with a young prostitute on a street in London.

A storm raged in the night
The rain poured heavily
On such a night, who knows why,
I wandered aimlessly.
Across the road she stood
Against the lamp-post,
her head leaned heavily,
as she waited
for a prospective client . . .
the makeup ran down her cheeks
in the pouring rain . . .
But when the rain had washed away
Those layers of makeup . . .
I looked at her closely.
A plain, simple face it was,
on those innocent features
surfaced the colours of youth
washed by the rain . . .
I felt as if she were
My own daughter
Whom I had lovingly raised
Carried in my womb.
Suddenly, my heart longed
To seize her in my arms . . .

I longed to turn my veil into my nest once again
I longed to shelter her in that nest once again.[28]

This poem reflects and draws upon experiences which transcend political geography, nationality and the linear progression of history measured by time. It conveys the commonality of female experiences across boundaries and borders.

Zehra Nigah has also written about the ill-fated Afghan war and its damaging consequences for Pakistan. As she said in the course of our meeting, 'Behind every small nation are the grand strategies of bigger, more powerful countries. The war that America waged in Afghanistan spelled disaster for Pakistan.' Poems such as 'Gulbaadshah' and 'Gulzameena' express with eloquent sadness the impact of the aggression on children:

Gulzameena, gulzameena,
with your delicate finger, what do you write on this pile of rubble?
Gulzameena raised her questioning eyes and answered,
A few days ago, this pile of rubble was my school
I would inscribe the Holy name of Allah on its wall
My paper, pens and books, my fellow companions have all been destroyed
I come here every day, and from the satchel of my memories, I pull out the last lesson I learnt
I write it on this pile of rubble and return
I know I am not destined to read
At least I can continue to write.[29]

Zehra Nigah's poetry demonstrates her skills as an accomplished lyricist and a fine poet capable of both intensity and subtlety. The fact that in the sixty years of her writing career she has published only three volumes of poetry speak eloquently for the precedence she gave to domesticity over poetry: a sacrifice that was evidently not without some pain. Her poems are traditional, both in form and content; they stay well within the bounds of 'protest' expected and permitted in women's writing from the subcontinent. They illustrate the power of the forces to which women must submit rather than the energy, anger or defiance that is apparent in the works of more political poets like Kishwar Naheed.

As feminists, these poets have used their writing to rework and redefine subtly the complex relationships between women and men and also gender and the state in Pakistan. They have used poetry especially at crucial historical junctures in Pakistan's history to express and discuss intimate issues of self, emotions and nationalism which could not have found a voice in any other genre, given their socio-historical and cultural condition.

In conclusion it can be said that poetry is arguably the most personal mode of writing. In situations/locations that circumscribe the freedom of expression, the essentially symbolic nature of poetry offers a subterfuge for personal and communal disaffections and serves as a creative outlet for suppressed tropes of thought and feeling.

Notes

1. 'Speech No. Twenty Seven', *Penguin Book of Modern Urdu Poetry*, selected and ed. Mahmood Jamaal, Harmondsworth: Penguin, 1986, p. 138.
2. Alberto Manguel (ed.), *Other Fires: Short Fiction by Latin American Women Authors,* Torento: Random House, 1992. Quoted in the Editorial, *Pakistani Literature*, Special Issue, 'Women's Writings', vol. 3, no. 2, 1994, p. 15.
3. N.K. Agarwal, 'Interview with Fawzia Afzal Khan', *Asiatic*, vol. 3, no. 1, June 2009, p. 97.
4. Rukhsana Ahmed (ed. and tr.), *We Sinful Women,* Ann Arbor: The Women's Press, 1991, p. 1.
5. Christina Oesterheld, 'Urdu and Muslim Women', *Islam in Contemporary South Asia*. Quoted in Valerio Pietrangelo, 'Urdu Literature and Women', *The Annual of Urdu Studies*, vol. 19, 2004.
6. Ahmed, pp. 20–1.
7. 'How Crazy Are Those Who Love You So Much', *Penguin Book of Modern Urdu Poetry*, selected and ed. Mahmood Jamaal, Harmondsworth: Penguin, 1986, p. 140.
8. 'The Night Cometh', *Masterpieces of Modern Urdu Poetry,* Selected and Edited by K.C. Kanda, New Delhi: Sterling, 1998, p. 345.
9. 'Kishwar Naheed', in *Modern Urdu Poets*, ed. Yunus Ahmar, Karachi: Royal Book Company, 1995, pp. 62–3.
10. Interview to Asif Farrukhi, quoted in Asif Farrukhi, ed., Karachi: Oxford University Press, 2005, 'Introduction', *Kishwar Naheed: The Distance of a Shout,* ed. Asif Farrukhi, Karachi: Oxford University Press, 2005, p. xi.
11. Ahmed, p. 59.

12. Anita Anantharam, 'Engendering the Nation: Women, Islam and Poetry in Pakistan', *Journal of International Women's Studies,* vol. 11, no. 1, November 2009, p. 213.
13. The word *hadd* literally means boundary or limit, and the term *hadd* implies a maximum penalty fixed by the Sharia for a particular offence.
14. Ahmed, p. 31.
15. Quoted in 'Introduction', *Kishwar Naheed: The Distance of a Shout,* p. xi.
16. Ahmed, p. 47.
17. Ibid., p. 43.
18. Ibid., p. 55.
19. Ibid., p. 47.
20. Farrukhi, *The Distance of a Shout,* p. xiv.
21. Anantharam, 'Engendering the Nation', p. 211.
22. Ahmed, p. 113.
23. Ibid., p. 115.
24. Ibid., p. 134.
25. Ibid., pp. 137-8.
26. Anita Weiss, 'Islamic Influences on Socio-legal Conditions of Pakistani Women', in Magnus Marsden, ed., *Islam and Society in Pakistan,* Karachi: Oxford University Press, 2010, pp. 59-60.
27. Ahmed, p. 119.
28. Ibid., pp. 125-9.
29. 'Gulzameena', my translation.

CHAPTER 10

Coke Studio
A Musical Identity

Bidisha Mukherjee

PAKISTAN – A WORD, a name, a country, conjures up myriad images in the minds of rest of the world, with varied perspectives. History makes its way through twists and turns, carves out a valley of images about Pakistan is – a non-democratic state, to some even a failed state, with growing fundamentalism, a breeding ground of terrorists and suicide bombers; poor citizens in *burqa* and *pathani salwar* and a rich elite class. This, however, is the surface. If we scratch beneath and delve deeper into the nation state of Pakistan, like any nation state we will find its distinct characteristics, with good, bad, ugly woven together in a beautiful tapestry. It is essential to gain a deeper understanding about Pakistan by not only studying its politics, economics and society but also its popular culture, art, literature, lifestyle and also the emerging, vibrant mass media. In fact, Pakistan, since its creation out of partition of the British empire in the subcontinent, has always tried vehemently to come out of the popular prejudices and stereotypes through every means possible, whether political, commercial or cultural.

If we look into the struggle of Pakistan to establish a sound identity in this world, we have to rewind into history to have a brief idea about the ideology with which this state began its journey, which to a large extent, has shaped its identity. Born in 1947 out of the division of British India into a Muslim Pakistan and predominantly Hindu India, Pakistan has been searching for its identity since its very inception. Many of Jinnah's statements suggest that he intended a non-theocratic, even secular and democratic, state for Muslims to live in, wishfully thinking that religious distinctions would wither away with time into a more wholesome Pakistani identity. For numerous reasons this vision never materialized in any substantive way and soon after Jinnah's death, non-democratic and theocratic forces began to envisage a very different Pakistan, most strongly voiced thirty years after Jinnah's death in the slogan popularized by General Zia-ul-Haq's dictatorial regime, '*Pakistan ka matlab kya? La ilaha illallah*' (What is the meaning of Pakistan, there is no God but the God).

Helping the Taliban in Afganistan, acquiring nuclear capabilities, and allowing the rise of intolerance and sectarian violence internally under the banner of fundamentalist Islam have all contributed to an image problem of considerable proportion. The 9/11 episode has worsened it. Former president General Pervez Musharraf tried to peddle a softer more liberal image by publicly endorsing theatre and film festivals, and by trying to promote women's participation in politics. He made frequent reference to Jinnah's pronouncements and ideals, visualizing a very different Pakistan from the one that now exists.

It was very interesting to observe how the dynamic persona of Jinnah is still capitalized upon in order to win the heart of the young Pakistani, inspire them with fresh zeal and of course to create that identity of a different Pakistan. The introduction of youthful and dashing Jinnah as the poster boy entering urban Pakistan public space was the private and voluntary initiative of an internet company *World on Line* based in Lahore in 2005-6. Those responsible for the project stated that they want the country's youth to be inspired by the person they call Quaid-i-Azam (although he had not become one when the pictures were taken) and believed that the young cannot identify with what they call the *baba* figure of the aged *Quaid*. With over 200,000 posters printed and distributed across urban Pakistan, this was a project in nationalism of a very different kind.[1]

Zarminae Ansari writes:

> Our identity displayed proudly in the ads, celebrates a glorious past. It is interesting to note that the chosen past representing cultural identity is religious, not regional. Islamic history is extensively used: when regional references are made, they are from a particular era in history – the Mughal period . . . as opposed to Mohenjo-daro, the Hindu Shahiya Temples of Salt Range, or the Gandhara ruins in Taxila. Not just in ads . . . but also in every sphere of our public lives, we tend to ignore the varied strains of

religion or region, and consciously choose, cultural elements conforming to an Islamic identity.[2]

Every identity in Pakistan, whether a product or an airline, is not merely a business decision. It has an underlying effort to construct a national identity. Faraz Maqsood Hamidi in his essay writes, when Negus was commissioned to develop the corporate identity for Pakistan International Airlines (popularly known as PIA) the creator knew that he was branding much more than a fleet of aircraft – he was branding a nation that had only recently 'shed blood for a corner of the sky'. In a feat of cultural orchestration, PIA's identity was launched on 7 April 1976. The bottle green and gold combination resonated across the country and earned adulation across the world. The new logotype pioneered a new chapter in aviation branding by raising itself from a commodity to an experience. 'As the country's most visible icon, the PIA fleet radiated two strategic messages: Pakistan International is an international carrier while Pakistan is an international country.'[3]

Another mass identity was created through the very popular drink called Pakola. With the new born country trying to develop its indigenous products, in the 1950s the migrant Memon brothers of the Teli family from Surat created a unique flavour which readily appealed to the common people and it soon became a brand icon for the country. Entrepreneur Seth Haji Muhammad Ali Teli refined the formula of soft drinks of international companies which became extreme popular with the ordinary Pakistan.

In those early days, Pakistan was high on patriotism and he formulated the perfect colour suited to the time – Green (as green equals Pakistan) and nothing could have inspired more than a Pakistani Cola or Pakola! Pakola was launched on 14th August 1950, the third anniversary of Pakistan's creation, in Karachi (the then capital of Pakistan), at the Pakistan Air Force Base in the presence of the Prime Minister of Pakistan, Liaqat Ali Khan. And thus was forged an enduring association between brand and country.[4]

In the late 1970s and early 1980s the Cola War was engulfing the soft drink market of Pakistan, with Coca-Cola and Pepsi vying to get consumer attention. Given the huge capital the brands were capable of muscling of their way into the retail outlets. However, Pakola was not forgotten. Even though the golden days were over, what saved Pakola from oblivion was the strong branding and marketing legacy left by Seth Haji Muhammad Ali Teli. However, the young grandson of the creator of Pakola today faces numerous challenges in this globalized market but he can fight his way through with the belief that he carries the legacy of a great Pakistani brand.[5]

This reference to Pakola and the Cola Wars brings us to the main part of our text which tries to see whether international brands have in any way contributed to the national image creation. International soft drinks like Coca-Cola started their journey in Pakistan as a foreign product and were identified with being 'imported'. This aligned with Coca-Cola corporation's centralized global marketing structure at that time. It was a time when desiring the image of Coke was inextricable from the distances one felt from its cultural point of origin. In this distance there was a space for desire and difference. But multinational consumerism has grown in contemporary times and is more 'at home' in Pakistan's national cultural imagination than ever before. That is to say in more recent times, global corporations have assigned strategic importance to vernacularizing the image and experience of their commodities.[6]

These days the company is keener to appeal to the demographic target group (youth) through various means. What appeals to youth more than music? And with Pakistan's rich musical tradition the strategy of promoting products through music has become a trend in Pakistan, with Pepsi's Battle of the Bands and Levi's Original Music, and topping the charts is Coke Studio. But does this kind of programme, more precisely, Coke Studio, just publicize a soft drink in a 'softer way'? Or does it actually help promote and protect the local culture of Pakistan, giving a strong un-Islamic national identity to its own people and to the rest of the world? Hence I took up Coke Studio as a case study to delve deeper and trying to identify a real Pakistan through it.

Before talking about Coke Studio, it is useful to go through a brief history of popular music in Pakistan after its formation. The multi-ethnic formation of Pakistan had churned a beautiful, eclectic musical tradition that has an extremely rich amalgamation of classical, folk and popular music ranging from various parts of South Asia as well as Central Asian, Persian, Turkish, Arabic, and modern-day Western popular musical influences surviving side by side. With these manifold influences, a unique Pakistani musical culture has been formed. From Pakistan's inception, music was a form of entertainment like anywhere else. But unlike Pakistan's hardliner-Islamist image today, society was a bit different back then. In spite of the erratic political landscape, the back and forth swing from democracy to military dictatorship, the tradition of Pakistani music remained sturdy.[7]

The 1940s saw Alam Lohar, a cult Punjabi-folk favourite, who wooed the crowd with the song *Jugni* which still is extremely popular with some help from Coke Studio. With a few exceptions, minorities in Pakistan appeared frequently on TV during the 1950s, singing some of the great music to come out of the entertainment industry. Sunny Benjamin John and Irene Perveen, singers belonging to Christian families, stole the hearts of young Pakistanis with their heartfelt music. The 1960s, considered a golden age by many, was a happy time in Pakistan. Music in the 1960s took a turn around the world. With the Beatles in the West, Pakistan produced Ahmed Rushdi in the East – arguably, the first disco star of his generation. *Ko-ko-Korina*, a song that earned a Platinum Jubilee, was so popular in the region it escalated the Pakistani movie industry to great heights. Many versions of the song appeared in the next few decades both domestically and in India too.

The 1970s gave rise to a popular, risqué trend called the 'hair dance'. To do the hair dance, one had to shed all inhibitions, and shake it, literally. To any Pakistani who grew up in the 1980s, the words *Vital Signs* were not measures of physiological statistics, but a musical band of heartthrobs who sang *Dil Dil Pakistan*. These young, leather-jacket-wearing-motorbike-riding men were patriotic, and Pakistanis realized, 'You know what? It's cool to be Pakistani.' Styled in Ray-Ban sunglasses, the band members of *Vital Signs* challenged General Zia-ul-Haq's strict regime and introduced Pakistanis to the world of pop music. Because it was a patriotic song, it remained uncensored. Earlier in the decade, Nazia Hassan sang *Disco Deewane*, a song which made it to the US Billboard charts, a first for any Pakistani singer. In the 1990s the U2 of Pakistan, Junoon struggled to promote their music. The US invasion of Afghanistan left much violence on the streets of Pakistan and thus began a long, on-going stretch of political instability. One band member, Salman Ahmed, said he made his first political statement by creating a rock band. Junoon's music, which highlighted the corruption of Pakistan's elite, got the group into trouble and it was banned. Junoon's vocalist Ali Azmat considered himself and the band to be 'musical guerillas', but the ban only escalated their popularity as counter-culture heroes.[8]

In the early 2000s, the explosion of information technology gave young artists an opportunity to showcase their talent. Strings and Jal made their mark in the international music market. A plethora of TV channels saw the emergence of fresh, new faces that are now household names in Pakistan. Halfway through the decade, Coke Studio was launched.

Coke Studio is a musical programme, originating from Karachi, and is aired in 27 television channels and 11 radio stations across the country at present.[9] It is a show of live musical performance and recording session, where singers and musicians perform together on the same platform, creating a flavour of *jugalbandhi*. Coke Studio is an international franchise that was produced in Pakistan by Rohail Hyatt, of *Vital Signs* fame, and his wife Umber Hyatt in 2008. Its featured artists on each episode were backed by a house band and guest artists. Even though it is an inspiration from the original Brazilian show named Estúdio Coca-Cola,[10] it is fundamentally different from the original version. In the Brazilian edition the show was a concert-style show whereas the Pakistani adaptation records its shows inside a closed studio. The programme focuses on a fusion of the diverse musical influences in Pakistan, including eastern classical, folk, pop, rock and contemporary popular music. Even flamenco influence is also acknowledged in the session *Jo Merey* by *Noori* in Season Two, Episode Three. The show provides a common platform for famous as well as forthcoming and lesser known artists, from a variety of genres and regions, to team up musically in live studio recording sessions. There are debut songs, traditional folk, Sufi, popular songs, along with 'remixes' which are an attempt to pay tribute to musical geniuses like Nusrat Fateh Ali Khan along with Michael Jackson in *Waasta Pyar Da* by Atif Aslam or *Ae Wattan Kay Sajeelay Jawanon*, a tribute by Amanat Ali to the legendary Noorjehan.

Coke Studio has been popular, receiving critical acclaim and frequently being rebroadcast on television and radio in Pakistan. The official Facebook Page of Coke Studio has more than 1.3 million 'likes' till September 2012. The current 'likes' of this page is 3.1 million as of 12 February 2014. The videos are also available on Youtube, which have frequently been viewed and commented on, with most videos counting over a million hit. The number of news channel broadcasting Coke Studio has grown over time with internet and audio-visual media Coke Studio is spreading out far and wide. There is no doubt that this massive popular appeal is due to the multicultural nature of the programme.

Coke Studio was launched on 8 June 2008 and has aired for five seasons so far with 24 episodes. The first season started off with four episodes and a live audience. The mood was experimental and the anticipation and optimism of a 'would-be-parent' was felt. Season Two premiered on 14 June 2009 a new logo and without a live audience, eliminating the associated background noise and providing a more intimate atmosphere.[11] From this season onwards Coke Studio has transformed itself from an arrangement to a thought process. Each of the five episodes was given a name and a brief justification for the respective names. Starting with *Identity* – 'acknowledgment of the power of individuals', *Harmony* – 'individuals coming together to create a common ground that is in harmony with itself and each other', *Equality* – equalizing music, its boundaries and genres, *Spirit* – as in human spirit. The Coke Studio journey completed its course on the 14 of August, with a special 90-minute Independence Day episode titled *Unity.* Debuting in this episode, Atif Aslam sang *Humain kya hua*, a distinct patriotic number; this song dares our conscience, probes indifference and intends to incite unity. '*Humain kya hua* is a rousing wake-up call, both musical and lyrical'. This same episode showcased Noori's *Kedaar*, which was exclusively composed for this session, *Kedaar* means powerful and invincible. Ali Hamza says, 'Coke Studio is one of the birth pangs for an awakening Pakistani conscience'.[12]

Similarly Season Three had episode named – *Reason, Will, Conception, Form* and *Realisation.* The first episode centred around the reason for being or the reason behind embarking on any venture. The second one emphasized on the force behind attainment, which is, will. Conception follows the natural course of evolution, and arrives at that third crucial stage when the combining of reason and will lead to an idea taking tangible form. The last episode is the realization of goals and dreams. To further strengthen the bond with the audience, Coke Studio introduced lyrics of featured songs in its website with Urdu and English translation. The deep thought and hard work behind conceptualizing and executing each season shows that this is not an ordinary musical endeavour.

A word should be mentioned about Coke's sponsorship of this musical endevour. Fusion music was proposed to them by the executive producer and visionary of the show Rohail Hyatt when he was the music consultant for Coca-Cola but it wasn't really perceived as a good idea. Then, he drew their attention to the brand charter where it says that Coca-Cola sought to encourage inclusiveness, not exclusiveness.[13] Coca-Cola websites mention nothing about Coke Studio, nevertheless it can be assumed that, the company saw this unique endevour reaching out to its favourite target group of youth by vernacularizing its product in a market where a rival company is the leader. In the Coke Studio website it is mentioned that 'Coca-Cola believes that music can bridge barriers, celebrate diversity and bring out something greater than the sum of its parts.' It further says, 'Coke is proud to have created the platform where renowned and upcoming musicians from various genres can collaborate to realize their dreams.' Hence, a product reaches its target audience, new musicians get a chance to showcase their talent, audience receive awesome musical experience. Everyone is happy. A symbiotic relation has been discovered. However, it has more to offer.

The Coke Studio website goes like this:

Coke Studio embodies a musical fusion of exciting elements and diverse influences, ranging from traditional eastern, modern western and regionally inspired music. Bringing alive the magic of live recordings and performances, Coke Studio prides itself on providing a musical platform, which bridges barriers, celebrates diversity, encourages unity and instills a sense of Pakistani pride. Coke Studio is an inspired step by Coca-Cola for having created a platform where renowned as well as upcoming and less mainstream musicians from various genres can collaborate musically.

In each season, Coke Studio spirals to encompass a wider arc of diversity as the voyage of discovery continues in an exploration of the next wave of musical styles and influences. We also learnt that Coke Studio, in the fourth season, offered content sung in nine different languages including Brahui, Seraiki, Hindi, Punjabi, Farsi, Poorvi, Urdu and Marvari,[14] etc.

Coke Studio One was the first step in the realization of a dream, one which merged tradition with modernity, consistency with change. It also marked the commencement of the journey into the core of live music.... Most importantly, though, the first season essentially put on the map the Coke Studio philosophy of peace and harmony, and celebrating life.

For the third season the website reads, 'Come and be a part of the sea change as once again we connect distinct and varied styles, ethnicities and identities and link them with that one common denominator – Music.'

Coke Studio embarks on its fourth season with a heightened awareness of the invisible depths of the musical foundations upon which it stands. Expanding on the experiences of the previous three seasons, Coke Studio now continues along the path of self-discovery with a fresh perspective on the scale of diversity – of music, poetry, cultures and languages - that exist in Pakistan.

In the description of each season we see, apart from this remarkable musical dedication and enthusiasm to revive a traditional music, a distinct message, an assertion; rather a plea exists to recognize Pakistan in this true light of a phenomenally prosperous musical tradition, not as a terrorist making nation.

The diversity of singers and musicians of this show truly resembles a palette. For instance, in Season Five, which was first aired on 13 May 2012, 16 artistes of various genres of music, region, *gharana* and age were brought together for yet another marvellous production. While one artist of the show is inspired by video games, another loves bringing back Pakhtun folk.

Rohail Hyatt portrays his brainchild in a different way. In an interview to *Dawn.com* he voices his strong opinion that:

When foreign publications tried to portray Coke Studio as a sort of anti-terrorism resistance, it was horrific. I mean here's someone totally changing what we're trying to do, and encapsulate it into what they think is going on, and as a story just totally ruining it. You know it's not about trying to bring in an alternative thought process – it's totally different, it's free from all that. That is its beauty. It's free from purpose to change, free from purpose to dictate, it's got nothing of that embedded in it anywhere.[15]

In contrast, other contributors to Coke Studio are of the opinion that seems to harp on the age-old fight to create an identity, more so a non-religious, common identity for their beloved country.

Bilal Khan in an interview with *Dawn.com* was asked, why does an artiste want to be a part of Coke Studio? He said:

Coke Studio is a platform. Given the current atmosphere in Pakistan where on a social, political and economic scale we have experienced and seen so much, it comes as a relief. It has the power to unify this fragmented nation of ours. It is no accident then that there is a fusion of sounds, colours, genres and styles of music on the show. That is all meant to translate into the real-life experience of the average Pakistani. And for me it was the most important thing to be a featured artiste on such an ambitious television programme. The music of my debut album centers on the search for hope in times when all dignity feels lost. And that is what CS has and continues to do for Pakistan.[16]

Model, actress, singer Meesha Shafi comments, '. . . at a time like this it is very important that it is keeping the music industry going and growing, as events and concerts are at an all time low unfortunately. It couldn't have come at a better time. It's doing a lot for a lot of people including me.'[17]

Adnan Malik, Associate Video Producer and the Behind the Scenes Producer of Season Two, in an interview to *Changing Up Pakistan* blog was asked about the final episode of Coke Studio's Season Two which was aired on 14 August, Pakistan's Independence Day, and was aptly titled, *Unity*. He was asked how the show embodied this spirit of unity and what message it gave out. He replied that:

My favorite aspect of this show is its engagement in helping define a Pakistani identity. We are clearly at a crossroads in terms of a collective cultural ethos, and I believe that this show is an example of how we should engage with our past, present and future. The music takes from both current Western influences and indigenous classical and folk influences to create a truly 'contemporary' and 'universal' sound. The music is an honest representation of where we are today, it's both timely and timeless; both purely Pakistani and palatably global. Coke Studio is all about Unity – the collaboration of big-hearted, open-minded Pakistanis to create something unique, beautiful and truly our own. The effort shows that it is possible to work together and create amazing things with pure intentions and dedicated hard work. At a micro level, Coke Studio is also a metaphor for nation building. It has captured the imagination of the whole nation and collectively brought us together from all corners to appreciate and celebrate the diversity of our country.[18]

Again in an article of *Dawn.com*, Murtaza Razvi writes,

Rohail Hyatt and his talented House Band don't need to compose patriotic songs that for a long time now have rung hollow; they, instead, are doing us proud by concentrating on what they're good at: making music.

They don't have to come up with soppy, *watan*-loving numbers or statements like 'This is not who we are'; statements that have ceased to work now. . . .[19]

From the above comments we can arrive at a point that Coke Studio is not screaming out patriotism. Rather by upholding the rich musical tradition of the country it is very genuinely appealing to the patriotic heart of a Pakistani national as well as striking a chord in music lovers' hearts across the borders. It's serving both the purpose of solidifying the identity and soothing heart with its musical marvel.

In the Independence Day episode of *Unity*, all the featured artists kept harping on one phrase – 'let's change ourselves' instead of blaming and criticizing others. It is notable to see that standing at this juncture of history, these young musicians, a representative of the young generation, are tired of the doldrums, exhausted from the blame game, disillusioned about the intentions; they want a change. For these people, serving quality music to the audience is their unique way of doing it.

Music in Pakistan has done what the country was unable to do through its politics, i.e. to give a sense of belonging and pride to its people and be a cultural representative across borders with the help of musical geniuses like Abida Parveen and Nusrat Fateh Ali Khan, Rahat Fateh Ali Khan and others. Following Mohammad A. Qadeer we can say, 'These are symbols of the national consciousness'. The scene is similar even in this new decade, where amidst chaos and political instability, Coke Studio manages to give Pakistanis something to proudly call their own. The show gets a major boost because of its easy accessibility online and a huge following on social networking sites. Some of these comments on the Coke Studio's Channel YouTube[20] and some blogs go like this:

excaliburkz

Coke Studio is a ray of light that emanates from the heart of Pakistan and touches the rest of the world – forcing it to see us differently; forcing us to look in the mirror and realize that what we possess is important and worth fighting for.

LittleAngel3006

One of such great things we are proud to have in Pakistan! A great matter of pride for every Pakistani child, young and old that culture and art still prevail in our society, at such high level. Feel proud to be a citizen of Pakistan!

Ammarttitude

Best music of the world is being produced by Pakistan. . . .

Pakistan Zindabad.

ssssaaaa10

Indeed the best . . . !!! coke studio has made us proud . . . !!! PAKISTAN ZINDABAD . . . !!

codename22111991

Whenever Pakistan is pressed down to nothing we bring out new more powerful gems to show the world what we can do and how well we can do it. Pakistan is an undying gem, it is like a diamond in the rock being polished by each hardship it faces. Pakistan always gives you the best quality and not focusing on quantity at all. Pakistan Zindabad, cokestudio is yet another success.

Kalsoom

I really loved the different themes of Coke Studio and how it was more representative of Pakistan as a nation. The show was very popular esp. among young Pakistanis and I think it's very indicative of Pakistan's past, where we are, and where we want to go.

Its YouTube channel has 124,793 subscribers (as on 17 September 2012). Although most of the videos on the channel have subtitles in only English and Urdu, it is the universal appeal of the music that has enabled it to garner such an overwhelming response from people all over the world. Many of the comments on the videos are from Indians who are pleasantly surprised to discover the distinct style of Pakistani music. Contemporary Pakistani singers are relatively well known in India, but now due to the widespread appeal of Coke Studio, folk singers are also becoming household names across the border.

Although this number nationally and internationally may seem to represent only a miniscule elite compared to the vast population of the country, nevertheless, the importance of the show cannot be ignored, as owing to technological advancements it is reaching out to thousands within minutes. Keeping in tune with Ian Talbot it can be said that apart from commercial bonanza emanating from this kind of programme, an assertion of national identity can also be felt.[21] After the launch of Coke Studio in 2008, the morale of the Pakistani urban youth is changing. For the youth commenting on these websites, blogs, social networking sites or web magazines it seemed like a 'historical impact'. Most of the comments equate Coke Studio with changing the face of Pakistan in the international arena and as Hamayoon Khan in Season Five mentioned, the show offers songs which are 'truly Pakistani'.[22] It gives the Pakistani listeners a sense of belonging, pride and reinvented musical brilliance.

The show upholds an unprecedented national identity which includes the various tribal traditions, folk music, Sufi music, pop, rock, classical music – kind of 'unity in diversity' feel. To an outsider, it's like music has stitched together the far-flung areas of Pakistan; in the words of Mohammad A. Qadeer, it's a 'convergence of ethnicities'. Along with the audience the singers themselves feel this new found 'unity'.

Sanam Marvi, a young Sufi singer from Sindh, says:

> I have seen many people saying that 'you are from Sind, you are from Punjab'...what is Punjab? What is Sindh? Everyone is Pakistani. This is our home. Just like father-mother-sister-brother stay together in a home, we too are like one family. We should not think whether I am from Sindh or Punjab. We are all brothers and sisters and we must do something together for our country, whether through music, or business or through Islam.[23]

Famous Pakistani folk singer Arif Lohar, son of Alam Lohar, describes his experience in Coke Studio through a beautiful couplet:

Hum Pakhtun na Punjabi
Sindhi na Balochistani
Ek Khuda aur Ek Naadi, Hum saab Pakistani

This means, that we are neither Pakhtun nor Punjabi nor Sindhi nor Balochistani, we have one God and one river, we are all Pakistani.[24]

This opulent store of Pakistani music is presenting Pakistan in a new light to the world. As an outsider, the picture of rural Pakistan is pretty bleak in our minds and the advent of Taliban has all the more depressed that picture. However, in Coke Studio when the folk singers of Balochistan deliver an extraordinary musical exhibition, may be, somewhere, our one-dimensional perspective about these areas change, and so for Pakistan. The music lifts us to a different world, and we forget the pressing social problems for a while, nay, we get optimistic. For instance when contemporary pop singer Komal Rizvi shares the same platform with renowned Balochi folk legend Akhtar Chanal Zahri or when the Chakwal Group is accompanied with Meesha Shafi, the co-existence bespeaks of the eternal truth that tradition and modernity go hand in hand complementing and in this case, complimenting each other. In the fusion song *Daanah Pah Daanah* (Multitude of Grains) Brahui, Balochi, Punjabi, Persian and Urdu are used. This folk song is written and composed by Akhtar Chanal Zahri, and tells the story of a shepherd introducing his beloved to the wonders of his land, invoking famous rivers and mountains of Balochistan. 'Through this patriotic anthem, imbued with shades of a pastoral romance, the poet presents a message of friendship and amity.' The sense of belonging is found in the great singer's voice when he says, 'I was listening to the world and observing that no one was looking at us, no one is thinking about us. . . . I am deeply grateful to everyone for calling from Balochistan.'[25]

As music is contagious, the idea of Coke Studio is spreading afar. Along with Coke Studio@MTV, the Indian version and Coke Studio Middle East have also captured attention. In the introduction section of the Coke Studio Middle East, Coca-Cola goes on to say:

> Coke Studio inspires teens of the Arab world with the Coca-Cola point of view about positive change. Teens have been struggling between two worlds, a world of tradition, heritage, and pride contrasted with another world of modernity, progression and connection to the world. Coca-Cola demonstrates via Coke Studio that positive change happens when we connect with others and open up to the world. Coke Studio proves, through music, that Local and International music are as good and as beautiful when mixed together, that tradition doesn't contradict modernity but makes it even better, that 2 different cultures can come together in a beautiful way and share a common core. Coke Studio expresses what Coca-Cola and music have in common: it is Inclusive. Connected. Authentic. Uplifting. Happy.[26]

The reason for this spread can be attributed to the growing popularity of Coke Studio Pakistan. In fact Coke Studio Pakistan is taken as a benchmark.[27]

The unresolved ideological contradictions have created a persistent identity crisis in Pakistan.[28] Since nationalism is a subject very close to the heart of a Pakistani, it has been consciously and unconsciously used many times, through many products or endeavours to catch a glimpse of the public. Coke Studio has subconsciously catered to the hungry heart of a patriot in a bleak time when the world is up against Pakistan, especially after the behind-the-scene role of some agencies to support cross-border terrorism. The discovery and ultimate killing of Osama-bin-Laden in Abbotabad (northern Pakistan) has brought the international image of Pakistan to an all time low. Music, at this time, brings the rare thing called Hope. It's like saying to the world 'we have something nice also'. National unity was often defined in the idioms of homogenization. It was seldom conceived as unity built on diversity.[29] Although the process of integration is still going on in the economic and political realm, elements within the society are definitely scoring a goal in terms of promoting the balancing of diversity of the civil society. Although there are provincial discontents, in platforms like these, national integration is occurring fairly well.[30] Politically and economically speaking Pakistan has miles to literally feel 'unity in diversity' and uphold a consensus on national identity. However, through the soft power like music, the integration is more willful, happier and perhaps enduring. On the other hand, music in Pakistan needs to free itself from the clutches of Bollywood music to evolve on its own. In fact, along with other contemporary musical endeavours, Coke Studio has started doing exactly that, emancipating itself from borrowed ideas and establishing a distinct, independent musical identity for the nation. With Coke Studio, the heart of Pakistani nationals has been lit with a renewed hope that finally the world will come to know of Pakistan as a country with beauty and harmony in its legacy.[31]

Notes

1. S. Akbar Zaidi, 'Re-imaging the Image', in Saima Zaidi, ed., *Mazaar, Bazaar: Design and Visual Culture in Pakistan,* Karachi: Oxford University Press, 2009, pp. 188–91.
2. Zarminae Ansari, 'Rooh-Afza, Drink of the East! A Case Study of Iconography and Successful Branding', in Saima Zaidi, ed., *Mazaar, Bazaar: Design and Visual Culture in Pakistan,* Karachi: Oxford University Press, 2009, pp. 151–5.
3. Abbas Ali and Faraz Maqsood Hamidi, 'Brand Take-Off: Pakistan International Airlines', in Saima Zaidi, ed., *Mazaar, Bazaar: Design and Visual Culture in Pakistan,* pp. 165–75.

4. Mariam Ali Baig, 'The Pakola Tale', in Saima Zaidi, ed., *Mazaar, Bazaar: Design and Visual Culture in Pakistan*, pp. 157-63.
5. Ibid.
6. Tahir H. Naqvi, 'Cultural Politics of Hope and Coke: Media, Marketing and Citizenship in Pakistan', *Economic and Political Weekly*, vol. 40, no. 40, 1 October 2005, pp. 4316-19.
7. Rafaya Sufi, 'The Musical history of Pakistan', Asia Society, http://asiasociety.org/blog/reasia/musical-history-pakistan (accessed on 20 June 2011).
8. Ibid.
9. Coke Studio On Air Schedule, http://www.cokestudio.com.pk/season5/schedule.html (12 September 2012)
10. Anonymous, 'Coke Studio (Pakistan)', Wikipedia: The Free Encyclopedia, http://en.wikipedia.org/wiki/Coke_Studio_(Pakistan) (accessed on 10 August 2011).
11. Ibid.
12. Anonymous, 'Season Two, Episode Five', Coke Studio, http://www.cokestudio.com.pk/Season.aspx?SeasonId=2 (accessed on 10 November 2011).
13. Ahemer Naqvi, 'The Artist must shine', Blog.Dawn.Com, http://www.dawn.com/2011/08/07/%E2%80%98the-artist-must-shine%E2%80%99.html (accessed on 7 August 2011).
14. Guitar_freak, 'Rohail Hyatt talks about Coke Studio S4 and more', http://www.koolmuzone.com/2011/05/rohail-hyatt-talks-about-the-coke-studio-s4-more-interview/ (accessed on 31 May 2011).
15. Naqvi, 'The Artist must Shine', Blog.Dawn.Com.
16. Shahzeb Shaikh, 'Spotlight: When There's Hope', http://www.dawn.com/2011/06/12/spotlight-when-theres-hope.html (accessed on 21 June 2011).
17. Meesha Shafi, Message, Coke Studio- Season 3 http://www.youtube.com/watch?v=aaf0hEdnVW8 (10 November 2011).
18. Kulsoom, 'Behind the Scenes at Coke Studio: An Interview with Adnan Malik', CHUP!- Changing Up Pakistan, http://changinguppakistan.wordpress.com/2009/08/20/behind-the-scenes-at-coke-studio-an-interview-with-adnan-malik/ (accessed on 10 August 2011).
19. Murtaza Razvi, 'Unity unlabelled', blog.DAWN.COM, http://www.dawn.com/2011/06/08/unity-unlabelled.html (accessed on 21 June 2011).
20. Cokestudio's Channel YouTube, http://www.youtube.com/user/cokestudio (accessed on 14 August 2011).

21. Ian Talbot, *India and Pakistan,* New York: Oxford University Press, 2000, p. 225.
22. BTS: Larsha Pekhawar Ta, Hamayoon Khan, http://www.cokestudio.com.pk/season5/episode1.html?WT.cl=1&WT.mn=Episode%201 (accessed on 12 September 2012).
23. Sanam Marvi, Message – Coke Studio Season 3 http://www.youtube.com/watch?v=KCzZHcwvXU8 (accessed on 13 November 2011).
24. Arif Lohar, Message- Coke Studio Season 3 http://www.youtube.com/watch?v=QUGBPDRFYNY (accessed on 13 November 2011).
25. Behind the Scene, *Daanah Pah Daanah*, Komal Rizvi and Akhtar Chanal Zahri http://cokestudio.com.pk/Episode.aspx?SeasonId=4&EpisodeId=15 (accessed on 13 November 2011).
26. Coke Studio Middle East http://www.cokestudiome.com/en_EG/about.html?WT.cl=1&WT.mn=About (accessed on 12 September 2012).
27. Nupur Amarnath, 'Coke Studio India Season 2: A Platform for Dying Traditions and Independent Music', http://articles.economictimes.indiatimes.com/2012-06-29/news/32472490_1_carnatic-singers-harshdeep-kaur (accessed on 17 September 2012).
28. Mohammad A. Qadeer, *Pakistan: Social and Cultural Transformations in a Muslim Nation,* Abingdon: Routledge, 2006, p. 62.
29. Ibid., p. 64.
30. Ibid., p. 76.
31. Alnas Zia, 'In Pakistan, Coke Studio Hits High Note', Aslan Media, http://www.aslanmedia.com/music/306-music-artist-profile/2849-in-pakistan-coke-studio-hits-a-high-note (accessed on 21 June 2011).

CHAPTER 11

Understanding Pakistani Cinema

A Peek from Across the Border

Shalmaly Mukherjee

A Quick Glance at the History Pakistani Cinema

In Pakistan most films are in Urdu and many are in Punjabi language, but there are also films in Pashto, Balochi, Sindhi and English languages.[1] Before the separation of Bangladesh in 1971, Pakistan had three main film production centres: Lahore, Karachi and Dhaka.[2] The area comprising what is now Pakistan was a well-established film production centre before 1947. In undivided India, Lahore, situated in Punjab, was an established film-making centre. There were studios, cinemas, producers, and distributors. Punjabi film production was particularly well established here and there were three major studios in Lahore in the mid-1940s.

The Partition of India into two independent states – India and Pakistan, caused irreparable damage to film production in Lahore. Most of Lahore's film producers were Hindu and as the city fell to the side of the Islamic state of Pakistan, they migrated to India. This deprived Lahore – more famously referred to as Lollywood in the film circles – of much needed investment and expertise in film production and distribution. After Partition, some film talent in Lahore left for Bombay (presently known as Mumbai), some talent moved from Mumbai to Karachi and some to Lahore. Some of the major names migrating from Mumbai to Lahore included singer-actress Noorjehan and her director-editor husband Shaukat Hussain Rizvi, actor-director Nazir Ahmed Khan and his actress wife Swaran Lata, composers Ghulam Haider and Khursheed Anwar, and producer-director W.Z.

Ahmed.[3] Ahmed directed several blockbuster movies including *Roohi* – the first film to be banned by the Film Censor Board of Pakistan. The government said the film generated 'class hatred', and portrayed a 'rich married woman having an affair with a young, unmarried man'. The film was later released with 'required' editing.[4]

After the dust of Partition settled down, this new pool of film talents who migrated to Lahore and the people of the film fraternity who were still there started to build film studios and cinemas and restore the old ones. In the early 1950s, Pakistan saw the country's first film studio, Shahnoor, opened by Shaukat Rizvi and Noorjehan. Following it were G.A. Gul's Evernew Studios, Bari Malik's Bari Studios and Shabab's Shabab Studios.[5]

Teri Yaad which was released in September 1948 was the first commercial release in the newly-independent Pakistan. It was a pre-independence venture, directed by Dawood Chand, starring Nasir Khan, Pran and Asha Posley. Unfortunately, the film received bad reviews and proved to be a flop in the box office.[6] Films such as *Hichkolay* (1949), *Shahida* (1949), *Sachai* (1949), *Ghaltfehmi* (1949), *Pherey* (1949) and *Mundri* (1949) closely followed *Teri Yaad*.[7] In these early years of film production, Bombay and Lahore followed the same genres: love, romance, tragedy, and melodrama with similar black-and-white portrayal of hero and villain, good vs. evil, betrayal, death, loyalty with dedicated heroines and later – a home-wrecking vicious vamp. In the early period Punjabi films rose to popularity due to their soft action sequences where the villain and hero would fight with sticks and with time gradually evolved to swords, guns and assault rifles and explicit graphic details of gory bloodbath in the later period.[8] Anwar Kemal Pasha rose to be Pakistan's first multifaceted filmmaker who scripted, produced and directed his own films. He also had his own distribution office at Lahore. Anwar Kemal's films dealt with issues of poverty, love, social strata, suicide, moral decay and death. His notable films included *Gumnam* (1954), *Qatil* (1955), *Sarfarosh* (1956) and *Anarkali* (1958).[9]

In the late 1950s and the 1960s, Pakistan saw a new and energetic brand of directors in the industry, namely Masood Pervez, Khalil Qaiser, Riaz Shahid, S. Suleman, Hassan Tariq and Pervez Malik who gave the country several blockbusters and issue-based films. Khalil Qaiser and his screenwriter Riaz Shahid were branded as rebellious filmmakers as they made films against the evils of the society, such as poverty, corruption, the atrocities of the British Raj, even on oil in the

Middle East with films such as *Shaheed* (1962), *Farangi* (1964) and *Zerqa* (1969). Based on Rajinder Singh Bedi's short novel, Sangeeta in 1978 made *Muthi Bhar Chawal.* Though colour films became a regular trend in Pakistan by the early 1970s, the first indigenous colour films of the country came out in the mid 1960s – *Sangam* (1964) and *Naila* (1965). *Heer Ranjha* (1970) by director Masood Pervaiz and producer-actor Ijaz and Hassan Tariq's *Eik Gunah Aur Sahi* (1975) became milestones in Pakistani colour films. Nazrul Islam joined these directors in the 1970s and gave such exceptional films as *Ehsas* (1972), *Haqeeqat*, *Aina* (1974), *Zindigi* and later *Bandish* (1980) and *Nahi Abhi Nahi* (1981). Javed Shaikh, Syed Noor, Shamim Ara and Javed Fazil have become the most prominent directors in the last 20 years.[10]

The Martial Law in 1977 changed the scenario of film making in Pakistan with a renewed interest in the action genre. Punjabi films became synonymous with violence, revenge, scenes of carnage to serve justice by the muscle power of the protagonist.[11] By 1978, Sultan Rahi was on his way to becoming the ultimate macho hero ever to be produced by Pakistan cinema and the most profitable name in the film industry until his tragic untimely death in the 1990s.[12] The 1980s and 1990s saw a decline in filmgoers as, uncensored and smuggled video and satellite TV infilterated Pakistani homes. Today, the film business in Pakistan is facing challenges from Cable TV, VCD, and DVD. The CD channels of Cable TV are showing latest Indian and Hollywood flicks illegally.[13]

Pakistan always had a firm and concrete roots in commercial cinema which was one of the major reasons for the insignificant numbers of alternate films and also the lack of film societies in Pakistan. There are various attempts to produce alternate films by screenwriters, producers and directors but most of the efforts have largely failed both commercially and critically. Director A.R. Kardar's *Jago Huwa Savera* (1959) and *Qasam Aus Waqt Ki* (1970) were total disasters due to harsh realism and poor screenplay respectively. Ashfaq Malik's *Dhoop Aur Saey*, Hamid Akhtar's *Sukh Ka Sapna* (1962) and Riaz Shahid's *Susral* (1962) did not pay back either.[14]

Matinee Idols: The Cult Heroes

Indo-Pakistani cinema has witnessed many glamorous and larger than life screen figures, but only some became matinee idols – the cult heroes. Actors like K.L. Saigal, Dilip Kumar, Waheed Murad,

Amitabh Bachchan and Sultan Rahi are some cult figures that found a following on either side of the border and affected the style and trends of the film industry in both India and Pakistan. Evidence of this is the uncountable number of enthusiastic fans, another is the number of clones they have on either side of the border. Santosh Kumar, Nadeem and Hanif are some of the heroes in Pakistan who were heavily influenced by Dilip Kumar. And Izhar Qazi of Pakistan followed Amitabh Bachchan. Pakistani heroes had the disadvantage of a cinema that sought to cover a limited market. In spite of this India could not remain blind to the charismatic heroes such as Waheed Murad and Sultan Rahi.[15] The personal style and acting of Waheed Murad inspired Jeetendra in India.[16]

According to noted Pakistani film historian, educationist and playwright Khurram Ali Shafique, the cinematic era of Waheed Murad in Pakistan should be 'seen in the perspective of military dictatorship within the country and a general trend of permissiveness that marked the 1960s all over the world'.[17] The non-political and pseudo-democratic order made the youth of Pakistan turn away all of its attention from the economic and political issues of the society to the unreal but pleasant pastures of fantasy. 'The release of *Arman* (1966) was the grand explosion of Waheed Murad syndrome clearing the ground for films that could take escapism to its most delightful heights.'[18]

The most successful of Waheed Murad films, such as *Arman, Andaleeb* (1969), *Anjuman* (1970), etc., bypassed the economic issue as they placed the hero in a stable position in society.[19] Being naturally suave and charming, Murad was tailor-made for such roles. The hero depicted by him was the ultimate escapist who at the slightest sign of trouble drowned himself in alcohol and fits of melancholy. It was up to the heroine to take charge of things. Thus, it was the era of Waheed Murad which gave Pakistani cinema some of the strongest female characters in films such as *Arman* and *Andaleeb*.[20]

For a long time, Pakistani cinema was dominated by the 'dacoit' (bandit) genre, and during the 1980s, the presence of the country's two biggest film stars, Sultan Rahi and Mustafa Qureshi, besieged the box office with a traditional brand of rural identity that appealed to a wide section of the population.[21] In the British Film Institute's (BFI) guide to contemporary South Asian cinema, the Pakistani journalist,

Sajid Iqbal underlines the cultural significance of Pakistani cinema's most successful film:

But the best was yet to come two years later with the release of Punjabi film *Maula Jat* featuring violent hero Sultan Rahi. The running period of this movie at cinema halls was so long that people simply lost track. This was undoubtedly the most successful film ever made in Pakistan. The typical axe (called *gandasa* in Punjabi and Hindi) held high by the character Maula Jat is an accepted symbol of violent protest against the cruel military regime by the poor masses. It established Sultan Rahi as the most successful film personality of Pakistan.[22]

For all its iconic status,[23] *Maula Jat* (1979) is reviewed to be a poorly directed film that features some wonderfully over-the-top performances. It is a very violent film and borrows heavily from the Western genre but the exploitative tone maintained throughout what is a meandering narrative transforms *Maula Jat* into a film that is defined by a populist appeal rather than its unsatisfactory technical achievements.[24]

Women in Pakistani Cinema

To see how women appear in these collective daydreams can be very interesting. Khurram Ali Shafique has studied Pakistani cinema through its history and worked to trace some patterns between the images of women appearing in it. According to him, *Saat Lakh* (1958), *Armaan* (1966), *Aina* (1977) and *Kalay Chore* (1990) were not only the most popular movies of the respective decades, the heroines of these films can be called the four basic prototypes on which the rest of the female characters in Pakistani films are modelled. This also shows us that the model for the public fantasy can be quite different from one decade to that of another.[25]

Kausar, the heroine of *Saat Lakh* (played by Sabiha Khanum) is an heiress to a large estate and a sophisticated woman who would not take on the matrimonial mantle easily. She decides to hire a man to pose as her husband as her father's will states that she will be deprived the inheritance unless she marries. Further in the story, she falls in love with the same man and love transforms melting her indifference and apathy into submission and tender longings. The other female film characters of the period share various characteristics of Kausar among them – 'inexperience, naive, playfulness, innocence, and the dependence of all these women on a man for their understanding of the outside world as well as their own personal feelings'.[26]

Saheli (1960) created another type of women who's by nature profound and prudent. Heroines such as Nayyar Sultana and Shamim Ara contributed much to the development of this kind of women, but the most accepted of them was Zeba playing Najma, the heroine of *Arman*.[27] Najma can be called the Pakistani take on Cinderella, minus the fairy god mother. She is an orphan who lives with her wealthy but less-than-kind relatives, practically being a house-maid. One of her cousins gives birth to an illegitimate child; Najma protects the family name and the mother-child duo by making sure the baby lives undiscovered. She accepts the proposal of the 'right' man without much fuss. The baby is discovered during her marriage and to save her cousin's name, she acknowledges the baby as her own, exposing herself to trouble, humiliation and rejection by her lover. Her miseries keep mounting until a stroke of luck resolves the plot bringing out her true story. She even saves the hero when he is about to toss himself off a cliff. In the entirety of film the main point is the heroine's control over everything that is happening around her. Her misfortunes are of her own choice that she accepts as part of her position. Her generosity and noble soul stop her from letting down her family which gave her shelter. She is mature and prudent and can see more than one aspect of reality – love, honour, gratitude, values, life are all important in their own place, but family is her first priority. Her commitment to this institution is unquestionable. As discussed above it is the hero in *Arman* who is running away from responsibilities: his leading lady is the agent of his metamorphosis into a more thoughtful person. Zeba, Shamim Ara and Shabnam played a variety of Najmas in other films around the same period such as *Doraha* (1967) and *Andaleeb* (1969).[28]

The 1970s saw the vamp of the earlier movies like *Dil Mera Dharkan Teri* (1967) and *Aag* (1967) evolving into the heroine with films like *Mohabbat Zindagi Hai* (1975), and finally *Aina* (1977). The mod/bad girl became the third model of leading woman in public fantasy. Rita of *Aina* (played by Shabnam), the heroine of the 1970s, is actually the bad girl of the 1960s.[29] She speaks English, drives alone late at night, dresses in Western outfits, and drinks once in a while. She leads a Westernized lifestyle in a lavish bedroom, bathroom fitted with a bathtub where the audience can find her sleeping in some scenes. Rita and her lover do not exchange the conventional love-talk either. When the rich father tries to be traditional with *'yeh shadi nahin ho sakti'* Rita does not worry about *'log kya kahengey'* and finds its quite natural to leave her house and arrange her marriage herself. The father looks for the opportunity to get the two separated and when her personality clashes with her husband's, succeeds for some time, takes away her child and lets her believe that the baby is dead while all the time the child is under the care of its father. However, when Rita discovers the truth, she not only returns to her husband and child but also slaps her father. The disruption of family as an institution is apparent where this woman of the 1970s can find a sanctuary neither in her parents' nor her own home. Motherhood is still important to her as she conceives her child against the wishes of her parents but it cannot be enough stressed that this idea of motherhood – the woman being in the control of the decision to give birth or not without her parental support – was something new in Pakistani cinema.

Action films were gaining momentum and movies such as *Parakh* (1978) and *Miss Hong Kong* (1980) were in the making. The action-oriented heroine grew in popularity with the advent of the violent 1980s and a fourth and completely different type of woman was emerging. Perfected in *Kalay Chore* (1990), the most popular movie since *Aina*, this heroine could seduce men and fight them at the same time, without being fazed. Neeli played the dual roles of Lachi and Honey – merely two reflections of the same image.[30] The 'Lachi-Honey' woman is a logical impossibility – a distorted fantasy who can churn out improper phrases and make obscene gestures without any uneasiness, face sexual advances without feeling harassed, and can defend herself and help her male counterpart with firearms and karate. She is not a character growing out of feminism but a male identified as a woman. It may be seen as the collective daydream of a nation faced with the reality of prohibition and drug trafficking, *hudood* ordinance and Nawabpur rapes.[31]

It should be noted in here that these four models of women, namely the characters Kausar, Najma, Rita and Lachi-Honey, can very well be applied to the whole of South Asian cinema. The cinema of this region emphasizes so much on love stories that it can certainly be used for analysing the images of female sexuality in the male mind. In a way these women reflect what the male species of the Indian subcontinent may like to escape to – the four milestones in their collective psychology. The differences between these characters also reflect upon differences between the society and the situation of each period. The woman of cinemas has yet to be born in Pakistan. The films made are manifestations of the male unconscious because all movies are fashioned by men's choices and all female roles appearing within them are 'male-identified' or 'women as perceived by men rather than women as they really are'.

Pakistani Film Industry: Observations

To most Indians, the Pakistani film industry is almost non-existent, and the industry there doesn't have a great future. One could argue that Indians' widespread contempt for Pakistan's cinema is motivated by the ongoing political enmity between the two nations. However, Pakistanis seem to agree with Indians' assessment of Lollywood. Pakistani film has not always been such an endangered species. In the face of stiff competition from Bollywood and pirated Bollywood videos, and the recent spread of cable television, Lollywood's annual output has dropped radically.[32] In the prime years of Pakistani cinema, the industry produced more than 200 films annually; today it is as less as one-fifth of what it used to be. The Pakistan Bureau of Statistics shows from more than 700 cinemas operating in 1990s in the country, this number has dwindled down to less than 170 by 2005.[33]

Pakistan's only internationally recognized film festival, the Kara Film Festival,[34] takes place annually in Karachi which is located in the province of Sindh. Established in 2001, the festival shows a broad range of films from mainstream Hollywood blockbusters to more specialized world cinema. Karachi has never shied away from tackling social taboos and unlike the feudalism of Punjab, the emergence of an intellectual middle class has meant a far greater level of involvement with theatre, television and cinema. However, it is not solely Karachi that has continued to offer a pluralistic vision of what might be possible if the government was to get behind artists; Lahore's intellectual circles have also had success with television drama, taking on a broad range of social issues in a very melodramatic manner.

There is an argument to be made that when the government fails to provide moral, social or political direction and support to its people then traditional institutions like the media and film in particular are able to respond to crises, concerns and anxieties in both an allegorical and populist way. The Pakistan film industry must be recognized and held responsible for its rise and fall. The government played practically no positive role except to censor films and issue censor certification. However, for all the suppression, be it religious and social, that has permeated Pakistani society for a number of decades now it is difficult to account for the consistent failure of film makers to act upon such misgivings in a constructive way. In times of political and social failure, it is the responsibility of a nation's film industry to demonstrate on screen, the problems and inequalities that are evident in society. Yet no such aspiration or didactic impulse has really ever existed in Pakistani cinema. Perhaps it is to do with the reality that an orthodox religious fervour affects life in such a way that images are regarded somewhat suspiciously, and possibly associated with an outdated, decadent view of a corrupted Western society. But this argument seems invalid when one looks at Iran after Khomeini swept to power through Islamic revolution; the new Iranian cinema based on neo-realist principles has taken it to new heights in world cinema.

Many continue to refer to Pakistan as a new nation yet this seems like an awkward scapegoat for the poor economic support and creative discouragement expressed by a government to indigenous film-makers. Several of them have to work in the television industry for need of better option. With such a young population, it is surprising that the youth are not being actively encouraged to engage with film as a career choice. The steady decline of cinema in Pakistan over the years is alarming and makes for grim analysis of the current dire state of an industry which is in desperate need of modern infrastructure and support system including funding and film courses. The regime of General Zia-ul-Haq, VCRs, film piracy, the introduction of entertainment tax, and Islamic laws have been some of the many obstacles to the industry's growth. A radical and orthodox Islamization of the industry can be noticed which tries to exploit the conservative fundamentalist ideology to cash in on the box-office. The mainstream commercial film *International Gorillay* (1990)[35] is the ideal example. The film cashed on the *Satanic Verses* fiasco and portrayed denounced author Salman Rushdie as an anti-Islamic incarnation of evil, complete with a personal evil army and secret foreign base, who wants the downfall of Pakistan, the stronghold of Islam. Once thriving, the cinema in Pakistan now barely exists. Pakistan and India are two hostile neighbours in the South Asian region and in nearly every field the tension can be witnessed. However, the one field in which India seems to surpass Pakistan is showbiz, while Pakistan's film industry is yet to make it big in the region. The loss of Lollywood is the gain of Bollywood. In fact, actors, directors and cinema owners in Pakistan's struggling movie industry in Lahore accuse India of stealing its best actors and hijacking screens,[36] causing massive loss of revenue and business, taking more blood out of Pakistan's already anaemic film industry. It is in need of immediate and serious attention, interest and support from the government, corporate sector and the cine-goers of Pakistan.

Notes

1. Pakistan film magazine http://mazhar.dk/film/
2. Uzma Zafar, 'Lollywood to Regain Its 1948 Glory With Viewers' Support', *The Daily Mail,* online edition (4 August 2010), http://dailymailnews.com/0810/04/ShowBiz/index.php?id=4 (accessed on 20 September 2011).
3. Mushtaq Gazdar, *Pakistani Cinema: 1947-1997*, Karachi: Oxford University Press, 1997, p. 24.
4. Aijaz Gul, 'Cinemas of the South: A Short History of Pakistani Films', Fédération Internationale de la Presse Cinématographique International Federation of Film Critics (FIPRESCI), 2006, http://www.fipresci.org/world_cinema/south/south_english_asian_cinema_pakistan_history.htm (accessed on 20 September 2011).
5. Gazdar, *Pakistani Cinema: 1947-1997*, p. 25.
6. Ibid., p. 30.
7. Ibid., pp. 24-38.
8. Masoom, 'History of Pakistan: Short History of Pakistani Films', http://masoom-historyofpakistan.blogspot.in/2010/02/short-history-of-pakistani-films.html (accessed on 20 September 2011).
9. Gazdar, *Pakistani Cinema: 1947-1997*, p. 33.
10. Ibid., pp 104-47.
11. Masoom, *'History of Pakistan: Short History of Pakistani Films.*
12. Cineplot.com, Sultan Rahi (27 December 2009), Retrieved from the website of Cineplot.com http://cineplot.com/sultan-rahi/ (accessed on 20 September 2011).
13. Gul, 'Cinemas of the South: A Short History of Pakistani Films'.
14. Ibid.

15. Khurram Ali Shafique, 'The Rise and Fall of Cult Heroes', *Tuesday Review, Dawn*, 24-30 October 1995. Retrieved from the official website of Khurram Ali Shafique – *The Republic of Rumi* www.therepublicofrumi.com/khurram/cinerama1.htm (accessed on 20 September 2011).
16. Omair Alavi, 'Waheed Murad', *Dawn* (28 September 2009), retrieved from the website of Cineplot.com http://cineplot.com/waheed-murad (accessed on 20 September 2011).
17. Shafique, 'The Rise and Fall of Cult Heroes', *Tuesday Review, Dawn*, 24-30 October 1995.
18. Ibid.
19. Muhammad Rizwan Anjum, 'Waheed Murad: A Legend Hero' (Gujrat, Pakistan), retrieved from the website of Pakistan Film Magazine http://mazhar.dk/film/stars/waheedmurad.html (accessed on 20 September 2011).
20. Shafique, 'The Rise and Fall of Cult Heroes', *Tuesday Review, Dawn*, 24-30 October 1995.
21. Cineplot.com, 'Sultan Rahi' (27 December 2009).
22. Sajid Iqbal, '*Pakistani Cinema*', British Film Institute (BFI) (July 2007), retrieved from the website of BFI http://www.bfi.org.uk/features/imagineasia/guide/contemporary/pakistani.html (accessed on 20 September 2011).
23. Gazdar, *Pakistani Cinema: 1947-1997*, p. 166.
24. Cineplot.com, 'Maula Jatt' (1979) (4 January 2010), retrieved from the website of Cineplot.com http://cineplot.com/maula-jatt/ (accessed on 20 September 2011).
25. Khurram Ali Shafique, 'Importance of Being Eve', *Tuesday Review, Dawn*, 31 October-6 November 1995, retrieved from the official website of Khurram Ali Shafique, *The Republic of Rumi* http://pakistanspace.tripod.com/khurram/cinerama2.htm (accessed on 20 September 2011).
26. Khurram Ali Shafique, 'Women and Cinema in Pakistan', *The News International: You* (vol. 3; no. 11), 1993, retrieved from the official Website of Khurram Ali Shafique – *The Republic of Rumi* http://pakistanspace.tripod.com/khurram/womencinema.htm (accessed on 20 September 2011).
27. Ibid.
28. Shafique, 'Importance of Being Eve', October-November.
29. Shafique, 'Women and Cinema in Pakistan'.
30. Shafique, 'Importance of Being Eve'.
31. Ibid.

32. Alex Rodriguez, 'Pakistan's Film Industry is in Collapse', *Los Angeles Times* (8 November 2009), retrieved from the website of http://articles.latimes.com/2009/nov/08/entertainment/ca-lollywood8 (accessed on 23 September 2011).
33. Sara Faruqi, 'In-Depth: Pakistan's Film Industry and Cinema Culture', *Dawn.com* (15 December, 2010), retrieved form the website of Dawn.com http://dawn.com/2010/12/15/in-depth-pakistans-film-industry-and-cinema-culture/ (accessed on 23 September 2011).
34. See Official Website of the Kara Film Festival, Karachi, Pakistan http://www.karafilmfest.com/ (accessed on 23 September 2011).
35. IMBD page of the Pakistani film *International Gorillay* (1990), http://www.imdb.com/title/tt0251144/ (accessed on: 23 September 2011).
36. Rob Crilly, 'Bollywood is Killing Our Film Industry, Say Pakistan's Actors', *The Telegraph* (24 September 2010), retrived from the website of the *Telegraph* (UK) http://www.telegraph.co.uk/news/worldnews/asia/pakistan/8023072/Bollywood-is-killing-our-film-industry-say-Pakistans-actors.html (accessed on 23 September 2011).

MINORITIES AND SECTARIANISM

CHAPTER 12

Religious Minorities in Pakistan

Aspirations and Challenges

Shiraz Sheikh

Introduction

PAKISTAN WAS ENVISIONED as a democratic state where equal rights for minority would be assured as expressed by Mohammad Ali Jinnah in his speech to the Constituent Assembly in 1947: 'You may belong to any religion, caste or creed – that has nothing to do with the business of the State ... we are starting with this fundamental principle that we are all citizens, and equal citizens of one state.'[1] Also Article 20 of the 1973 Constitution of Pakistan guarantees 'freedom to profess religion and manage religious instructions' while Article 25 guarantees 'equality of all citizens'. In spite of a secular vision of the founding father and constitutional protection, the religious minorities in Pakistan have suffered severe discrimination under authoritarian regimes and under elected governments as well.

The issue of minorities is associated with Pakistan's notion of nationhood and its self-perception of identity. As created *de jure* in the name of Islam, Article 2 of the Constitution of Pakistan declares that 'Islam shall be the state religion of Pakistan' and Article 41(2) states 'a person shall not be qualified for election as head of the state unless he is a Muslim'. Though the constitution as noted above guarantees equality for all citizens and protects discrimination against minorities such provisions have never been implemented in practice. Both the democratic and military regimes discriminated against the religious minorities in order to appease extremist Muslim groups and for calculated political gains. Rasul Bakhsh Rais argued that the unsettled issue of religion, identity politics and Islamic radicalism have caused marginalization of religious minorities[2] in Pakistan.

General Ayub Khan constituted the Council of Islamic Ideology (CII) in the 1960s to neutralize the vocal religious groups. During his period traditional *ulema* were poorly represented as his main objective was 'reinterpretation of Islam according to modernist parameters . . . to legitimise national policies in Islamic terms.'[3] Zulfikar Ali Bhutto also enforced the prohibition of alcohol in 1977 as prescribed by the CII to appease the Islamic groups, especially those who were leading the campaign against him. Bhutto under the pressure of religious groups also declared the Ahmadis[4] as non-Muslims and enacted a series of laws limiting their freedom of thought, expression and association.

The worst came under General Zia ul-Haq, who for his political mileage and under the pressure of extremist groups revived the discriminatory scheme of separate electorates and made the Blasphemy Law[5] more stringent. Both the laws made religious minorities second-class citizens and pushed the minorities out from the mainstream of the country. The civilian governments of Benazir Bhutto and Nawaz Sharif after the death of General Zia did nothing to annul institutional segregation, legal bias and societal discrimination against the religious minorities. Though General Pervez Musharraf abolished the separate electorate system[6] the discrimination and violence against minorities has multiplied in the last few years both in number and severity.[7] The Human Rights Commission of Pakistan's (HRCP) 2010 report suggested that 'there were even worse time ahead'.[8]

Social Background and Demographic Profile of Religious Minorities

The regions which comprise Pakistan today were the land of many religions in the past. Before the arrival of Aryans who established Hindu Vedic era it was the land of Dravidians.[9] The post-Aryan period saw the proliferation of Buddhist and Zoroastrian civilization but later was recaptured by Hindu dynasties.[10] By the seventh century AD Punjab became an objective of the vice-regents of the Umayyad Khalifa. In the latter period Muslim rulers like the Khiljis, the Lodhis, the slave dynasty (*Ghulam Vansh*) and the Mughals ruled India from 1192–1858 (666 years), their empires extending to the whole of India. Consequently Islam was diffused to a great extent. After the decline of Mughal rule the colonial period not only resulted in exploitation of the resources of the subcontinent but also saw the spread of Christianity through missionaries. During the fifteenth and sixteenth centuries a religion, Sikhism, emerged in Punjab – divided at the time of Partition.

In 1947 Pakistan came to its existence as a result of the partition of British India. One of the imperatives of Partition was migration of people, one of the largest in the history of the Indian subcontinent. Millions of Muslims migrated to Pakistan while a huge number of Hindus and Sikhs moved into India. Many Christians, Hindus and Sikhs with other smaller religious groups like Parsis and Buddhists also remained in Pakistan. According to the census of 1951 there were around 97,70,000 Hindus and 5,41,000 Christians remaining in Pakistan.[11] Majority of the Hindus were in East Pakistan, comprising around 22 per cent of the total population while majority of the Christians were in West Pakistan and constituted 1.3 per cent of the total population.[12] By the time of the 1961 census the total number of Hindus increased to 1,00,01,574 and was largely concentrated in East Pakistan.[13] From 1951 to 1961 Christians increased by 35.8 per cent and largely located in Lahore Division.[14]

The new statistics on religious minorities is confusing as different sources exhibit unmatched figures. The official census figure of 1998 counted religious minorities as 3.73 per cent of the total population.[15] The latest figure available at the Ministry of Minority Affairs is lower than the official census.[16] Another source, the International Religious Freedom Report 2010, released by the US Department of State, counts religious minorities at around 5 per cent of the total population.[17]

Hindus are the largest religious minority in Pakistan. According to the 1998 census Hindus are 1.6 per cent of the total population. They are mostly settled in Sindh and Baluchistan. Economically and socially they are at the lower rung of the social stratification. A large number of Hindus work as bonded labour in farms or brick kilns in Sindh and Baluchistan. Christians are the second largest religious minority following the Hindus. Catholics and the Protestants constitute 50 per cent each of the community. They are settled mostly in Bahawalpur, Peshawar, Hyderabad, Rawalpindi and Quetta. They are engaged mostly in lower-grade service sector. Iftikhar H. Malik noted that the notion of Pakistani identity on Islamic uniformity in the post-Partition phase has added to an anti-Christian sentiment.[18] He observed that many

Christians in Punjab were originally peasants but after 1947 many of them became landless and had to work as sweepers which further stigmatized their social status. Sikhs are mostly Punjabis with smaller traditional groups residing in Karachi and Khyber Pakhtunkhwa. There are a few Sikhs in the tribal areas; they are bilingual and have a close relationship with the Sikhs in Afghanistan. During the Taliban ascendancy, many Afghani Sikhs migrated abroad, with a small number coming to Pakistan. The Sikhs remain reasonably secure compared to other religious minorities.

The Ahmadis are the new religious minority forcefully created against their will. Both the Shias and Sunnis do not accept them within the fold of Islam.[19] The Ahmadis call themselves Muslim but do not believe in *Khatm-e-Nabuwwat* (finality of Prophethood). They believe Mirza Ghulam Ahmad from Qadian, a nineteenth-century cleric as their prophet. After the creation of Pakistan, the Majlis-i-Ahrar (Council for Liberation) and the Majlis-e-Khatm-e-Nabuwwat (Council for the Finality of Prophethood) demanded that the Ahmadis be declared as non-Muslims. The demand was accepted in 1974 by the then prime minister Zulfikar Ali Bhutto to appease the religious groups. Later General Zia inserted Section 298-C in the Pakistan Penal Code. The induction of this section made it a punishable offence for Ahmadis to call themselves Muslims, profess their religion, using Islamic greetings or using *Azan* . . . by words, either spoken or written, or by visible representation.

The Ahmadis are not allowed to have public places of worship, and thus are confined to their homes for worship. They are the only group which is not allowed to promote its faith as guaranteed by the Constitution of Pakistan. Ahmadis are also barred from obtaining a Pakistani passport. To obtain a passport one has to pledge to not being an Ahmadi. They are also prevented by law from marrying a Muslim, and have to produce a certificate of conversion if they want to marry a Muslim. They are also prohibited from observing Islamic festivals and doing Haj. Intermarriages and open social interaction remain minimal. They neither openly profess their identity nor congregate visibly to avoid hostile attention.

Apart from these major religious minority groups there are other smaller and politically insignificant religious minorities. The Parsis are urban-based business families mostly concentrated in Lahore and Karachi. They are less visible in public sphere and there are no reports of violence against them. Bahais are another small group of people who keep a very low profile. They are hardly visible in the public sphere and are not targeted by other religious extremist groups. Zikris are another minority group mostly residing in south-western Baluchistan which is their spiritual centre, Koh-i-Murad. They are called Zikris because they do *zikr* (a process of constant recitation of the God's name) either individually or in a group.[20] Apart from the surroundings of Koh-i-Murad Zikris are also living in Karachi and Quetta. Due to the fear that they will be declared a religious minority like the Ahmadis Zikris are largely under-represented.[21] Another understudied minority group is Kalasha – locally called *kafir* – living in the three landlocked hamlets at the foothills of Chitral across the Durand Line. Because of their insignificant number which is about 3,000 only, national statistics ignores them.[22] There are other smaller religious minorities like Buddhists and Jains in the Himalayan region; they are mostly understudied and usually not visible.

Aspirations of Religious Minorities in Pakistan

The aspirations of any minority group – ethnic, linguistic or religious – can be categorized into the following categories: recognition, access, participation, autonomy and independence. These aspirations and demands are standalone and also interconnected to each other. The type of demand varies depending upon the size and capacity of the minority group. Other important factors which drive the aspirations of minority groups are: (1) the socio-economic positions of the minority groups, (2) the government's policies towards the minorities and, (3) the behaviour of the majority communities towards the minority groups.

The grievances of the minorities include the demand for equitable share of national resources and more economic and political opportunities. Another force which governs the minority aspirations is the nature of political organization and mobilization within the minority groups. More the minorities are consolidated and organized there are more possibilities of increased participation in mainstream politics and social affairs. Unfortunately the religious minorities in Pakistan are territorially scattered and largely heterogeneous socially, which further discourages minorities to voice their collective demands.

One usual demand of minorities is recognition of the community as minority. This is linked to policy making which gives more concession and opportunities to them for their upliftment. But in specific cases it is also possible that recognition may lead to more discrimination and compartmentalization which the minority does not want. In Pakistan the Ahmadis and Zikris are two such religious minorities which clearly do not want recognition as minorities from the majoritarian society to avoid persecution and discrimination.[23]

It is unlikely that a mere 5 per cent (taking the higher estimate) of religious minorities in Pakistan which is also fragmented and unorganized would ever demand any form of separation or autonomy. Also, in a society like Pakistan, where religious intolerance is so high, it is unlikely that a religious minority would get any significant concession. Religious minorities can demand proportional representation. In this regard, the political system of Pakistan allows only token representation. Through his presidential order General Zia reserved 10 seats in the National Assembly. Hindus and Christians were given four seats each, one seat was given to Ahmadis and one seat was reserved for Sikhs and Parsis together.[24] Similarly some seats were also kept reserved for minorities in Provincial Assemblies. But this token reservation of seats has not brought any political or social change for the minorities.

Religious minorities in Pakistan can only seek autonomy in their social sphere and cannot have any political and economic autonomy. Since religion is a very strong driving force of politics in Pakistan which also organizes social behaviour, it is unlikely that minorities ever get autonomy even in social sphere. The Human Rights Commission of Pakistan (HRCP) has noted that even the religious sphere of minorities is controlled by the state in Pakistan. The Evacuee Trust Property Board (ETPB), a body created after the Partition to protect the land and property related to non-Muslim religious sites, is engaged in selling these properties to Muslims.[25] The state also controls the publication of religious texts of the non-Muslims and many a times bans them. Ahmadis are one such religious minority who are not allowed to profess and promote their religion.

In many cases, minority communities resort to violence as the ultimate course to pressurize the government for concession. But in the case of Pakistan where the legal system and government along with the majority is violent against the minority, it is unlikely that minorities would resort to violence. Since minorities are territorially dispersed and lack spatial consolidation, consequently lack collective bargaining capacity to further their interest, it is unlikely that they are given any special benefits like reservation or special schemes. In such circumstances only a compromised arrangement, political or social, seems possible for them.

Challenges Faced by Religious Minorities in Pakistan

Political Order

The political order in Pakistan has always been a challenge for religious minorities. The military has ruled the country for a longer period than democratic regimes. For half of the last six decades since its creation, Pakistan has remained under direct military domination and the rest under its indirect shadow. Military regimes which have been cyclic in Pakistan turn into the dominant actor in the power structure and their own agenda has always shaped the national policies. Further the military, dominated by Punjabi Muslims,[26] has alienated the interests of not only the religious minorities but also the other ethnic communities. Unlike a democratic government which is accountable to its voters and may do something to appease them, the military regimes in Pakistan have controlled the power as arbitrator and not been accountable to anyone.

General Zia-ul-Haq who saw himself as the *Amir-ul-Momineen*[27] tried to shape the society on religious lines which made the life of the minorities difficult. The Zia period witnessed the Islamization of the legal system, public policy and popular culture. Pakistan National Alliance (PNA), the main opposition to the Bhutto regime once promised to enforce *Nizam-e-Mustafa* (Islamic system) in Pakistan at the earliest, welcomed the process of Islamization.[28] This provided much needed social legitimacy to the martial law regime. General Zia revived the separate electorate system which divided the society into Muslim and non-Muslim voters. He also introduced new clauses in the Blasphemy Law which created immense difficulties for the minorities.

Separate Electorates

Pakistan adopted a scheme of separate electorates in 1948 but switched over to the scheme of joint electorates in 1957. Deviating from separate electorates, which was termed as a 'colonial heritage', the 1962 constitution maintained the scheme of joint electorates.[29] Following that, general elections were held in 1962, 1965, 1970 and 1977 on the basis of joint electorates. After the revival of the separate electorate system by General Zia-ul-Haq – through Presidential Order No. 14 in 1985 which amended the Articles 51 and 106 of the constitution of Pakistan – four subsequent elections in 1988, 1990, 1993 and finally in 1997 were held on the principle of separate electorates. It was argued that separate electorates were meant to safeguard the interests of minority and not majority community, like in British India. General Musharraf in the January 2002 election through the Conduct of General Election Order 2002 abolished the separate electorate system but he also excluded Ahmadis from its remit.[30]

Under the system of separate electorates the entire society was compartmentalized into five groups: Muslims, Christians, Hindus, Ahmadis, and other smaller religious groups. In the separate electorate system a Muslim could vote only for a Muslim and a Christian only for a Christian.[31] Mohammad Waseem noted that General Zia reverted back to the separate electorates believing it would prevent religious minorities to vote for the Pakistan People's Party (PPP).[32] He further noted that the whole scheme of separate electorate and reservation for minorities had become a 'farce'. Aftab Mughal termed the scheme of separate electorates as 'religious apartheid' and believed that it was misused to marginalize the religious minorities.[33] Extending Mughal's proposition Fr. Bonnie Mendes called it 'nothing else but political order apartheid in the name of religion' and used for cutting off Christian and other minorities from the Muslim counterparts in the election.[34] The system of separate electorate violated the democratic rights not only of minorities but of all Pakistani citizens by denying them the right to elect representatives of their choice.

Blasphemy Law

Apart from imposing the separate electorate system, General Zia also proclaimed Ordinance XX in 1984, which amended the Pakistan Penal Code. It added two sections 298B and 298C; these provisions were specific to Ahmadis – who were already declared non-Muslims by Bhutto. These two sections of the Blasphemy Law further restricted the freedom of religion and expression of Ahmadis. Another section of

Blasphemy Law 298A is a Shia-specific provision that prevents Shias from vilifying some companions of the Prophet and other persons considered holy by the Sunnis. Observers believe that official Islam under General Zia's Islamization with stringent laws did not make people morally good: 'In fact, the crime rate for theft, robbery, adultery and drinking increased under the Zia government, reaching its highest point in 1985.'[35] With the growing religious intolerance the cases of blasphemy grew during and after the Zia period even though death penalty was made mandatory for blasphemy.[36]

Pakistan has multiple legal systems. At the federal level the Pakistan Penal Code and Sharia are the basis of the legal system and certain set of customary laws are practiced in the frontier and rural areas. Shias and other religious sects too have their own separate legal systems. The multiplicity of legal systems pose difficulties for minorities, specially the Christians and Ahmadis. Under Article 203-D of the Pakistan Constitution, the Federal Shariat Court operates as a parallel judicial system. It has authority to declare any law defunct if it seems to be repugnant to Islam. Moreover non-Muslims[37] under Article 203-E(4) are barred to plead as lawyers in the Federal Shariat Court even if a non-Muslim is a party.

Apart from the official policy of religious segregation of minorities from mainstream politics, the society in Pakistan in general has become intolerant to religious minorities. The systematic *gherao* of court premises during the hearing of blasphemy cases puts tremendous pressure on judges to pass any judgement in favour of minorities. Minorities in Pakistan live under constant fear and do not dare speak out and impose self-censorship. Fr. Mendes explains that common Pakistani Muslims have been made to understand that the country was formed for the Muslims alone, which is historically incorrect. They see minorities as second-class citizens. This situation has made the lives of minorities insecure at the community level.[38]

Societal Discrimination

Apart from the state and constitutional discrimination, the societal discrimination on account of one's faith is rampant and deep rooted in Pakistan. The ideological apparatus – education system and media – is largely controlled by the majority community at the state and private level. The textbooks and even the teachers at the elementary level preach segregation and hatred against minorities.[39] Organized hate speeches and campaigns continue through the use of stickers, wall graffiti and pamphlets. Urdu TV channels also spread hate messages against minority communities. Electronic media generally invite conservative religious leaders to their programmes.

The HRCP has noted that state officials hardly take any action against the promoters of hate speeches. Official impunity is also granted for murder of minority community people. Social boycott is another instrument used by the majority community to discriminate against the minorities. Political and religious groups too brand the entire minority community to be agents of another country. The HRCP noted that Hindus suffered 'reprisal attacks' after the demolition of the Babri Masjid in 1992. Faith-based discrimination is so deep rooted that even during calamities, the majority does not spare any chance of perpetuating violence. The HRCP noted that after the summer floods of 2010, '500 Ahmadi families displaced by the floods were denied relief goods and shelter by government officials and clerics on account of their faith.'[40] Hindus and Sikhs were pushed away from food distribution points.

There are built-in biases in the education system and public-sector jobs. Minorities are excluded from socio-economic life and higher positions in civil and military sectors.[41] In the education system non-Muslim students have the option of opting for ethics, but the Islamic Studies paper gives 30 per cent more marks which puts them at an obvious disadvantage. In the general knowledge papers of competitive examinations (Sindhi Public Service) many questions about Islamic Studies are asked. To get into cadet college candidates are required to appear in the paper of Islamic Studies. Atomic Energy Commission Institute in Sindh does not recruit non-Muslim candidates.[42] Christians are deemed unclean and often considered fit only to be sanitary workers. The HRCP observed that a considerable number of bonded labourers in Sindh were from the Hindu community. Political parties do not keep minorities in their agenda. Malik has noted that 'religious minorities have fewer chances to move up the socio-economic ladder. They are routinely kept out of higher positions both in the civil and armed forces – which feed into a greater sense of inequality.'[43]

Collective Violence as an Instrument of Social Control

In Pakistan the majority community has used collective violence as an instrument of social control over the minority communities. They have resorted to essentially two forms of violence, manifest and latent. According to Johan Galtung 'violence is present when human beings are influenced so that their actual somatic and mental realisations are below their potential realisations'.[44] Violence is here defined as the cause of the difference between the potential and actual, between what could have been and what it is. If resources are monopolized by a homogeneous group or class and are used for other purposes, then the actual level of realization falls below the potential level. Hence violence is present in the system.

Galtung made traditional distinction between two levels of violence, the manifest and the latent. Manifest violence, whether personal or structural, is observable. Latent violence is something which is not there, yet might easily come out.[45] It is further divided into physical and psychological violence – creating objective and subjective conditions to decrease mental and physical potentialities. Structural violence is silent, it does not show but creates all kinds of obstacles.[46] There may not be any person who directly harms another person in the structure. The violence is built into the structure and shows up as an unequal power and consequently as unequal life chances. Resources are unevenly distributed and the power to decide over the distribution of resources is also unevenly distributed.

Majority in Pakistan always used collective violence whether manifest or latent as a tool to control the behaviour of the religious minorities. The majority has shown tendencies of unleashing its anger not at the actual source of its despair but at the most vulnerable section of the minorities. Religious minorities become the scapegoat of the actions for which they are not responsible directly or indirectly.[47] The violence takes the shape of lynching, rioting, vigilantism, terrorism, and for women it is worse as they became victims of forced conversion and rape. The incidences of violence unleashed on minorities exhibit traces of both spontaneity and organization but in all cases have their roots in the collective sense of majority. The state attitude also encourages such violence in Pakistan. The state in most of the cases grants impunity to the predators engaged in violence against the religious minorities.[48] The administration in Pakistan remains indifferent to the grievances of the minority communities.

The impacts of majoritarian violence on religious minorities are manifold. Religious minorities in Pakistan live under constant sense of psychological insecurity, social stigmatization, their legal and economic positions degraded to the point of being second-class citizen. The National Commission for Justice and Peace, Pakistan (NCJP) has described their plight as:

> Pakistani society has visibly lost its religious diversity besides the acceptance and tolerance 1970s onwards. Demographic data is one indicator which shows that Pakistan would be loosing its Parsi, Buddhist population entirely in the near future. Kalash people are also on their way to extinction. The Hindu and Christian communities have suffered a degradation of their economic bases and opportunities, thus diminishing middle class which characterised their social standing so far.[49]

Minority groups are often subject to threats, harassment and violence. They live in continuous fear, provoked by the built-in official bias and courts ruling in favour of Muslims, which leads to a virtual impunity of predators of religious minorities.

The International Federation for Human Rights (IFHR) in its 2005 report titled *Freedom of Expression, of Association and Assembly in Pakistan* mentions a number of cases of faith-based violence against religious minorities in Pakistan. According to the Centre for Legal Aid Assistance and Settlement (CLAAS) – a non-governmental organization (NGO) rendering and advocating legal assistance to religious minorities – between 2001-5, there were nine attacks on Christian institutions and 52 Christians were killed.[50] The worrisome matter is that only two of these cases led to trial and conviction of the perpetrators. According the IFHR, on 4 October 2002, a Christian hospital in Bannu was attacked with a grenade, and on the 2003 Christmas day, a bomb was thrown at a church in Sialkot which killed two girls.[51] Not only minorities, the extremists target even Muslims who dare to speak their mind or exhibit any concern towards the plight of minorities in Pakistan. On March 2004, Sajid Ishaq, director of *Islamabad Rozgar Markaz* was threatened after he conducted a press conference on issues related to minorities.[52]

The HRCP has noted that extremists have used the provisions of Blasphemy Law as an instrument to settle personal scores and victimize minority and vulnerable communities. People were lynched after being implicated in blasphemy cases. The minority individuals who were allegedly accused of blasphemy cases and their families were vulnerable to the extent that they faced collective violence even before the allegations were proven. In July 2010, two Christian brothers Sajid and Rashid Emmanuel who were accused in blasphemy cases were shot on court premises in Faislabad when they were in police custody.[53] The extremist religious groups have created a climate of terror and instilled fear among investigating officers. This fear obstructs impartial investigation in matters related to Blasphemy Law as many of the investigation officers do not dare to bring the truth for fear of personal security. The HRCP noted that the government was being blackmailed by extremist elements . . . judges dared not ask mobs to leave the proceeding in blasphemy cases. Judges hearing blasphemy cases feared for their own lives, and a high court judge was killed.[54]

Ahmadis are the most vulnerable group whose life is at risk in Pakistan. In an HRCP assessment, by 2010 as many as 202 Ahmadis were killed in faith-based attacks since the promulgation of Prohibition of Qadiyaniat Ordinance 1984. Out of this as many as 99 Ahmadis were killed in the year 2010.[55] The same report also found that 1,468 news reports, editorials and articles which promoted hate and intolerance towards Ahmadis were published in Urdu newspapers in 2010.[56] In 2009 there was a series of attacks on Christians in Gojra, Punjab. More than a year since the gory anti-Christian violence took the life of eight Christians including four women and a child no person has been found guilty.[57] In early February 2010 three Sikh men were kidnapped by Taliban militants in Orakzai Agency. The abductors demanded Rs. 20 million for their release by 20 February. When the ransom amount was not paid, one among the three Sikhs, Jaspal Singh was found beheaded on 21 February.[58] The members of Sikh community living in Orakzai for many years were asked to flee the area or pay the *jizya*.

The religious extremist groups can make any small incident a pretext to unleash violence on minority groups. The 1999 report of NCJP noted that in 1999, 11 non-Muslim Pakistanis were killed for smallest of reasons like 'shouting on street, refusing to sell on credit, "bribe", or for cracker hitting the bicycle.'[59] Apart from direct physical violence, abduction and killing, the extremist groups have also used weapons like forced conversion, rape, denial of admission in schools and refusal of using Muslim graveyard to Ahmadis as noted by the NCJP.[60]

The 2010 prediction of the HRCP that there is bound to be worse time ahead seems to be true in 2011. Radicalization and religious intolerance of the society has grown in recent times. Any voice speaking for minorities or against radicalization is silenced by the fundamentalists. The present time is proving to be the one of the worst times for the religious minorities in Pakistan. Today there is visible tussle between the liberal secular space and the religious radical space. The liberal space has shrunk as there is no collective voice against the overt radicalization of Pakistan society. The recent killings of Salman Taseer – the governor of Punjab – and Shahbaz Bhatti – the minister of minority affairs – by radicals for speaking against the controversial Blasphemy Law and the subsequent happenings followed by the killings exhibit the plight of the shrinking liberal space. Amid these events it will be premature to assume any peaceful time for minorities in the near future.

Notes

1. Quoted from Mohammad Ali Jinnah, 'The President's Address' at the Constituent Assembly on 11 August 1947, cited in Z.H. Zaidi (ed.), *Jinnah Papers: Pakistan at Last, 26 July-14 August 1947*, Series 1, vol. 4, Islamabad: Qaid-i-Azam Papers Project, 1999, pp. 535-8.
2. Rasul Bakhsh Rais, 'Islamic Radicalism and Minorities in Pakistan', p. 448, http://www.apcss.org/Publications/Edited%20Volumes/ReligiousRadicalism/PagesfromReligiousRadicalismandSecurityinSouthAsiach19.pdf (accessed on 28 August 2011).
3. Jamal Malik, *Colonization of Islam: Dissolution of Traditional Institutions in Pakistan*, New Delhi: Manohar, 1996, p. 35.
4. Ahmadis are one religious minority group in Pakistan who claim that they are Muslims, but do not believe in *Khatm-e-Nabuwwat* (finality of Prophethood). They were declared non-Muslims in 1974 by then Prime Minister Zulfikar Ali Bhutto for the same reason.
5. See Blasphemy Law, available at http://www.pakistani.org/pakistan/legislation/1860/actXLVof1860.html (accessed on 30 August 2011).
6. See The Conduct of General Elections Order, 2002. Available on the Internet at http://publicofficialsfinancialdisclosure.worldbank.org/

sites/fdl/files/assets/law-library-files/Pakistan_Conduct%20Of%20 General%20Elections%20Order_2002_en.pdf (accessed om 20 August 2011).

7. Human Rights Commission of Pakistan (HRCP), 'Life at Risk: Report of HRCP Working Group on Communities Vulnerable Because of their Beliefs' (Lahore: HRCP, April 2011), p. 9. Available on the Internet at www.hrcp-web.org/pdf/life%20at%20risk.pdf (accessed on 28 Aug-ust 2011).
8. Human Rights Commission of Pakistan (HRCP), 'State of Human Rights in 2010', (Lahore: HRCP, April 2011), p. 124. Available on the Internet at www.hrcp-web.org/publications/AR2010.pdf (accessed on 28 August 2011).
9. Iftikhar H. Malik, 'Report: Religious Minorities in Pakistan' (London: Minority Rights Group International, September 2002), p. 4. Available on the Internet at, cdn.criticalppp.com/wp-content/uploads/ 2010/06/PakistanReport.pdf (accessed on 15 August 2011).
10. Ibid.
11. E.H. Slade, *Census of Pakistan, 1951,* vol. 1, Karachi: Government of Pakistan, 1951, p. 8.
12. Ibid.
13. A. Rashid, *Census of Pakistan Population 1961,* vol. 1, Karachi: Government of Pakistan, 1961, pp. 11-23.
14. Ibid.
15 *Census of Pakistan 1998*. Available on the Internet at, http://www.census.gov.pk/Religion.htm (accessed on 31 August 2011).
16. 'Population of Minority Communities and Religious Demography', Ministry of Minority Affairs. Available on the Internet at, http://www.minorities.gov.pk/ (accessed on 1 September 2011).
17. Bureau of Democracy, Human Rights, and Labor (BDHRL), 'International Religious Freedom Report 2010' (Washington D.C. US Department of State, 17 November 2010), p. 2. Available on the Internet at http://www.state.gov/drl/irf/2010/148800.htm (accessed on 15 August 2011).
18. Malik, 'Report: Religious Minorities in Pakistan', p. 13.
19. Rais, 'Islamic Radicalism and Minorities in Pakistan', p. 455.
20. Malik, 'Report: Religious Minorities in Pakistan', p. 11.
21. Ibid.
22. Ibid.
23. One example of such behaviour can be seen in the fact that during Zia's period one seat reserved for Qadianis in the 1985 national elections went vacant as no one filed nominations for it.

24. Tahir Mehdi et al., *National Assembly Elections in Pakistan 1970-2008: A Compendium of Elections Related Facts and Statistics*, Lahore: Church World Service Pakistan/Afghanistan and Free and Fair Network, 2010, p. 184.
25. HRCP, 'State of Human Rights in 2010', p. 129.
26. Stephen P. Cohen, *The Pakistan Army*, Karachi: Oxford University Press, 2002, p. 105.
27. Shuja Nawaz, *Crossed Swords: Pakistan, its Army, and the Wars Within*, New York: Oxford University Press, 2008, p. 380.
28. Ibid., p. 360.
29. Mohammad Waseem, 'Joint or Separate Electorate', *Pakistan Christian Voice*, Internet Magazine, October and November 2000. Available on the Internet at, http://www.suffrage-universel.be/res/pkmi03.htm (accessed on 1 July 2011).
30. The Conduct of General Election Order 2002, by which the joint electoral system was adopted, excluded Ahmadis from its remit, and their names have been transferred to a list designated as 'non-Muslim' comprising Ahmadis only.
31. Mehdi et al., *National Assembly Elections in Pakistan 1970-2008: A Compendium of Election Related Facts and Statistics*, p. 184.
32. Waseem, 'Joint or Separate Electorate'.
33. Aftab Mughal, 'System of Religious Apartheid', *Pakistan Christian Voice*, Internet Magazine, October and November 2000. Available on the Internet at http://www.suffrage-universel.be/res/pkmi03.htm (accessed on 1 July 2011).
34. Bonnie Mendes, 'Political Order Apartheid in Pakistan in the Name of Religion' *Pakistan Christian Voice*, Internet Magazine, October and November 2000. Available on the Internet at http://www.suffrage-universel.be/res/pkmi03.htm (accessed on 1 July 2011).
35. Rubya Mehdi, *The Islamisation of the Law in Pakistan*, Richmond: Curzon Press, 1994, p. 154.
36. From 1948-79, 11 cases of blasphemy were registered. Only three were reported from 1979-86. Forty-four cases were filed from 1987-99. In 2000, 52 cases were registered - 43 against Muslims and nine against non-Muslims. See Mohammad Shahzad, 'The Impact of Blasphemy Law,' *Dawn*, 18 July 2002, Available on the Internet at, http://www.thepersecution.org/ news/dawn020718.html (accessed on 5 July 2011).
37. The constitution also defines the basic belief of a professing Muslim and provides a definition of a non-Muslim. The 1973 constitution,

Second Amendment, Article 260 reads: (a) 'Muslim' means a person who believes in the unity and oneness of Almighty Allah, in the absolute and unqualified finality of the Prophethood of Muhammad (peace be upon him), the last of the prophets, and does not believe in, or recognize as a prophet or religious reformer, any person who claimed or claims to be a prophet, in any sense of the word or of any description whatsoever, after Muhammad (peace be upon him); and (b) 'non-Muslim' means a person who is not a Muslim and includes a person belonging to the Christian, Hindu, Sikh, Buddhist or Parsi community, a person of the Qadiani Group or the Lahori Group who call themselves 'Ahmadis' or by any other name or a Bahai, and a person belonging to any of the Scheduled Castes.

38. Mendes, 'Political Order Apartheid in Pakistan in the Name of Religion'.
39. HRCP, 'Life at Risk', p. 18.
40. Ibid., p. 20.
41. Malik, 'Report: Religious Minorities in Pakistan', p. 21.
42. HRCP, 'Life at Risk', p. 24.
43. Malik, 'Report: Religious Minorities in Pakistan', p. 12.
44. Johan Galtung, 'Violence, Peace, and Peace Research', *Journal of Peace Research*, vol. 6, no. 3, 1969, p. 168.
45. Ibid., p. 172.
46. Ibid.
47. Malik, 'Report: Religious Minorities in Pakistan', p. 22.
48. The International Federation for Human Rights (IFHR), 'In Mala Fide: Freedom of Expression, of Association and Assembly in Pakistan', no. 408/2, January 2005, pp. 26-37.
49. National Commission for Justice and Peace, Pakistan (NCJP), 'Human Rights Monitor 2009-10, A Report on the Religious Minorities in Pakistan' (Lahore: NCJP, Catholic Bishops' Conference, 2010), p. 38. Available on the Internet at, www.ncjppk.org/HRM%20find%20June%2009-2010.pdf (accessed on 31 August 2011).
50. IFHR, 'In Mala Fide: Freedom of Expression, of Association and Assembly in Pakistan', p. 60.
51. Ibid.
52. Ibid.
53. HRCP, 'Life at Risk' p. 28.
54. Ibid., p. 31.
55. HRCP, 'State of Human Rights in 2010', p. 127.
56. Ibid., p. 128.

57. Ibid., p. 129.
58. BBC, 'Kidnapped Political Sikh Beheaded in Khyber Region', Available on the Internet at 2011, news.bbc.co.uk/2/hi/8527614.stm (accessed on 28 November).
59. Malik, 'Report: Religious Minorities in Pakistan', pp. 24-5.
60. See NCJP, Human Rights Monitor 2009-10, 'A Report on the Religious Minorities in Pakistan'.

CHAPTER 13

The Blasphemy Laws and the Minorities in Pakistan

T.K. Jabir

Introduction

RELIGION IS A KEY existential symbol of majority of the Muslim states in the world. The Muslim states in general are synonymous with dictatorship – either military or monarchical – repression, social injustice and corruption, in contrast to democracy, human rights and multiculturalism of the West. These predicaments have been intimately related with the colonial and post-colonial relationship between the Muslim states and the West. This is particularly true when states become the principal carriers of the secular policies internally and externally. The political manifestation of secularism, wherever it has not been an indigenous theme, if associated with colonial inducement would have been in a bewildering position. The political question of majority community versus minority community becomes prominent and troublesome even in a society with one dominant religion, which implies the dearth of multiculturalism. In the states of South Asia, this is unambiguous. This subject is a greater divisive force in states where religion is the source of political legitimacy or the basis of a state's identity. Religion turns out to be a treacherous political weapon when the majority religious community endeavours to personify the state's culture, social institutions and the state itself according to a specific belief system. Separate electorates was enshrined in the character of the Pakistani state following its creation in 1947. When the Muslims became a majority, Pakistan had a formidable task of reassuring its religious and ethnic minorities and integrating them into mainstream national politics. In the 1956 constitution, and later in the amended 1973 constitution under the Zia-ul-Haq regime, Pakistan practiced separate electorates against the will of its minorities. Today Pakistan has become a battlefield between two factions. One clings to religion for the justification of its identity; on the other side is a small group of vocal liberals. Meanwhile, the majority of the country fends off poverty and starvation, and is too busy making ends meet to bother with candle-lit vigils to protest against discriminatory legislation.

In the following analysis, I will examine what sorts of marginalization and exclusions various minority communities have been undergoing under the Blasphemy Laws in particular and other discriminating laws in general and what are the solutions for this problem in Pakistan.

The Islamic State, Minorities and Modernity

The concept of *dhimmi* or protected communities has been the traditional concept used to address non-Muslims in Islamic states, who are granted fewer rights than Muslims. The traditional political Islamists have defended it, however, writers on the far right and people like Moulana Abul Ala Mawdudi do not feature it in their centre-right version of the Islamic state. A reformed Islam can fully accommodate minority and human rights. The Muslim state that rests on progressive Islam can treat all its citizens fairly – Muslims and non-Muslims who share the same human values and commitment to justice and equity.[1]

Muqtedar Khan argues that Islamic states inevitably treat non-Muslim citizens as less than equal. He cites blasphemy and apostasy laws as well known for the problems they cause minorities and says that narrow interpretation of the role of women in Islamic societies has also restricted the scope for non-Muslim women.[2] In his view, in seeking to impose Islamic law and create an Islamic state, Islamists are in direct opposition to the spirit and letter of the Quran, which explicitly states 'there is no compulsion in religion[3] and exhorts peoples of the book to live by the laws revealed to them'.[4] In these verses it is unambiguous that an Islamic state must advocate religious pluralism and inclusive citizenship. According to Khan, the ideal model is represented by the federal state of Madinah, which was based on a real and actual social contract agreed upon by Muslims, Jews and others that treated them as equal citizens. Divine law was applied but only after consultation and with consent of all citizens regardless of their faith. The difference between this and contemporary Islamic states is that the latter apply Islamic law without consent or consultation and often through coercion.[5]

In the modernized world system the fundamental right of citizenship is the right to live and work in a country. The citizens must be entitled for suffrage, and to contest elections and enter into certain occupations, either military or state service, which may not be entitled to non-citizens. Legal citizenship only designates a formal status, without in anyway indicating what the citizen feels and whether she/he is a member of a political community. So, citizenship must always have a subjective or psychological component. In the case of legal rights, mere possession of that would not ensure that individuals will feel themselves to be the citizens of that country.

In the theory of multiculturalism and minority rights, Will Kymlicka differentiated three kinds of minority rights that were to be accorded to ethnic and national groups: self-government rights, poly-ethnic rights, and special representation rights. Self-government rights require the delegation of powers to national minorities, such as indigenous peoples. These rights are not entitled to other cultural minorities who have immigrated into the country. The latter would be entitled for poly-ethnic rights, which guarantee financial support and legal protection for practices peculiar to some ethnic or religious groups. Both indigenous peoples and immigrant minorities might also be eligible for special representation rights which guarantee places for minority representatives on state bodies or institutions. The principal argument of Kymlicka's theory of differentiated rights is a distinction between two kinds of minorities: national minorities and ethnic minorities. National minorities are peoples whose previously self-governing, territorially concentrated cultures have been incorporated into a larger state. In Kymlicka's theory, the minorities have very different legitimate claims to make, and understanding this should make clear that national minorities need not fear that policies of multiculturalism would reduce them to the status of migrants, just as other citizens need not fear that multiculturalism implies that immigrants have a legitimate claim to self-government. Kymlicka's arguments based on the modern liberal tradition, have a history of recognizing group differentiated rights. In his view it is, 'the orthodox liberal view about the right of states to determine who has citizenship rests on the same principles which justify group differentiated citizenship within states, and that accepting the former leads logically to the latter'.[6]

It can be epitomizing the predicament of multiculturalism and citizenship of minorities in Pakistan. The minorities have been undergoing alienation from their state, hence social disadvantage and religious and ethnic discrimination directly from the people and indirectly from the government. In such situations individuals could not be exactly considered as 'full citizens' or enjoying active citizenship, even though they may enjoy certain formal entitlements. Not uncommonly, such people regard themselves as 'second-class' citizens, if not as third-class citizens.[7]

The State and the Composition of Pakistani Society

The demise of the British Indian empire brought with it the deadly partition of India and Pakistan in 1947. Millions of people were forced to leave their homes on either side of an arbitrarily drawn border. Muslims moved from India to either to West or East Pakistan (later Bangladesh), and a large proportion of Hindu and Sikh populations left the newly-founded Pakistan for India. Yet the issue of minority rights had been at the forefront of political discussion well after the creation of Pakistan in 1947. It is often argued, in fact, that the tensions exposed and played out during this period set in place a template for communal strife based on religion. After Independence, some leaders of the Pakistan movement continued to press for the continuation of separate electorates, others pushed for ideological consistency, while still others aimed to ensure adequate representation of minorities in the elected bodies of the country. The idea is that, separate electorate system considered as a solution towards the political stability of the state. On the issue of separate electorates, the views of the leaders of East Pakistan, where there was a sizeable Hindu minority, were different from those of the leaders of West Pakistan. While the West Pakistanis stressed the need for separate electorates, the East Pakistanis insisted on joint electorates. Members of the minority communities were also of the view that separate electorates would cast them off mainstream national politics. They demanded equal political, civic and legal rights that could be guaranteed only under the joint electorate system.

Subsequently, the civil war between East and West Pakistan ended with India's intervention in 1971, East Pakistan became the new state, Bangladesh, which led to more trans-regional migration. While East Bengalis left West Pakistan for Bangladesh, Pakistan accepted the repatriation of several thousand Urdu-speaking East Pakistanis, also called Biharis. Most of these new immigrants settled in Karachi, increasing the number of Urdu-speakers in urban Sindh. Following friction over the question of language between Sindhis and Urdu-speakers in 1972, Pakistan became reluctant to accept any more migrants from Bangladesh.[8] The Iranian revolution of 1979 and the Soviet invasion of Afghanistan created millions of refugees who added to Pakistan's population, and to its ethnic and linguistic diversity. So, Pakistan has had radical demographic changes within a few decades of its formation and its ramifications have fed into the already highly competitive and volatile inter-community relationships. Pakistan remains a populous country covering a substantial terrain and it is currently the sixth most populous state in the world and, after Indonesia, the most populous Muslim state. It lacks a coherent structure, although some consciousness about common social institutions did evolve in the course of the struggle for independence. The provincial societies have been fully organized historical formations. They constitute the building blocks of the emerging Pakistani society. Integration of the provincial communities has been one of the abiding themes of national development and a crucial process of Pakistan's social history.[9] Pakistan has striven from its independence, at least in the political rhetoric provided by both civilian and military leaders, for democracy, liberalism, freedom of expression, inclusiveness of minorities, and secularism. It is appropriate to bring up here the famous and oft-quoted statement of the founder of Pakistan:

> You are free now; you are free to go to your temples, you are free to go to your mosques or to any other places of worship in the State of Pakistan. You may belong to any religion or caste or creed – that has nothing to do with the business of the State. . . . We are starting with this fundamental principle: that we are all citizens and equal citizens of one State. Now, I think we should keep that in front of us as our ideal and you will find that in course of time Hindus would cease to be Hindus and Muslims would cease to be Muslims, not so in the religious sense because that is the personal faith of each individual, but in the political sense as citizens of the state.[10]

However, the country has drifted toward increasingly authoritarianism, religious extremism, and intolerance of minorities. This rift between animated political rhetoric and grim political reality has confused the world as much as the Pakistanis themselves.[11] Complex historical and social factors, anti-colonial movements, religion and language have shaped the interaction between religion and politics in Pakistan. Islam was at the heart of the political struggle for the creation of Pakistan and has remained the central theme of post-Independence political discourse. Still, the debate on the role of Islam in national politics makes complex the political scenario of the country. Even after six decades, the relationship between religion and state is still as ambiguous as the nature and direction of the democratic enterprise. The question of what type of polity Pakistan should be, liberal democratic or Islamic, evokes different responses from different social sectors and political interests. Military leaders, mainstream political parties, and Islamists have all attempted to define this relationship according to their vision of democratic development and the role of religion in society and state affairs.[12]

After 10 years of military rule, in 2008 democratic rule was restored in Pakistan through elections that international observers considered as competitive and reflective of the people's will. The Pakistan People's Party (PPP) and its federal coalition partners controlled the executive and legislative branches of the national government and three of the four provincial assemblies.

The Religious Minorities

The hounding of minorities in the name of religion dates back to the founding of Pakistan in 1947, created after a bitter struggle for independence by the Muslims of India, who were a minority themselves. Following the country's creation, the notion of Pakistan as a land solely for Muslims began to dominate the public narrative and translated into massive political, economic and social biases against religious minorities, particularly Christians, Hindus, Sikhs, Ahmadis, Shias and Zikris.

Hindus

The largest religious minority in Pakistan is the Hindu community. They live mostly in Sindh, Peshawar and Balochistan. Since atrocities and abduction for ransom have been rising, hundreds of Hindu families from Balochistan had migrated to India recently, acknowledges the Minority Affairs Ministry. The Babri Masjid dispute in India triggered the demolition of many temples in Pakistan. The Allahabad court verdict in August 2010 on Babri Masjid dispute in India was highly intimidating to Hindus in Pakistan.

Christians

The second largest religious minority in Pakistan are Christians, their history dating back to centuries. The communities includes Anglicans, Protestants, Catholics, Armenian Orthodox, Assyrians or Chaldeans, smaller number of Nestorians and more recent Evangelical sects. They are represented in many fields of Pakistani society and have to some degree, achieved higher positions in the government, bureaucracy and businesses. The events of 11 September 2001 saw many atrocities being committed on the Christian community. The issues of land disputes have often lead to the robbing and torching of residences of Christians. Two major incidents include the Shanti Nagar massacre in 1997 in which 2,500 Christians had to flee their village, and the Gojra riots of 2010, when eight Christians were buried alive.[13]

Sikhs

Sikhism itself originated in the Punjab province. The population of Sikhs in Pakistan is 13,640. The holy sites of the Sikh community have been frequently targeted, many Sikh families have been forced to flee their homes. Sikhs from Orakzai, a place near Afghanistan where they have been living for generations were forced to flee the area after Taliban militants asked them to pay *jizya* or leave the area.

Ahmadis

Ahmadis are a minor sect of Muslims in the Punjab province of Pakistan. Their basic difference with the Muslims is in the finality of Prophet Muhammad. Hate speech, intimidation and violence against the Ahmadis have been a norm in Pakistan. Since the promulgation of the 1984 Prohibition of Qadiyaniat Ordinance until the end of the year 2010, hundreds of Ahmadis had been killed in faith-based attacks. The year 2010 was the worst year in terms of the number of killings since

1984; as many as 99 Ahmadis were killed in 2010 itself. The religious political parties frequently threaten a movement against the Ahmadi community if it 'did not accept its minority status' and the government keeps silent about their blasphemous and unconstitutional activities.

Shias

Shias is a minority Muslim sect which makes up an estimated 5-20 per cent of the total Muslim population. The majority of Pakistani Shia Muslims belong to the *Ithna Ashariyyah* law school, with significant minority groups who practice Ismailism, which is composed of Nizari (Aga Khanis), Mustaali, Dawoodi Bohra, and others. The Sunni militant groups have assaulted various holy places and disturbed the rituals of the Shia sect.

Zikris

Zikris are predominantly in south-western Balochistan where their spiritual centre, Koh-i-Murad, is located. They are a Baloch ethnic group in Makran and the adjoining areas, and fear that they will suffer the fate of the Ahmadis, as there are demands from certain Sunni groups for their designation as a non-Muslim minority. The Zikris have generally subscribed to the idea of a revealed *imam, Mahdi* (promised Messiah) and, while believing in all the basic tenets of Islam, they consider Syed Muhammad Jaunpuri, a contemporary of the Mughal Emperor Akbar in the sixteenth century, to be their *Mahdi*. According to them, the imam appeared on Koh-i-Murad, an arid hilltop near Turbat in Balochistan, where he performed religious and spiritual rites before disappearing in Afghanistan. They remember and constantly recite the names and attributes of God, either on an individual basis or collectively.[14] Most Zikris are poor peasants or nomads.

There are some other minority religious communities like Zorastrians, Bahais, Buddhists, Kalashas, Jains and Makranis who represent a very small denomination, have not been an exception to victimization.

Islamization of Pakistan Society

On 25 January 1948 just months before Mohammad Ali Jinnah's final exit from politics, he publicly retracted his earlier commitment to democratic citizenship by declaring that Pakistan's constitution would be based on Islamic law (Sharia) 'to make Pakistan a truly great Islamic State'.[15] Pakistan has had three constitutions since its independence. The first 1956 constitution declared Pakistan to be an Islamic republic and the Pakistan government granted equal citizenship rights to all men. However, by and large, the document did not formally commit itself to religion-related exclusions of minorities. Indeed, in 1962, General Ayub Khan who introduced his own constitution dropped the word 'Islamic' from the country's title and sought to make it more liberal in character. For example, progressive Islamic laws in the sphere of marriage and divorce were adopted in the new constitution. Ayub Khan encountered religiously inclined Islamic parties and institutions. To challenge the hegemony of Islam, his government nationalized religious endowments and assumed guardianship of religious shrines. He also sought to regulate religious education.[16] In 1962, the Council of Islamic Ideology (CII), Pakistan's top constitutional advisory body was established for Islamic order be perpetuated in the state. The council's current functions include recommending laws to the parliament and provincial assemblies that conform to the Quran and *Sunnah* (Prophet's Tradition), making recommendations to bring current laws to conform to Islamic injunctions and advising the parliament, provincial assemblies, or other government functionaries on proposed laws and whether they are in accordance with Islamic injunctions or not. The 1973 constitution under Articles 228-31 had the job of identifying laws repugnant to Islam, and then recommending ways to bring them in conformity with Islamic principles to this council.

President General Zia-ul-Haq (1977-88) amplified the magnitude of the council and used it to legitimize and promulgate controversial legislations like the *hudood* ordinance. For the Pakistan's social and political system, Zia began to give an altogether dissimilar direction, which was Islamic and in its most conservative tradition. His ordinances, laws, actions, and acts of omission and commission were passed through the Eighth Amendment into the Constitution when the National Assembly was convened after the 1985 non-party elections. By this Gen. Zia consolidated the separate electorates of the minorities in the 1973 constitution. The wave of religious intolerance and extremism began with Zia courting the religious constituency for political support and legitimacy.[17] The Soviet military intervention in Afghanistan and the Mujahideen resistance based in Pakistan were also factors that influenced the growth of religious militancy. The flow of arms and money from the oil-rich West Asian countries to the Islamic *madrasa* (religious school) network further contributed to the power and influence of religious organizations and the militant groups.

The religious-oriented parties like Jamaat-i-Islami and Majlis-i-Ahrar, advocated the Islamization of the country. Such ideological groups demanded holistic socio-political reorientation of Pakistan. However, they were not the only ones who sought a systemic change; even the ruling political and civil elite soon began to seek out legitimacy and national cohesion through selective use of Islamic ethos.[18] They sought to eliminate vestiges of the British-derived civil and criminal laws and create a state based upon *Shariat*. Most liberal Pakistanis repeatedly rejected the imposition of *Shariat* law, despite the incessant demand for it by all Islamist parties. They stoutly demanded the Islamic provisions to be included in the yet-to-be adopted constitution. In response to the Islamists in Pakistan, the Muslim League leaders gradually viewed Islam as an acceptable vehicle for nation-building. By this time several Western social practices had been altered or abandoned in the name of Islam, notably the public consumption of alcohol, gambling, and co-educational classrooms, except in some of Pakistan's Westernized cities, such as Islamabad, Lahore, and Karachi.[19]

Islamists have played a significant role in Pakistan since the 1970s, providing the framework through which the country has defined its national interests and worked out its domestic and international politics.[20] Islamism has also enlarged Pakistan's regional power by opening new foreign policy possibilities of Islamabad, most notably in using Islamist activism to deal with developments in Afghanistan and Kashmir.[21] It is interesting to note the observation of Ayesha Jalal, that Pakistan could not be 'national' and 'Islamic' state. It could not be 'national' hence in the traditional Islamic conception of the state, non-Muslims do not have equal rights of citizenship; and it could not be 'Islamic' if the boundaries of the nation state, as opposed to religious affiliations, were to distinguish citizens from non-citizens.[22]

The Blasphemy Laws

Blasphemy laws in the developed world have had as grave social and psychological implications for religious minorities as the blasphemy laws in Pakistan. These laws cover acts that may fall within the offences of blasphemy, the violation of which carries extended prison sentences and death by hanging. The prevention of blasphemy, or irreverence towards holy persons, religious beliefs, customs and artefacts as currently articulated in Pakistan's Penal Code (PPC), finds its roots in colonial legislation drafted in 1860. This Indian Penal Code of 1860, prepared by the First Law Commission chaired by Lord Macaulay, criminalized the act of damaging or defiling a place of worship or a sacred object under Section 295. Section 295A was added to provide for the offence of 'outraging religious feelings'. Penalties for such offences, included imprisonment for a term extending upto two years, a fine, or both. Pakistan inherited this code at independence and amendments made over the years transformed the legislation into the Offences Relating to Religion as set out in the PPC.[23]

Pakistan government under Gen. Zia ul Haq introduced relentless penalties including life imprisonment and death penalties were drafted into the legislation. The PPC Ordinance 1982 amended Section 295B to include life imprisonment, providing that, 'Whoever wilfully defiles, damages or desecrates a copy of the Holy Quran or any extract thereof or uses it in any derogatory manner or for any unlawful purpose shall be punishable with imprisonment for life.' Ordinance XX, which added Sections 298 B and C to the PPC, sealed the expulsion of Ahmadis from the Pakistani state in 1984. Any Ahmadi Muslim community member, preaching or propagating his faith, or outraging the religious feelings of Muslims, or referring to herself or himself as a Muslim is now liable to three years imprisonment.

In 1986, the Criminal Law Act III provided a further amendment to Section 295C by criminalizing defamation against the Prophet and providing that, 'Whoever by words, either spoken or written, or by visible representation, or by any other imputation, insinuation, directly or indirectly, defiles the sacred name of the Prophet Muhammad shall be punished with death or imprisonment for life, and shall also be liable to a fine.' It is under this section that Aasia Bibi became the first Christian woman to be sentenced to death for blasphemy in November 2010. Nawaz Sharif's government in 1992 removed the option of a life sentence from Section 295C and imposed a mandatory death sentence, thereby giving more power to those who wished to use this law. One of the first fatal assaults against Pakistan's Christian minority community triggered by the blasphemy laws took place soon after the enactment of the 1992 amendment.

The indistinct terminology of the current legislation enables the misuse of Sections 295–298 of PPC, and has allowed the persecution of minorities and the poor by providing unscrupulous complainants with a mechanism for settling personal vendettas through the justice system. The law has manifested in society as a tool for promoting intolerance. Even though a majority of those charged under this law are Muslims, the law has made non-Muslims even more susceptible. In addition, the manner in which the law is propagated by the religious groups in Pakistan has led to vigilantism and mob violence. The state has consistently failed to intervene and protect anyone against violence by maliciously motivated elements and the certainty of impunity has encouraged them to commit lawlessness. Reported incidents reveal that those accused of blasphemy are killed in jail often even before they are sentenced. On 14 November 2010, the accused in a blasphemy case was shot dead near his house in Lahore after being granted bail. Other examples include incidents on 30 July and 1 August 2009, when dozens of people were injured after riots broke out over allegations of blasphemy against the Holy Quran.[24] Since 1986, nearly a thousand cases of blasphemy have been registered in Pakistan. Of these, 476 have been registered against Muslims, 479 against Ahmadis and 180 against Christians. In 2010, over 32 people were killed extra-judicially by angry mobs or individuals on the basis of allegations of blasphemy and 64 people were charged under the blasphemy law.[25]

Article 20 of the 1973 constitution contains the following major provision on religious freedom: 'Subject to law, public order and morality,(a) every citizen shall have the right to profess, practise and propagate his religion; and (b) every religious denomination and every sect thereof shall have the right to establish, maintain and manage its religious institutions.'[26] Two points have to be kept in mind here. Firstly, Article 20(a) is expressly available only to citizens of Pakistan. Secondly, this is a constitutional right, yet it is subject to law. This signifies that subconstitutional legislation, for reasons of public morality or public order, may regulate this right. In theory, the practice of every religion, including Islam, is subject to this provision. But case law indicates that these restrictions have only been applied to the time, place, and manner of certain religious celebrations. More often than not, such restrictions have been applied to Muslims who belong to certain sects. As such, it can be asserted that this provision has generally not been utilized to the detriment of the non-Muslim minorities.[27] If the Christians and Ahmadis profess, practice or propagate their religious principles, involuntarily it would become blasphemy in Pakistan; hence the blasphemy laws are illogically coded, and the Christian religious principles have some similarities with Islamic principles and Ahmadi principles have more similarity with Islam.

The blasphemy laws are incompatible with international human rights standards not only because they impose undue restrictions on freedom of expression, freedom of religion, and other human rights, but also because they are discriminatory in their effect. The government lacks the necessary safeguards against abuse, providing no clear definition of what constitutes blasphemy, weak evidentiary standards for convictions in lower courts, and no criminal intent requirement.[28] This makes it possible for the laws to be exploited to persecute minorities or to carry out revenge in personal disputes. The blasphemy laws have also been invoked to instigate and justify sectarian or communal conflict, with allegations of blasphemy often serving as the trigger for mob violence that has in some cases been implicitly, if not explicitly, condoned by police and government officials.[29]

The blasphemy laws lack on what constitutes a violation. This determination is left to the police and judicial officials to make, often relying on their own personal beliefs and interpretations of Islam. Nina Shea has argued that 'interpreting what falls under Pakistan's anti-blasphemy laws is essentially a theological question and, since there is no black-letter definition of the crime in the Quran or other authoritative Islamic sources, it is one that remains unsettled.'[30] Moreover, the blasphemy laws lack the safeguard to prevent the law's abuse. The penalties for violating these laws have been excessively severe. The due process and fair trial protections are often lacking in blasphemy cases, and the UN member states have made clear that such guarantees are essential when dealing with death penalty: 'Capital punishment may only be carried out pursuant to a final judgment rendered by a competent court after legal process which gives all possible safeguards to ensure a fair trial, at least equal to those contained in Article 14 of the International Covenant on Civil and Political Rights.'[31]

Despite the perceived legitimacy in Pakistan, the blasphemy laws clearly run afoul of various international human rights instruments. Firstly, the blasphemy laws circumvent Article 55(c) of the UN Charter[32] and Article 18 of the Universal Declaration of Human Rights

(UDHR), to which Pakistan is a signatory. This is especially troubling since Pakistan was once firmly committed to abide by the Charter and Declaration. Secondly, the anti-blasphemy laws circumvent Articles 18, 19, 20 and 27 of the International Covenant on Civil and Political Rights (ICCPR), to which Pakistan is a signatory.[33] The ICCPR concretized the basic freedoms of religion and conscience articulated in the UDHR and made its signatories legally bound by it. In addition to prohibiting state coercion that would impair a person's freedom to practice or adopt a religion or belief of one's choice, the ICCPR also prohibits states from denying religious minorities the right, in community with other group members, to enjoy their own culture, profess or practice their own religion, or to use their own language. All these principles have been violated by the blasphemy laws in Pakistan.

Misusing or misinterpretations of blasphemy laws are large in number and any fresh case which lacks any solid evidence. For example, in December 2010, Dr. Naushad Ali Valliani, a physician from Hyderabad, was accused of blasphemy. He was arrested for throwing a visiting card belonging to a Muhammad Faizan in the dust-bin. The guilty act was throwing a card bearing the name 'Muhammad'. He apologized for throwing the card in the dustbin, insisting that he had no intention of insulting the Prophet, but local religious leaders insisted on further action and an FIR under Section 295C of the Pakistan Penal Code was registered against him. This blatant abuse of the law against innocent people only highlights the necessity for reform and increased scrutiny.[34] The Human Rights Commission of Pakistan (HRCP) reported in 2006 that while minority groups were often victims of false blasphemy accusations, it observes that the number of instances in which blasphemy laws were abused to settle petty scores with other Muslims had risen sharply over the past years.[35]

Advocates of the blasphemy laws belong to all sects of Muslims – Sunni, Shia, Barelvi, Deobandi and Ahle Hadith. Despite intersect hatred, extremists from each group have been united in discriminating against Pakistan's religious minorities. Some liberal factions have stood to oppose them, including human rights activists and people from the educated middle-class. Generally, the impact of blasphemy laws is a serious erosion of the rule of law itself. The police and courts have been apparently at the mercy of Islamist extremists and other extralegal forces.

Personal Laws

There have been numerous personal laws for the minority communities. For the Hindu community, there is the Hindu Disposition of Property Act 1916, Hindu Gains of Learning Act 1930, Hindu Inheritance (Removal of Disabilities) Act 1928, Hindu Law of Inheritance (Amendment) Act 1929, etc. For Christians, there is the Christian Marriage Act 1832 and Christian Marriage Act 1872. There have been only minor changes to the personal laws relating to Christians, Hindus and other minorities since the Partition.[36] Particularly, the Hindu community does not have any specific codified laws relating to family matters, which are governed by customs and traditional laws. However, members of minority communities can approach the country's regular family courts since the Family Courts Act 1964 does not restrict its jurisdiction to Muslims alone. One of the central concerns for religious minorities such as Hindus, Sikhs and Baha'is is the lack of a mechanism for registration of marriages. Married couples do not have any official certificate showing that they are married, which is a hurdle for married women in acquiring passports or any other such certificate. The couples have to make individual petitions in courts and although the courts issue such orders, they apply only to the petitioners and are not the ideal solution to the absence of a marriage registration mechanism. Lack of registration of marriages also has implications for legal recourse for spouses in case of matrimonial disputes. The religiously stirred milieu of the Pakistani judicial system pushes them to adopt their own customs or traditional laws. Most of the issues are settled through community forums.[37] Akbar S. Ahmed observes the predicament of laws in Pakistan, citing that at times four distinct laws overlaps. These are the British colonial law, which by and large was the basis in 1947 for Pakistan's penal code and criminal procedure code; then Islamic Sharia law, tribal law, which applies to certain areas of the country; and state law, which is codified by each state's local ruler. The application of the law has never been fully resolved.[38]

Hate speech is another method harassing minorities and vulnerable communities in Pakistan. The hate speeches by clerics at religious congregations and Friday prayer sermons are extremely condemnable. Some of the mainstream newspapers are also partly responsible for the hate campaigns against members of minority faiths as they often brand members of entire minority communities as agents of other countries.[39] The minority communities have been victimized by all these sorts of discriminations – admission to schools, attaining public sector jobs, getting senior-level jobs in the private sector, etc. The minorities are politically disadvantaged, economically pitiable and socially segregated and only have limited opportunities for menial jobs, bonded labour, low wages. Kidnapping of young minority women and forced conversions are widespread phenomena. The curriculum in educational institutions promotes intolerance towards minorities and cultural diversity. The minorities have been frightened everywhere in Pakistan, and deep social insecurity has forced them to flee abroad. However, this is limited to the economically well-off people among the minority. It is largely a passive citizenship that has been enjoyed by the minority communities.

Attempts to Save the Minorities

The doomed history of the minorities in Pakistan has a contradictory reality associated with its founder Jinnah, as he belonged to a minority Shia sect of Muslims. However, soon after his death, the principle of equality he instituted was disregarded by the majority community. Former President General Pervez Musharraf had taken a few measures to give a progressive twist to the amendment of blasphemy laws. In April 2000, he announced a proposal to make an administrative change in the procedure for registration of cases under the blasphemy law. It aimed at reducing the misuse of this law to settle personal scores. However, he retreated in the face of opposition from some religious groups, as he did in March 2005 after Islamist groups had raised their voice against the deletion of the column on religion in new Pakistani passports.[40]

The remarkable initiative taken to protect minorities had inverted in 2002. This constitutional amendment was inserted by the Chief Executive, that guarantees the reservation of seats for minorities in Provincial and National Assemblies. It can be acknowledged that in April 2010, the Federal Ministry of Minorities announced that ten religious festivals of the minorities would be celebrated officially in Pakistan. The festivals included Baisakhi, Diwali, Holi, Eid-e-Rizwan, Chelumjust, Nauroz, Christmas and Easter. To recognize the contribution, services and sacrifices by the minorities in the creation of Pakistan and to highlight the vision of Jinnah on religious freedom and tolerance, elaborated in his address to the Constituent Assembly on 11 August 1947, it was decided to observe 11 August as 'Minorities' Day'.[41] The minority communities have been demanding separate marriage laws and the matter was to be addressed in a Minority Protection Bill, the government was working on announced by the Federal Minister for Minorities in 2010, but this is yet to be tabled in the National Assembly. In 2010 April, the government decided to reserve four seats for minorities in the Senate.

In 2011, Sherry Rehman, Member of Parliament, of the Pakistan People's Party, who had proposed the amendments in a private member's bill, announced that she will not pursue the legislative process. Even for this effort, Mrs Rehman had received many death threats from the militants and she reportedly took the decision after Pakistan's prime minister said there was no scope for discussion on changing the law. As long as the blasphemy provisions remain in the statute books, they provide legitimacy to groups who use violent means to oppress minorities. The government's position provides a green light to vigilantism, which was proposed by the Minority Rights Group International to United Nations High Commissioner for Refugees (UNHCR). There have been several protests by some Islamic groups against attempts to change or repeal the various provisions of Section 295. In January 2011, the Governor of Punjab province, Salman Taseer, and in March, Minority Affairs Minister Shahbaz Bhatti were shot dead by fundamentalists. Both had long-standing initiatives to amend the draconian laws of blasphemy. These killings had a huge impact and halted the work of the already lagging commission for minority affairs and to its ministry.

Every minority community in Pakistan firmly identifies its national identity as Pakistani, but their religious or ethnic identity is being questioned by the dominant community. For the security of all minority groups, state cohesion and the democratization of the state are to be ensured. The Government of Pakistan should have the political determination to contain the growth of religious militancy and terrorism.

Conclusion

It is obvious that the identity of the religion of the state has been fuelling as an exclusionary discourse in Pakistan and it lacks mass nationalist legacy and mass anti-colonial tradition grounded in strong nationalist narrative to grow as a modern nation state. The social and political exclusion of minorities in particular has had a direct impact on the weakening of state power. The declining power of the state due to the merging of the religious factors had been employed for political legitimacy by various governments, both military rulers or civilian rulers right from the formation of the state. The Pakistan society's reluctance to engage with modernity has been a key impasse to the waning of civilian politics. In the case of Pakistan, there is a significant contrast between its rulers and the ruled, the former have almost been elite educated at institutions in the West, and the latter have always been either from various seminaries (*madrasas*) or nothing.

Many Muslim theologians in states like Pakistan in particular, and South Asian states in general, even today not only reject the socio-political ideals of modernity but also reject any idea about the plurality of Islam. For them Islam is a monolithic phenomenon and any intellectual inquiry of plurality is on the path of error, and anyone accepting plurality may even be denounced as *kafir* (unbeliever). As Karen Armstrong says, 'Judaism, Christianity and Islam are rooted in a profound fear of annihilation, a conviction that the liberal, secularist establishment wants to wipe out the religion. This is as true of the militant Christian groups in the United States as it is of Muslim extremists in Egypt and Iran.'[42] This is epitomized in the scantiness of religious reformation, especially in Islam and its versions in Pakistan in particular. Its religious scholars depict Islam as a static religion rather than a dynamic one. The primary audience for fundamentalists are members of their own faith who are deemed to have gone astray and lack sufficient piety to attain personal salvation. Fundamentalists are against the idea of pluralism in matters of faith while firmly believing that there is only one correct school of interpretation of scriptures, religion, and law.[43] The modern societies have acknowledged the significance of pluralism as being universal and ideological monolith is being rejected. Modernity uses the dialect of rights whereas theological discourse is entirely built around the language of duties. Thus traditional Islam imposes duties and rejects the idea of rights, and the Islamists never recollect the ideas of Prophet Muhammad's authentic traditions, of establishing that a society of consensus and negotiating with all religious communities. So multiculturalism presumes that Islam as a religion is embedded in a distinct culture that maintains itself from one generation to the next. One can be a good citizen and at the same time identify primarily with a culture that is not the dominant one. In other words, the citizen's relation to the nation can be mediated by a communitarian sense of belonging. In the Muslim societies the transformation from feudal to democratic society is far from complete and hence the empowerment of people, particularly its minorities and women remains incomplete. Participatory politics and civic culture with a focus on citizenship rights have suffered gravely due to the bureaucratic-military nexus, which was exposed by the frequent military takeovers of the civilian government, and which led to the breakdown of the democratization process in Pakistan. In the vacuum of democracy, this was paving ways for various kinds of militant Islamism, like its latest version, the Tehreek-e-Taliban Pakistan (TTP).

The Pakistan state was created in 1947, however the nation-building process in Pakistan is an awfully sluggish process. It is not as simple as replacing the civilian government and conducting the elections, strengthening the civil society and building secular political parties as a countervailing force in Pakistan, which can contain the demands for Islamization by the religious parties and radical Islamist groups. For a democratic society, it is indispensable to constitute modern democratic tradition which include active citizenship, equality, rights and individual freedom, and repealing of draconian legislations like the blasphemy laws. The need to reinterpret of the classical Islamic texts, the *Ijtihad,* has been overdue for some centuries, for the texts to be re-read contextually with the help of a dynamic methodology. The individualization and repositioning of religion from the public sphere has been the momentous paradigm which manifested in the 'Arab Spring', particularly in Egypt and in Tunisia and that should be a lesson for the future nation and state building process in Pakistan.

Notes

1. Clinton Bennet, *Muslims and Modernity: An Introduction to the Issues and Debates,* London: Continuum, 2005, p. 160.
2. Muqtedar Khan, 'The Islamic State and Religious Minorities', Available on the Internet at www.islamfortoday.com/khan06.htm (accessed on 20 August 2011).
3. Quran 2: 256.

4. Ibid., 2; 5: 43, 5: 47.
5. Khan, 'The Islamic State and Religious Minorities', p. 2.
6. Will Kymlicka, *Multicultural Citizenship: A Liberal Theory of Minority Rights,* Oxford: Oxford University Press, 1995, p. 124.
7. Andrew Heywood, *Political Theory: An Introduction*, New York: Palgrave Macmillan, 2004, p. 207.
8. Ashok Kapur, *Pakistan in Crisis*, London: Routledge, 1991, p. 8.
9. Mohammad Abdul Qadeer, *Pakistan: Social and Cultural Transformations in a Muslim Nation*, London: Routledge, 2006, p. 2.
10. Mohammed Ali Jinnah's speech at the First Constituent Assembly of Pakistan, on 11 August 1947, cited in Eshrat Hussain Basri, 'Constitutional Provisions for the Rights of the Non-Muslim Minorities in Pakistan', *Journal of Humanity and Islam*, vol. 1, no. 1, April 2011, pp. 1-10.
11. Ravi Kalia, 'Introduction', in *Pakistan: From the Rhetoric of Democracy to the Rise of Militancy*, New Delhi: Routledge, 2011, p. 1.
12. Anwar Syed, *Pakistan: Islam and National Solidarity,* Lahore: Vanguard Books, 1984, pp. 74–100.
13. Rabia Mehmood, 'Pakistan Blasphemy Laws Retake Centre Stage', 22 February 2011, Available on the Internet at http://www.pbs.org/wnet/need-to-know/security/pakistan-blasphemy (accessed on 21 November 2011).
14. A.G. Baloch, *Zikri Firqa Ki Tarikh* (*The History of Zikri Sect*), Urdu, Karachi, 1996, p. 51 cited in Iftikhar H. Malik, 'Religious Minorities in Pakistan', *Minority Groups International*, September 2002.
15. Farzana Shaikh, *Making Sense of Pakistan*, New York: Columbia University Press, 2009, p. 45.
16. Rajiv Bhargava, 'Inclusion and Exclusion in South Asia: The Role of Religion', *Background Paper for HDR 2004*, United Nations Development Programme, p. 23
17. Mumtaz Ahmad, 'Revivalism, Islamization, Sectarianism and Violence in Pakistan', in Craig Baxter and Charles H. Kennedy, *Pakistan: 1997,* Boulder: Westview Press, 1998, p. 118.
18. Iftikhar H. Malik, *The History of Pakistan*, London: Westwood Press, 2008, p. 134.
19. Stephen P. Cohen, *The Idea of Pakistan*, Washington DC: Brookings Institution Press, 2004, p. 168.
20. Seyyed Vali Reza Nasr, *Islamic Leviathan: Islam and the Making of State Power*, New York: Oxford University Press, 2001, p. 112.
21. Vali Nasr, 'National Identities and the India–Pakistan Conflict', in T.V. Paul (ed.), *The India–Pakistan Conflict: An Enduring Rivalry,* Cambridge:

Cambridge University Press, 2005, p. 184, cited in Marvin Weinbaum, *Pakistan and Afghanistan: Resistance and Reconstruction*, Boulder: CO: Westview Press, 1994.

22. Ayesha Jalal, *Democracy and Authoritarianism in South Asia: A Comparative and Historical Perspective,* Cambridge: Cambridge University Press, 1995, p. 234.
23. 'A Question of Faith', *A Report on the Status of Religious Minorities in Pakistan*, Jinnah Institute Report, 2011, p. 12.
24. Ibid., p. 40.
25. State of Human Rights in 2010-11, Human Rights Commission of Pakistan, p. 7.
26 Pakistan Constitution Article 20 reprinted in 14 Constitutions, *supra* n. 5 in Safdar Mahmood, Constitutional Foundations of Pakistan 46 (2nd revd. edn. 1990) cited in Farooq Hassan, 'Religious Liberty in Pakistan: Law, Reality, and Perception (A Brief Synopsis)', *Brigham Young University Law Review,* 2002, pp. 283-300.
27. Ibid., pp. 283-300.
28 US Commission on International Religious Freedom (USCIRF), 'Pakistan', in *2009 Annual Report* (Washington, D.C.: USCIRF, May 2009). Available on the Internet at http://www.uscirf.gov (accessed on 12 October 2011).
29 'Policing Belief: Pakistan', *Freedom House Publication 2011*, Available on the Internet at http://freedomhouse.org/template.cfm?page=576 (accessed on 17 August 2011).
30 'Testimony of Nina Shea, Director of Hudson Institute's Centre for Religious Freedom, before the Tom Lantos Human Rights Commission of the Committee on Foreign Affairs of the US House of Representatives: Pakistan's Anti-Blasphemy Laws', Hudson Institute, 8 October 2009. Available on the Internet at http://www.hudson.org (accessed on 29 August 2011).
31. 'Safeguards Guaranteeing the Rights of Those Facing the Death Penalty, Approved by Economic and Social Council Resolution 1984/50 of 25 May 1984', available on the Internet at http://www2.ohchr.org/english/law/protection.htm. (accessed on 21 September 2011.
32. See U.N. Charter Article 1, para 3; U.N. Charter Article 55, para c.
33. See International Covenant on Civil and Political Rights, Articles 18, 27, G.A. Res. 2200A (XXI), U.N. GAOR 21st Sess., Supp. No. 16, at 52, U.N. Doc. A/6316 (1966), 999 U.N.T.S. 171 (entered into force 1976).
34. 'A Question of Faith', p. 40.

35. Human Rights Commission of Pakistan, *State of Human Rights in 2006,* Lahore: Human Rights Commission of Pakistan, January 2006, p. 141. Available on the Internet at http://www.hrcp-web.org. (accessed on 10 October 2011.
36 Family Laws and Minority Women in Pakistan, available on the internet at www.hisoft.us/sites/mrcpak/publications/minority_women (accessed on 24 September 2011).
37. 'A Question of Faith', p. 40.
38. Akbar S. Ahmed, 'Pakistan's Blasphemy Law: Words Fail Me', *The Washington Post Outlook*, Sunday, 19 May 2002.
39. Annual Report 2010 of the Human Rights Commission of Pakistan, Available on the Internet at http://www.hrcp-web.org/Publications/AR2010.pdf (accessed on 11 October 2011).
40. Gilles Boquérat and Nazir Hussain, 'Enlightened Moderation: Anatomy of a Failed Strategy', in Ravi Kalia, ed., *Pakistan: From the Rhetoric of Democracy to the Rise of Militancy*, New Delhi: Routledge, 2011, p. 178
41. Annual Report 2010, the Human Rights Commission of Pakistan.
42. Karen Armstrong, 'Is a Holy War Inevitable?' *GQ Magazine*, January 2002, pp. 122-3. Also see, Karen Armstrong, *The Battle for God: Fundamentalism in Judaism, Christianity and Islam*, New York: The Random House Publishing Group, 2001, pp. 135-364.
43. Nader Hashemi, *Islam, Secularism, and Liberal Democracy Toward a Democratic Theory for Muslim Societies*, Oxford: Oxford University Press, 2009, p. 42.

CHAPTER 14

Religious Extremism and Sectarian Violence in Pakistan

Revisiting Islamization

Azhar Ali

RELIGION IN PAKISTAN has been a contested issue since its inception. It was even created, claiming, as the homeland for South Asian Muslims. The Pakistan movement was also carried out under the shadow of Muslim identity. The Islamic identity and consciousness of its people have been dominant influences on their history throughout. Indeed, without that particular background, there could have been no Pakistan. Pakistan is probably the first state in the world carved out in the name of Islam. This is the irony in the history of Pakistan that its founding father, Mohammad Ali Jinnah, never emphasized on an Islamic state or a state based on religious values. Jinnah envisaged for a secular democratic state where everyone will enjoy equal rights. But Jinnah's death soon after Partition left the country directionless in its efforts to establish a viable governing system. Pakistan suffered a lack of pragmatic political leadership after Jinnah. This political crisis worsened when the military took over power in the late 1950s. Weak political leadership and institutions and time-to-time military intervention blocked its way to become a viable political entity. Apart from history and ideology, Pakistan's geographical location has also profoundly affected its fortunes as an independent state.

However, religion in Pakistan had never been a dominant force in politics until the Soviet invasion in Afghanistan where Pakistan played a vital role with covert American support. In fact, until this time religion was seen as the binding force in uniting the whole country. It was a force to undermine the ethnic and secessionist aspirations. But the 1971 breakup of East Pakistan and the emergence of a new state, Bangladesh was a big blow to the Islamic identity of Pakistan. It was also a big blow to the two-nation theory as well, which was being propagated during the Pakistan movement. Moreover, Gen. Zia's idea of Islamization of Pakistani society unleashed religious extremism in Pakistan rather than giving it viability. Religion became a force to influence political process. Use of religion in politics further witnessed the rise of sectarian violence in the country. A good number of scholars have, so far, commented on religion and religious extremism in Pakistan. But there are still concerns regarding the much debated issues of religious extremism and Islamization in Pakistan. Was the process of Islamization, essentially initiated during the Zia period, natural, or a state set-up to gain regime legitimacy? Whose interests, indeed, are protected through the use of religion? Can one find class interests behind the manipulation of religion involved in the process of Islamization? A focused attempt is made here to understand these vital questions.

Though the notion of class system is often disregarded in Pakistan, the analysis of alliance and affiliation among various groups and classes reveals interesting relationship to violence and religious extremism in the country. This article explores the vested interests of certain classes which aligned themselves with each other in a complex way.

Social Formation and Class Alignment

Noted Pakistani scholar Hamza Alavi has identified class system in Pakistan in an interesting way. Class formation in Pakistan is complex, since most of the post-colonial states are identified as the peripheral capitalist states and Pakistan is no exception. So discussing the class system in a literal way would be a difficult task and perhaps confusing. According to Hamza Alavi, landlords are the most powerful indigenous class in Pakistan. Electoral politics being highly biased towards rural areas, landlords predominate in the political leadership. Alavi also adds that members of the bureaucracy and the army are also part of this class. This class also dictates the peasantry and poor people as they are dependent on it for livelihood. These peasantry and poor people constitute a subordinate class to the landlords due to which landed elites dominate politics and society as well. Landlord power is also reflected in the failure to implement land reforms, despite the rhetoric of some governments. Politically landlords are the most effective organized class in the country.

Similarly, another dominant class is the Salariat class. The term 'Salariat' was coined by Hamza Alavi. According to him Pakistan movement was the movement of the Muslim Salariat in India, the educated lower middle classes whose main avenue for livelihood and upward mobility was to secure salaried jobs in the colonial and post-colonial state apparatus.[1] These people mainly were Urdu speakers who migrated from Uttar Pradesh in India at the time of Partition. In Marxian terminology, the Salariat class is identified as similar to the auxiliary class, whose role in society can be fully understood only with reference to fundamental classes to which it relates. This Salariat class which, itself, is divided into two strata *vis-à-vis* the bureaucracy at the top which wields power and the ordinary scribes below them. Nevertheless, it looms large in colonized and post-colonial societies and dominates their urban life and political debates.

The third important class which has been identified is the indigenous bourgeoisie. This class consists of those engaged in commerce and trade. It is argued that in the context of Pakistan this class has suffered most due to migration. Large number of business communities who were mainly Hindus had to leave the region and only a small number of business class was left in Pakistan. Those Muslim business communities who migrated from India were largely Gujarati-speaking traders, i.e. Memons, Bohras, Ismaili Khojas and Ithna Ashari Khojas. These Gujarati-speaking business communities in Pakistan had no political representation as such. They were left at the mercy of the bureaucracy. They were represented collectively through chambers of commerce and the influential Pakistani Federation of Chambers of Commerce and Industry. Given the political isolation and weakness of the trading communities in Pakistan, it is quite remarkable to see how the state authorities in the country set about the task of turning them into an industrial bourgeoisie. The government embarked on a desperate drive for industrialization, because it believed that without industries Pakistan would not be economically viable. Pakistan did witness some growth during Gen. Ayub's period but it was not sustained in the following regimes.

Thus, class formation in Pakistan is both interesting as well as complex. Apart from class formation and characteristics, this article further attempts to examine the rise of religious extremism and sectarian violence.

Seeds of Religious Extremism and Sectarian Violence

Historically, Islamist parties in Pakistan, i.e. parties that use Islamic beliefs or values as the bases of their political agenda, initiated their demand for converting Pakistan into an Islamic state soon after its Partition from India in 1947.[2] However, they were unable to generate popular support for their aim as the ruling elites did not give much space to them to manoeuvre. It was not until the Islamization project of Gen. Zia-ul-Haq that the concept of Islamic state began to acquire substance and the Islamic parties began to move to the centrestage of Pakistani politics. The general who had deposed an elected prime minister in 1977 and later had him executed by manipulating the judicial process could turn nowhere but to religious sanction to legitimize his dictatorial rule.[3] The centrepiece of the Islamization process was a selective implementation of the Shariat laws. The Soviet invasion of Afghanistan further extended the space for religious forces as they were cynically pumped into the Afghan war. The Soviet invasion of Afghanistan laid the foundation of the notion of Jihad. The US desperately supported Pakistan in the Afghan war to downplay the influence of Soviet Union in South Asia. The religious forces in Pakistan with the state and US covert support, proclaimed the fight against the communist regime as Jihad. The space for religion in politics was further extended by Gen. Zia-ul-Haq during his rule. He introduced the idea and started the process of Islamization of both society and politics in Pakistan. This process was supported and promoted as the current situations were in favour. Also Islam was seen as an effective means to ease the soaring ethnic tension within Pakistan.

It is often recognized that military and bureaucratic oligarchy are the ruling class in Pakistan. They ruled longer than any democratic regime, through coups. During Gen. Zia's period the process of Islamization was seen as a source of state power. Gen. Zia took over power from Prime Minister Zulfikar Ali Bhutto. Bhutto's failure to save the country from breaking up and his policies of socialism led to his downfall. Bhutto's populism had affected the industrial elite in particular through nationalizing of industries and championing the cause of labour. Also the continued domination of the public sector caused unhappiness among the industrial elite and the entrepreneurial class that had expected wide-scale privatization of national industries. As a result, from early on the industrial elite and the entrepreneurial classes became a critical source of opposition to Bhutto. In opposing him, they joined hands with the lower middle-class merchants and more importantly, with Islamist forces. Throughout the 1970s, businessmen and entrepreneurs provided financial and logistical support to the Islamist opposition to Bhutto.[4] Therefore, it can be argued that religion, as a force, was being employed to destabilize the then regime. It is discernible why Gen. Zia opted for Islamization as a viable source for his regime. He also saw the private sector as an important base of support for his regime. It was the powerful economic class that was opposed to Bhutto and his policies. It was closely tied with Islamist forces and these Islamist parties that spearheaded the fall of Bhutto. The private sector was also a key to Gen. Zia's attempt to create a middle and lower middle-class base for his regime as a counterweight to the Pakistan People's Party's (PPP) lower-class base support.[5]

Gen. Zia replaced Bhutto's idea of socialism with his idea of Islamization. He was keen to undertake political and economic reforms in order to undo the effect of Bhutto's populism. He held the view that only Islamic law can help the state to go further. In doing so, he intended to gain legitimacy for his regime. The idea of Islamization not only helped him to gain support but also aided him to suppress political opposition. The military regime furthermore created the institutional means to organize Islamist interest groups within the state and encouraged them to participate in politics though these institutions. Gen. Zia was an admirer of Moulana Abul Ala Mawdudi, who was the founder of the Jama'at-e-Islami (JI). He had looked at the JI as an intellectual force that could serve the same function in his regime as the left had done in PPP during the 1969-79 periods. The JI's ideology supported authoritarianism and contained a powerful critique of both the left and western democracy to the advantage of the military.

Gen. Zia's Islamization was essentially seen as more of securing his regime rather than creating a theocratic state based purely on religion. Though the military-bureaucratic regime attempted to Islamize the state institutions and society it could not gain currency as it was not inclusionary or cohesive enough to accommodate the aspirations of others. Every move taken in the course of Islamization was essentially based on either regime's interest or its aligned class's interest. The Federal Shariat Court was instituted and granted appellate jurisdiction over convictions and acquittals from district courts involving newly-implemented Islamization schemes. In fact, the Federal Shariat Court was in the end used less as a means of creating an ideological system of justice and more as a powerful tool of social control in the hands of state leaders. Gen. Zia directly appointed the court's judges and the court closely followed the military's agenda. It is also argued that the Islamization of the judiciary was a cover for curbing its powers. During the first years of military rule the judiciary rather than political parties and actors served as the main source of resistance to it. Therefore, the weakening of the judiciary in turn impaired civil society institutions before the state and made the extension of the state's reach into society easier.

However, the course of Islamization unleashed sectarian violence in Pakistan as the process was not cohesive enough to accommodate the aspirations of all sects of Muslims and minorities. In fact Islamization was seen as an imposition of a single sect over others. Consequently, it created tension in Shia-Sunni relations as Zia's Islamization was largely a Sunni affair and hence viewed Shia activism as a threat. Contrarily, there have been equally strident demands that Pakistan be declared a Sunni Hanfi republic and the Hanfi *fiqh*, or legal code, be made the law of the land, that all other sects be declared minorities and be given second-class citizenship. This has led to a great deal of sectarian violence.[6] But these developments are the logical extension of the Zia regime's decision to impose Islamic law in Pakistan. The question is 'which Islamic law'? Indeed, one can see differences within the Sunni sects, leave apart the Shias. There are traditionalist Deobandi Ulema, traditionalist Barelvi Ulema and Jama'at-i-Islami, who differ in their beliefs and creed and are incompatible with each other. In such a situation one cannot expect positive results or constructive outcome for state and nation-building.

Furthermore, the affiliation of religious parties and organizations with particular classes and political parties raises several concerns regarding the authenticity of Islamization. It is believed that these religious organizations and groups have become very effective instruments to exploit political situations. For instance, the assassination of Punjab governor Salman Taseer had shaken the state. But the case here is about the individual, Malik Mumtaz Qadri, who killed him, his religious affiliation to one particular sect and the possible politics behind the assassination. Salman Taseer was assassinated for his comments over the much debated 'Blasphemy Law'. The assassination was described by commentators in Pakistan and elsewhere as an example of rising religious extremism. Qadri is said to have his religious allegiance to Jama'at Ahle-e-Sunnat, a leading Barelvi sect. This became apparent when some 500 religious clerics of Jama'at Ahle-e-Sunnat forbade its followers to pray for or attend the funeral of Salman Taseer. The veteran civil rights activist of Pakistan, I.A. Rehman commented that the unprecedented edict issued by several hundred clerics means that the Ahle-e-Sunnat which had been relegated hitherto to a secondary status *vis-à-vis* the smaller but richer and better armed Deobandi factions now felt strong enough about its faithfuls.[7] Similarly, Arif Jamal, the author of *Shadow War: The Untold Story of Jihad in Kashmir,* also shared his views. According to him sectarian divisions are deep and different sects would be at each other's throats as soon as this cause goes away. Elaborating on the dynamics among the various sects, particularly the existential threat posed to Barelvi and Shia sects by the petro-dollar inspired Wahhabi and Deobandi schools, he said that the Barelvis had been trying to assert themselves.[8] One expression of Barelvi assertion was the establishment of the Sunni Tehreek in the 1990s. A large number of Dawat-e-Islami cadres – Qadri is allegedly one of them – have been joining the avowedly violent Sunni Tehreek.

However, rising sectarianism has also made inroads into trade and businesses. An Urdu journalist from Karachi, Said Akhter Khan, reports that many sectarian organizations are backed by business houses that fund them and in turn use them against their business rivals.[9] He said that he personally knew leaders of Sunni Tehreek who had admitted as such to him. The Tehreek leaders took a large sum of money from a share company to malign its rival, accusing it of manufacturing shoes carrying the name of Allah on the soles of the shoes. Sipah-e-Sahaba, another Sunni sectarian organization prepared a list of goods manufactured in factories owned by Shia business community. Similarly, Tehreek-i-Jafferia, a Shia sectarian organization, accused some factory owners of blasphemy against their *imam*. Akhter warned that there is a greater trend of such activities in Karachi than elsewhere in the country. And backing by big businesses has played a significant role in nurturing sectarian organizations.[10]

Gen. Zia's project of Islamization also enabled *madrasa*s to proliferate. Given the fact, *madrasa*s in Pakistan have been traditional sources of knowledge, as economic backwardness never allowed the state to modernize and upgrade its educational system. In most of the rural areas basic education is still provided through these *madrasa*s. Due to the prevailing conservative attitude of the system the students of these *madrasa*s often disregard the modern view of the society. On the contrary, it is also true that in the backward areas these *madrasa*s play the role of a welfare institutions. Their system of providing free education often attracts the poor and marginalized classes in order to avail at least basic education. After the end of the Afghan war, the *madrasa*s gained popular support within the society. However, these institutions unfortunately became the instruments of religious and sectarian politics by various political parties and organizations. The condition of these *madrasa*s from the point of view of quality education is also a matter of concern. Therefore, several scholars and religious experts have expressed their opinion for the need of revising *madrasa* curriculum. For instance, Moulana Wahid Khan says that those who are passing out every year from the *madrasa*s do not seem to be able to meet the requisites of preaching Islam. Similarly, a prominent cleric linked to Jamat Ahle Hadees, emphasized that the standards of *madrasa*s are falling. His reasons for the falling standard of *madrasa*s is that the owners of the *madrasa*s keep busy in pulling students towards their own institutions and pay more attention to politics and funds than to education. Even the Shariat Council of Pakistan has recommended that the *madrasa* curriculum needs changes to meet current requirements.

Thus, one can argue that the seeds of extremism were sown by the political establishment itself. Successive regimes used religion to gain legitimacy through incorporating religious values and norms in the political system and institutions. The political vacuum, which had been created due to the lack of pragmatism among the political actors, was filled in by religious forces. Interestingly it is also a fact that despite much religious extremism, religious parties have not won even 10 per cent of the total number of parliamentary seats in any elections except the 2002 elections, which was a doctored one, in the political history of Pakistan.

Conclusion

One can conclude by saying that the project of Islamization has proved counter-productive instead of becoming a binding force. It has not only weakened state power but also fragmented the society itself. Indeed, Gen. Zia was clever enough to exploit the political crises existed at that point of time. He used religion to gain legitimacy and also to destroy support bases of political parties, notably the PPP. Perhaps, Zia tried to institute only those religious norms or legal codes to which he is said to have had allegiance. It was his regime's drawback that it did not pay attention to the aspirations and the faith of other sects within the same religion. Instead of incorporating the needs and aspirations the authoritarian regime tried to impose the norms and values of a single sect. Zia might have not thought that his long-term process, Islamization, based on short-term interests would yield fatal outcomes. The process of Islamization exposed the state to face long term consequences. It is now strongly realized among the political elites in Pakistan that the state seems weak against religious forces. This is also because of the greater network of these forces at the global level. There are certain organizations which have acquired the capability to wage war against the state. In recent developments in the Swat region, Pakistan establishment's decision to declare Sharia law as a governing system was seen as the outcome of a weak state. The state was in a compromising position instead of getting the region out of this condition. Not only this, in all of it the democratic institutions have lost their essence.

Thus, one can argue on the bases of established facts that the rising extremism and sectarian violence is the result of interests of certain groups and classes, who brought and supported the very idea of Islamization. The politics of interest sustain religion as a dominant force. The affiliation of political parties with sectarian groups helps them to gain political benefits. Similarly, business communities also align themselves with ruling elites and religious forces in order to extend and protect their interests. So it is important to discern what is meant by islamization and whose interest it serves largely. Therefore, scholars such as Paul A. Baran argue in the larger context of the Third World that the ruling class in underdeveloped countries spare no energy and receive a greater deal of American support for their efforts to strengthen the sway of religious superstitions over the minds of their starving subjects. This view of the manipulation of religion in the Third World perfectly fits the context of Pakistan.

Notes

1. Hamza Alavi, 'Authoritarianism and Legitimation of State Power in Pakistan', in Subrata Mitra, ed., *The Post-Colonial State in South Asia*, London: Harvester Wheatsheaf, 1990, p. 4.
2. Hassan N. Gardezi, 'The Politics of Religion in Pakistan: Islamic State or Sharia Rule' (web source, http://www.sacw.net/new/Gardezi140403.html)
3. Ibid.
4. Syyed Vali Raza Nasr, *Islamic Leviathan: Islam and the Making of State Power*, New York: Oxford University Press, 2001, p. 134.
5. Gardezi, 'The Politics of Religion in Pakistan: Islamic State or Sharia Rule'.
6. Hamza Alavi, 'Pakistan and Islam: Ethnicity and Ideology', in Fred Halliday and Hamza Alavi, eds., *State and Ideology in Middle East and Pakistan,* London: Macmillan, 1988, p. 80.
7. Anita Joshua, 'Liberal Pakistan Shaken to the Core', *The Hindu*, 15 January 2011.
8. Ibid.
9. Muhammad Amir Rana, *A to Z of Jehadi Organizations in Pakistan*, Lahore: Mashal Publication, 2005, p. 145.
10. Ibid., p. 12.

PAKISTAN, AFGHANISTAN, US AND THE WAR ON TERROR

CHAPTER 15

Pakistan's Afghan Policy

The Dynamics of Continuity and Change

Anwesha Ghosh

Introduction

RELATIONS BETWEEN Pakistan and Afghanistan have essentially remained estranged – despite their shared geography, ethnicity and faith. The only departure perhaps would be the four years of Taliban rule. While the principal historical cause of this has been the unresolved issue of the Durand Line. Tensions and suspicion between Pakistan and Afghanistan have also emanated from their divergent strategic outlook and dissimilar national ethos. It is important to note that Afghanistan was the only country to oppose Pakistan's admission to the United Nations, conditioning its recognition upon the provision that the right of self-determination be given to the people of Pakistan's North West Frontier Province (NWFP).[1] Afghanistan can be seen as a 'hyphen' between the South and Central Asian security networks. With India in the east, Pakistan can ill-afford an irredentist neighbour in the west. Since 1947 both countries have interfered in each other's domestic affairs. The Soviet invasion of Afghanistan gave Pakistan suitable opportunity to wage a proxy war in Afghanistan, garnering the support of Western and Arab allies. Since the end of Cold War, Pakistan has been more conscious and proactive about maintaining her influence and control over Afghanistan, the result being the creation and support of the Taliban.

Post the 9/11 terrorist attacks, Pakistan had to make an uneasy choice of abandoning the Taliban and joining the US-led coalition to destroy al-Qaeda and terrorism. With developments such as al-Qaeda supremo Osama-bin-Laden's killing in the Pakistani heartland and subsequent deterioration in the relations between the two allies, and the American decision to withdraw troops from Afghanistan, it is likely that Afghanistan's neighbours like Pakistan will become more conscious of the benefits of the greatest share of the 'Afghan pie'. This article looks at Pakistan's Afghanistan policy over the years. It also takes into account the converging factors between the two neighbours and tries to analyse whether the future approach of Pakistan towards her western neighbour would be marked by 'continuity' or 'change' from her previous approaches.

Because of the buffer status thrust upon it by the nineteenth century-colonial rivalry between the British and the Czarist empires, known as the 'Great Game', Kabul assiduously avoided the temptation to rely on foreign influence to ensure its survival.[2] Though inextricably tied on the basis of commonalities namely religion (Islam), several ethnic groups (Pashtun and Baloch), thousand miles of border and also a border region that has never come under the control of any government, yet the divergent approaches have been a marked feature in the dealings of these issues. While commenting on one such common factor between the two neighbours, that is the shared faith, Marvin Weinbaum perceptively noted:

> The ideal and rationale of Pakistani state is an Islamic consensus that is expected to transcend geographic and ethnic divisions. [In contrast], the Afghan state has found its legitimacy in satisfying and balancing the interests of competitive ethnic and tribal communities [as a result] the relationship between ethnicity and politics has been virtually reversed from one state to the other.[3]

Dissimilarities in their levels of socio-political structure, socio-economic development, and Pakistan's repeated interference in the internal issues of Afghanistan have contributed in causing irritation in the relation between the two countries. The dynamics of continuity and change have marked Pakistan's interaction with Afghanistan and the character of these ties has been decisively shaped by Islamabad's quest for a friendly regime in Kabul which would allow Pakistan to escape the nightmare of being sandwiched between a hostile India in the east and an irredentist Afghanistan in the west.[4]

Afghanistan-Pakistan Relations in Post-Independence Pakistan

'Few other countries are closer to Pakistan in culture and history than Afghanistan. (Yet), the hope for friendly operation was however, vitiated at the start,' says Abdul Sattar.[5] Since its inception, Pakistan's relations with Afghanistan have been on a low key due to its persistent attempts to influence the course of events in Afghanistan. Two areas – NWFP and Baluchistan have long been complicating Afghanistan's relations with Pakistan. Controversies involving these areas date back to the establishment of the Durand Line in 1893 dividing Pashtun and Baloch tribes living in Afghanistan from those living in what later became Pakistan. The Afghans never accepted the Durand Line. After the British withdrew from the Indian subcontinent and the Pakhtun areas were transferred to Pakistan, Kabul refused to accept it. Afghanistan also rejected the 1947 referendum held in the NWFP as it had not provided Pakhtuns the option to join Afghanistan. Afghanistan's National Assembly in a resolution in 1949 had repudiated all agreements concluded between British India and Afghanistan. Afghanistan's demand for Pakhtunistan and refusal to recognize the Durand Line posed a threat to Pakistan's security on its western borders in the early days.

The deteriorating Pakistan-Afghanistan relations were further fuelled by Pakistan government's proposal of 27 March 1955, to include Pakhtunistan into the new 'One-Unit West Pakistan Province'. The proposed act, which came into force on the midnight of 13-14 October 1955 by the Establishment of West Pakistan (Administration) Order, 1955, led to strong protests in Afghanistan as it never accepted Pakhtun areas as part of Pakistan.[6] In the aftermath of the Pakistan government's action, Afghanistan recalled its minister in Karachi, Sardar Mohammed Atiq Khan Rafiq. The Afghan prime minister, Sardar Mohammed Daud, refuted Pakistan government's action over Radio Kabul on 30 March 1955. He stated that 'the announcement made from Karachi on March 27 (1955) showed that the Government of Pakistan (violated) all international laws and regulations, and without paying any heed to the rights of the people of (Pashtunistan) to decide their own destiny, and without paying any attention. . . , thus annihilating the freedom of their (Pashtun) brothers.'[7] He reiterated Afghanistan's stand on the crisis and remarked, 'I wish to make it clear in the most explicit words to the world that Afghanistan does not at all consider (Pashtunistan) as a part of Pakistan.' Pakistan, he declared, would be responsible for any eventual 'undesirable consequences' which could occur due to this treacherous act.[8] However, the most serious crisis was from 1961 to June 1963, when diplomatic, trade, transit and consular relations between the countries were suspended.

Relations in the Soviet Era

> Afghans are fighting the war for Pakistan. We must support them. American interest has been regenerated because of Afghanistan. Let us cash in on this.
>
> President Zia-ul-Haq[9]

During the 1970s, Pakistan was reeling under the effects of US economic sanctions imposed due to concerns about its nuclear programme. But soon after the 1978 communist coup in Afghanistan, Pakistan found it opportune to get the US to lift its sanctions. High-ranking Pakistani officials urged the US government to forgo its past reservations about Pakistan and pay attention to the threat which the Soviet client regime in Afghanistan posed to US interests in the region.[10] Pakistan at that time tried to position itself as the regional bulwark against communism. From that time, Pakistan's involvement with Afghanistan was focused on training, equipping and planning of operations for the resistance fighters to tie down the Soviet Union.[11] It was during this period that the US and others used this to their advantage in funding, via Pakistan, groups of Mujahideen, or Islamic holy warriors, based in the region that could easily cross back and forth between the two countries. This continued right through the decade-long insurgency against the Soviets in Afghanistan. Later when it became clear that the Soviet Union may leave, Pakistan became more ambitious and worked to have a client regime which would not only give it 'strategic depth' against India but would also help stabilize its volatile western border. In 1988, when the Soviet withdrawal was imminent, the ISI and CIA predicted that the Najibullah regime will crumble quickly.[12] In May 1988, President Zia promised US Congressman Charles Wilson that 'I will give you Jalalabad as a Christmas present, with Hekhmatyar in charge'.[13] In 1989, during Prime Minister Benazir Bhutto's first term in office, US and Pakistan agreed on the plan of a Jalalabad offensive –

to make the city a base for the interim government, but for different reasons. Americans wanted to see humiliated Soviets clinging to their helicopters as this would be a befitting revenge of Vietnam. Pakistan on the other hand saw it as an opportunity for some 'holy warriors' of the defence establishment to conduct a victory parade by entering Kabul as a modern-day Saladin and earning the lofty title of 'Victors of Kabul'.[14] The then ISI Chief, Lt. Gen. Hamid Gul, told the Afghan Cell that the city could be taken in a week 'if the government was prepared to allow for a certain degree of bloodshed'.[15] The irritant of bloodshed was not too significant a factor as it was Afghan blood that was to be shed. Some commanders in the field were furious about ISI's decision of frontal attack on the city and considered it a 'dumb' idea, as it was not wise to lose 10,000 lives.[16] In another commentator's words 'a major Afghan decision was taken by the Pakistanis with no Afghan present, but with the US ambassador looking on'.[17] Therefore it would be fair to say that with Soviet occupation of Afghanistan, Pakistan's foreign policy objectives in its western neighbour became more ambitious. Pakistani leaders became more determined to dominate Afghanistan to neutralize its irredentist claims and transform it into an ally against rival India. President Zia's words were reflective of this:

> We have earned the right to have friendly regime [in Afghanistan]. . . . We took risks as a frontline state, and we won't permit it to be like it was before, with Indian and Soviet influence there and claims on our territory. It will be a real Islamic state, part of a pan-Islamic revival that will one day win over the Muslims in Soviet Union, you will see it.[18]

Buoyed by Pakistan's newly acquired military capabilities and proxy influence in Afghanistan, Chief of Army Staff, General Mirza Aslam Beg (1988-91) created the doctrine of 'strategic depth' against India. This doctrine called for the dispersal in Afghanistan of Pakistan's military assets and personnel well beyond the offensive capabilities of the Indian forces, since Pakistan's geographic width was perceived to be inadequate for a prolonged defense against India.[19] Pakistan's strategic depth in Afghanistan entailed 'sanitizing' the latter of any outside influence in particular that of India and using Afghan territory for Pakistan's unconventional proxy conflict in Kashmir against India.[20] Training camps were established in the Pashtun regions of Afghanistan to prop up Pakistan-sponsored insurgency by groups like Hizb-ul-Mujahideen affiliated to Jamaat-e-Islami.

Many Afghans resented this blatant interference and several commanders were alienated. In October 1990, Afghans blocked the participation of ISI Chief Lt. Gen. Asad Durrani in the *Shura*, a meeting of national commanders, in Kunar. It also opposed the ISI's plan of direct attack on Kabul.[21] By 1994, Pakistan was disgusted with the civil war and disappointed due to constant failure of their main ally Gulbuddin Hekmatyar and his Hezb-i-Islami, and started looking for new 'potential Pashtun proxies in Afghanistan'.[22]

Dynamics during the Taliban Period

The Taliban emerged out of the plans conceived by the ISI, grew through the chaos and anarchy of various brawling Mujahideen groups, was recruited by the Jamiat Ulema-e-Islam led by Maulana Fazlur Rahman from the Afghan refugee camps in NWFP and Baluchistan.[23] The ISI took charge of providing logistic support and broker alliance between General Abdul Rashid Dostum, General Shahnawaz Tanai, former commander Jalaluddin Haqqani and the Taliban.[24] These alliances were vital and provided the Taliban with necessary material and technical edge to defeat its rivals. Close alliance with religious seminaries in Pakistan provided it with the required foot soldiers. The ISI instructed governments in Balochistan and NWFP to ensure that no political activities against the Taliban gain ground. Many anti-Taliban individuals were asked to leave Pakistan to prevent any organized opposition. 'The Taliban were born in Pakistani refugee camps, educated in Pakistani Madrasas and have learnt their fighting skills from mujahideen parties based in Pakistan.'[25] Another view is that Taliban was yet another product of the inventive minds at Pakistan's ISI, a sort of crusading army that would rid Afghanistan of anarchy, rapine and banditry - all real plagues at the time.[26] Cash was used to buy commanders. The first two provinces, Uruzgan and Zabul were taken without firing a shot. Former Pakistani Interior Minister, Major Gen. (Retd) Naseerullah Babar, after years of denying, while addressing a rally in Gujranwala admitted that the student militant group of Taliban was trained by Pakistan's army. Pakistani military ruler Gen. Zia extended his support to Mullah Omar, the founder of Taliban because of his cultural affinity with the latter and he was 'an orthodox Sunni Muslim' himself.[27] Given the fact that Taliban's main benefactor and its leaders were from Pashtun community, most of the Taliban belong to 'Sunni Muslim, predominantly of (Pashtun) origin. The Taliban practice of Islam Puritanism is nurtured in the *madrasas* of the Jamiat-ul-Ulama-e-Islam (JUI) in the northwestern province of Pakistan,' where they received their "military" and "religious education".'[28] Even an apologist for Pakistan like Gen. Kamal Matinuddin had to admit, 'One thing is certain: that without outside agency the Taliban themselves did not have the ability to organize a full-fledged fighting force. The training needed to operate sophisticated military hardware and the logistics required to sustain a conflict for so long were surely beyond the capacity of these new entrants to the battlefield.'[29]

Pakistani writers and journalists have documented the extent of Pakistani influence and material support to the Taliban. Going by Ahmed Rashid, in 1998 the cash-strapped finance ministry of Pakistan authorized Rs. 300 million in salaries for the Taliban administration in Kabul. In 1997-8 Pakistan provided Taliban $30 million in aid. This included 6,00,000 tons of wheat, diesel, petrol and kerosene; fuel was partly paid by Saudi Arabia.[30] In 1998 after the capture of Mazar-e-Sharif, the Taliban had gained control of almost 90 per cent of Afghanistan though the areas controlled by Ahmed Shah Masood remained out of their reach. Thus Pakistan had been among the only three nations which had recognized Taliban. In the midst of the ongoing war, the *Washington Post* portrayed Taliban as the handiwork of Pakistan. It reported in one of its issues, 'Most Taliban members are young Afghan refugees who were enrolled in religious schools in northern Pakistan. Many are ethnic Pashtuns from southern Afghanistan.'[31] Many believe Pakistan was building up the Taliban because Pakistan 'was trying to act as the puppet master in Afghanistan' and as such it 'has furnished money, weapons and logistical support'.[32] Noted Indian security analyst C. Raja Mohan expressed a similar view, 'After the collapse of the Soviet Union, Afghanistan has emerged as critical to the Pakistani political ambitions in Central Asia. The Pakistani strategic dream is to control the trade and transit routes in and out of Central Asia.'[33]

Shift in Pakistan's Afghan Policy post-9/11

After the 9/11 attacks, when the United States decided to confront Osama bin Laden and his Taliban host, Pakistan had to make difficult decisions – either make common cause with Washington in its war against the al-Qaeda network based in Taliban-controlled Afghanistan or persist with its pro-Taliban Afghan policy and as a consequence, suffer international condemnation for guilt by association. President Pervez Musharraf announced on 13 September 2001 that Pakistan would lend its 'unstinted cooperation' to America. He told Washington that his army-led regime would open Pakistani airspace for American air and missile strikes against landlocked Afghanistan, share 'information and intelligence' and offer 'logistical support' to American military force. These decisions marked a paradigm shift in Islamabad's thinking towards the Taliban. Christophe Jaffrelot, analysing the political situation in Pakistan, stated that in the prevailing economic and political environment, Pakistan had no other choice but to swing with the US.[34] Taliban for Pakistan then became a strategic liability rather than an asset.

Following the 2001 US operations in Afghanistan and the resultant fall of the Taliban, Pakistan recognized the transitional administration led by Hamid Karzai and offered significant amount of aid and continued relief to Afghan refugees living in Pakistan. However Afghanistan's administration remains suspicious as Pakistan's past role in supporting the Taliban remains the source of most ill-feeling.[35] Yet Afghanistan has consistently provided Pakistan with evidence of the support that the Taliban enjoys within its territory only to be categorically rebuffed by the Pakistani military regime, which seems to be keeping its Taliban option alive. While such an option becomes viable in the case of the withdrawal of the United States from the region, it also accrues huge military and economic aid from the US for Pakistan's role in the global war on terrorism (GWOT). In fact post-9/11, Pakistan emerged as one of the world's leading recipients of US aid, obtaining more than $2.6 billion in direct US assistance for FY 2002-FY 2005, including $1.1 billion in security-related aid.[36] It was only in 2011, after the Abbottabad 'reality check' that the US decided to cut down on its aid to Pakistan. US-Pakistan relations were in crisis even before the circumstances of the killing of Osama-bin-Laden became known. Amid a rapid unraveling of ties between Washington and Islamabad, the principal architect of the US military partnership with Pakistan, US Joint Chief of Staff Admiral Mike Mullen, has bitterly accused the country of using terrorism as a policy weapon and said it has 'lost the bet' to be a regional player of consequence because of it.[37]

While addressing the Senate in September 2011, Mullen said 'the government of Pakistan, and most especially the Pakistani army and ISI, jeopardizes not only the prospect of US strategic partnership but Pakistan's opportunity to be a respected nation with legitimate regional influence'.[38] But analysts say that the US would continue to lean on Pakistani army operationally and support the civilian government though the relation is expected to remain uneasy amid efforts to avoid a complete breakdown.

While the Taliban remains a constant 'irritant' in the Pakistan-Afghanistan relationship, narco-trafficking and smuggling along their borders also remains a serious problem. Afghanistan has emerged as the world's leading source of opiates, supplying three quarters of the global market in 2003. The UN estimates indicate that nearly 80 per cent of the income from narcotics did not go to the farmers but rather to the traffickers themselves, some of whose profits support armed groups and warlords.[39] In addition to covert state support, armed groups including the Taliban-al Qaeda have relied on a combination of cross-border ethnic ties, the parallel economy, and the drug trade leading to an unending vicious cycle of conflict.

Today, Afghanistan is clearly a part of the dominant conflict in South Asia 'Afghanistan . . . in many ways has replaced Kashmir as the main arena of the still-unsolved struggle between Pakistan and India'.[40] From Pakistan's perspective, its own support for the Taliban government was essentially helpful in two ways. Firstly, it relieved the pressure arising from Afghan-Pakistani border dispute and Pashtun Nationalism and secondly, it helped her gain long-sought 'strategic depth' *vis-à vis* India. Though there are arguments in favour of the refugee crisis unleashed on Pakistan by the Soviet invasion of Afghanistan and the subsequent civil war which were strong factors behind Pakistan. Propping up the Taliban, the more recent academic work in Pakistan indicates that undue attention has been accorded to the 'strategic depth' theory and there is a need to move away from that obsession. However in the post-9/11 era, Pakistan suffered heavy losses on every conceivable field after the exit of Taliban and the entry of Karzai administration, whose foreign policy agenda is pro-Indian and at least rhetorically fixed on conflicts in its relationship with Pakistan.[41] Unstable Afghanistan could mean refugee influx into Pakistan, into Pashtun-dominated FATA (Federally Administered Tribal Areas) and NWFP yet Pakistan's interests were and are so very linked with Afghanistan's instability that it opposed

Indian involvement in Afghanistan from the very beginning. It is not surprising, therefore, that Pakistan sees India's growing influence in Afghanistan as a threat. Pakistan cannot afford a situation when the devil of the Durand Line and other issues will be raised. Conversely, the Indian government's sustained support for perceptibly anti-Pakistani forces in Afghanistan has been interpreted as 'strategic encirclement' by Pakistan.[42] Presently, India is heavily investing in the reconstruction of Afghanistan. To demonstrate its assistance, it is spending millions of dollars in various projects as a goodwill gesture. These developments have caused enough worry for Pakistan despite Karzai's categorization of India as a 'good friend' and that of Pakistan as a 'twin brother . . . we are conjoined twins, there's no separation' in his March 2010 address.[43] Reiterating a similar thought during his last visit to India in October 2011, Karzai mentioned that 'Pakistan is a twin brother, India is a great friend. The agreement we signed with our friend will not affect our brother.' On the same occasion he expressed that 'We have decided not to talk to Taliban...we've decided to talk to Pakistan . . . between countries rather than with organizations or individuals who we cannot find.'[44]

The Unavoidable India Angle

It is often argued by one school of thought that Pakistani actions in the South Asian region are relate to balancing the country's security fears *vis-à-vis* India. Seth Jones has argued that Pakistan government's strategy in Afghanistan has for decades 'been to balance India and keep the foothold in Afghanistan'.[45] Before 9/11, Pakistan supported the Taliban to achieve its strategic objectives in Afghanistan, especially to curb the potentials of India. Militant groups, including Arab mercenaries, were encouraged to operate in Pakistan and set up training camps to train young people for the struggle not only in Afghanistan but also in Kashmir. After 9/11, as a result of intensive pressure from the United States, President Musharraf banned the operation of some of the more militant groups that started appearing on the global list of terrorism. These gestures were not always sincerely pursued though. It is argued that he took such steps because he wanted Pakistan to get back into the mainstream and frustrate Indian eagerness to get Pakistan declared as a terrorist state. He feared that India might seek US assistance to crush the freedom movement in Kashmir. As Matinuddin says, 'He was also concerned about the safety of the strategic assets, which could come under the attack if he refused to cooperate with the United States.'[46] India's lavish assistance programme in Afghanistan post-2001 has been reported to range from helping political candidates (during the 2004 presidential and 2005 parliamentary elections), to construction activities like building the parliament, roads, including in the borders, to giving educational scholarships to Afghan nationals to get education at different levels. These moves have raised Pakistan's concern. Indo-Afghanistan Strategic Partnership Agreement signed in 2011 promises to deepen Pakistan's worries. Pakistan all this while has accused India, particularly since 2003, of using its consulates in Jalalabad, Kandahar and Herat to launch and promote terrorist activities in Pakistan, particularly in the strife-torn province of Baluchistan and FATA.

Report of the European Council for Foreign Relations explains Pakistan's fears 'of encirclement of India'. The report indicates that Delhi's assistance to Afghanistan has been considerable with Indian-donated Tata buses (among many such initiatives) forming an obvious part of Kabul's public transport system. India is also making important contributions to other sectors to make its presence felt in Afghanistan. According to ABC poll conducted in December 2008 and 2009, 74 per cent of the Afghan population held favourable opinions about India, while only 8 per cent held favourable opinions about Pakistan.[47] The president of Afghanistan himself was educated in India and has visited Delhi several times since 2002. But India's support to Kabul is seen in Islamabad – and perhaps more in Pakistani military head-quarter in Rawalpindi – 'as part of a deliberate strategy to encircle Pakistan'.[48]

There have been debates within Pakistan over India's alleged involvement in Baluchistan. Rehman Malik, the Interior Minister, directly accused India and Afghanistan of supporting the Baluch National Army. He also accused Baluch Liberation Army (BLA) of the February 2009 kidnapping of UNHCR official John Solecki, saying the BLA wants to draw world attention to its demands of secession. This accusation came during the investigation into the death of Baluch politicians in the province.[49] Given the long-term India-Pakistan competition, Pakistan now seeks to hobble India's expanding strategic, diplomatic and economic ties with the states of Central Asia and Afghanistan. There are certain very significant converging factors between the relationships shared by the two countries which often overshadow the disgruntlements which the people of Afghanistan might possess towards their next door neighbour.

Converging Factors in Pakistan-Afghanistan Relations

Notwithstanding the issues of Durand Line and Pakhtunistan, there are a number of factors which affect Pakistan-Afghanistan relations in a positive way.[50] These could be termed as converging factors in Pakistan-Afghanistan relations, which have had the centrifugal pull to keep both countries close to each other.

Economic Factor

Being land-locked, Afghanistan, for trade, relies on the port of Karachi for the majority of its imports and exports. This has traditionally been the greatest point of leverage with Pakistani authorities whenever Afghanistan has created trouble on the border, or raised the issue of Pakhtunistan. The Afghan business class has a considerable stake in re-exporting/smuggling items imported through this arrangement back into Pakistan. Moreover, Pakistani currency is freely exchangeable anywhere in Afghanistan. Wheat, edible oil and petroleum products are imported exclusively from Pakistan, and the NWFP government, generally, includes Afghan wheat requirements in its provincial forecasts. Most Afghan men have, traditionally, sought temporary employment in Pakistan during winters, especially in the NWFP.[51]

Refugee Factor

After the Soviet invasion of Afghanistan, 3.5 million refugees entered Pakistan. Despite not being a signatory to the Geneva Convention on Refugees (of 1951), Pakistan was actively involved in the rehabilitation of refugees. The Afghan Refugee Commissionerate was established for the welfare and rehabilitation of the refugees. A huge number of Afghans have grown up in Pakistan, and have been educated in Pakistani schools, colleges and universities.[52]

Religion, Culture and Ethnicity Factors

Traditionally, the Afghan clergy have looked towards the subcontinent for their religious education. The Darul Ulum Haqqania in Akora Khattak, near Nowshera in Pakistan is the alma mater of most Afghani scholars.[53] Religious affinity, strengthened by ethnic bonds, provides the strongest bond between Afghanistan and Pakistan. Pakistanis consider themselves émigrés from Afghanistan, or some other part of Central Asia. The ethnic identity of the major ethnic group, i.e. Pashtuns, is based upon a complex mix of various factors, such as history, language, the commonality of racial stock and traditions. Despite the existence of the Durand Line, there was no government-imposed restriction on movement across the line. Therefore, tribes on both sides still engage in travel and trade. Whereas the majority of Pashtuns find assimilation on either side unproblematic, their orientation has remained strongly towards Pakistan.[54]

Conclusion

The US President Barack Obama's proclamation that US has largely achieved its goals in Afghanistan and his subsequent intention of 'ending the war responsibility' has set in motion a substantial withdrawal of troops in an acknowledgement of the shifting threats and the fast changing politico-economic landscape in war-weary America.[55] The US has admitted the Taliban as being a part of the Afghan nation and concluded that it does not threaten America's 'homeland security' and has stressed on reconciliation with the Taliban and expressed optimism about the peace process. These developments quite evidently have generated new concerns among the regional players with stakes in Afghanistan who have started formulating new strategies in order to establish their respective influences. Going by the past, Pakistan would be exceedingly keen to recover the position which it had lost after the fall of Taliban. Inspite of huge US financial assistance to Pakistan, the country's insecurity has only increased. Pakistanis appear to be more distrustful of the United States than they are of the al-Qaeda.[56] Pakistan's intentions and security perceptions are the crux of her problem. Pakistan has to understand that shutting down militant groups in its territory is in its core national security interests. Until its strategic managers and citizenry alike embrace this belief, Pakistan will not strategically renounce militancy as a tool of foreign policy. The 2008 Mumbai attacks, along with the countless suicide and other attacks within Pakistan itself, demonstrate the capacity of Pakistani militant groups to undermine regional security. Despite the clear danger they pose, there are few facile means to eliminate them. The international community is reluctant to isolate Pakistan over its ongoing support for militant groups, including the Taliban, because it needs continued access to and assistance from Pakistan for the war in Afghanistan. Considering the government within Afghanistan is fragile and Karzai himself is not secure in his space as a result of intense turmoil in the political process within the country, it is likely that Pakistan would again get an opportunity to cast her influence on her western neighbour. It would be interesting to see whether the post-US withdrawal Afghanistan policy of Pakistan would be one of 'change' from what she has maintained in the past or 'continuity' of the same.

Notes

1 S.M. Burke, *Pakistan's Foreign Policy: An Historical Analysis,* Oxford: Oxford University Press, 1991, p. 73.
2 J.N Dixit and Anand Giridharadas, eds., *Afghanistan and 9/11*, New Delhi: Roli Books, 2002, p. 60.
3 Marvin Weinbaum, *Pakistan and Afghanistan: Resistance and Reconstruction*, Lahore: Pak Book Corporation, 1994, p. 1.
4. J.N Dixit and Anand Giridharadas, eds., *Afghanistan and 9/11*, p. 60.
5. Hafeez Malik (ed.), *Pakistan: Founder's Aspirations and Today's Realities,* Karachi: Oxford University Press, 2001, p. 381.
6. 'New West Pakistan', *Asian Recorder*, vol. 1, no. 41, October 1955, p. 458.
7. 'Demonstrations Against Pakistan's One-Unit Move', *Asian Recorder*, vol. 1, no. 13, 1955, p. 137.
8. Ibid.
9. Rizwan Hussain, *Pakistan and the Emergence of Islamic Militancy in Afghanistan*, Hampshire: Ashgate, 2005, p.115.
10. Ahmed Shayeq Qassem, *Afghanistan's Political Stability: A Dream Unrealized*, Hampshire: Ashgate, 2009, p. 81.
11. Arpita Basu Roy, *Contemporary Afghanistan: Conflict and Peace-Building*, New Delhi: Har-Anand, 2010, pp. 114–20.
12. Basu Roy, *Contemporary Afghanistan: Conflict and Peace-Building*, p. 115.
13. Robert D. Kaplan, *Soldiers of God,* New York: Vintage Books, 2001, p. 137.
14. Basu Roy, *Contemporary Afghanistan: Conflict and Peace-Building,* pp. 115–20.
15. Iqbal Akhund, *Trial and Error: The Rise and Eclipse of Benazir Bhutto*, Oxford: Oxford University Press, 2000, p. 92.
16. Kaplan, *Soldiers of God,* p. 254.

17. Dennix Kux, *The United States and Pakistan 1947-2000-Disenchanted Allies*, Karachi: Oxford University Press, 2001, p. 298.
18. Diego Cordovez and Selig Harrison, *Out of Afghanistan: The Inside Story of the Soviet Withdrawal*, New York: Oxford University Press, 1995, p. 92.
19. Hussain, *Pakistan and the Emergence of Islamic Militancy in Afghanistan*, p. 172.
20. Qassem, *Afghanistan's Political Stability: A Dream Unrealised*, p. 81.
21. Barnett R. Rubin, *Fragmentation of Afghanistan: State Formation and Collapse in the International System*, New Haven: Yale University Press, 1995, p. 255.
22. Ahmed Rashid, *Taliban, Militant Islam, Oil and Fundamentalism in Central Asia*, New Haven: Yale University Press, 2000, p. 298.
23. K. Warikoo, *The Afghanistan Crisis: Issues and Perspectives,* New Delhi: Bhavana Books, 2002.
24. Basu Roy, *Contemporary Afghanistan: Conflict and Peace-Building*, pp. 114-20.
25. Rashid, *Taliban, Militant Islam, Oil and Fundamentalism in Central Asia*, p. 186.
26. William Maley, ed., *Fundamentalism Reborn? Afghanistan and the Taliban*, New York: New York University Press, 1998, p. 49.
27. Muntaz Ahmad, 'The Crescent and the Sword: Islam, the Military, and Political Legitimacy in Pakistan, 1977-1985', *Middle East Journal*, vol. 50, no. 3, Summer 1996, p. 374.
28. Ahrari M. Ehsan, 'China, Pakistan and the "Taliban Syndrome",' *Asian Survey*, vol. XL, no. 4, July/August 2000, p. 663.
29. Warikoo, *The Afghanistan Crisis: Issues and Perspectives,* p. 66.
30. Rashid, *Taliban, Militant Islam, Oil and Fundamentalism in Central Asia*, p. 186.
31. 'Pakistan Funded Taliban', *Asian Recorder*, vol. XXXXI, no. 12, 19-25 March 1995.
32. 'Logistic Support', *Asian Recorder*, vol. XXXXI, no. 12, 19-25 March 1995.
33. 'Pak Foray into Afghanistan', *Asian Recorder,* vol. XXXXII, October 1996, p. 259.
34. Mohammad Waseem, 'The Dialectic between Domestic Politics and Foreign Policy', in Christophe Jaffrelot, ed., *Pakistan: Nationalism Without a Nation?,* London: Zed Books, 2002, p. 265.
35. *Afghanistan,* Country Profile 2005, The Economist Intelligence Unit, United Kingdom, 2006.

36. Shanthie Mariet D'sauza, 'The Taliban Factor in Pakistan-Afghanistan Relation', *Institute of Peace and Conflict Studies* (IPCS) website, 6 November 2006. Available on the Internet at http://www.ipcs.org/article/pakistan/the-taliban-factor-in-pakistan-afghanistan-relations-2143.html (accessed on 8 August 2011).
37. 'US Signal Break with Pak over Terror Links', *The Times of India*, 24 September 2011.
38. Ibid.
39. Shanthie Mariet D'sauza, 'The Taliban Factor in Pakistan-Afghanistan Relation'. IPCS website, 6 November 2006. Available on the Internet at http://www.ipcs.org/article/pakistan/the-taliban-factor-in-pakistan-afghanistan-relations-2143.html (accessed on 8 August 2011).
40. Barnett R. Rubin and Ahmad Rashid, 'From Great Game to Grand Bargain: Ending Chaos in Afghanistan', *Foreign Affairs,* vol. 87, no. 6, 2008, pp. 30–4.
41. Barnett R. Rubin and Abubakar Siddique (eds.), 'Resolving the Pakistan-Afghanistan Stalemate', *United States Institute of Peace Special Report,* 2006, p. 176.
42 Barnett R. Rubin and Ahmad Rashid, 'From Great Game to Grand Bargain: Ending Chaos in Afghanistan'. *Foreign Affairs*, vol. 87, no. 6, 2008.
43. Tanvir Ahmed Khan, 'Pakistan-Afghanistan: Towards Mutual Security, Stability and Trade', Working Paper, Institute of Strategic Studies, Islamabad, November 2010. Available on the Internet at http://www.issi.org.pk/old-site/photos/ALL%20SPEECHES%20-%20CONFERENCE%2012-13%20NOV%202010.pdf (accessed on 9 August 2011).
44. 'Karzai Calls off Talks with Taliban', *The Times of India*, 6 October 2011.
45. Seth Jones, 'Pakistan's Dangerous Game', *Survival,* vol. 49, Spring 2007, p. 18.
46. Kamal Matinuddin, 'Post 9/11 Afghanistan', *South Asia Journal*, January-March 2004.
47. Anthony Cordesman, 'Afghan Public Opinion and the Afghan War: Shifts by Region and Province' (Breakout of the data in ABC News Poll, CSIS Report, 10 April 2009), p. 40.
48. Daniel Korski, 'Afghanistan: Europe's Forgotten War', Policy Paper, European Council on Foreign Relations, London, January 2008, p. 26.
49. 'Afghanistan and India behind BLA: Malik', *Dawn,* 23 April 2009.

50. Inam ul Haque, 'Afghanistan Crisis–Challenges', *South Asia*, Research Paper, National Defense College, 2003-4.
51. Ibid.
52. Khawar Hussain, 'Pakistan's Afghanistan Policy', dissertation submitted to Naval Post-Graduate School, California, USA, 2005, p. 61.
53. Hussain, 'Pakistan's Afghanistan Policy', pp. 60-4.
54. Ibid., pp. 69-70.
55. 'Obama Plan: Cut war Spending and Invest More in America', *The Times of India*, 24 June 2011.
56. Christine Fair, 'Time for Sober Realism: Renegotiating Pakistan Relations with US', *Washington Quarterly*, Taylor & Francis Online, 2009.

CHAPTER 16

Pakistan

Islamic Identity, Jihadist Upsurge, and the War on Terror

Yaqoob-Ul-Hassan

Ever since Pakistan has come into existence as an independent entity, it has been in a state of chaos and conflict, often termed as world's first failed nuclear state. The mêlée is between Islamists who claim that Pakistan was founded on the basis of Islam, says that Jinnah, the founder of the nation, never used the word secularism, and those liberals who believe that Pakistan was championed as a modern, democratic, progressive state who often quote Jinnah's 11 August speech. Throughout its troubled history Pakistan has been a state in search of its identity and ideology. According to Zahid Hussain:

> This is in essence the same struggle currently playing out between the radical Islamists spearheading the insurgency and the Pakistani state, and understanding the longer history of this struggle is crucial to understanding why the Islamic military and extremism have gained such momentum, and why they were allowed to rage out of control. It is vital to understanding why the Pakistani state, and more particularly the military and the government, was so quick to welcome the jihadis into the northern territories in the fight against the Soviets, and why the state then threw its support behind the Taliban. And it is vital to understanding why the Musharraf government was so reluctant to take decisive action against the Islamic extremist and militant groups.[1]

In this article, an attempt has been made to examine the role of religion in the creation of Pakistan, the rise of Jihadism and the present unending War on Terror in Pakistan and the mutual interplay among them.

The present crisis of Pakistan is because its founders bothered less to discuss and debate the identity and ideology of Pakistan; as it was created in a very short period of time, from the 1940 Lahore Resolution to its formal creation in 1947. Throughout the Pakistan movement, there never was a uniform vision of Pakistan or the role of Islam. This means that Pakistan was and remains a contesting vision between the liberal and Islamist schools of thought. It was created by the imagined community, 'then Pakistani nationhood was indeed insufficiently imagined'.[2] The most formidable task that confronted its founding fathers was the question of the infant nation's identity. Islam provided a natural anchor to this identity problematique, with all its subsequent and attendant dilemmas. Of late, a scholar of repute, Saadia Toor, has underlined the salience of the latter in her work titled *The State of Islam: Culture and Cold War Politics in Pakistan*. She asserts that the forms of Islam deployed in Pakistan were neither consistent nor permanent as the organizing ideology of the nation-state, and the meaning of religion has been deeply contested, from the Left and from the Right, at every stage of the nation's development.[3] This contrasts to India, which had already worked on the objectives of the new nation for almost half a century before, and had already, laid down the philosophy of how to run a new nation.

Role of Religion

During the British rule three schools of thought emerged among the Muslims; one was the Aligarh tradition which balanced selectively, embracing the Western notion of modernity and religion; the second was the Deobandis, who seek salvation in Islam and reject Western mores as deviation from religious orthodoxy;[4] the third group was, what Hamza Alavi called the Salariat, which later joined the Muslim League for their expediencies.[5] So in order to understand Pakistani polity it is imperative to examine this schism both at the level of the state and society. Since Pakistan's inception as an independent entity, religion has been exploited to boost national cohesion and favourable regional environment. During the demand for the creation of Pakistan, the Muslim League appealed to religious sentiment in order to secure Muslim support. The Indian National Congress secured assistance of 'Nationalist' Muslim clerics organized in the Jamiatul-Ulema-e-Hind to attack Jinnah and other Muslim League leaders. The Muslim League responded by relying on its own theologians.[6] Jinnah assured the religious leaders that Pakistan would follow Islamic laws, which is revealed in a letter written by Jinnah to the Pir of Manki Sharief. In it the Muslim League leader clearly stated in November 1945: 'It is needless to emphasize that the Constituent Assembly which would be predominantly Muslim in its composition would be able to enact laws for Muslims, not inconsistent with the Shariat laws and the Muslim will no longer be obliged to abide by the Un-Islamic laws'.[7]

This was further elaborated by Afzal Iqbal:

> The spectacular victory of the Muslim League in the Punjab elections in 1946 (79 of 86 Muslim seats as against only 2 out of 86 Muslim seats in 1937) can't be understood only in terms of Quaid-i-Azam's charisma. One cannot ignore the use that was made of the religious emotions by the ulema [Islamic scholars], the sajjada nashins [hereditary heads of Sufi shrines] and their supporters.The thrust of their message was simple; those who vote for the Muslim League are Muslims, they will go to Heaven for this good act.Those who vote against the Muslim League are Kafirs[non-believers], they will go to hell after their death.They were to be refused burial in a Muslim cemetery. . . . The Quaid-i-Azam was not unaware of the use of religion in this manner by the Muslim League, although on principle he was opposed to mixing religion with politics. . . . And yet it is the fact that the people of Pakistan talked in the only idiom they knew. Pakistan was to be the laboratory of Islam, the citadel of Islam.[8]

On 14 August 1947, Lord Mountbatten offered Akbar, the Mughal ruler, as the role model for Pakistan, in his speech to the Constituent Assembly of Pakistan, while officially transferring the power to the new state. It was the litmus test for Jinnah's secular credentials which most scholars think the leader had revealed in his 11 August speech to the nation. However, not only did Jinnah revert to his earlier speech but also dismissed Akbar as the role model for the nascent nation; on the contrary, Jinnah chose the Prophet Muhammad (PBUH) as the role model:

> The tolerance and goodwill that great emperor Akbar showed to all non-Muslims is not of recent origin. It dates back thirteen centuries ago when our prophet not only by words but by deeds treated the Jews and Christians, after he had conquered them, with the utmost tolerance

and regard and respect for their faith and beliefs. The whole history of Muslims, wherever they ruled, is replete with those humane and great principles which should be followed and practiced.[9]

Thus Jinnah's speech was unambiguously couched in Islamic terms reflecting the historical, cultural and civilizational ethos of the Indian Muslims, and drawing its inspiration from the Koran and the holy Prophet:

This is the vision of an Islamic society which would be equitable, compassionate and tolerant, and from which mismanagement and inefficiency would be eradicated. Pakistan itself would be based on the high principles laid down by the Prophet in Arabia in the seventh century. Although Jinnah had pointed out the flaws in Western-style democracy, it was still the best system of government available to Muslims.[10]

Although Jinnah was also against the theocratic state, which he revealed in a broadcast to the people of the United States of America recorded in February 1948:

In any case Pakistan is not going to be a theocratic State to be ruled by Priests with a divine mission. We have many non-Muslims – Hindus, Christians and Parsees – but they are all Pakistanis. They will enjoy the same rights and privileges as any other citizens and will play their rightful part in the affairs of Pakistan. [11]

Thus, from the aforesaid passage, it is clear that while Jinnah was not a religious fanatic, he was also not a secularist. His vision of Pakistan was of a democratic, pluralistic and progressive Muslim state.

Jinnah's death created a political vacuum and changed the course of Pakistan's history. His successor Liaquat Ali Khan was the one who brought for the first time religion into politics.

His alliance with the Mullahs produced the 'Objectives Resolution', which declared Pakistan to be an 'Islamic State'. Common perception holds Zia or Bhutto responsible for mixing religion and politics, but it was Liaquat Ali Khan under whose leadership mullahs were given entry into politics and the right to decide the fate of nation.[12]

Thus, after the creation of Pakistan, the Ulema knocked on the door of Pakistan consistently. They managed to get an insertion in the opening sentence of the Objectives Resolution: 'The sovereignty over the whole universe belongs to God Almighty alone, and the authority which he has delegated to the state of Pakistan through its people for being exercised within the limits prescribed by Him is a sacred trust.' For the minorities it was a matter of concern, although they were assured by the moderates in the Constituent Assembly of Pakistan (CAP) that the Objectives Resolution will not find a place in the constitution.[13]

During its early years, Pakistan was confronted with a number of controversies: the Urdu language, Kashmir imbroglio and the identity question. So religion was used for political legitimacy and national integration by both the political and military elites. This unholy nexus between military and mullahs started with the anti-Ahmadi demonstrations in 1953 when serious riots broke out in Lahore. Leading from the front was the founder of Jamaat-i-Islami (Party of Islam) Moulana Mawdudi who was opposed to the creation of Pakistan initially and considered Pakistan as '*na Pakistan*' (impure land).[14] As Lawrence Ziring has asked, 'why the political leadership after Jinnah allowed those heretofore opposed to the Pakistan idea, namely the Muslim clerics, to intrude themselves into the nation's constitution making activities?'[15] The Jamaat-i-Islami was demanding to declare the Ahmadis as non-Muslims. 'Thus the state apparatus used religious groups for a political purpose. The extent of the religious groups' influence and the sentiment unleashed by them could not be controlled. And the Military stepped in to deal with the symptoms of the chaos generated by religious-political agitation, without any effort to deal with its causes.'[16] The lack of quality leadership after the departure of Jinnah could have done much to control and maintain the law and order, but the successors of Jinnah found it an opportunity to exploit this chaos. According to Hassan Abbas:

> In these circumstances the only commonly shared notion of nationhood was Islam. Thus the political leadership of the day was frequently forced to fall back on the slogan of Islam to bring order out of chaos. And here lay the central dilemma of the Pakistan Muslim League and other like-minded parties, a majority of whose leadership in these early years was either secular, or at the very least moderate enough to abhor the prospect of religion being formally inducted into politics. They wanted to appeal to the slogan of Islam to forge national unity and discipline, but they did not want it to go any further than that. But the moment this slogan was out of

the bag, it was up for grabs, and none but the religious parties were better qualified to pick it up and take it to its natural conclusion, that is, the call for an Islamic state with an Islamic constitution.[17]

Thus, when finally the constitution of Pakistan was drafted in 1956, the Objectives Resolution got the place of preamble, Constituent Assembly became the National Assembly and declared Pakistan's official name to be 'Islamic Republic of Pakistan'. Thus Pakistan became the first Muslim country to use religious description in its constitution. Even the powerful military-bureaucracy nexus supported religious sentiments from time to time to counter communism during the entire period of Cold War.

Jihadism

Jihadism is often referred to as another name of Pakistan. Nowadays it is a highly debated but most misinterpreted term both in academic and diplomatic fields. The literal meaning of *jihad* is to '*strive*'. The verbal root means to '*exert effort*'; such effort includes *jihad* by the tongue and even by heart.[18] In the history of the Muslim communities Jihad had acted as a social reality. It was employed against the colonial powers in the service of liberation and acted as an antidote to subjugation. That is why the Western interpretation of Jihad reifies and renders it with violence. The modern interpretation of Jihad which completely identifies it with violence was the contribution of Pakistani theologian Moulana Mawdudi and Sayyid Qutb from Egypt. In contrast to the classical doctrine which referred to *jihad* as struggle with one's self or to bring religion in practice, Mawdudi and Qutb argue that Jihad is an imperative that applies not between Muslims and non-Muslims (Dar-al-Islam and Dar-al-Harb), but also between the Muslims and the so-called Muslims who follow the Western code of life by betraying the percepts of Islamic sovereignty and opening the door to *Jahiliyya* (pre-Islamic period of ignorance).[19] As Roxanne L. Euben has vividly put it:

By reinscribing the cosmic battle between the Abode of Islam and the Abode of War inside the Muslim community, Qutb and Mawdudi represent part of what Emmanuel Sivan characterized as a sea-change in Jihad mythology, a massive inward turning in the postcolonial era. In this sense, then, they marked a significant departure from antecedent doctrine and prevalent practice regarding the scope and purpose of Jihad.[20]

Militant Islamism has its own intellectual history, in which Islamic Jihadism is a recent phenomenon. Jihad has always been intrinsic to Islam. It has been creatively made use of in modern times in various Muslim countries. It has emerged in a systematic way in Egypt as part of the broader Islamic revival spawned by the humiliating defeat of the Arab armies in the 1967 war with Israel. With the revival of Muslim Brotherhood, which President Anwar Sadat exploited and supported in order to suppress communists on the Egyptian streets, the Jihadists demanded that Egypt be transformed into an Islamic state. Sadat resisted and was assassinated in 1981 by the world's largest Jihadist organization. The word Jihadist entered the world's vocabulary.[21] Competing with the rise of the Jihadist movement in Egypt was the evolution of Shia Jihadism in Iran.[22] 'It was not bin Laden who focused jihadist attention on America but rather Ayatollah Khomeni.'[23] Jihadists have a series of demands: ending of US support for Israel, withdrawal from Saudi Arabia, broader American disengagement from the Islamic world.[24]

Jihadism in Pakistan is not a new phenomenon. Providing sanctuary and protection to the religious men from outside who were fighting against the foreign power was always a tradition among the tribals, for example, the shelter given to the followers of Sayyad Ahmad Shaheed Barelvi or the Hindustani Mujahideen in the Ambala war of 1863 against the mighty British Army.[25] According to Sultan-i-Rome:

> In this scenario, the role of Sufi Muhammad, Fazlullah, and other such religious figures or those who advocated armed struggle on religious grounds; gave and provided asylum and sanctuary to foreigners and non-locals; and associated and cooperated with likeminded people from India and Afghanistan or other countries, was neither unique nor a new development or phenomenon.[26]

Jihadism in Pakistan is not confined with any specific class or sect, nor are they limited to one part of the country. There are several kinds of militant groups operating in Pakistan,[27] however the following categorization into three types are based on their allegiance to various Islamic sects or movements, their theatres of operation, the ethnic background of their members and their objectives:[28]

(1) Firstly, the Pakistan Salafist Jihadists who have ethnic links with the Afghan Taliban and popularly represent the Tehrik-e-Taliban Pakistan (TTP). While they sympathize with the Afghan Taliban and consider Mullah Omar as their primary leader, they operate mainly in Pakistan in the areas bordering Afghanistan.
(2) Secondly, there are three main Sunni Deobandi Jihadi groups operating in the rest of Pakistan, with heavy concentration in Punjab and Sindh. The three groups are: Sipah-e-Sahaba Pakistan (SSP), Lashkar-e-Jhangvi (LeJ), and Jaish-e-Moahammad (JeM).
(3) Finally, there is the Lashkar-e-Taiba (LeT), the only major Wahabi/ Ahl-e-Hadith Jihadi outfit which was created during 1989 and 1990 in Afghanistan's Kunar province. It has become increasingly recognized for its attacks in India.[29]

Nevertheless, the above categorizations are not necessarily mutually exclusive, they often overlap in membership, communication help and come to each other's rescue when the need is felt. Later it was Abu Ali Tunisi, an al-Qaeda linked *jihadi* hailing from Tunis, who managed to bring the rebels of four militant groups - Harkatul-Jihad-ul-Islam, Harkat-ul-Mujahideen, Jaish-e-Mohammad, and, Lashkar-e-Jhangvi – under the fold of al-Qaeda.[30]

The Afghan Jihad

The year 1979 saw tumultuous events in the Islamic world – revolution in Iran and Soviet occupation of Afghanistan. Iranian revolution re-shaped and altered the strategic landscape of both the Persian Gulf and the Middle East. In Pakistan the critical change in the role of religion came in the wake of the Iranian revolution and the Soviet invasion of Afghanistan. Pakistan became a proxy battleground between Iran and Saudi Arabia as both wanted to proliferate their own religious influence.

The Soviet invasion of Afghanistan and subsequently the resistance movement was the turning point in world politics in general and Pakistan in particular. The Reagan-Zia collaboration gave a new interpretation to the concept of war that was *jihad,* a holy war, against the godless Soviets. *Jihad* for Gen. Zia no longer remained defensive, it became an offensive war, as Tauqir Hussain vividly put it, 'Thus during

Zia's time was born Pakistan-style Jihadist Islam, spawning a whole generation of militants'.[31]

The Afghan Jihad became the major cause of Pakistan's religious radicalization. The military used the tag of religion and pretending to be an army of Islam, brought new radical revolutionaries and a new breed of military adventurers under its realm. The retired heads of army and ISI were brought back with full control and authority.[32] The Soviet movement became the *intifada* [emphasis added] for the whole Muslim world exploited by the ISI and CIA, who trained and financed the Mujahideen. According to one senior ISI directorate commander at that time, the ISI trained 80,000 fighters from 43 countries.[33]

Mujahideen were also recruited from the madrasas and Afghan refugee camps, where Pakistani mullahs preached Deobandism (a branch of Sunni Islam) in order to provide raw material for the Afghan *jihad*. The *jihad* was also preached in mosques – a call for holy war became a permanent feature of sermons. The Pakistani military which is said to be the only secular institution was also radicalized during Gen. Zia's time. Islamic training and philosophy were made a part of the curriculum at the Command and Staff College.[34] The officers were required to read *The Quranic Concept of War*, a book written by Brigadier S.K. Malik. For promotion an officer was required to be a devout Muslim.

With growing military success of Taliban, its puritanical and fanatical Islamic code of life was highly applauded by their Pakistani godfathers. Many Islamists in Pakistan saw the imposition of Sharia in Afghanistan as somewhat of a 'divine' effort by their fellow believers. As Mariam Abou Zahab has candidly summed up:

> The chickens are coming home to roost: Talibanization has started spreading across the border. The Afghan war has left an indelible imprint on Pakistan's cultural, economic and political life, especially in the tribal areas bordering Afghanistan and even in the adjacent settled districts.[35]

The success of Afghan *jihad* became the inspiration of the young, radical Pakistani Islamists, who wanted to liberate the Muslims all over the world. The Afghan *jihad* privatized the concept of jihad. However the exit of Gen. Zia from the political scene did not end the jihad launched by ISI and military but it was endorsed as a regional policy by both civil and military regimes, both in Kashmir and in supporting

Taliban. The military-*mullah* activization of religiosity as a tool of resistance against Soviet infidels left a drastic impact on Pakistani society in general and Pakhtun and Federal Administrate Tribal Area (FATA) regions in particular:

> For a whole decade, power hungry generals, mullas and politicians kept playing with the fate of innocent Pakhtun Muslims by indoctrinating jihadi philosophy in the youth. With the departure of Soviets from Afghanistan, transnational Islamic revivalism gained momentum and NWFP became a safe hatchery for them. The emergence of the Taliban (Pakhtuns in majority) and their control of Afghanistan was seen, all over NWFP, with unprecedented religious enthusiasm. The Taliban movement of Afghanistan featured the political use of Islamic revivalist ideals in the tribal areas of NWFP and the whole belt converged to host transnational Islamic extremists under the umbrella of Pakistan's military establishment.[36]

During the post-Afghan *jihad*, 10,000 Pakistanis received military training in Afghanistan in order to wage religious wars in Afghanistan, Kashmir (Al Badr-1 and Al Badr-2 in Zawar, Paktia) and in tribal areas of Pakistan where Jamaat-i-Islami and Lashkar-e-Taiba (LeT) members were trained for the Kashmir *jihad*. When Taliban captured Kabul, slogans were chanted in Pakistan by their god fathers, '*Kabul kay Bad Islamabad*' (after Kabul Islamabad).

After 11 September 2001, the US invasion of Afghanistan, there was an influx of Taliban and al-Qaeda militants into FATA that consolidated the extremist control of the region. This further led to the Talibanization of Pakistani society (it also meant Islamization of Pakhtun nationalism).[37]

The largest component of foreign fighters in Afghanistan was not Arabs or Uzbeks, but Pakistanis. According to *Jane's World Armies*, on the eve of 9/11 there were as many as 7,000 Pakistanis fighting in the ranks of the Taliban.[38] Later the anti-American sentiments in the context of Afghanistan, Iraq war, and the issue of Palestine was greatly cultivated and exploited by the religious parties in Pakistan.

Madrasa students provided cannon fodder to the Taliban in its fight first against the various warlords and against the NATO. However, all *madrasas* are not preaching Jihadism; there are about 10-15 per cent of them – which can be easily recognized – that have sectarian and international terrorist links. However, they must not be confused with those that are a normal part of Pakistani life.[39] Thus, it is this small but extremely potent minority that provides a pool of graduates for transnational terrorist networks. The financial backing from Saudi Arabia and other Gulf countries breed the violent jihadi culture (Wahhabism/Salafism) that has eroded Pakistan's South Asian identity of (Sufism) while promoting an '*Arabist Shift*'.[40] As Arshi Saleem has meticulously revealed:

The inherent danger posed by the Islamic groups is that there has been a fundamental shift in their agenda. Simply, there is now a distinction between what can be termed 'Old' and 'New' Islamists in Pakistan. New Islamists (Pakistani Taliban, jihadi organizations, Islamists), who were initially inspired by Mawdudi's Islamic liberation theology and later developed their own interpretations are generally protagonists of Political Islam, that is, they seek to transform politics through religion and religion through politics. They are unlike Old Islamists (traditional Islamic Madaris/ Ulemas/Pirs/ Sufis and mainly Baralvi religious parties) who were accommodated by the secular elites, and thus, avoided political confrontation. Islamist organizations are based mainly in the economically marginalized and socially traditional regions of Pakistan. The new Islamists in Pakistan were to attempt to capture civil society institutions with a view to eventually capture the state.[41]

Moreover, the present recruits for *jihad* are not coming from the madrasas; of course they provide the radical literature, but the modern jihadists came from the elite classes. Even the 11 September hijackers were drawn from the strata of angry professional and Westernized Muslims.[42] According to Zahid Hussain, the new generation of al-Qaeda is strongly committed to the cause of global *jihad* and has acted as a magnet for radicalized Muslims, including a number of American Muslim citizens who have travelled to Pakistan to receive training in al-Qaeda camps for carrying out attacks within the United States.[43]

However, Islamism is not the only source of extremism in Pakistan. On the one side, extremism has gained by better organization or patronage provided by the religious parties. On the other hand, relative inaction of governments to counter them, as well as the apathy of the masses towards their activities has given the extremists a boost.[44] Apart from religion, Islamization, mullahs, and madrasas, there are some other root causes of extremism in Pakistan. The economic disparities within the provinces in Pakistan have resulted in great violence against the state and the citizens of the country. The areas most affected by extremism are mostly backward areas of the country.[45] An Iranian journalist, Gul Jammas Hussain identified economic disparity as a definite reason behind the growing Talibanization in the tribal regions of Pakistan. He identified the in-built feudalism that continues to rule the roost in these areas, 'Pakistan has to uplift its underprivileged areas, which are the main breeding grounds for the militancy. Unemployment, poverty, lack of quality schools, massive corruption, a low standard of living, and the millennia of debilitating feudalism has accelerated the Talibanization of the country.'[46] He further stated:

> One reason why so many people have joined various Taliban groups in the Swat Valley – an area that is home to 1.3 million people with fertile land, orchards, vast plots of timber, and lucrative emerald mines – is that the Taliban have successfully exploited the profound differences between wealthy landlords and their landless tenants. The Taliban seized power from about 50 big landlords who ruled the Swat Valley and then organized the long-suffering peasants into armed bands. The entire landowning clique fled the Valley, and the Taliban offered the economic spoils to the landless peasants of Swat Valley.[47]

War on Terror

After 9/11, the diplomatic costs of Pakistan's *jihadi* strategy started to mount. For Washington terrorism became the top priority and Islamabad's diplomatic notion of the distinction between 'freedom fighters and terrorists' no longer held water. Pakistan was compelled to shun its ties with Taliban. 9/11 put states like Pakistan and Afghanistan in the spotlight. After Pakistan joined the US-led War on Terror, that began with the bombing of Afghanistan in November 2001, the gap between the public's perception and Islamabad's interpretation of terrorism widened. The result has been the erosion of stability and security at all levels including political, social and economic, ethnic and individual – across the country. The prospects of a consensus-based pace remains elusive in Pakistan.[48] After the US-led War on Terror, the Islamist parties, their splinter groups and sympathizers opposed the US attack and occupation of Afghanistan, staging street demonstrations mainly in the North Western Frontier Province (NWFP) now renamed as Khyber Pakhtunkhwa (KP). Initially these groups established the

Afghanistan Jihad Council and later on, they established the Muttahida Majlis-e-Amal (MMA) to contest the general elections in 2002.[49] The MMA government in NWFP (2002-7) maintained a supportive attitude towards the Taliban.[50]

The Afghan and the NATO officials believe that the threat to Afghan stability comes from across the border where the militants are enjoying safe havens, especially in Quetta, from where Taliban *Shura* under Mullah Omar operates. According to one estimate there are 15-20 small, local militant groups in South Waziristan Agency and twelve in North Waziristan, which are not closely coordinating their operations, but have committed themselves to come to each other's rescue if needed, and are highly inspired by the Taliban.[51]

Terrorism poses a grave threat to the stability of Pakistan, but the military is still following a pick and choose approach to countering terrorism; it kills or captures foreign militants, but provides the sanctuary to the Afghan Taliban for '*strategic depth*' in Afghanistan. The doctrine now stands for denying India a foothold in Afghanistan. This became possible only after the dismantling of the Taliban regime, and now there is growing influence of India in Afghanistan, which is investing both in economic and social sectors. Pakistan now treats India as an enemy rather than the Taliban in Afghanistan. US targets al-Qaeda and its allies while Pakistan distinguishes between 'good and bad Taliban'; it targets the 'bad' Taliban because they kill people inside Pakistan through terrorist bombings. It does not target the 'good Taliban' who attack the Americans in Afghanistan.

Pakistan has suffered a lot since it joined the US-led war on terror and began militarily engaging with militants in the tribal areas of Pakistan. During 2010 alone, there were 1,986 terrorist incidents, wherein 478 security personnel and 1,361 civilians lost their lives, while another 1,316 security personnel and 3,744 civilians were injured. Thus, since 9/11, 34,000 Pakistanis have lost their lives. Its economy has suffered a loss of US $43 billion since 2001.[52]

Today FATA is regarded as the epicentre of international terrorist activities, providing safe haven to different international terrorist groups including the al-Qaeda and Islamic Movement of Uzbekistan (IMU). Most of the top militant commanders mushroomed in FATA and NWFP after 9/11.[53]

However, the post-9/11 operations in the tribal areas of Pakistan have been broadly unpopular and characterized as 'Washington's War'. The common people of Pakistan share the perception that there is Indo-US-Israeli nexus in the militancy in FATA and Balochistan as well as the growing incidents of suicidal attacks across Pakistan.[54]

Several factors account for the varied outcomes of operations by Pakistani security forces against foreign and indigenous Islamists, criminals and insurgent groups in FATA and other parts of Pakistan, including NWFP since 2011.

Firstly, Pakistani establishment has never accepted the War on Terror as their own war and have never embraced counter- insurgency doctrinally and operationally.

Secondly, US succeeded in changing Pakistan's Taliban policy but fell short of altering its Afghan policy. There is a growing divergence of interests between Washington and Islamabad *vis-à-vis* the end game in Afghanistan.

Thirdly, the military is reluctant to use force on its own people. Some have accused the government of conducting them at Washington's behest. Defections have been reported within the army itself. Prior to 9/11, the army as an institution was regarded as the only secular institution in the state apparatus. Now the same institution has been infiltrated and that has been demonstrated by the various attacks against military.

Finally, the ruling elite has not been able to integrate economic, social and political instruments into their operations.[55]

Once Pakistani military started operations on the insistence of America in the Tribal areas, religious militias or mujahideen increasingly became violent and manifested itself in the emergence of numerous theatres of militant resistance to successive federal governments.

The aggressive rise of Taliban in NWFP and the country-wide acts of terrorism and sabotage over issues of military operations in the entire FATA and adjacent districts, particularly Swat, were signals of a civil war.[56] Pakistan witnessed bloody episodes of extremist violence. What made them disturbing was that the assailants and suicide bombers came from the tribal areas and hid in the urban centres of the country after carrying out operations.[57] So far, most terrorist attacks in the region from 2002 onwards have been suffered by Pakistan, totaling up to 2,273 followed by Afghanistan (2135).[58] The Lal Masjid episode was the turning point in the definitive rift between *jihadi* groups and the establishment. Before the operation there had been 12 attacks in

Pakistan, while in the first year following the Lal Masjid siege, there had been more than 88 bombings that killed 1,188 people, and wounded 3,209, an average of three people wounded everyday from July 2007 to July 2008.[59] The Lal Masjid siege also prompted the formation of the most notorious alliance of various local militant groups under the loosely affiliated Pakistan Taliban or TTP under the leadership of Beitullah Mehsud.[60] This was the turning point in the rise of terrorism in Pakistan that seems to have no end. The operations against the militant groups have not only failed to stop the attacks, but have led their dramatic escalation. The TTP is said to have representatives from each of the Pakistan's seven tribal agencies and from the settled districts of the FATA. The group's principal aims are threefold:

(1) Uniting disparate pro-Taliban groups active in the FATA and NWFP;
(2) Assisting the Afghan Taliban in its conflict across the international frontier; and
(3) Establishing a Taliban-style political dispensation in Pakistan and perhaps beyond.[61]

The TTP is regressively committed to supporting the *jihad* in Afghanistan and is now committed to Islamist revolution or establishing a Caliphate in Pakistan. Its enforcement of *Sharia* but mixed with the *Pashtunwali* made them popular among the people;

> Taliban tax the drugs trade passing through their territories (because they don't care if Westerners take drugs), they crack down very hard on local drug dealing, thereby earning much credit in the local population and especially from parents. So if the Taliban are bandits, they are often what Max Weber called 'rational bandits' – and rational banditry in his view was the original basis of taxation and the state.[62]

Un-manned Airborne Vessel (UAV) or drones have been used by the US to target suspected terrorists in Pakistan since 2004. No doubt a number of top al-Qaeda operatives along with lesser figures have been killed and many bases and safe havens have also been destroyed. But the success of these drones has come at high human and political costs. According to one estimate, more than 70 strikes between 2006 and 2009 killed around 700 civilians and 14 al-Qaeda leaders, and in July 2009 the Brookings Institution in Washington released a report stating that 10 civilians died in the drone attacks for every militant killed.[63] These drones are counterproductive; they have created more militants than they have killed. This has further led to the growth of anti-Americanism in Pakistan, especially in the tribal areas. The perception that Western forces want to eliminate Pashtuns has now become entrenched following increasing collateral damage caused by the drones.

Thus, there seems to be no end to this ideological war and its impact on Pakistani state both economically, socially and politically. As history has shown terrorism or Jihadism in Pakistan can't be completely eliminated but can be reduced to some extent. It is more than an insurgency or war; it is now a full-fledged ideology and can't be confronted or defeated by force alone, by killing or capturing the Jihadists. But when their ideology is discredited, when their tactics are seen to have failed and when they come to find more promising paths of dignity, respect and opportunities.

Relevance of Religion

Moreover, a clear demarcation has to be drawn between how the Pakistani nation perceives the proper role of Islam and the Taliban who seek to create an extremely conservative theocratic Islamic state. A recent survey conducted by Gallup Pakistan, the affiliate of Gallup International, revealed that 67 per cent wanted Islamization of society, 13 per cent said they believed that there is no need for Islamization, while 20 per cent gave no response. Forty-eight per cent respondents said steps to Islamize the society should be taken one by one, while 31 per cent said steps should be taken at once while 21 per cent gave no response to a question on the process of Islamization.[64]

Thus, it is clear from the above survey that the majority want that the country be governed according to Islamic principles. They want to see *Sharia* or Islamic law play a larger role in their country than it does today. But even the majority of those who favoured a greater role for *Sharia* oppose an increase in Talibanization and support reforming conservative structures dating from the time of General Zia. A joint study conducted in 2008 by the World Public Opinion and the United States Institute of Peace revealed that only 15 per cent want Talibanization of daily life whereas 59 per cent expressed opposition of Talibanization. Majority of the Pakistanis have faith in their version of democracy; interestingly those who wanted a larger role for Islam had an exceptionally strong desire for greater democracy. But the Pakistani people have little faith in the present political institutions, such as prime minister, president or National Assembly.[65]

From the very creation of Pakistan, Islam has been and will remain a central social and political force. Now the question is not whether religion has a role in Pakistani polity, but how it can be channeled as a force for positive change. As Ziad Haider has candidly summed up:

> Whereas once Islam underpinned the state's flawed narrative of nation building and strategic security, non-state actors have hijacked that narrative with an extremist interpretation of Islam for a variety of motives, including the pursuit of a new Islamic order. It is this hijacking of the national Islamic narrative that is the defining feature of Pakistan's current troubles.[66]

An accommodationist posture is required on the part of the state to draw various shades of scriptural interpretations into an integral whole. If this is accomplished, every segment of the Pakistani society will feel that it has a stake in the stability of the system governed by the Islamic ethos. Thus, much depends on focusing on building an inclusive and robust Pakistani state by invoking progressive Islamic values.

However, the contemporary circumstances have forced academia to revisit the philosophical moorings of secularism in the context of non-European societies, particularly in Muslim countries where religion is controlled by the state from above.

> The current backdrop for debates on secularism in both academic circles and in popular political discourse is provided by the anxiety generated by the role of Islam in world politics in the post-Cold War era. The wars in Afghanistan and Iraq, the 'war on terror' and the fear of religion – particularly Islam – as a potentially irrepressible source of violence and disorder in a capitalist world, has sparked new interest in secularism as an ideology of stability.[67]

The strict compartmentalization of the public and the private spheres – the basic tenet of secularism – may not serve as a guide to society. A holistic perspective which integrates human affairs is capable of addressing and finding solutions to a range of dilemmas engulfing the Pakistani society.

Conclusion

In Pakistan, the problem is not Islam, but its polity that is based on the patronage and kinship of various landlords and a few mercantile families. Political parties in Pakistan have amassed provincial or ethnic interests rather than national interests. People have taken recourse to religion when their identity or ideology is perceived to be under threat. From time to time, Pakistani leaders have invoked religion as the sole response to all challenges by ignoring other equally relevant factors.

However, there is a growing realization in the West that if Pakistan is a problem it is also a part of the solution. If Pakistan is destabilized, it will definitely draw the whole region into its vortex. The ramifications on India will be extremely serious. In the context of the precariousness of the Pakistani state, it will be a risky affair for any external power to exert undue pressure on it. The US has to refrain from issuing public rebukes because they are counter-productive. If greater coercion is deemed necessary, it should be applied through greater engagement between the two nations, rather than threatening to cut off assistance or imposing sanctions.

The world community in general and the US in particular in collaboration with Pakistan has to deal with the issues of energy, education, health and basic infrastructure, facilitate trade contacts with US and European markets and assist flow of foreign direct investment into viable projects in Pakistan.

The military as an institution will be central to any political reforms the government pursues and the *ulema*, has to play a great role in defining the contours of state policy by voicing greater assertiveness in Pakistan's political future. Reforming *madrasa* education, tax reforms, judicial reforms and bringing tribal areas under direct control of the centre are prerequisites for any change in Pakistani polity. Under judicial reforms, the traditional, time-tested institution of *Jirga* can be given a constitutional status. The *Jirga* system has been indigenously evolving over a period of time. It's a system with which the whole population is familiar. Such a system may be likened to India's historic institution of Panchayats. It is worth noting here that since 1993, India's Panchayati Raj system has been accorded a constitutional status.[68]

Some progress towards a resolution of the Kashmir conflict could induce Pakistan to scale down its military behemoth. It could potentially reduce the attractiveness of using militancy as an instrument of foreign policy. The US has to take Pakistan into confidence in any resolution of the Afghan imbroglio; if Afghanistan becomes the contested zone for Pakistan and India, we can be certain that the country would return to the 1990s. Any new steps therefore would require the US to do an even tougher job alleviating Pakistan's concerns *vis-à-vis* India in Afghanistan.

Notes

1. Zahid Hussain, *The Scorpion's Tail: The Relentless Rise of Islamic Militants in Pakistan – And How It Threatens the World*, New York: Free Press, 2010, pp. 41-2.
2. Farhat Haq, 'Pakistan: A State for the Muslims or an Islamic State', in Ali Riaz, ed., *Religion and Politics in South Asia*, London: Routledge, 2010, p. 133.
3. Saadia Toor, *The State of Islam: Culture and Cold War Politics in Pakistan*, London: Pluto Press, 2011, p. 252.
4. Ziad Haider, 'Ideologically Adrift', in Maleeha Lodhi, ed., *Pakistan: Beyond the Crisis State*, New Delhi: Rupa, 2011, p. 128.
5. For details, see Hamza Alavi, 'Class and State', in Hassan Gardezi and Jamil Rashid, eds., *Pakistan – The Roots of Dictatorship: The Political Economy of a Praetorian Sate,* London: Zed Press, 1983, pp. 40-93.
6. Husain Haqqani, *Pakistan: Between Mosque and Military*, Lahore: Vanguard, 2005, p. 7.
7. Quoted in Ishteyaq Ahmed, 'Spectre of Islamic Fundamentalism (1947-2007)', in Rajshree Jetly, ed., *Pakistan in Regional and Global Politics*, New Delhi: Routledge, 2009, p. 157.
8. Husain Haqqani, *Pakistan: Between Mosque and Military,* pp. 8-9.
9. Quoted in Akbar Ahmad, 'Why Jinnah Matters', in Maleeha Lodhi, ed., *Pakistan: Beyond the Crisis State*, India: Rupa, 2011, pp. 25-6.
10. Ibid., p. 28.
11. Ibid.
12. Riaz Shahid, 'Reassessing Liaquat Ali Khan's Role', *Daily Times*, Lahore, 15 February 2010.
13. Hassan Abbas, *Pakistan's Drift into Extremism: Allah, the Army and America's War on Terror*, New York: M.E. Sharpe, 2005, p. 20.
14. Ibid., p. 22.
15. Lawrence Ziring, *Pakistan in the Twentieth Century: A Political History*, London: Oxford University Press, 1997, p. 146.

16. Husain Haqqani, *Pakistan: Between Mosque and Military*, pp. 8-9.
17. Hassan Abbas, *Pakistan's Drift into Extremism: Allah, the Army and America's War on Terror*, p. 30.
18. M.A.S. Abdel Haleem, 'Qur'anic "Jihad": A Linguistic and Contextual Analysis', *Journal Of Quranic Studies*, vol. 12, 2010, p. 147.
19. Abul Ala Maududi, *Jihad Fi Sabilillah (Jihad In Islam)*, 'Translated by Khurshid Ahmed' (U.K.I.M. Dawah Centre), pp. 1-23.
20. Roxanne L. Euben, 'Killing (For) Politics: Jihad, Martyrdom, and Political Action', *Political Theory*, vol. 30, no. 1, February 2002, pp. 14-15.
21. Monte Palmer and Princess Palmer, *Islamic Extremism: Causes, Diversity and Challenges*, New Delhi: Cambridge University Press, p. 121.
22. Ibid., p. 124.
23. Ibid., p. 125.
24. Steven Simon, 'The New Terrorism: Securing the Nation Against a Messianic Foe', *The Brookings Review*, vol. 21, no. 1, Winter 2003, p. 21.
25. Sultan-i-Rome, 'Swat: A Critical Analysis', Institute of Peace and Conflict Studies (IPCS), Research Papers, no. 18, January 2009, p. 5.
26. Ibid.
27. For details see, Mohammad Amir Rana, *The Gateway to Terrorism*, London: A New Millennium Publication, 2003.
28. C. Christine Fair, 'Lashkar-e-Tayiba and the Pakistani State', *Survival*, vol. 53, no. 4, August-September 2011, p. 34.
29. Ayesha Siddiqa, 'Jihadism in Pakistan: The Expanding Frontier', *Journal of International Affairs*, Fall/Winter 2009, vol. 63, no. 1, pp. 63-4. And also see, C. Christine Fair, 'Lashkar-e-Tayiba and the Pakistani State', *Survival*, vol. 53, no. 4, August-September 2011, pp. 29-52.
30. Syed Mazar Abbas Zaidi, 'Organizational Profiling of Suicide Terrorism: A Pakistani Case Study', *Defense Studies*, vol. 9, no. 3, September 2009, p. 429.
31. Tauqir Hussain, 'Post-1979 Pakistan: What Went Wrong?', in 'The Islamization of Pakistan, 1997-2009', View Points from *The Middle East Institute Washington* (special edition, 2009), p. 9.
32. Ibid., p. 10.
33. Quoted in Bruce Riedel, 'Armageddon in Islamabad', *The National Interest*, no. 102, July-August 2009, p. 9.
34. Stephen Cohen, *The Pakistan Army*, Lahore: Oxford University Press, 1968, p. 95.

35. Mariam Abou Zahab, 'The Regional Dimension of Sectarian Conflicts', in Christophe Jaffrelot, ed., *Pakistan: Nationalism Without a Nation*? New Delhi: Manohar, 2002, p. 124.
36. Omar Farooq Zain, 'NWFP and the Scourge of Talibanization', *Pakistan Horizon*, vol. 62, no. 4, October 2009, p. 31.
37. Vali Nasr, 'Military Rule, Islamism and Democracy in Pakistan', *Middle East Journal*, vol. 58, no. 2, Spring 2004, p. 205.
38. 'Foreign Pro-Taliban Fighters Inside Afghanistan Pre-hostilities', *Jane's World Armies*, 8 August 2001.
39. 'Pakistan: Madrasas, Extremism and the Military', International Crisis Group, Asia Report No. 36, 29 July 2002, p. 2.
40. Suroosh Irfani, 'Pakistan: Reclaiming The Founding Moment', in 'The Islamization of Pakistan, 1997-2009', View Points from *The Middle East Institute Washington* (special edition, 2009), p. 16.
41. Arshi Saleem Hashmi, 'Pakistan Politics, Religion and Extremism', *Institute of Peace and Conflict Studies (IPCS)* Research Paper, no. 21, May 2009, p. 11.
42. Stephen Cohen, 'The Jihadist Threat to Pakistan', *Washington Quarterly*, vol. 26, no. 3, Summer 2003, p. 11.
43. Zahid Hussain, *The Scorpion's Tail: The Relentless Rise of Islamic Militants in Pakistan – And How It Threatens the World*, p. 81.
44. Shahid M. Amin, *Realism in Politics*, Karachi: Royal Book Co., 2005, p. 303.
45. Shahid Javed Burki, 'Economics and Extremism', *The Dawn,* 5 January 2010.
46. Quoted in Ramtanu Maitra, 'Pakistani Economy at the Midst of an Existential Crisis', *Aakrosh*, vol. 12, no. 44, July 2009, p. 14.
47. Ibid. p. 14.
48. Shabanna Fayyaz, 'Post 9/11 Peace Narratives In Pakistan', *Pakistan Institute of Peace and Security* (*PIPS*), January-March 2009, p. 1.
49. Omar Farooq Zain, 'NWFP and the Scourge of Talibanization', *Pakistan Horizon,* vol. 62, no. 4, October 2009, pp. 32-3.
50. Ibid. p. 33.
51. 'Pakistan's Tribal Areas: Appeasing the Militants', International Crisis Group, Asian Report, no. 125, 11 December 2006, p. 21.
52. Ehsan Mehmad Khan, 'Internal Security Strategy for Pakistan', *PIPS,* January 2011.
53. Maqbool Khar Wazir, 'Geo-Politics of FATA After 9/11', *Islamabad Peace and Research Institute* (*IPRI*), vol. XI, no. 1, Winter 2011, p. 66.
54. Ibid., p. 71.

55. Christine Fair and Seth Jones, 'Pakistan's War Within', *Survival*, vol. 51, no. 6, December 2009-January 2010, pp. 162–3.
56. Omar Farooq Zain, 'NWFP and the Scourge of Talibanization', *Pakistan Horizon*, vol. 62, no. 4, October 2009, pp. 33–4.
57. Ibid., p. 34.
58. Mohammad Fayyaz, 'The Global War on Terror In south Asia', *Pakistan Horizon*, vol. 62, no. 4, October 2009, p. 40.
59. Zahid Hussain, *The Scorpion's Tail: The Relentless Rise of Islamic Militants in Pakistan- and How it Threatens the World*, p. 120.
60. Ibid., p. 121.
61. K. Alan Kronstadt and Kenneth Katzman, 'Islamist Militancy in the Pakistan- Afghanistan Border Region and US Policy', *Congressional Research Service*, 21 November 2008, p. 5.
62. Anatol Lieven, *Pakistan: A Hard Country*, London: Allen Lane, 2011, p. 422.
63. Zahid Hussain, *The Scorpion's Tail: The Relentless Rise of Islamic Militants in Pakistan-and How it Threatens the World*, p. 148.
64. *The Indian Express,* 2 June 2011.
65. For details see, C. Christine Fair, Clay Ramsay and Steve Kull, 'Pakistani Public Opinion on Democracy, Islamist Militancy, and Relations with the U.S.', *A Joint Study of World Public Opinion Org. and the United States,* Institute of Peace, February 2008.
66. Ziad Haider, 'Ideologically Adrift', p. 126.
67. Humeira Iqtidar and David Gilmartin, 'Secularism and the State in Pakistan', in *Modern Asian Studies*, vol. 45, no. 3, 2011, p. 492.
68. Anatol Lieven, *Pakistan: A Hard Country*, p. 92.

CHAPTER 17

War on Terror and Democracy in Pakistan

Ashish Shukla

SEPTEMBER 11 ATTACK was meticulously planned and executed by the al-Qaeda. It was originally aimed to shake three important pillars of American State – World Trade Centre, Pentagon and the White House. After the incident, there was overwhelming support for the United States (US) and condemnations for the terror incident worldwide. US did not take much time to determine that Afghanistan based al-Qaeda, headed by Osama bin Laden, was behind the attack and decided to build an international coalition to fight against terrorism which was later known as the 'coalition of willing'. This very attack on the sole superpower guided a structural change in the international system and subsequently US launched its 'Global War on Terrorism' (GWOT) to eliminate the top al-Qaeda leadership responsible for the event and dismantle the infrastructure of terror worldwide. In the history of international relations, it was the first war of its kind which was declared against a non-state actor – the al-Qaeda and its affiliates. Under severe international pressure and amidst fears of being declared a terrorist state, Pakistan entered into counterterrorism cooperation with the US and made a swift decision to officially abandon its longtime ally the Taliban through which it was trying to secure 'strategic depth' against its arch-rival India.

Gen. Musharraf's decision to side with the US was very calculated, as he knew that Pakistan would not be able to stand in the way of the United States, a wounded bear, which was certain to invade Afghanistan. Gen. Musharraf's calculations were that Pakistan had no choice but to side with the United States because of the three internal weaknesses of Pakistan; first, Pakistan's military was not in a position to defend its territorial integrity against the most powerful state of the international system; second, Pakistan's economy was in a very bad shape and; third, Pakistani society was fragmented and people were not united as a nation, even at the time when Pakistan was isolated internationally for supporting the Taliban and harbouring other terrorist groups as well.[1] Apart from it there were some other factors due to which Pakistan chose to go with the US; first, Pakistan wanted to save its strategic weapons at any cost which were a guarantee against perceived Indian aggression; second, India had already offered its unconditional support to the US which could jeopardize Pakistan's position on Kashmir and; third, Pakistan's already bad economy would have been decimated.[2]

On numerous occasions, Washington has publically acknowledged Pakistan's important role in fighting terrorism and propagated the idea that apart from dealing with terrorism in the region, it also aims to transform Pakistan into an economically sound and politically stable democratic state. However, historical facts, experiences and current American policies, actions, and activities in the region, especially in Pakistan and Afghanistan, tell us a different story. Historical experiences and facts suggest that as far as Pakistan and its democratization process is concerned, the United States has played a less than admirable role. Benazir Bhutto, a two-time prime minister, had occasionally expressed her suspicions that the CIA had been behind General Zia's coup which overthrew her father and later hanged him to death.[3] All these deliberate US approaches toward Pakistan produced grave distortions in the country and rendered Pakistani society even more ungovernable. In 1995, Benazir met Bruce Riedel in the historical Willard Hotel in Washington and during the discussion said that America was an unreliable ally and had not only betrayed democracy in Pakistan but also undermined the efforts of its restoration.[4] Farzana Shaikh argues that in Pakistan, the military plays a key role in determining the question of national interest and is successful in doing so due to the support of external powers, particularly the United States.[5] In public, Washington has always maintained a strong rhetoric about democratic transformation but on the ground it used its economic, military, diplomatic and political power repeatedly in favour of military dictators such as Ayub Khan, Yahya Khan, Zia-ul-Haq, and more recently Pervez Musharraf.

Moonis Ahmar claims that the fact that America maintains close relationship with the military establishment of Pakistan should not be viewed with surprise, as in most of the developing world authoritarian regimes flourish under Washington's patronage.[6] Bruce Riedel has revealed that he had heard all these arguments by various Pakistanis and also conceded that most of these were true.[7] Thus, the revelation by a former CIA officer who had guided four US presidents on South Asian affairs, matters and it exposes the real intentions of Washington – not let democracy flourish in Pakistan.

Pre-2002 Election Scenario

It was on 12 October 1999 that General Musharraf staged a coup against Prime Minister Nawaz Sharif and took power in his hands and declared himself – chief executive, while also made promises to root out corruption and reinvigorate democracy in Pakistan. Washington criticized the move and stressed the need to restore civilian rule as soon as possible.[8] State Department spokesman James P. Rubin said 'we would obviously seek the earliest possible restoration of democracy in Pakistan'.[9] However, within a few months, contrary to the wishes of Washington, Gen. Musharraf removed President Rafiq Tarar and made himself the president of Pakistan. In his autobiography, he has termed his act of grabbing power as 'countercoup' which is highly disputed. He has written that when the news came out that the army chief had deposed Prime Minister Nawaz Sharif, people from all walks of life joined the celebration and distributed sweets in joy because they were fed up with the regime.[10] But this military version of interpretation is only partially true and there were people in Pakistan and abroad who were shocked to hear the news, as they knew that a military government could not be justified over even a least functioning elected democratic regime. It is worthwhile to note that the US had prior knowledge about the deteriorating situation in Pakistan but it did almost nothing to prevent the crisis. The rift between Nawaz Sharif and General Musharraf was created over former's effort to negotiate with India without taking the military on board. General Musharraf was quite clear on the issue and had expressed his resentment over the peace process with India by refusing to attend the welcome ceremony for Atal Behari Vajpayee, the then prime minister of India, who had arrived in Pakistan for the historic Lahore Declaration.[11] The rift intensified when the army launched Kargil Operation without informing Nawaz Sharif, as claimed by Nawaz Sharif himself, while Musharraf says he had briefed the prime minister in this regard. It's still unclear which version is true. Realizing the danger Nawaz Sharif sent his brother Shahbaz Sharif to the US in the summer of 1999. Shahbaz met with Karl Inderfurth, Assistant Secretary of State for South Asia, and Bruce Riedel and delivered the message that Nawaz Sharif was convinced about a military coup in Pakistan by General Musharraf.[12] The reason behind making the US aware of the possible outcome was only to secure the superpower's opposition to any military take over. But unfortunately no substantial steps were taken by the US to avert the crisis and save an elected democratic regime in Pakistan.

In May 2000, Pakistan Supreme Court upheld the coup and justified the removal of Nawaz Sharif. It, however, placed two restrictions on Gen. Musharraf – first, it required him to hold general elections within three years from the time of coup, and second, it asked him not to introduce structural changes in the constitution.[13] Gen. Musharraf obeyed the court's order of conducting elections within the specified time but cleverly bypassed the second restriction with the help of some special provisions.

Military's Manipulation in the 2002 Elections

Gen. Musharraf issued the Legal Framework Order (LFO) hardly two months before the elections, which allowed the president to make necessary laws to facilitate general elections. Under the LFO, in August 2002, Musharraf introduced 29 sweeping constitutional amendments which empowered him as president to dismiss the prime minister and dissolve the National Assembly; in a way he re-established the Eighth Constitutional Amendment. Hardly two weeks before the October 2002 general elections, the US gave $230 million for military spare parts which was indeed an indication that US endorsed the policies of Musharraf.[14] There evolved a popular joke in Pakistan – Mush and Bush have entered in an electoral alliance. Elections of 2002 cannot be considered free and fair because the army had not only manipulated the election process but also controlled the lead-up to the elections. No one was satisfied, except the military, with the elections, including the opposition and the domestic and foreign observers. The European Union (EU) termed the voting as 'deeply flawed', and raised serious questions over the military regime's intentions. The pre-poll rigging and widespread irregularities prompted local and international human rights groups to condemn the entire electoral process.[15]

Despite all these manipulations, election results were quite surprising and to some extent disappointing for both Pakistan's military regime and the US, as no one had expected that religious parties would perform well in the democratic process because historically people had never voted for them. Though PML-Q managed to win 118 seats in the National Assembly, PPP stood second with 81 seats but to everybody's surprise Muttahida Majlis-e-Amal (MMA), an Islamic coalition of six religious parties, emerged as the third largest party with 63 National Assembly seats in its hands. At the provincial level, it formed government in the North West Frontier Province (NWFP), now Khyber Pakhtunkhwa, on its own and a coalition government in Baluchistan. People who had a close eye on Pakistan affairs made it clear that the unprecedented performance of the religious parties was the result of the military regime's effort to marginalize mainstream political parties and barring their main leaders (Benazir Bhutto and Nawaz Sharif) from contesting and campaigning in the election process. The military regime successfully disqualified many mass leaders by making graduate degree mandatory for contesting the elections. This very requirement of a bachelor's degree created controversy and people questioned the relevance of such a provision in the country where only 3 per cent people even today have a bachelor's degree.[16] However, it recognized *madrasa* degrees as equivalent to BA which helped many Islamists contest the election. It also disqualified many people who had been convicted on corruption charges or had abused their power, defaulted on a bank loan or absconded from court proceedings.[17] It also did not lift the ban on political activities until early September and thus mainstream political parties were allowed to campaign only for six weeks before the elections.[18] The National Accountability Bureau (NAB), working under a senior general, was also used to coerce and harass politicians by instituting cases against them and seeking their disqualification through the national accountability courts.[19] Former prime minister Yousaf Raza Gillani was also victimized on the charges of misusing official cars and telephone facilities.

Besides making such arrangements, Musharraf created a new political party – Pakistan Muslim League-Quaid-e-Azam (PML-Q), widely known in Pakistan as King's Party, by clearing its members of charges of corruption. When the army failed to get the desired results, despite all its manipulations, it made a successful attempt to split Benazir Bhutto's PPP. Under intense fear of losing privileges, being involved in court cases, or victimized by NAB, 20 members of the PPP defected and formed a new group called Pakistan People's Party Patriot (PPPP) and later supported King's Party (PML-Q) to get the necessary numbers to form the government.[20] This change of loyalties by the elected members of PPP is an extraordinary example of the military regime's political manoeuvring.[21] Zafarullah Khan Jamali, became the first Balochi prime minister of Pakistan in November 2002 and Gen. Musharraf proudly claimed to the world and Pakistan that he had transferred full executive powers to an elected representative parliament and restored the 1973 constitution, as per the direction of Supreme Court. Thus, the so-called democratic restoration by the 2002 elections had only established, argues Veena Kukreja and M.P. Singh, a 'puppet democracy' through cosmetic 'civilianization' and the General was quite busy concentrating all the powers in his hands and those of the military and intelligence establishments.[22]

Free Hand to Musharraf on Domestic Front

It is now widely accepted that under the dictatorial regime of General Pervez Musharraf, the military acquired the central stage in Pakistan's state structure and polity, more decisively and unashamedly than it had enjoyed in the past.[23] Though various Pakistani governments, especially the military, have always followed the US line, the military regime headed by Musharraf had left all of them behind in appeasing the United States. When Musharraf announced his decision to join the US-led War on Terror, religious right and fundamentalist forces severely criticized him but liberals in Pakistan welcomed the decision and were hopeful for a positive change on both democracy and terrorism fronts. However, later the military dictator disappointed people on both the fronts. Shrewd generals in the army including Musharraf sensed a great opportunity, in the War on Terror, to get rid of all progressive forces and carve out a permanent role for the army in Pakistani polity. Pro-democracy voices in Washington were silenced in the wake of 9/11 events and the al-Qaeda with its affiliates acquired the centrestage in US policies in the South Asian region, more specially Pakistan and Afghanistan. To pursue this important retaliatory goal, Washington sought Pakistan Army's cooperation and eased the pressure to democratize and to rebuild civilian national institutions. The new situation suited both Gen. Musharraf and the army who were, in any way, not ready to give substantial space to the civilian democratic leadership in Pakistan. When Washington found that Gen. Musharraf was ready and more or less delivering on the promise of fighting against al-Qaeda terrorists, no one from Washington raised the issue of democracy with the dictator. Ahmed Rashid has claimed that some of the officials at the State Department, the Pentagon, and the National Security Council told him that Gen. Musharraf was indispensible for the US and in fact the White House had no desire to see the return of civilian leadership at the helm of affairs.[24]

How ironical had been the policies of Bush administration with regard to Pakistan is evident from the fact that soon after 9/11, the US administration started making arguments that global Islamic *jihad* was the product of the repressive authoritarian societies in the Islamic world and propagated the idea of promoting democracy in order to get rid of such kind of problems, but followed an exceptionally different policy in the case of Pakistan. In June 2002, in a commencement speech at West Point, Bush called for 'the rule of law, limits on the power of the state, free speech and equal justice . . . across the Islamic world.'[25] Again in January 2005 in his State of the Union address, he outlined his policy of establishing democracy in the Middle East and emphasized that the way forward to human rule in the region lay through democracy.[26] However, the problem, argues Bruce Riedel, was that Bush had no desire of pushing his new friend General Musharraf to follow his freedom and democracy agenda and he did very little to push the general to restore democracy.[27] Gen. Musharraf found the situation in his favour and moved for a reshuffle in the army, to tighten his grip on the institution, and promoted 27 officers to the rank of major general, organized local body elections, extended his term for the next five years with a fraudulent referendum, and later manipulated the election process and ultimately managed to secure a razor thin majority for the PML-Q in the parliament. He even tried to silence the media, which was becoming critical of his regime and policies, and other vocal people by promulgating the Defamation Ordinance 2002.

American Aid to Pakistan

Pakistan, since very early, has been the recipient of US aid which started in 1951 in the form of bilateral aid. However, the aid has been intermittent and heavily dependent on US interests in the region and Pakistan's behaviour. When it agreed to follow the line, as per Washington's desire, US became generous in providing economic and military aid to Pakistan. However, the moment the US realized that it had fulfilled its objectives and did not need to take Pakistan on board anymore, it abandoned the country and in some cases also imposed sanctions on it. For example, at the time of USSR's invasion of Afghanistan, the US sought Pakistan's help to counter the communist threat but soon after achieving the objective of defeating the Soviets through proxy war, left Pakistan alone to bear the brunt. Almost a decade later, in the wake of 9/11 events, Washington felt that for the successful execution of the War on Terror Pakistan's cooperation was necessary. This time US militarily threatened and diplomatically pressurized Pakistan to join the War on Terror as a frontline ally. Pakistan had no option but to concede US demands which paved the way for the removal of all US sanctions of the preceding decade including one that required stopping aid to countries where a military coup had replaced a civilian regime.[28] After receiving directions from the administration, the United States Agency for International Development (USAID) sought to engage Pakistan and reopened a mission in 2002 to help stabilize the country and initiated various programmes to address the issues of poverty, education, and health.[29] The *Times of India* reported on 23 February 2010 that in the post-9/11 period Pakistan received around $ 18 billion as aid from the US of which $11.5 billion was given as military assistance.[30] Shuja Nawaj also claims that since 2001, the US has provided Pakistan a sum of $13 billion in military aid and $6.6 billion in economic assistance, with more to come.[31] These economic assistances were widely reported in the Western media which attempted to make people believe that the US was helping Pakistan stabilize.

Indeed the post-9/11 US assistance to Pakistan was not intended to transform the nature of Pakistani state or society or strengthen Pakistan's internal stability but was a 'thank you' to Musharraf's military regime for its role in the OEF.[32] This was the reason behind 9/11 commission members' observation that US assistance had not 'moved sufficiently beyond security assistance to include significant funding for education efforts'. It is quite ironical that a state which publically claims to have intentions of democracy promotion and empowering people in another state, provides massive amount of aid to strengthen the military not the civilian institutions. Azeem Ibrahim, in a Discussion Paper titled 'U.S. Aid to Pakistan: U.S. Taxpayers Have Funded Pakistani Corruption', argues that of the aid which US provided to Pakistan in the post-9/11 period, only 10 per cent was actually meant for development programmes.[33] Shah, a 71-year-old man, says about US and its aid to Pakistan that 'everyone here hates the American Government' and 'I haven't seen a penny of this US assistance'.[34] Tariq Fatemi, former Pakistani ambassador to the US, has also questioned US aid policy toward Pakistan and asked 'How many dams were built? How many highways? Can you touch anything that was built with US assistance?'[35]

Enhanced Partnership Act 2009

Enhanced Partnership Act 2009 is better known as Kerry Lugar Berman Act or Peace Act which was passed by the US Congress and signed by President Obama in November 2009. The stated objective of the act is to help civilian regime with financial assistance that will be used to empower people and to develop civilian infrastructure such as building schools, roads, hospitals, reforming police service, improving services in education and health sector and delivering better services to the people of Pakistan. Ishtiaq Ahmad argues that the $7.5 billion civilian aid under the Kerry Lugar Act is a tangible manifestation of the broad support for Pakistan.[36] Apart from it, there is a democracy bonus of $1 billion every year if the president of the US certifies to the Congress that Pakistan is a democracy.[37] Though the initial commitment is only for five years, there is a 'performance clause' in the act which states that the aid may be extended for another five years if Pakistan's performance and atmosphere is satisfactory. It will provide Pakistan's democratic regime $1.5 billion annually. But it is not as easy as it looks. It places certain conditions on Pakistan which requires a certification from the US Secretary of State under the direction of the president that Pakistan is honestly fulfilling the conditions attached with. The act requires that Pakistan military and intelligence agencies ensure their honest participation in fighting the al-Qaeda, Taliban, and other terrorist groups that threaten international forces in Afghanistan from their bases in the tribal areas of Pakistan. It also requires the military and intelligence agencies to work for the consolidation of democratic rule and maintenance of law and order in Pakistan. It makes it clear that aid will flow only if conditions are met and the US president asks the Secretary of State to give a certificate in this regard.

These conditionalities generated a controversy in Pakistan and people in the country accused the US of micromanaging the state's internal affairs. Pakistan army, the most powerful institution in the country, criticized the bill by expressing 'serious concerns' over some of the provisions and pressurized the civilian government to seek a review. In the wake of criticism from the army, the Pakistani government made it clear that the legislation was not an ideal document and was not binding on Pakistan. Yousaf Raza Gillani, the then prime minister, informed the media that the Kerry-Lugar Bill's conditions were not binding on Pakistan and that the government would seek to forge consensus on the issue among political parties and all stakeholders.[38] Responding to the critics of Kerry-Lugar Bill, Salman Taseer, the former Punjab governor, had said, 'It does not interfere with Pakistan's economic programme or development schemes rather it is directed towards investing in the vital social sector and human beings. It is a poverty alleviation programme'.[39] In the end a joint explanatory Congressional Statement clarified that the legislation 'does not seek in any way to compromise Pakistan's sovereignty, impinge on Pakistan's national security interests, or micromanage any aspect of Pakistani military or civilian operations'.[40]

Thus, it was a timely, important and welcome move on the part of the United States to strengthen the civilian regime in Pakistan but let's not forget that the aid is meant for civilian purposes but conditions have been imposed on the performance of military and intelligence agencies. It is ironical that you are giving aid for a civilian purpose and have linked it with the performance of military and intelligence agencies. It cannot be guaranteed that military and intelligence agencies will play their part honestly in the coming years and the flow of aid will continue. Osama-bin-Laden was killed in an unilateral American operation in Abbotabad, half a kilometre away from Pakistan Military Academy (PMA), Kakul. No one is ready to accept that the military and intelligence top brass did not know about Laden's hiding at such a place which is very close to the military academy. It shows that the US has not been receiving full cooperation of the Pakistani military and spy agencies which may create problems in the successful implementation of the Kerry-Lugar Bill. It would have been better for both Pakistan and US if such conditions are attached with military aid and assistance.

Judicial Crisis and Imposition of Emergency

Judges of Pakistan's Supreme Court are usually considered conservative because of their act of justifying every military coup in Pakistan under 'doctrine of necessity' and they never stood up firmly against any military dictator. For the first time in the history of Pakistan, in 2007, Chief Justice (CJ) Iftikhar Mohammad Chaudhry not only refused to bow against the will of a dictator but also showed courage to fight him directly in the public and in full glare of the national and international media. This all happened because of Musharraf's unilateral and authoritarian rule and policies which he was pursuing either for gaining more legitimacy in the eyes of people at home and abroad or eliminating his political rivals and critics for strengthening his hold on Pakistani politics. After becoming a frontline ally of the US, the Musharraf regime, under the garb of War on Terror, started a brutal crackdown on its domestic critics including political opponents, members of Sindhi and Baloch nationalities.[41] Hundreds of people were falsely linked to the terrorist activities and were detained by the security agencies at undisclosed locations, denied access to lawyers, families and courts, and in some cases subjected to inhuman torture also. The Human Rights Commission of Pakistan (HRCP) had estimated that the military regime had abducted at least 400 critics of Musharraf government and detained them without filing any charges.[42] The Supreme Court under Chief Justice Iftikhar Mohammad Chaudhry took serious notice of such cases and started regular hearings and ordered government officials to appear in the court and give clarification regarding the disappearances. In early October 2007 the CJ made it apparent that he will summon the heads of the intelligence agencies to testify and take legal actions against them if needed.[43] This brought him in direct conflict with the military establishment and resulted in his suspension on 9 March 2007. This led to a severe political crisis in the country and provoked countrywide protests from lawyers who were later joined by members of civil society. In July, he was reinstated by the Supreme Court.

On 3 November 2007, fearing of the court's ruling in coming days over his eligibility for presidential election and on the issue of holding two powerful posts, Musharraf proclaimed a state of emergency. Under the emergency rule, he sent the entire judiciary home and brought several amendments to the constitution. The majority of people were against the emergency and 67 per cent of people expressed their anger against Musharraf.[44] The president unsuccessfully attempted to explain his decision of imposing emergency by charging that the SC was 'working at cross purposes with the Executive and the Legislative in the fight against terrorism' but the people were not convinced with his explanation. Though the cases that were put up before the SC or on which SC took *suo motu* actions were deliberate acts of Pakistani establishment, especially the military and intelligence agencies, they did not give a clean chit to its partners engaged in the War on Terror. Amnesty International report claimed that Pakistan's foreign allies, mainly the US and the UK, actually encouraged, condoned or acquiesced in grave violations of human rights[45] and these allies who pretend to be the promoters and facilitators of democracy, freedom, justice and human rights worldwide, intentionally did not put pressure on the military to observe restraints in this regard. Several individuals who were victims of such acts and somehow survived enforced disappearance in Pakistan and were released from detention later revealed that they were being interrogated by foreign intelligence personnels.[46] The report, which made it apparent that Pakistani state was severely indulged in gross violation of human rights and was behind several disappearances in the country, was not true in the eyes of both the military establishment of Pakistan and US officials who insisted that the acts of intelligence agencies were part of ongoing intelligence cooperation. Former US Undersecretary of State Nicholas Burns visited Pakistan in 2006 and was confronted by the HRCP with the evidences of human rights violations by the Musharraf regime, which was using US-supplied aircrafts and other equipment on Baloch people and sought US intervention in the matter.[47] But Burns rejected the HRCP's pleas for the US intervention by saying that US would not 'meddle in Pakistan's internal affairs'. It makes clear enough about the US' real intention and role in democracy promotion in Pakistan.

Benazir-Musharraf Deal

When Washington realized that Gen. Musharraf is losing his grip on power in Pakistan, it tried hard to secure him and secretly worked out the modalities of a prospective deal between the dictator and the self-exiled former Pakistani Prime Minister Benazir Bhutto. John Negroponte, former US permanent representative to the UN and an experienced Indian Foreign Service officer, was tasked to mediate in the 'arranged marriage' between the two.[48] Initially Gen. Musharraf was reluctant to negotiate with his political foe but under severe pressure from the United States and Britain he agreed to hold secret talks with Benazir in a third country. With positive encouragement and assurances from the United States of expected outcome both the leaders secretly met in Dubai to see if they could meet the expectations of each other. And at the end of the meeting both realized that there were strong possibilities of a deal that would be in the interest of the people of Pakistan and democracy in the country. In the meeting Gen. Musharraf agreed to quit from the post of COAS and also accepted her other demands including dropping corruption charges on her and her husband, while in return Benazir reluctantly agreed not to come to Pakistan before elections.[49] In order to concretize the process of negotiations, on 4 September 2007, PPP leader Benazir Bhutto and emissaries of Gen. Musharraf met in Dubai to discuss terms and conditions of a power sharing agreement between her and Musharraf which was confirmed by Tariq Azeem, then Minister of State for Information, who said that in the meeting three most contested issues were discussed; first, resignation of Gen. Musharraf from the post of COAS before his re-election; second, constitutional amendment to deprive the president of the power to dissolve the National Assembly; and, third, lifting the ban on becoming third-time prime minister.[50]

Though both the leaders were sceptical of each other, finally they entered into a power sharing deal in 2007. Later, contrary to the agreement, Benazir decided to return to Pakistan before the scheduled elections. Gen. Musharraf granted, through a presidential ordinance only on the eve of her return, Benazir and other opponents amnesty from all pending corruption cases.[51] Till the last moment, Musharraf unsuccessfully tried to persuade her not to return to Pakistan before elections and in the end even warned Benazir that her security was based on the status of her relationship with him. It was a crucial and tough time for Benazir. To ensure her physical survival Benazir approached the United States to intervene and ensure her security on the ground in Pakistan. She met John Kerry, Chairman of Senate Foreign Relations Committee, and urged him to press her request that United States guarantee her safety in Pakistan. She even approached Vice-President Dick Cheney in this regard and requested him to call Gen. Musharraf to provide her full protection. But she failed to get her request accepted on both the occasions.[52] Despite the danger of being killed, she reached Karachi airport and made her first phone call to US Ambassador to Pakistan Anne Peterson and complained that she was not satisfied with the security arrangements.[53] However, no special arrangements were made and she luckily escaped unhurt when her vehicle was targeted by two bombs. Assassin succeeded on 27 December in the second attempt when she was about to leave Liaquat Bagh (Rawalpindi) after a successful election rally.

The assassination of Benazir Bhutto was a tragic incident for both Pakistan and democracy. A United Nations (UN) enquiry later found that Gen. Musharraf had not made appropriate arrangements to protect Benazir and that was the reason for her assassination. The UN report stated that 'Ms Bhutto's assassination could have been prevented if adequate security measures had been taken.' It also stated that the federal government was fully aware of the threat but did little more than passing the information to her.[54] One thing which the UN report did not cover is that the assassination could have been averted if the US had considered Benazir's repeated requests for her safety and guaranteed her security. Wikileaks later made some secret cables public which reveal that Benazir Bhutto even requested the US, after a suicide attack on 18 October 2007, to provide security but the US refused to accept her demand by saying that it would not be good for her political interests, as people would see her being protected by US security guards.[55]

2008 General Elections

General elections of 2008 were a major test for Pakistan and the future prospects of democracy in the country because these elections were held at a time when people were politically charged due to the assassination of Benazir Bhutto. Though, there was a popular resentment against Gen. Musharraf's despotic rule, the political parties were fragmented and there were different issues in the election manifestos of the parties. The PPP under Asif Ali Zardari's leadership was using the slogan of 'Pakistan Khappay' while Nawaz Sharif's PML-N was more concerned with the restoration of judges. There were also some very common and important issues like dealing with radical extremism, constitutional changes made by Gen. Musharraf, disputed War on Terror and nuclear issues but the parties had different perceptions and approaches as well.[56] This was making the situation more complicated and tensions were growing day by day before the scheduled date of the elections and people feared violence and large-scale rigging. But at the end various national and international observers conceded that the elections were relatively free and fair.

It was a watershed in the history of Pakistan which produced a peaceful transition of power. Election results were a serious blow to the Mush-Bush alliance. The PPP emerged as the single largest party with 120 seats closely followed by the PML-N with 90 seats; King's Party the PML-Q got only 51 seats which was followed by the MQM with 25 seats and Awami National Party with 13 seats. Though the people of Pakistan did not give any single party the mandate to rule over them they unanimously rejected Musharraf's policies and agendas. Ignoring popular resentment against Gen. Musharraf, Condoleezza Rice, the then US Secretary of State, came out in support of Musharraf and said that 'Musharraf is the president of the country and the US would continue to deal with him and pursue its interests for a stable and democratic state'.[57] In the days after the declaration of results foreign envoys including those from the US, the UK and France held a flurry of meetings with key players who were supposed to run the country soon such as Asif Ali Zardari and Nawaz Sharif, and requested both the leaders not to impeach Musharraf for the suspension of judiciary.[58] These attempts were made amid demands for Musharraf's resignation on moral grounds, which makes it amply clear that the US administration wanted Gen. Musharraf at the helm of affairs for an indefinite period.

Formation of a Coalition Government

Soon after the declaration of election results, pragmatism prevailed over the usual enmity of PPP and PML-N and leaders of both the parties buried their longstanding differences and stood together to form a coalition government for the sake of the future of democracy in the country and to keep Gen. Musharraf out. It was not an easy task for them to oust Gen. Musharraf from the presidential seat because the US was making attempts to retain him at the helm of affairs and Musharraf himself was busy creating hurdles in the formation of a new civilian government by the forces hostile to him. It was a time when the political atmosphere was completely against Musharraf and at this crucial point the military, led by General Kayani was not ready to stand firmly behind him. Nawaz Sharif was pushing for the impeachment of the dictator while Zardari was hesitant but pressure from the PML-N was such that it appeared that he would not be able to handle the pressure for a long time. Gen. Musharraf sensed the situation at the right time and in an emotional, though pre-recorded, televised speech to the nation stepped down from the office of the president.

Future of Democracy

Frederic Grare claims that though Pakistan is not a military dictatorship since 2008, it is also not a democracy, instead it is still a 'praetorian state with only a democratic façade'.[59] Predicting anything about Pakistan has always been a difficult task but it seems that the future of democracy in the country still remains fraught with danger. There are a number of issues that have made the situation complex for democracy, such as rising Islamic militancy, deepening of poverty, economic fragility, and anti-government feelings. Pakistan's dependence on US for economic assistance is another problematic issue because without such assistance it would be difficult for the civilian regime to cope with the problems that are persistent at the moment. But one cannot forget that US assistance comes with certain hidden conditions that sometimes create unfavourable atmosphere for the civilian regime at home. If we compare US drone attacks in military and civilian regimes, we'll be able to find that the CIA more vigorously pursued the policy of targeting militants through UAVs under the democratic regime (see Fig. 17.1). Drone attacks in Pakistan started in 2004 under the Musharraf regime, and there were only ten such attacks till 2007. But these attacks dramatically rose to 35 in 2008, in post-Musharraf period, 53 in 2009, and 117 in 2010 and more than 20 attacks have been reported in the first quarter of 2011.[60] What does all this mean? It means that when Musharraf was in power, the US was more comfortable with Pakistan and targeted

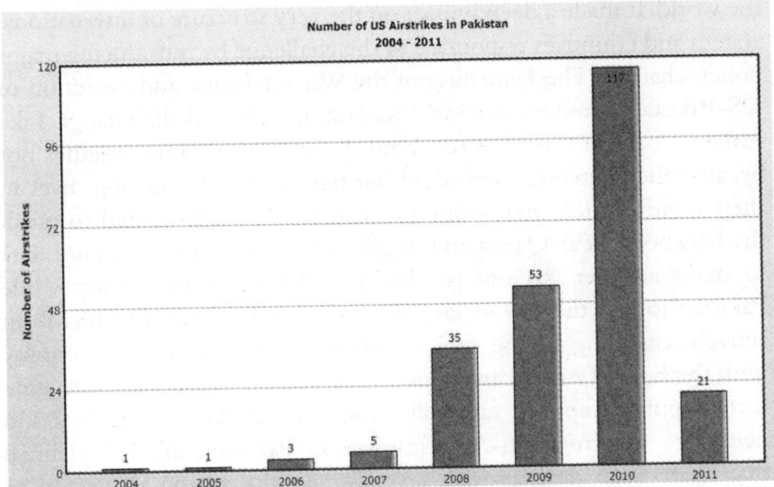

Source: http://www.longwarjournal.org/pakistan-strikes.php

FIG. 1: DRONE ATTACKS INSIDE PAKISTAN

militants by UAVs only occasionally but with his departure from the scene it lost the greater leverage on Pakistan and intensified its drone attacks to target militants. This breaching of Pakistani sovereignty by a foreign power has a negative impact on the legitimacy of civilian government in Pakistan. Recently the US Navy SEALs conducted a unilateral operation to kill Osama-bin-Laden which was broadly criticized by Pakistanis on the ground of violating sovereignty. Ashley Tellis, an American expert on South Asian affairs and senior associate at the Carnegie Endowment for International Peace, has recently argued that in the changed circumstances for maintaining its credibility, the Pakistan Army is trying to overthrow the elected civilian regime.[61] Given the situation, it can be said that though there is a civilian regime at the helm of affairs only time will tell how long it'll continue.

Conclusion

The September 11 attack on the US was a landmark event in the history of international relations when al-Qaeda under the leadership of Osama-bin-Laden successfully executed a terrorist attack deep inside America and in a way challenged the supremacy of American power in the world. It made a deep impact on the very structure of international system and countries responded to the challenge by introducing major policy changes. The launching of the War on Terror and evolution of US-Pakistan counterterrorism cooperation reflected the change. Like earlier occasions this time too both the countries came together not because their interests converged but both had different objectives in their minds which they wanted to fructify. The US wanted to break the backbone of al-Qaeda and its affiliates so that they could not dare to make another attempt to challenge American hegemony, while Pakistan joined the US to save its nuclear weapons, oust India from actively engaging in the region and to revive the fragile economy with the help of American economic assistance. In order to gain some sort of public support, especially from the liberal constituency, and neutralize growing anti-Americanism in Pakistan, the US claimed that apart from dealing with terrorism in the region it wanted to transform Pakistan into an economically sound and politically stable democratic state. However, it did not take substantial steps to support its rhetoric. Instead the US privately encouraged Gen. Musharraf and made him believe that as long as he appeared to be cooperating in killing al-Qaeda terrorists Washington would give a free hand to him on domestic affairs. General Musharraf exploited the opportunity in the form of War on Terror and left no stone unturned to consolidate his own and army's position in Pakistani polity. Under the garb of War on Terror the Pakistani army launched a brutal crackdown on the domestic critics and political rivals of Musharraf. It not only falsely linked a number of people in terrorism but also detained around 400 people at undisclosed locations and subjected them to inhuman torture. Pakistan's Western allies including the US and UK, instead of putting pressure on Musharraf, actually encouraged, condoned or acquiesced in grave violations of human rights which later led to a severe judicial crisis and imposition of emergency in the country.

In the wake of protests against Musharraf and his government, the US realized that the general was losing his grip on power and needed outside backup to sustain his presidency. At this crucial juncture Washington secretly worked out a possible deal between Gen. Musharraf and Benazir Bhutto which was aimed to make Benazir the prime minister in return for her support to Musharraf's presidency. However, things did not go according to plan and the situation changed dramatically when Benazir returned to Pakistan before the scheduled elections and got killed in Rawalpindi after addressing a successful election rally. The UN report on Benazir's assassination later made it amply clear that the Pakistani government had not made adequate security arrangements and that was the reason she got killed. The elections of 2008, which took place in a politically charged atmosphere, made it amply clear that Musharraf would no longer be able to sustain his position. This time again, it were US officials who requested the major political parties that were to form the new government, not to impeach Musharraf for his previous acts and facilitated Musharraf's safe exit from Pakistan. Thus, in a nutshell, there are enough evidences to claim that the War on Terror and subsequent American policies negatively affected the democratization process of Pakistan.

Notes

1. Pervez Musharraf, *In the Line of Fire: A Memoir*, London: Simon & Schuster, 2006, p. 202.
2. Ibid.
3. Benazir Bhutto, *Daughter of the East: An Autobiography*, London: Hamish Hamilton, 1988, pp. 76-8.
4. Bruce Riedel, *Deadly Embrace: Pakistan, America, and the Future of Global Jihad*, Noida: HarperCollins, 2011, p. 37.
5. Realist school has been dominating the discourse in world politics since very early and emphasizes that decisions related to foreign policy are taken on the basis of national interest. If Pakistan's army is shaping the national interest of the country, then it is obviously controlling the foreign policy of Pakistan and also other domestic policies. In its quest for dominance the military is helped by the United States. For details see, Farzana Shaikh, *Making Sense of Pakistan,* New York: Columbia University Press, 2009, p. 12.
6. Moonis Ahmar, 'Perceptions on Pak-US Relations After 9/11', in M. Saleem Kidwai, ed., *US Policy Towards South Asia: Focus on Sixty Years*, Delhi: Academic Excellence, 2008, pp. 223-37.
7. Riedel, *Deadly Embrace*, p. 37.
8. James Wynbrandt, *A Brief History of Pakistan* (New York: Facts on File, 2009), p. 254.
9. Jonathan S. Landay, 'Pakistan Coup Poses Danger, But U.S. Has Little Leverage', http://articles.philly.com/1999-10-13/news/ 25508814_1_ pakistan-coup-india-and-pakistan-nuclear-tests. (accessed on 13 May 2011).

10. Musharraf, *In the Line of Fire*, p. 127.
11. Riaz Ahmed Shaikh, 'A State of Transition: Authoritarianism and Democratization in Pakistan', *Asia Journal of Global Studies*, vol. 3, no. 1, 2009, pp. 4-21.
12. Riedel, *Deadly Embrace*, p. 63.
13. Musharraf, *In the Line of Fire*, pp. 151-2.
14. Ahmed Rashid, *Descent Into Chaos: How the War Against Islamic Extremism is Being Lost in Pakistan, Afghanistan and Central Asia*, London: Allen Lane, 2008, p. 157.
15. Aqil Shah, 'Pakistan's "Armored" Democracy', *Journal of Democracy*, vol. 14, no. 4, 2003, pp. 26-40.
16. Ijaz Shafi Gilani, *The Voice of the People: Public Opinion in Pakistan 2007-2009*, Karachi: Oxford University Press, 2010, p. 69.
17. Mohamed A. El-Khawas, 'Musharraf and Pakistan: Democracy Postponed', *Mediterranean Quarterly*, vol. 20, no. 1, 2009, pp. 94-118.
18. Ibid.
19. Shaikh, 'A State of Transition', p. 17.
20. Ibid.
21. M.H. Askari, 'The Trauma of 1971 and After', *Dawn*, 19 December 2003.
22. M.P. Singh and Veena Kukreja, 'Introduction', in Veena Kukreja and M.P. Singh, eds., *Pakistan: Democracy, Development and Security Issues*, New Delhi: Sage, 2005, p. 18.
23. Akbar S. Zaidi, 'State, Military and Social Transition: Improbable Future of Democracy in Pakistan', *Economic and Political Weekly*, vol. 40, no. 49, 2005, pp. 5173-81.
24. Rashid, *Descent Into Chaos*, p. 149.
25. Riedel, *Deadly Embrace*, p. 75.
26. Mohammad Waseem, 'Functioning of Democracy in Pakistan', in Zoya Hasan, ed., *Democracy in Muslim Societies: The Asian Experience*, New Delhi: Sage, 2007, pp. 177-218.
27. Riedel, *Deadly Embrace*, p. 75.
28. Teresita C. Schaffer, 'U.S. Influence on Pakistan: Can Partners Have Divergent Priorities?', *The Washington Quarterly*, vol. 26, no. 1, 2003, pp. 169-83.
29. Balfer Center for Science and International Affairs, 'Report on U.S. Aid to Pakistan', Cambridge: Harvard University, 2009, available on internet at http://belfercenter.ksg.harvard.edu/files/Final_DP_2009_06_08092009.pdf (accessed on 5 October 2011).
30. See 'Pakistan Got $18 bn aid from US since 2001', *Times of India*, 23 February 2010.

31. Shuja Nawaz, 'The Pakistan Dilemma',http://www.foreignaffairs.com/print/67756 (accessed on 4 May 2011).
32. Craig Cohen and Derek Chollet, 'When $10 Billion is Not Enough: Rethinking U.S. Strategy Toward Pakistan', *The Washington Quarterly*, vol. 30, no. 2, 2007, pp. 7-19.
33. Balfer Center for Science and International Affairs, 'Report on U.S. Aid to Pakistan'.
34. Griff Witte, 'Billions of Aid Dollars buy U.S. Little Goodwill in Pakistan', *Washington Post*, 24 August 2010.
35. Ibid.
36. Ishtiaq Ahmad, 'The U.S. Af-Pak Strategy: Challenges and Opportunities for Pakistan', *Asian Affairs: An American Review*, vol. 37, no. 1, 2010, pp. 191-209.
37. Riedel, *Deadly Embrace*, p. 86.
38. See 'Kerry-Lugar Bill Not Ideal Document: Pak', *Times of India*, 8 October 2009.
39. See 'Opponents of Lugar Bill "Armchair Critics"', *Dawn*, 6 October 2009.
40. Ahmad, 'The U.S. Af-Pak Strategy', p. 201.
41. Amnesty International, 'Report on Enforced Disappearances in Pakistan' London: Amnesty International Publications. Available on the internet at http://www.amnesty.org/en/library/asset/ASA33/018/2008/en/0de43038-57dd-11dd-be62-3f7ba2157024/asa330182008eng.pdf (accessed on 5 September 2011).
42. Selig S. Harrison, 'Global Terrorism: US Policy After 9/11 and its Impact on the Domestic Politics and Foreign Relations of Pakistan', in Rajshree Jetly, ed., *Pakistan in Regional and Global Politics*, New Delhi: Routledge, 2009, pp. 20-44.
43. Center for International Policy, Special Report on Pakistan, Washington D.C.: The Center for International Policy. Available on internet at http://www.bso-na.org/files/pakistan_the_state_of_the_union.pdf (accessed on 10 October 2011).
44. Ijaz Shafi Gilani, *The Voice of the People*, p. 71.
45. Amnesty International, 'Report on Enforced Disappearances in Pakistan'.
46. Ibid.
47. Center for International Policy, 'Special Report on Pakistan'.
48. J. Andrew Greig, 'U.S. and Pakistan: Relations During the Bush-Musharraf Years', in Ravi Kalia, ed., *Pakistan: From the Rhetoric of Democracy to The Rise of Militancy*, New Delhi: Routledge, 2011, pp. 194-216.

49. Zahid Hussain, *The Scorpion's Tail: The Relentless Rise of Islamic Militants in Pakistan And How It Threatens the World*, New York: Free Press, 2010, p. 127.
50. Nirupama Subramanian, 'Musharraf-PPP Talks Resume in Dubai', *The Hindu*, 5 September 2007.
51. Wynbrandt, *A Brief History of Pakistan*, p. 275.
52. Ron Suskind, *The Way of the World: A Story of Truth and Hope in an Age of Extremism*, New York: Harper & Row, 2008, pp. 262-5.
53. Hussain, *The Scorpion's Tail*, p. 137.
54. See 'Report of the United Nations Commission of Inquiry into the Facts and Circumstances of the Assassination of Former Pakistani Prime Minister Mohtarma Benazir Bhutto', available on internet at http://www.un.org/News/dh/infocus/Pakistan/UN_Bhutto_Report_15April2010.pdf (accessed on 21 May 2011).
55. Nirupama Subramanian, 'Benazir Asked U.S. for Security, Was Turned Away', *The Hindu*, 22 May 2011.
56. Ashok K. Behuria, 'From Fragmentation to Coalition: End of General Musharraf's Politics?', *Strategic Analysis*, vol. 32, no. 3, 2008, pp. 329-38.
57. Abdus Sattar Ghazali, 'Pakistan's Post Election Scenario', http://www.opednews.com/articles/opedne_abdus_sa_080228_pakistan_s_post_elec.htm (accessed on 21 May 2011).
58. Ibid.
59. Frederic Grare, 'Pakistan's Pursuit of Democracy', in Ravi Kalia, ed., *Pakistan: From the Rhetoric of Democracy to the Rise of Militancy,* New Delhi: Routledge, 2011, pp. 160-76.
60. Bill Roggio and Alexander Mayer, 'Charting the Data for US Airstrikes in Pakistan, 2004-2011', http://www.longwarjournal.org/pakistan-strikes.php (accessed on 22 May 2011).
61. See, 'Sarkar Giraneke Prayas Me Pak Sena', *Dainik Jagran*, 2 July 2011.

CHAPTER 18

Terrorism in Pakistan and Fragile Counter-terrorism Strategy

Nishu Sharma

Introduction

TERRORISM HAS FOR long been part of human society, but of late it has assumed even more horrific proportions. In the post-Cold War period it has achieved the status of a critical threat. Terrorism is a complex phenomenon and a method whereby an organized group seeks to achieve its avowed goals, chiefly through the systematic use of violence. There are many causes for the rise of terrorism, such as social, economic, cultural and political. Any nation that has not satisfactorily attended to these problems makes itself a potential target for the emergence of terrorism. If people do not find the system or the political processes compatible to their demands, they may opt for terrorism as a weapon to change the system. The terrorists' aim is to replace the present governmental system with their own regime, and to run the political system according to their understanding.

Terrorists see non-combatants as the softest and easiest target for their aims. Terrorism is a random process. During the attack the terrorist does not aim at any particular person but attacks randomly. It is a premeditated criminal act, politically motivated, potentially including religious, philosophical, ideological, or culturally symbolic motivations. The true target of terrorism remains society as a whole.[1]

There is as yet no consensus among scholars on the definition of terrorism. The Federal Bureau of Investigation (FBI) defines terrorism as 'The unlawful use of force or violence against persons or property to intimidate or coerce a government, civilian population, or any segment thereof, in furtherance of political or social objectives'.[2] The FBI further describes terrorism as either domestic or international, depending on the origin, base and objectives of the terrorist organization. The United Nations defines a terrorist as

> any person, who, acting independently of the specific recognition of a country, or as a single person, or as a part of a group not recognised as an official part or division of a nation, acts to destroy or to injure civilians or destroy or damage property belonging to civilians or to governments in order to effect some political goal.[3]

The US Department of Justice describes terrorism as premeditated, politically motivated violence perpetrated against non-combatant targets by sub-national groups or clandestine agents, usually intended to influence an audience. The US Department of Defense notes that the calculated use of violence or threat of violence by terrorists to inculcate fear is intended to coerce or to intimidate governments or societies in the pursuit of goals that are generally political, religious, or ideological.[4]

Terrorism and Pakistan

Pakistan has constantly been contemplated as an active sponsor and exporter of terrorism, especially support to militant activities in India and backing the Taliban regime in Afghanistan. In relation to Kashmiri refugees, training has been provided to Pakistani and international volunteers by the country itself, and to those who sympathized with their Muslim brethren.[5] But the state government has constantly denied its direct involvement in supporting militants, emphasizing the indigenous character of the Kashmiri resistance and holding private citizens and groups responsible for any support mobilized in Pakistan for the Kashmiris.

Pakistan has looked upon militant Islam as a strategic option which has been proved during the 1971 war, where Pakistan's military rulers had helped in the creation of volunteer militias of Bengali Islamists to fight the pro-Bangladesh militia and Indian troops. Instead of accepting political negotiations with Bengali politicians who secured a majority in that election, the West Pakistan-led military chose to define the issue as a religious war between Islamic Pakistan and Hindu-backed Bangladesh. Islamists were the most dependable political allies of the

Pakistani state, especially in resisting Indian ascendancy in South Asia.[6] Insurgent supporters within Islamabad's policy making circles said that Islamic militants would serve as an important fifth column for Pakistani soldiers, sabotaging the much larger and better equipped Indian army, in case of war.[7]

The rise of Islam and Pakistan's support for terror has affected the relations between Pakistan and Afghanistan as well. The increasing Taliban activities in the provinces of North West Frontier Province (NWFP) and Baluchistan sharing borders with Afghanistan, also in the Federally Administered Tribal Areas (FATA), has affected the relation between the two. 'The rise of the Taliban – and their rule in Afghanistan from 1996 until 2001 – was the product of Pakistani backing, support from Afghanistan's Pakhtun community, and the war-induced displacement, anarchy, and militancy that became a way of life.'[8] The Afghan President Hamid Karzai has several times accused and asked Pakistan to stop Taliban's incursion into Afghanistan but Pakistan's responses remained feeble which disappointed Afghanistan. President Karzai stated that Pakistan had not cooperated on security issues. He also condemned Pakistan's 'double game' on terrorism in Afghanistan. Many Afghans are suspicious of Pakistan's connections to the Taliban-led insurgency in their country. 'Pakistan has not supported our efforts to bring peace and security to Afghanistan, which is very unfortunate'.[9]

Today Pakistan is confronting the same challenge in its own territory. Terrorism in Pakistan has become a major and highly destructive phenomenon in the recent years. The state had aided terrorist organizations like al-Qaeda and Taliban for its benefits but presently they have turned against the government and become involved in terrorist activities inside the country. The situation in Pakistan is that of increasing economic and political instability and destabilized government losing its control. The biggest threat Pakistan is confronting today is growing hegemony of Taliban and allies of al-Qaeda.

Causes of Terrorism in Pakistan

Sectarianism

Sectarian terrorism in Pakistan has been an outcome of some historical and regional rivalries. There are four different schools of Muslim thought in Pakistan – Barelvi, Deobandi, Ahle Hadith and Shia. The first three are commonly grouped as Sunni but their thinking and expressions are wide apart. There are differences between Sunni and Shia thinking and intra-Sunni factionalism which has been historical but they have generally co-existed peacefully. The prolonged Iraq-Iran war and the post-Afghan *jihad* rivalries between Northern Alliance, pre-dominantly Shia and orthodox Sunni backed by Saudi Arabia and Pakistan, had adversely affected sectarian harmony in Pakistan.[10]

The communal schism on sectarian lines was the outcome of the process of Islamization of laws in Pakistan which was introduced by President Zia-ul-Haq in 1977–88; sectarian violence was very rare before that period.[11] The Shias, feeling empowered after the 1979 Iranian revolution and embittered over Gen. Zia's Islamization (in practice, Sunni-ization) programme, created an organization named Tehreek-e-Nifaz-Fiqah-e-Jaffria (Movement for the Imposition of Shia Law) and protested against the president's policies. They were successful in securing escape clauses in the new Islamized laws for themselves and in having the Shias in general exempted from certain aspects of those laws.[12]

Socio-economic Problems

Poverty is the biggest social problem in any society. The distinction between urban and rural poverty is important in Pakistan. Nearly two-thirds of the population and 80 per cent of the country's poor people live in rural parts of the country. Most of them do not have access to adequate basic needs of life.[13] The sense of deprivation leads to their exploitation by any of the extremist groups, in lieu of financial prosperity. Urban poverty remains lower than both overall and rural poverty because of the relatively easier accessibility to resources and opportunities in these areas. High incidence of poverty in rural regions can be linked to inadequate infrastructure, lack of opportunities and resources. The FATA is the most backward region in Pakistan with 60 per cent of the population living below the poverty line. Per capita public expenditure in the region is one-third of the average for Pakistan. Poverty and lack of opportunities is a major contributing factor to the growing militancy in FATA.[14]

The *World Bank's Task Force on Food Security* had put the ratio at 33.8 per cent in 2007-8 and 36.1 per cent in 2008-9. Such estimates placed 62 million people of the country Below the Poverty Line (BPL) in 2008-9. The new assessments say at least 20 million people might have joined the previous headcount on BPL population. The poverty increase is as follows: 22.3 per cent of the population in 2005-6 to between 30-5 per cent in 2008-9; now this population is beyond 40 per cent.[15] Pakistan's feudal system, which deprives large numbers of people from owning land, is another major contributor to poverty.

Illiteracy is yet another problem of Pakistan. The educational divide in Pakistan has created a deeply polarized society serving as a prominent cause of terrorism. Many people can be misguided by some radical groups as they do not know even the basics of Islam. A major portion of Pakistan's population consists of youth and a large number of young people who have the ability and are willing to work, are unemployed. Therefore, high levels of unemployment enable militant organizations to recruit even the better educated, mature and experienced young people of the society. The unemployment rate of Pakistan has been constant at 6.2 per cent since 2008.[16]

Corruption in government departments is deep-rooted. There is a lack of accountability due to which wealthy people are sure that they cannot be held responsible for their deeds. They keep looting the national exchequer and find ways to legalize their black money. According to the latest report of *Transparency International*, Pakistan has been ranked 34th among the most corrupt nations of the world in the global corruption index.[17]

Political Instability

Political stability is vitally important for the attainment of nation building, such as political development and national integration, which has direct influence on the formation of political parties. The development of states – modern or modernizing – takes place due to varying degrees of political stability. There are five issues, according to Leonard Binder, which many states face while trying to maintain the stability needed in their political systems. These areas are: identity crisis, legitimacy crisis, penetration crisis, participation crisis and distribution crisis. Without any doubt these play a significant role in creating political instability.[18]

In Pakistan, the imposition of one unit in 1955 the introduction of the 1962 constitution by Gen. Ayub Khan, frequent constitutional amendments by Zulfikar Ali Bhutto and distortion of the 1973 constitution by Gen. Zia-ul-Haq are closely related events in the context of political instability in Pakistan. The political leadership in Pakistan has remained weak and its structure has always been top down. The leadership in Pakistan is based on heredity/family patterns. Since people are not satisfied with the actions of political parties and governments, they start thinking about their existence and identity which generate negative feelings amongst people for government and all systems.[19]

Next contributing factor to the instable political conditions in Pakistan is the weak organization of political parties. The parties lack structure, there is absence of party elections, and domination of one family or ethnic group and which limits the scope of the party in terms of its voters and narrows its aims and objectives, thereby depriving it of a national character. It also affects policy making in both internal and external arenas.

The *jihadi* terrorism is also posing a threat to the national security of Pakistan. The epicentre of *jihadi* terrorism is Afghanistan. Initially, it was directed towards infidels and occupation forces but gradually it turned towards Pakistan, because of its alliance with the West in the War on Terror. The *jihad* of 1980s, against the Soviet occupation of Afghanistan, degenerated first into infighting on ethnic lines and ethnic terrorism and then to sectarian terrorism with the arrival of Taliban on the scene. The Taliban took upon themselves the so-called divine duty of enforcing Islamic order with the force of arms. Their narrow, myopic and ultra-orthodox view of Islam becomes a force of regression and decadence. When the resistance movement against American occupation of Afghanistan started engulfing Pakistan also, the perpetrators of *jihadi* terrorism were out to chastize the Muslims of Pakistan. The march of *jihadi* terrorism towards Pakistan has refuelled sectarian terrorism as well, witnessed in the most lethal combination of these two evil forces:

> The scene in Pakistan resembled a jungle in which everyone was fighting at times everyone else. The terrorists were making money by drug trafficking and gun running, so they were heavily armed. Their operations endangered the very existence of the state, and no one put an estimate even remotely how many people were killed in this fighting.[20]

Terrorist Groups active in Pakistan

Lashkar-e-Omar (The Army of Omar) is a Pakistani Islamic fundamentalist terrorist organization. The group, formed in January 2002, is a mixture of elements from three other terrorist groups: Harkat-ul-Jihad-al-Islami, Lashkar-e-Jhangvi, and Jaish-e-Mohammad. It also includes members of the Taliban and al-Qaeda.[21]

Lashkar-e-Taiba (LeT), active since 1993, was formed as the military wing of the well-funded Pakistani Islamist organization Markaz-ad-Dawa-wal-Irshad. The group, one of the largest and most proficient of the Kashmir-based terrorist groups, has claimed responsibility for a number of high-profile attacks on Indian targets in Jammu & Kashmir (J&K), as well as within India. The Indian government alleges that LeT was responsible for coordinating the 2008 Mumbai attacks.[22]

Jaish-e-Mohammad (JeM) was founded in 2000 by Maulana Masood Azhar, a Pakistani cleric. The group seeks to incorporate Kashmir into the state of Pakistan and has openly declared war on the US. The JeM has carried out attacks on Indian targets, the Pakistani government, and various sectarian minority groups within Pakistan. Acts of terrorism attributed to the group include the 2001 attack on the Indian parliament and a series of assaults in 2002 on Christian sites in Pakistan. The Pakistani government has also implicated the JeM for the two assassination attempts on former Pakistani President Gen. Pervez Musharraf. According to the US State Department, the group has at least several hundred armed supporters as well as tens of thousands of followers.[23]

Harkat-ul-Jihad-al-Islami (HuJI) is a Pakistan-based terrorist group with an affiliate in Bangladesh. The HuJI supports, like the other Pakistan-based terrorist groups want the secession of J&K from India and its eventual accession to Pakistan, essentially through violence. It also propagates the idea of Islamic rule over all parts of India. Among the other objectives of the HuJI is the Islamization of Pakistani society.[24]

Harkat-ul-Mujahideen (HUM) is a Pakistan based terrorist organization. The group is responsible for the December 1999 hijacking of an Indian airliner and numerous attacks on Indian troops and civilians in Kashmir. Harkat members have participated in insurgent and terrorist operations in Myanmar, Tajikistan, and Bosnia. These groups have focused on Indian targets since the days of the 1990 Kashmir jihad.[25]

Tehrik-i-Taliban Pakistan (TTP): Based in FATA, TTP is a string of loosely tied jihadi groups that operates all over the country and attacks Pakistani targets.

Sipah-e-Sahaba Pakistan (SSP) and Lashkar-e-Jhangvi (LJ): Headquartered in Jhang in south Punjab, SSP is a major sectarian militant outfit. Both SSP and LJ tend to carry out attacks against Shias.[26]

Counter-terrorism

Counter-terrorism is the method which follows the path of policies to combat both domestic as well as international terrorism. Counter-terrorism is an application of policies which can control terrorist activities. Bruce Newsome describes counter-terrorism as 'defensive and offensive measures against political violence. It is a method to deal with threat which has achieved the status of a most "critical" threat of the post-Cold War period. But if we look at the nature of the threat and its ability to inflict large scale damage of a nation-state, the requirement is to tackle it with a cognitive approach.'[27]

Counter-terrorism is a process which includes a broad spectrum of responses, from conventional war against states that harbour or sponsor terrorists through law enforcement to arrest terrorists within the country. It is decidedly a proactive function which contains both intelligence gathering and analysis of security-related information or 'intelligence'. It takes the fight to the terrorists with offensive military activities, covert operations and law enforcement efforts. Ideally, comprehensive and coordinated intelligence activity guides all three tasks and helps link them together. But to make it effective these tasks need to be combined into a comprehensive plan, a grand strategy combining various elements of national power to defeat terrorism.[28]

The counter-terrorism strategy involves diplomacy, intelligence, law enforcement, and financial efforts intended to defeat international terrorism. Due to the changing character of terrorism international coordination becomes the most important aspect of counter-terrorism. Over the last decade terrorists have become much more international forcing counter-terrorism strategies also to become international. This in a way helps to trace terrorist networks, which were referred earlier through intelligence sharing.[29] The internationalization of terrorism has compelled the nations to work together which has resulted in the existence of various international counter-terror policies and treaties.

Counter-terrorism requires a number of observations prior to its implementation – whether they are within the framework of rule of law and human rights or not. Framing counter-terrorism structures is not an easy task; the framework created for it should keep in mind societal demands because without human rights and rule-of-law-based framework for counter-terrorism, the states will appear hypocritical in their denial of basic rights to terror suspects. There will also be the danger of a drift towards autocratic rule, as basic rights and freedoms are sacrificed for the sake of spurious or ill-defined national security interest.[30]

The primary objective of counter-terrorism strategy is the protection and maintenance of liberal democracy and the rule of law. It is difficult to find out the exact linkages within a terrorist group due to its *ad hoc* structure and this often leads to huge investments in counter-terrorism strategies. That is why most of the counter-terrorism strategies are incremental, pragmatic and defensive with marginal pay-offs.[31]

Intelligence is the key concept in counter-terrorism. Nations that have suffered or are suffering from the evil of terrorism intercept communications, and trace persons; these in fact are the central activities of combating terrorism. But these actions are not enough to meet the growing challenge of terrorism. There is a need for new technologies, effective law enforcement and expanded range of military operations because if we talk about terrorism in the present context, the structure and demands have changed. Thus, with the growing rate of violence there is a need to frame more versatile and elaborate counter-terror policies which can deal with this menace.

Counter-terrorism: Responses and Measures

Scholars have enumerated many measures to combat terrorism. Counter-terrorism responses can be broadly divided in two models – the Criminal Justice Model (CJM) and War Model (WM). The CJM regards terrorism as a crime and functions on the fundamental premise of preservation of democratic principles in the fight against terrorism. Arrest and penalization of terrorists are the aims of CJM when terrorists adhere to the 'rule of law'. It possesses rigid constitutional boundaries and its nature is circumscribed by the standard rule of authority. This being the fundamental premise, it is safeguarded even at the expense of effectiveness of counter-terrorist measures.[32]

The WM considers terrorism as a tactic exercised in guerrilla activities or even acts of rebellion. It aims at the apprehending of terrorists and eliminating terrorism. It gives preference to restraining and countering terrorism rather than upholding liberal democratic principles. In WM the onus for response lies in the mechanism of use of force, which lies with the military and the special units.

However, due to shortcomings and certain grey areas in both the above responses, nations usually opt for the Expanded Criminal Justice Model (ECJM), which is a hybrid of CJM and WM. The ECJM regards terrorism as an exceptional phenomenon that is not necessarily an act of war, yet also deviated from the standard definition of a felonious crime. Its objective is arrest and penalization of terrorists. Under ECJM the forces responding are primarily police and secret services which are occasionally complemented by special anti-terrorism units. The nature of response includes preventive arrests, surveillance techniques and gathering intelligence data where typical methods are used by secret services with the intention of bringing a suspect to trial.[33]

When it comes to counter-terrorism measures we mean both defensive measures, to reduce vulnerability to terrorist acts, and offensive measures, to prevent, deter, and respond to terrorism.[34] The offensive measures also carry a contingency plan which enables a nation state to respond and address the challenge of any terrorist incident. There is need for these diverse responses due to the dynamic nature of terrorism and its capability to act at various planes and levels.[35] Now we will take various counter-terrorism measures into consideration.

POLITICAL MEASURES

A number of political measures can be used to counter terrorism and to resolve its causal factors. But states need to address the terrorists' specific political, economic, or social grievances by changing their policies to accommodate the terrorists or by offering some kind of concessions. By addressing a group's legitimate grievances, the state shows that it has done something in response; then, if the groups persist they may lose support and credibility. The state can also appease the general populace. If grievances are social or economic, engaging in measures that are seen to redress grievances through employment schemes, anti-discrimination measures, poverty reduction schemes like land redistribution, and opening legal economic alternatives to black-market activities, etc., can work effectively.[36]

Conflict resolution is also a political measure and includes public dialogue, secret mediation or negotiation to try and initiate peace processes. Steps can be taken to encourage opposition groups or to develop alliances with opponents of terrorist groups in order to decrease the appeal of the group. Even amnesties can be used to weaken the groups and their cause. Banning membership to such groups and their forefront organizations can work effectively as well declaring political and military wings illegal. But the important thing is to ban their sponsors also and not only the groups. Diplomacy and foreign liaison between intelligence and counterterrorist agencies are also important measures as diplomatic pressure can be used to lever state sponsors to decrease their support by expelling diplomats from states supporting terrorist organizations.[37]

JUDICIAL MEASURES

A judicial measure is one of the major tools to combat terrorism and includes the signing and ratification of international conventions and protocols. There has been an expansion of extradition treaties and efforts to increase compliance with well founded extradition requests for suspected terrorists. There are also efforts on to enhance mutual legal assistance and exchange of information with the judiciaries of other countries. For effective judicial measures, empowered criminal courts need to be established.[38]

PUNITIVE MEASURES

Punitive measures play a vital role in countering terrorism. A key aspect of countering terrorism is the severing of a group's financing by banning fund-raising and transfer of funds from potential front organizations, both nationally and internationally. Reducing bank secrecy is one of the measures, by facilitating exchange of information between states on the movement of funds between groups suspected of supporting terrorism. Financial rewards may also be offered for information leading to the arrests of terrorists. Punitive measures include economic sanctions like arms embargoes, freezing assets and diplomatic boycotts. Blocking the assets of states sponsoring terrorism can also become bargaining too also.

MILITARY

The role of the military in combating terrorism is advantageous as military can be incorporated into the civil system and can perform peace-keeping duties like helping the police in patrolling areas and searching for weapons, and assisting in cross-training. By making use of military skills, resources, and experience, civil powers can avoid spending money to duplicate and develop similar capabilities in other agencies and services. If we examine various uses of special forces, the 'willingness to take the fight to the terrorists; to meet them on their own ground rather than passively wait for them to strike', has led to the major counterterrorist successes. Military can make contribution in countering terrorism through cross-training and establishing links for cooperation, both domestic and international, and all these would help in formulating a valuable counter-terrorism capability.[39]

INTELLIGENCE AGENCIES

There are a number of arrangements and resources that have been developed to counter-terrorism and the highest priority among these is intelligence. The importance of intelligence in countering terrorism cannot be overemphasized.[40] Valuable information can be turned into intelligence, can be acquired and gathered through signals, electronic communications, and human source agents, as well as through open sources, surveillance and a variety of other means. But what is important is to ensure that intelligence agencies have plenty of personnel with diverse experience; agents and analysts need to have linguistic, cultural and regional expertise in all the geographical areas. These are needed for a variety of reasons:

> to infiltrate terrorist cells, recruit agents/informers, and acquire information to understand the nature of terrorist objectives and plans, their political motivations and alignments, the leadership and membership, the logistic and financial resources, the links with other terrorist groups, terrorist states, and international organised crime which would help in to prevent terrorist acts.[41]

MOVEMENT RESTRICTION

Movement restriction is also an important tool to control terrorism. Globalization, the reduction in trade barriers and borders and ensuring freedom of movement have benefited terrorists and allowed them to move not only themselves but also move funds, materials and equipment more easily. So to reduce terrorism more effective travel and immigration measures should be introduced.[42]

THE MEDIA

The media can convey the terrorist's message and can spread fear and terror in society. This should be considered significant because the public's fear of terrorism and sense of insecurity influence political, social and economic decisions, regionally and internationally. One may therefore 'win the battle' against terrorism by thwarting terror attacks, but 'lose the war' when the threat of terrorism succeeds in disrupting the daily life of civilians. Media can assist in countering terrorism but only to some extent; otherwise it plays a bigger role in spreading terrorism.

The relationship between publicity and terror is paradoxical. Publicity focuses attention on a group, strengthening its morale and helping to attract recruits and sympathisers. But it also helps an outraged public to mobilise its vast resources and produces information that the public needs to pierce the veil of secrecy all terrorist groups require.[43]

COUNTER-PROPAGANDA

Propaganda and publicity to the terrorist are paramount and the importance of countering such propaganda, from a counter-terrorism perspective, is extremely valuable and beneficial. The conflict resolution techniques encourage and facilitate dialogue, mediation and negotiation which are important in breaking down negative stereotypes of opposing factions that may perpetuate the use of violence. One of the tactics is to target those involved with the conflict or terrorist campaign by establishing and ultimately building on a common theme, belief, or value base. During the delegitimation of a group, it is important to convey and emphasize the inhumanity and immorality of the terrorists' activities while stressing that the actual impact is relatively small. These techniques help to reduce support as well as sympathy base and detract from any propaganda success through sensationalized media reporting.[44]

Hence preventing terrorism through placing and detonating of bombs is not sufficient. Instead there is a need to prevent financing, procuring, recruiting, researching, networking and mobility. Terrorism has become a headache worldwide and to counter it we need responses and a set of counter-terrorism measures. Due to its huge and diverse operations international measures and responses can counter such entities. So there is a need to frame such effective sets of measures and responses that could help in curbing this menace.

Pakistan's War on Terror: Fragile and Feeble

Pakistan appears to lack clarity about how to define the threat it is facing and what should be the attainable objectives. The primary flaw of Pakistan's counter-terrorism policy is that it is defined and driven by the military and its strategic objectives. The armed forces have a four-tiered approach: clear, hold, develop, and disintegrate, an approach used by the army in its operations in Swat in 2007 and in South Waziristan in October 2009. But, the army, however, is unwilling to extend its operation into North Waziristan as it is willing to adopt a careful and layered approach to counter-terrorism, which means it will check and destroy unfriendly forces before attending to other groups. The military is not inclined to cater to the US concerns about Taliban groups in North Waziristan, which have formal and informal agreements with the Pakistani army not to attack the state if the army does not attack them. Islamabad does not want to start a battle on all fronts and is willing to talk to militant forces that do not attack Pakistan.

There are three kinds of forces which operate inside Pakistan: the 'friendly' or good Taliban in North Waziristan; the 'unfriendly' or bad Taliban in North Waziristan, South Waziristan, Swat, and rest of the country in the form of the Tehrik-i-Taliban Pakistan (TTP); and other 'friendly' militants such as the Lashkar-e-Taiba (LeT), Jamaat-ud-Dawa (JuD), and Jaish-e-Mohammad (JeM). The army does not seem willing to develop public goodwill against these 'friendly' groups through a proactive use of public and private media, which were used effectively in the case of the Swat and South Waziristan operations. This is despite the fact that the army's main narrative revolves around presenting itself and the country as victims of terrorism.[45] Pakistan's army is equally unwilling to eliminate other militant groups which have found safe haven in mainland Pakistan. LeT, which came to international attention because of its involvement in the 2008 Mumbai attacks, and JeM have had a long partnership with the army for what Rawalpindi considers strategic reasons.

The 9/11 attack led Pakistan deliberately to participate in the US-initiated War on Terror. Pakistan's relationship with the US was strained after the events of 9/11, in part because of confusion and mistrust between the two sides till the death of bin Laden. The US knew bin Laden was hidden in Pakistan but the latter was not willing to hand him over and denied his presence in the country, the fact which strained US-Pak relations.

Many Pakistanis believe that the War on Terror was imposed on Pakistan by the Americans, while many in the US questioned Islamabad's sincerity in its commitment to fighting terror. In particular, Washington has not trusted Pakistan's security apparatus, especially the Inter-Services Intelligence (ISI), because of its alleged support of the Taliban by providing weapons, ammunition, intelligence and even direction to suicide bombings. The chief of the ISI, Lieutenant General Shuja Pasha, once declared Taliban leaders such as Fazlullah and Baitullah Mehsud as patriots and nationalists. In an interview to the German magazine *Der Spiegel*, Pasha similarly adopted a generous view of militant propaganda, terming it as a right in a democracy.[46]

In April 2011, during a visit to Pakistan, the Chairman of the Joint Chiefs of Staff Admiral Mike Mullen pointed to ISI's links with one such group, the Haqqani network. Recently, the US designated Pakistan-based Haqqani network as a terrorist group.[47] The killing of America's most wanted terrorist Osama-bin-Laden in a Pakistani military town not far from Islamabad raised new questions over army and ISI support for the al-Qaeda leader and the legitimacy of their counter-terrorism efforts. Laden was staying in Abbottabad, close to the Pakistan Military Academy, and the government and army were unaware of that fact. Shuja Nawaz, author of *Crossed Swords: Pakistan, its Army, and the Wars Within*, says the ISI 'has certainly lost control' of Kashmiri militant groups. 'According to Nawaz, some of the groups trained by the ISI to fuel insurgency in Kashmir have been implicated in bombings and attacks within Pakistan, therefore making them army targets.'[48]

The strategic community in Washington has also expressed disappointment with the level and quality of support from Pakistan and has raised concerns about the latter's potential for survival as a functioning state. The TTP is an umbrella terrorist group, believing in waging jihad even against Muslims who help non-Muslims or do not fight un-Islamic rule. Such beliefs compel them to wage war against Pakistani forces, as they are considered to be toeing the US line and fighting a war that is not Pakistan's. [49]

As long as the Pakistan army continues to differentiate among the various groups on the basis of their tactical position vis-à-vis the Pakistani state, terrorism will continue. There seems to be little intent to marginalize or eliminate the core militant groups operating inside Pakistan. The militants are considered a vital part of the army's operational plans to counter India. Overall, the India factor has led to the seemingly divided opinion amongst the Pakistani establishment about fighting militancy, especially given that there is a deep-rooted fear of the growing strategic relationship between the United States and India. The Pakistan army does not want to find itself in a situation where Islamabad does not have links with the Taliban and other warlords. The Afghan Taliban is a significant stakeholder in Afghanistan, and it is vital for Islamabad to keep ties with it. The Pakistan military went so far as to publicly admit that its forces arrested Mullah Baradar who was apparently engaged in a dialogue with the Karzai government in February 2010 to signal the Taliban that Islamabad would not allow militants to strike deals independently.[50] The US diplomats stationed in Pakistan believe that the continuation of the fight against terrorist organizations helps Islamabad extract money from Washington.[51] And in reality, Pakistani forces do not want the United States to leave the region.

Pakistan's present approach toward terrorism has disappointed the United States where President Barack Obama stated that Pakistan's counter-terrorism measures have failed to yield results with insurgent activities gaining ground and operational situation facing the military there continuing to deteriorate. The White House report sent by Obama to the Congress said, 'The return of militant-inspired violence after a four month lull following the 2010 floods demonstrated how insurgent elements have managed to survive and even return to many areas previously cleared by the Pakistan military.'[52]

One of the main problems while viewing counter-terrorism strategies and Pakistan-US relations is the incompetence exhibited by Pakistani institutions. Pakistan government has not dealt effectively with the public and with Washington and failed to remove the trust deficit that exists in both these spaces. The government has no aim when it defines its counter-terrorism strategy, and no ambition in combating the groups situated in North Waziristan. There is inertia when it comes to formulating policies against terrorism, and National Counter-Terrorism Authority (NACTA), an organization made to make this communication easier, has itself faced multiple disputes. The government is also blamed as an accomplice to some terrorist organizations that work in Kashmir and Afghanistan.[53]

Prevailing chaos and crisis in Pakistan are not merely a law and order problem, but the result of a covert war. Ironically, the national lawmaking institutions, political leadership, as well as the military establishment, have remained ignorant to this fact for the last decade. The changing tactics and targets of the various terrorist groups operating in the country are posing challenges to a police force which has limited resources, poor training, and inadequate equipments. Pakistan's civilian law enforcement structure has failed to develop any systematic and advanced counter-terrorism strategy owing to the lack of modern investigative tools, requisite skills, and incentives. In that case the judiciary remains as the only hope to keep intact the people's faith. But unfortunately, the judicial collapse that has emerged in Pakistan now is the worst one as faith of the masses in the judiciary has been shattered. This failure has led the whole nation to the brink of complete social anarchy. Inadequate and defective criminal justice systems are critical problems of Pakistan. The witness protection system in Pakistan is almost non-existent. Consequently, those who testify against powerful criminals and militants in courts receive no security. In dozens of cases, police officers investigating militants have been gunned down. Judges face similar security threats, and in many instances lower court decisions in terrorism cases are supposedly pending owing to such fears.[54]

The history of anti-terrorism laws in Pakistan explains the sheer lack of commitment and earnestness by the Pakistani politicians towards this issue. The last anti-terrorism act in Pakistan was promulgated in 1997 when special Anti-Terrorism Courts (ATCs) were established along with the Anti-Terrorism Appellate (ATA) tribunal. But it was declared unconstitutional by the Supreme Court of Pakistan right after it was enacted for the first time in 1997. The government again introduced Pakistan Armed Forces (Acting in Aid of Civil Power) Ordinance, 1998, through which broad judicial powers were given to the army units deployed in Karachi but before the military could bring about a positive change to the situation, the Supreme Court once again declared the ordinance as unconstitutional. It was repealed in April 1999. In August 1999, the original 1997 Act was amended to authorize the establishment of ATCs all over the country but decisions fail due to various factors.[55]

Pakistan's anti-terrorism laws are outdated as they were made before 9/11. The current anti-terrorism law addresses the prevailing security crisis as a law and order situation rather than encompassing terrorism and insurgencies as acts of war. More than 1,000 trained irregular war combatants, captured by the security forces during the daring operations in Swat and Bajaur, were released by the civil courts due to inherent legal flaws in the 'law of evidence'. Not a single terrorist has been convicted and sentenced to death in the last decade.[56] In the absence of a comprehensive judicial policy to combat terrorism and the foreign-funded war combatants, security forces take harsh decisions, which is used by the hostile forces and the compromised media elements to malign the establishment. The judicial failure has put the security forces and counter-insurgency operations in a very difficult position on the legal axis. Thus, Pakistan's feeble approach towards terrorism manifests itself in limited state capacity and willingness and overlapping geopolitical tensions undermining regional cooperation.

Pakistan has left the people at the mercy of terrorists as it has neither implemented the unanimous resolutions adopted by parliament to review the official policy on War on Terror nor enacted a piece of legislation to set up the NACTA despite an announcement made over two-and-a-half years back. Such is the level of indifference and apathy on part of the regime that despite a decision taken in 2008 for the constitution of NACTA and to raise a special squad to counter terrorism, the government did not enact any law yet. There is no counter-terrorism strategy framed so far though more than 35,000 Pakistanis have lost their lives as a result of terrorist activities.[57]

The NACTA was set up but remained ineffective in the absence of law that the government has failed to make in the last three years. Informed sources lament that while the innocent are killed everywhere, this important matter is delayed merely because of the tug of war between the Interior Ministry and the rest on the question as to who should lead this counter-terrorism body. The NACTA as envisaged would be a vital body not only to create a database of terrorists and terrorist organizations but will work for coordination and exchange of important information between the federal and provincial civilian agencies and security entities. The NACTA would not be an operational organization but would be a key body to conduct researches on counter-terrorism.

Conclusion

Pakistan is a state suffering from terrorism and dispersing it in the world but not willing to eradicate it due to its strategic benefits. It is a state possessing very feeble counter-terrorism strategy that only favours the terrorist organizations. Pakistan is a country suffering from socio-economic disparity leading to the emergence of terror outfits. There is, thus, a need to change the socio-economic imbalance and to create a new religious narrative. In spite of being a democratic country, every now and then, the reign goes into the hands of the army and they run the country. Weak judicial system is another flaw of the fragile counter-terror strategy.

Even the international community won't be able to solve the dilemma of terrorism until Pakistan acts against this menace. Thus, a regionally coordinated response to the threat of terrorism is essential. Measures should be taken to prevent and combat terrorism ranging from adopting effective legislation to denying the terrorists safe havens and support from the government, thereby ensuring effective international legal cooperation. In fact, countries in the South Asian region need to devise a holistic approach while addressing the terrorist threats which they confront, thus increasing the scope for regional cooperation. Overall, there is a need to develop an effective regional mechanism for fostering sustained counter-terrorism cooperation. It is clear from the ferocity and organization of the attacks in Mumbai that the potential of terrorism is not only challenging national security but threatening regional and international peace.

Notes

1. Brian T. Bennett, *Understanding, Assessing, and Responding to Terrorism*, New Jersey: John Wiley & Sons, 2007, p. 3.
2. Chris Quillen, 'A Historical Analysis of Mass Casualty Bombers', *Studies in Conflict and Terrorism*, vol. 25, no. 5, September-October 2002, p. 282.
3. Harold F. Tipton and Micki Krause, *Information Security Management Handbook*, 6th edn., New York: Auerbach Publications, 2008, p. 2875.
4. Bruce Hoffman, *Inside Terrorism*, New York: Columbia University Press, 2006, p. 31.
5. Ahmed Rashid, *Taliban: Militant Islam, Oil, and Fundamentalism in Central* Asia, New Haven: Yale University Press, 2000, pp. 186-7.
6. G.W. Choudhury, *The Last Days of United Pakistan*, Bloomington: Indiana University Press, 1974, pp. 229-39.
7. Karl Vick and Kamran Khan, 'Pakistani Ambivalence Frustrates Hope for Kashmir Peace', *Washington Post*, 29 June 2002.
8. Mohammad Waseem, 'Patterns of Conflict in Pakistan: Implications for Policy', http://www.brookings.edu/papers/2011/01_pakistan_waseem.aspx (accessed on 16 October 2011).
9. 'Pakistan is Playing 'Double Game' on Terror in Afghanistan: Hamid Karzai', http://timesofindia.indiatimes.com/world/south-asia/Pakistan-is-playing-double-game-on-terror-in-Afghanistan-Hamid-Karzai/articleshow/10224799.cms (accessed on 29 October 2011).
10. 'Terrorism: Major threat to Pakistan's National Security', http://pu.edu.pk/images/journal/pols/Currentissue-pdf/UMBREEN.pdf (accessed on 1 October 2011).
11. C. Jaffrelot, *Pakistan: Nationalism Without a Nation?*, London: Zed Books, 2002, p. 115.
12. Aarish Ullah Khan, 'The Terrorist Threat and the Policy Response in Pakistan' *Stockholm International Peace Research Institute*, Policy Paper no. 11, September 2005, p. 16.
13. 'Rural poverty in Pakistan', http://www.ruralpovertyportal.org/web/guest/country/home/tags/pakistan (accessed on 4 October 2011).
14. Nadeem Shinwari, 'Understanding FATA 2008', *CAMP*, October-December 2008, www.understandingfata.org (accessed on 5 August 2011).
15. Ikram Hoti, 'Statistics Reveal Stunning Increase in Poverty', http://economyofpakistan.blogspot.com/2010/02/statistics-reveal-stunning-increase-in.html (accessed on 9 October 2011).

16. International Monetary Fund (IMF) Report, 'World Economic Outlook October 2010: Recovery, Risk, and Rebalancing', http://www.imf.org/external/pubs/ft/weo/2010/02/pdf/text.pdf (accessed on 10 October 2011).
17. Transparency International Report, 'Corruption Perceptions Index 2010', http://www.transparency.org/policy_research/surveys_indices/cpi/2010. (accessed on 10 October 2011).
18. Leonard Binder, ed., *Crisis and Sequences in Political Development*, New Jersey: Princeton University Press, 1971, pp. 111-35.
19. Aslam Pervez Memon et al., 'Political Instability: A Case Study of Pakistan', *Journal of Political Studies*, vol. 18, Issue 1, pp. 31-43.
20. Walter Laquer, *No End to War, Terrorism in the 21st Century*, New York: The Continuum International, 2003, p. 181.
21. 'Terrorist Group of Pakistan Lashkar-e-Omar', http://www.satp.org/satporgtp/countries/pakistan/terroristoutfits/LeO.htm. (accessed on 11 October 2011).
22. Jamal Afridi, 'Kashmir Militant Extremists', http://www.cfr.org/kashmir/kashmir-militant-extremists/p9135 (accessed on 6 October 2011).
23. Mohammad Waseem, 'Patterns of Conflict in Pakistan: Implications for Policy'. The Brookings Project on U.S. Relations with the Islamic World, Working Paper, no. 5, January 2011, available at: http://www.brookings.edu/~/media/research/files/papers/2011/3/01/.20Pakistan%20waseem/01_Pakistan-waseem.pdf
24. 'Harkat-ul-Jihad-al-Islami (HuJI) (Movement of Islamic Holy War)', http://www.satp.org/satporgtp/countries/india/states/jandk/terrorist_outfits/HuJI.htm (accessed on 8 August 2011).
25. Jamal Afridi, 'Kashmir Militant Extremists'.
26. Mohammad Waseem, 'Patterns of Conflict in Pakistan: Implications for Policy'.
27. Paul J. Smith, *The Terrorism Ahead*, England: M.E. Sharpe, 2008, pp. 12-14.
28. Thomas R. Mockaitis, *The New Terrorism Myths and Reality*, London: Prager Security International, 2007, pp. 100-5.
29. Gautam Sen, *Impediments to National Security*, Pune: Envelop Mfg., 2007, p. 365.
30. Robert Imre, T. Brain Mooney and Benjamin Clarke, *Responding to Terrorism*, England: Ashgate Publishing Limited, 2008, pp. 192-3.
31. Sen, *Impediments to National Security*, p. 365.
32. Graeme C.S. Steven and Rohan Gunaratna, *Counter-Terrorism: A Reference Handbook*, California: ABC-CLIO Inc., 2004, p. 101.

33. Sen, *Impediments to National Security*, pp. 366-7.
34. Gunaratna, *Counter-Terrorism: A Reference Handbook*, p. 102.
35. Sen, *Impediments to National Security*, p. 368.
36. Gunaratna, *Counter-Terrorism: A Reference Handbook*, p. 102.
37. Ibid.
38. Ibid.
39. J.S. Adam, *Secret Armies*, London: Pan, 1989, pp. 81-2.
40. Stewart Foster, 'Maintaining a Co-ordinated Approach to Counter-Terrorism', *The Australian Quarterly*, vol. 58, no. 3, Spring 1986, pp. 321-5.
41. Gunaratna, *Counter-Terrorism: A Reference Handbook*, p. 111.
42. Ibid.
43. David C. Rapoport, 'The Media and Terrorism; Implications of the Unabomber Case', *Terrorism and Political Violence*, vol. 8, Issue 1, Spring 1996, pp. 7-9.
44. Gunaratna, *Counter-Terrorism: A Reference Handbook*, pp. 115-17.
45. The Brookings Project on US Relations with the Islamic World, Working Paper, no. 5, January 2011, http://www.brookings.edu/~/media/research/files/papers/2011/3/01%20Pakistanwaseem Mohammad Waseem, 'Patterns of Conflict in Pakistan: Implications for Policy' (accessed on 10 October 2011).
46. Ayesha Siddiqa, 'Pakistan's Counterterrorism Strategy: Separating Friends from Enemies', *The Washington Quarterly*, vol. 34, no. 1, Winter 2011, p. 156.
47. 'US Brands Haqqani Group as Terror Network', *The Indian Express*, 8 September 2012.
48. Jayshree Bajoria, 'The ISI and Terrorism: Behind the Accusations', http://www.cfr.org/pakistan/isi-terrorism-behind-accusations/p11644 (accessed on 8 October 2011).
49. Ibid.
50. Dexter Filkins, 'Pakistanis Tell of Motive in Taliban Leader's Arrest', *The New York Times*, 22 August 2010, http://www.nytimes.com/2010/08/23/world/asia/23taliban.html. (accessed on 16 October 2011).
51. Mohammad Waseem, 'Patterns of Conflict in Pakistan: Implications for Policy'.
52. Lalit K. Jha, 'Pak has Failed to Counter Terror', http://www.indianexpress.com/news/pak-has-failed-to-counter-terror/854764/ (accessed on 11 November 2011).
53. Ansar Abbasi, 'Govt Throws Nation at the Mercy of Terrorists',

http://www.pakistanherald.com/Articles/Govt-throws-nation-at-the-mercy-of-terrorists-2753 (accessed on 2 November 2011).

54. United States Institute of Peace Special Report, 'Reforming Pakistan's Police and Law Enforcement Infrastructure: Is it Too Flawed to Fix?', http://www.usip.org/files/resources/sr266.pdf (accessed on 6 November 2011).
55. Shahzad Masood Roomi, 'War on Terror and Collapse of the Judicial System', http://www.brasstacks.ca/?p=2293 (3 November 2011).
56. Ibid.
57. Ansar Abbasi, 'Govt throws nation at the mercy of terrorists', http://www.thenews.com.pk/today3printdetail.aspx?ID=6247&Cat=13 (accessed on 11 November 2011).

CHAPTER 19

US-Pakistan Relations

Retrospect and Prospect

Sumit Kumar Jha

TODAY, THE RELATIONSHIP between the US and Pakistan are at an all-time low. Both the countries do not enjoy the trust of each other. Rather, the clouds of distrust and suspicion are hanging over the relationship. Washington accuses Islamabad of not doing enough to contain terrorist activities operating from its soil and of not utilizing US aid for intended proposes. In fact, the American government has raised questions over Pakistan's commitment to apparently shared goals of defeating religious extremism since the killing of Osama-bin-Laden by American forces at Abottabad in Pakistan.[1] On the other hand, Islamabad blames Washington for violating its sovereignty by taking unilateral military actions against terrorist groups on its soil. In this regard, the drone strike by the North Atlantic Treaty Organization (NATO) forces on Pakistani posts near the Afghanistan border on 26 November 2011 proved to be a flash point between the two countries. The Pakistani government became so much angry at the incident that it asked the US to vacate its Shamsi Air Base in northern Pakistan within 15 days and blocked the supply route for NATO forces in Afghanistan. Prime Minister Yousaf Raza Gillani also warned the United States in a CNN interview that 'business as usual with the US will not be there'.[2]

Relations between the US and Pakistan have never been so fragile and estranged in the past. In fact, Pakistan had the privilege of being America's most important non-NATO ally during the Cold War period. Viewed in this context, the article tries to examine the nature of US-Pakistan relations since the Cold War. Divided into six sections, the first section is the introduction. The second section discusses US-Pakistan relations during the Cold War period. In the third section is about the relationship in the aftermath of 9/11 terrorist attacks. The fourth section analyses President Obama's policy towards Pakistan. The fifth section examines the recent factors for increasing distrust and suspicion between Islamabad and Washington. The sixth section tries to understand the future prospects of US-Pakistan relations and also recommend some policy initiatives for forging close ties and trust between the two countries. And finally the article concludes by arguing that acrimonious relations between the US and Pakistan are not good for both the countries' long-term national interests, or for security and peace of the South Asian region. Both the countries, therefore, should work towards developing strong and cooperative relations between themselves.

The Historical Background

Historically, there have been close engagements and estrangements between the US and Pakistan. However, what has been significant of US-Pakistan relations is that the US policy towards Pakistan has varied in response to the changes at home and abroad and it has never showed any genuine interest in forging durable relations with Pakistan. In fact, as time demanded, it has followed both engagement and containment policies towards Pakistan in order to achieve its objectives. On the other hand, Pakistan has always wanted to have a strong and cooperative relationship with the US for several reasons. Security concerns, financial assistance for economic growth and familiarity with the western instructions have been guiding factors for Pakistan in this regard. This was the reason when Liaqat Ali Khan, the first prime minister of Pakistan, visited Washington in 1950, he repeatedly expressed Pakistan's willingness to align itself with the United States, while also hinting on several occasions – both publicly and privately – Pakistan's desire to purchase large quantities of American arms.[3]

However, the US initially did not show much interest in South Asia in the post-Second World War years. In fact, as nearly all recent studies of American diplomacy during the late 1940s have shown, the Truman administration concentrated its attention on Europe and on the Middle East and East Asia. Virtually every place else appeared peripheral to core United States national security interest. Secondly, the US deliberately chose not to support either India or Pakistan in South Asia.[4]

But, the coming of the People's Republic of China (PRC) in 1949 forced the US to change its policy towards the South Asian region because the US policymakers feared the possibility of this region coming under the impact of communism. In such a volatile situation, India became the first preference for the US foreign policy makers to establish close relations with, considering its huge population, geography and its being a leader of the third world, among other things. However, Jawaharlal Nehru refused to the Truman administration's request to join its block and instead, adopted the policy of non-alignment.[5]

On the other hand, as maintained above, Pakistan had already expressed its desire to cooperate with the US in every possible way and openly supported the US foreign policy initiatives. Apart from this, Pakistan's near-contiguous border with the Soviet Union, its proximity to the Persian Gulf, and hence its potential role in the defense of Middle East oil fields also became another important factor for the US to tilt towards Pakistan.[6]

Within a short span of time, US–Pakistan relations improved drastically, resulting in the signing of the Mutual Defense Agreement in 1953 between the Eisenhower administration and Pakistan. Furthermore, Pakistan joined West-sponsored military alliances like the Southeast Asia Treaty Organization (SEATO) and Centre Eastern Treaty Organization (CENTO), becoming 'most allied ally of the US'.[7] In return, Islamabad could succeed in getting about $2 billion US assistance between 1955 and 1961, and $508 million military aid through the signing of a mutual defense assistance agreement between both the countries.[8] Not only this, American training teams also visited Pakistan, making presentations on a wide range of military and strategic subjects, including nuclear warfare and others. Pakistan also received diplomatic support on the contentious issue of Kashmir from the United States.[9]

Nevertheless, US–Pakistan relations suddenly got strained because of the US decision to provide military and economic assistance to India in the wake of China's attack on India in the north-east region in 1962.[10] In fact, Pakistan became so much disturbed with the US decision to support India that it approached China for assistance and started a bitter press campaign against the United States, openly accusing it of interfering in Pakistan's domestic politics and provoking conflict between East and West Pakistan.[11] The relationship further witnessed downturn when the US refused Pakistan's request to provide military assistance in the 1965 Indo-Pak war. It is true that the US withheld military supplies to both Pakistan and India during the war of 1965, yet Pakistan felt betrayed by this act because the most important reason for which it had joined the US camp was to meet any possible threat from India.

Despite acrimonious relations between Islamabad and Washington, some hopes of both the countries coming together became visible in early 1970 when Pakistan facilitated a secret dialogue between Washington and Beijing on the request of the US government. However, these hopes soon dashed in the wake of Indo-Pak war in 1971 resulting in Pakistan's partition and the formation of Bangladesh on 16 December 1971. During the war the US once again failed in helping out Pakistan, its closest ally in South Asia. Although the Nixon administration showed some tilt towards Pakistan, it did nothing substantive to preserve East Pakistan from dismemberment.[12] On the contrary, the US stopped economic and military aid for Pakistan.[13] On the other hand, the Soviet Union fully supported India by providing political, diplomatic and military support. The animosity between the two countries was further accentuated by the Pakistani government's decision to go for nuclear tests in 1974, which took place soon after the Indian nuclear tests. This resulted in the withdrawal of the earlier US-offer for the sale of A-7 aircraft to Pakistan and US-Pakistan relations reached their lowest level.

Notwithstanding the prevalence of deep distrust between the two countries, some signs of close cooperation began to surface in the early 1980s in the backdrop of the Soviet invasion of Afghanistan in 1979.[14] Both the countries perceived the invasion as a great threat to their interests. For the US, the success of the invasion meant the further expansion of Soviet power in the region, which was not acceptable to it. From Pakistan's point of view; its security became unsecured with the presence of over 80,000 Soviet troops in Afghanistan.[15] Of course, Pakistan could get huge amount of US military and economic assistance in return for its cooperation as well as other benefits.[16]

After having close alliance for a decade, cracks started reemerging in the relations between Washington and Islamabad. With the withdrawal of Soviet forces from Afghanistan, the former's disintegration and the end of the Cold War in the early 1990s, the US emerged as the sole superpower, resulting in the shift of the US policy in South Asia. This marked shift in the US policy affected Pakistan severely. Now it no longer remained a strategically significant frontline state of the US. In fact, the US started mounting pressure on Pakistan to toe its line on a number of issues. For instance, nuclear sanctions were imposed under the Pressler Amendment (1985) after the refusal of the US president to issue the required certificate in 1990. The United States also denied the transfer of 28 F-16 aircraft and military equipment for which Pakistan had paid $658 million in advance.[17] The relationship further deteriorated when the US imposed a second set of sanctions on Pakistan under the 1994 Glenn Amendment, following a series of nuclear tests by Pakistan in 1998.[18] Needless to add, the US coming out in support of India during the Kargil war in 1999 and the five day-visit of President Clinton to India in March 2000 and his just five hours' stay in Pakistan underlined the shift in the US policy on South Asia, which, further led to the shrinking of relationship between the US and Pakistan.[19]

The War on Terrorism: The Beginning of a Complex Relationship

Pakistan and the US entered the new century with their bilateral ties at an all time low. Yet, as had happened in the past, Islamabad and Washington appeared to be coming together afresh to forge cooperation between them, this time, to fight against terrorism in Afghanistan in the wake of the 9/11 attacks on the US, which were masterminded by a group of terrorists believed to be the members of the al-Qaeda led by Osama-bin-Laden. But this time the US did not approach Pakistan in the manner of request; instead it asked it to cooperate in eradicating the menace of terrorism by acting on at least six demands, which included:

1. Stop al-Qaeda operations on the Pakistani border, intercept arms shipments through Pakistan, and stop all logistical support to bin Laden.
2. Allow blanket over-flight and landing rights for US planes.
3. Allow access to Pakistan's naval bases, airbases, and borders.
4. Curb all domestic expression of support for terrorism against the United States, its friends, and allies.

5. Cut off Taliban's fuel supply and stop Pakistani volunteers going into Afghanistan to join the Taliban.
6. Break diplomatic relations with the Taliban and assist the United States in destroying bin-Laden and his al-Qaeda network.[20]

Sensing the future course of action of the US in case Pakistan declines to join the war against terrorism, Gen. Musharraf promptly decided to extend full cooperation to the US and clearly stated the reasons for this in an address to the people of Pakistan on 19 September 2001. The first concern for Gen. Musharraf was to secure Pakistan's strategic assets because he feared that if Pakistan did not join the war against terrorism, the US in retaliation would attack Pakistani nuclear assets. Second, he felt that going with the US would end Pakistan's isolation in the international arena, which it had been facing over a long time, particularly since the 1998 nuclear tests. Third, he feared that Pakistan's interests in Kashmir would be jeopardized if he did not sign up for the war on terrorism. Fourth, it was possible in the opinion of Gen. Musharraf that Pakistan would also be declared a terrorist state. Fifth, joining the US would help prevent an anti-Pakistani government from coming to power in Kabul. Lastly, over the last few years the Pakistani economy had become fragile and the country had been facing great difficulties in carrying out developmental work, pushing Pakistan to the verge of being a failed state. Thus, Gen. Musharraf anticipated that giving support to the US would enable Pakistan to get aid not only from the US but also from international financial institutions and other countries and thereby, Pakistan would re-emerge politically as a responsible and dignified nation.[21]

As also expected by a section of scholars on South Asia, Pakistan's joining the war against terrorism in Afghanistan could pave the way for both the countries to develop close ties once again. The US could secure valuable military and intelligence support from Pakistan. In the first few months of the war, over 28,000 sorties overflew Pakistani airspace from carriers in the Indian Ocean. Pakistan provided the US access to numerous military bases and helped establish a number of facilities including Intermediate Staging Bases at Jacobabad, Pasni, Dalbandin and Shamsi; Predator bases at Jacobabad and Shamsi, and access to other bases used by over 50 aircraft and 2,000 coalition military personnel. Pakistan provided fuel to aircraft, averaging

100,000 gallons per day, initially without any established repayment mechanism. It provided over 35,000 troops to protect these coalition bases and increased border security that reportedly resulted in the capture of 420 high value Taliban and al-Qaeda fugitives. Pakistan also provided intelligence support to coalition forces, most notably human intelligence which coalition forces desperately needed to complement their technical intelligence.[22]

In return, The US lifted economic sanctions on Pakistan and started providing economic and military support to Pakistan. In the first three years, the US extended $1 billion in grants, wrote off $1 billion in debt, provided $1.2 billion in arms sales, reinstituted a military training programme, and provided $3 billion for economic aid and security assistance.[23] The US government also genuinely sought to reduce Pakistan's foreign debt. Besides using its influence on G-8 countries for economic cooperation, the United States facilitated Pakistan's negotiations with the International Monetary Fund (IMF). America also reassured the Pakistani leadership that its nuclear weapon capability was acceptable and would not result in future roll-backs. The United States and Pakistan also started negotiation on matters related to nuclear non-proliferation, and agreed to resolve the proliferation issues involving Abdul Qadeer Khan, founder of Pakistan's nuclear weapons programme, in a mutually acceptable manner.[24]

Thus, the immediate outcome of Pakistan joining the US-led war against terrorism showed some good results for the people of Pakistan. For instance, in the following months the Pakistani economy started showing signs of improvement, which was one of the most vital issues in the country with high unemployment and inadequate infrastructure and other basic facilities. Pakistan's real GDP growth of 8.4 per cent in 2004-5 was the highest in two decades. Its debt burden came down and many mega projects like the port of Gwadar were started. The condition of schools was improved, leading to an increase in the enrolment of students at the primary level. Furthermore, the US assistance helped Pakistan launch large-scale economic and development projects, particularly in the areas bordering with Afghanistan which had been cleansed of terrorist cells. The construction of roads, schools, and hospitals in previously inaccessible regions helped bring local inhabitants into the mainstream of national life. This two-pronged strategy was developed to achieve both the short-term goal of defeating the terrorists and the long-term objective of eliminating the conditions that foster terrorism.

However, the process of establishing close ties between the two countries received a jolt, as the US started questioning Pakistan's commitment to and cooperation in, the war on terrorism.[25] US officials complained that Pakistani forces had not been aggressive enough in curbing the movement of the Taliban and the al-Qaeda militants out of Afghanistan and into Pakistan. Washington also criticized Islamabad for not persisting with attacks on militants within Pakistan.[26]

The US was not happy with the intelligence cooperation from Pakistan. In fact, there was fear that there were rough operations outside the control of Pakistani government that were undermining the war on terrorism and elements in the Pakistani establishment may be tipping off about impending US and Pakistan attacks and may also be continuing to support them with arms and money.[27] Washington was also very upset with the fact that the Pakistani government had not been doing enough to curb anti-American feeling in the country and the threats of jihad and terrorism against the US and its friends and allies. Washington expressed its concerns over Pakistan's nuclear programme and possible access of terrorist groups to nuclear weapons in the country.

On the other hand, the Pakistani government was upset with the fact the US was not recognizing and appreciating its cooperation in the war. It was also disturbed over US military action inside Pakistan, violating Pakistani sovereignty. The increasing collaboration between the US and India and the growing presence of the latter in Afghanistan were other matters of great concern for Pakistan. Along with it, the US maintaining distance on the issue of Kashmir continued to be an irritant in the relationship of Pakistan and the US. Apart from the deteriorating economy, political turmoil, increasing attacks by terrorists, the issue of unemployment and the failing education system were some other issues which further contributed to increasing rift between Islamabad and Washington.

The Obama Administration's Policy towards Pakistan

Against this background, one of the top priorities of the newly elected government under President Barack Obama was to prevent Pakistan from becoming a 'failed state' and to ensure the continuation of Pakistan's support in the war against terrorism in Afghanistan. Accordingly, President Obama came out with a new Af-Pak policy, which had a clear and focused goal: to disrupt, dismantle and defeat al-Qaeda in Pakistan and Afghanistan, and to prevent their return to either country in the future. At the same time, as explained above, the Obama administration also acknowledged the fact that the conflict in Afghanistan could not be resolved without addressing the sources of terrorism in Pakistan. In this context, the Obama administration not only appointed former Clinton administration diplomat Richard Holbrooke to be the Special Representative to Afghanistan and Pakistan (SRAP) to see that the new strategy brings the expected results. As a part of the new strategy, he announced to deploy 30,000 more troops in Afghanistan, but also restated the commitment to help Pakistani people to 'build a stable economy, a stronger democracy, and a vibrant civil society'.[28] As a result, Pakistan soon could get $1.5 billion economic assistance under the Kerry-Lugar Act over the next five years to build schools, roads, and hospitals and create opportunity zones in the border region to develop the economy and bring hope to places plagued by violence, military assistance to root out the terrorists, strengthen its democratic institutions.[29] President Obama also announced that a standing, trilateral dialogue would be launched among the United States, Afghanistan and Pakistan to discuss new developments in the region. He also maintained that enhanced intelligence sharing and military cooperation along the border must be ensured, while addressing issues of common concern like trade, energy, and economic development.[30] Despite his willingness to help Pakistan economically, President Obama publicly warned Pakistan of hard consequences by saying that gone are the days when blank cheques were given to Afghanistan and Pakistan. In his speech he outlined that Pakistan and Afghanistan had to perform, or aid would be stopped.[31]

In the following months the new strategy produced some good outcomes from the US point of view. For instance, the Pakistani security agencies took a more aggressive stance against militants, targeting them in key areas in the north and west (Swat, Malakand, South Waziristan, and Bajaur) in an attempt to wrest control from militants and 'reverse their momentum'.[32] The Pakistani military's large-scale domestic air and ground operations were unprecedented in the country's history and indeed, the ground offensives launched in 2009 garnered much praise from the US and other Western observers.

In fact, U.S. Central Command Chief General David Petraeus called the counter-insurgency operations in Swat and South Waziristan 'quite impressive' and said the tactics used would be studied for years to come.[33] On the other hand, Pakistan's gains were also eclipsed by more visible and pressing issues. There was national consensus on anti-terrorism operations. Swat was fast returning to normalcy, lawless areas of Waziristan were under control and the strategic strip of Malkand, Bajaur and Mohmand were brought under civil administration. What could be described as a very important success for both Pakistani and US interests and a psychological blow to the Pakistani Taliban was the killing of Baitullah Mehsud, the founding TTP chief, in a US-launched missile strike in August 2009.[34]

Furthermore, US Secretary of State, Hillary Rodham Clinton and Pakistan's foreign minister, Shah Mahmood Qureshi, held the US-Pakistan Strategic Dialogue in Washington during 24-5 March 2010.[35] The dialogue was seen as a major step towards overcoming the prevailing trust deficit between the two countries. The US once again acknowledged the contribution of Pakistan in the war against terrorism, assured it help on a number of issues and reiterated its commitment to enhancing the country's inherent capacities to realize the vision of a democratic, progressive state. The United States re-affirmed its resolve to assist Pakistan to overcome socio-economic challenges by providing technical and economic assistance and to enable Pakistan to build its strengths by optimal utilization of its considerable human and natural resources and entrepreneurial skills. The United States committed to work towards enhanced market access for Pakistani products as well as towards the early finalization of Reconstruction Opportunity Zones legislation. A Policy Steering Group was established to intensify and expand the sectoral dialogue process in the fields of economy and trade; energy; defense; security, strategic stability, and non-proliferation; law enforcement and counter-terrorism; science and technology; education; agriculture; water; health; and communications and public diplomacy.[36]

The Elements of Conflict and Mistrust

Despite these positive developments, the elements of conflict and mistrust have continued to affect the US-Pakistan relationship. For instance, Secretary Clinton told a House panel in April 2009 that 'the Pakistani government is basically abdicating to the Taliban and to the extremists'. Secretary of Defense Robert Gates followed it up with his own warning that US-Pakistan relations could suffer if Islamabad did not 'take appropriate actions' to deal with the militant threat.[37] Days later, President Obama himself expressed 'grave concern' about the situation in Pakistan, offering that the 'very fragile' civilian government there did not appear to have the capacity to deliver basic services to the Pakistani people. He did, however, acknowledge that the Pakistani military was showing more seriousness in addressing the threat posed by militants.[38] Thus the concerns expressed by the top three individuals, including the president underlined the fact about the prevailing trust deficit between the two countries.

The drift between Islamabad and Washington was further accentuated by the harassing of American diplomats by Pakistani military and intelligence elements, mainly through travel document delays, an effort that was resulting in significant delays to vital security and economic aid programmes. The US Embassy also formally complained that its diplomatic vehicles were subject to 'harassment' through 'contrived incidents'. While a State Department spokesman refrained from calling the development a 'deliberate campaign', he acknowledged that the backlog of 'several hundred' US visa applications and renewals was a 'big concern' that had been raised with Islamabad at 'very senior levels'.[39]

The arrest of David Coleman Headley in 2009 in connection with the 2008 terrorist attacks on Mumbai jolted the relations further. Headley's interrogation revealed that he had travelled to Mumbai five times from 2006 to 2008 as scout for the attack by the Pakistan-based Lashkar-e-Taiba (LeT) terrorist group; he subsequently pleaded guilty to the charges. Not only this, Headley's case became very important because of the fact that this was perhaps the first case in which a former Pakistani military officer has been directly linked to terrorist suspects in the United States. Headley and another Pakistan-born American, Tahawwur Rana, are believed to have reported to Abdur Rehman, a retired Pakistani major suspected of being a LeT contact.

Another factor for bitterness between the US and Pakistan was the increasing collaboration between China and Pakistan. Chinese companies and workers are now pervasive in the Pakistani economy. Beijing intends to build two new civilian nuclear reactors in Pakistan in what would be an apparent violation of international guidelines. During

Chinese Premier Wen Jiabao's December 2010 visit to Islamabad, the two governments signed 12 Memoranda of Understanding covering a broad range of cooperative efforts and designated 2011 as the 'Year of China-Pakistan Friendship'. Pakistani and Chinese businesses also signed contracts worth some $15 billion covering cooperation in oil and gas, mining, space technology, heavy machinery, manufacturing, and other areas. This added to the nearly $20 billion worth of government-to-government agreements reached.[40] In this context, there is not only a growing concern among American analysts about the utility of US assistance to Pakistan, but also a suspicion of Pakistan's real motive in the region.

However, what became a breaking point in the US-Pakistan relations was the case of CIA contractor Raymond Davis, who was arrested in Pakistan for shooting to death of the two Pakistanis who allegedly tried to rob him in downtown Lahore on 27 January 2011. Though, after days of tussle, the US could secure the release of Davis by paying $5 million 'blood money' to the families of the victims, yet the incident created bitterness between the two countries because the Pakistani government initially refused the US argument that Raymond Davis was an attaché to US embassy in the country. As a result of this development, while ISI restricted intelligence cooperation, the Americans responded inter alia by postponing an upcoming session of the Strategic Dialogue.[41]

Furthermore, the US apparently became very critical of the Sharia deal in Swat, which came into existence through the signing by President Zardari of a regulation in April 2009. A White House official said that solutions to Pakistan's security problems 'don't include less democracy and less human rights'. He further emphasized that the United States was 'very concerned' and maintained a view that 'violent extremists need to be confronted'. Prime Minister Gillani, however, dismissed US criticisms by claiming the issue was an internal matter and that his government had no alternatives given the circumstances.[42]

The issue of drone attacks emerged as another bone of contention between the US and Pakistan. In order to flush out terrorists in Pakistani regions bordering Afghanistan, the Obama administration resorted to drone attacks and by one assessment, 118 such drone strikes occurred in 2010 alone, more than during the preceding six years combined. Though the drone attacks have taken a significant toll on al-Qaeda and other Islamist extremist militants, a huge number of civilians have also been killed in attacks and this has generated extreme outrage among the Pakistani people against the US military. At the same time, the attacks have also been seen as a violation of the national sovereignty of Pakistan. In fact, reacting to the killing of 44 people in an apparent drone strike in North Waziristan, which took place just one day after Raymond Davis's release, the Foreign Ministry of Pakistan called the US action as 'flagrant violation of all humanitarian rules and norms'. In the same vein, referring to the US, Army Chief Gen. Ashfaq Parvez Kayani said in a statement that 'peaceful citizens' had been 'carelessly and callously targeted with complete disregard for human life' in an 'act of violence' that 'takes us away from our objective of elimination of terrorism'.[43]

Further, the gap between the US and Pakistan has widened after the killing of Osama-bin-Laden in Abottabad by US Special Forces on 2 May 2011. Though the Pakistani government expressed happiness over the killing of Osama, it criticized the US for violating the sovereignty of Pakistan and for not informing it about the operation. At the same time it became humiliating for the Pakistani military, for, the world's most wanted terrorist had been living for five years just a few hundred metres from the country's premier military academy. On the other side, the commitment of Pakistan to fight terrorism was widely questioned in the US. In fact, the Americans started raising questions about utility of continuing ties with, and providing financial assistance to Pakistan, which forced the Obama administration to suspend some $800 million in military transfers, including $300 million to reimburse Pakistan for expenses incurred in fighting the militants. In turn, Pakistan threatened to withdraw troops from the Afghan border and increased its efforts to establish close ties with China, bringing the relationship to an all time low.[44]

The Future Prospects

Though, Islamabad and Washington are facing the most difficult phase in their bilateral relations, it is unlikely that both the US and Pakistan can afford to be at odds with each other for a long time for many reasons. For instance, the US cannot win the war against terrorism in Afghanistan without the help of Pakistan. Similarly, Pakistan is very much dependent on the US for financial assistance.

Viewed in this context, it is imperative for the US and Pakistan to take steps to bring back the relationship on track, which can be started by taking the following initiatives.

The focus of American development assistance within Pakistan should be to broadly engage democratic leaders and civil society as well as continue funding for development and security purposes because it will create positive impression about the US in Pakistan, and also increase Pakistan's capacity to provide a stable civil government and take initiatives for repairing its torn economy. At the same time, the US should provide financial assistance to Pakistan for improving its education system, which in turn would help Pakistan to develop its people along the path of civil norms, peace and prosperity.

The US should not fruitlessly try to institutionalize political parties against the will of their leaders, fundamentally reshape Pakistani society, or place misguided faith in strategic communication and public diplomacy.

The US should start investment and potential trade agreements with Pakistan so that the Pakistani economy could improve, which will have very significant impact on the stability, peace and development in Pakistan. On the one hand, this would create jobs for the common people, and on the other the influence of terrorist groups will also decline in the country.

One challenging task that Washington needs to perform in order to establish a working relationship with Islamabad is to ensure a balance between the government and the military in Pakistan because there is a general perception in the country that Washington always likes Islamabad being ruled by the military. Secondly, it has also to ensure that the financial assistance given to Pakistan is not diverted for military purposes.

The US should facilitate normalization of the relationship between India and Pakistan because this would benefit the United States in more ways than one. It could, for instance, ease Pakistan's security fears and help lower the army's political profile, opening the way for democratization, and advance the prospects of an integrated South Asia market linked to the energy-rich Central Asia, increasing opportunities for US investment there. Peace between India and Pakistan will also ease fears of a nuclear war, may open up the possibility of their incorporation into the international nuclear community, and will help strengthen their command and control structure, which will encourage non-proliferation.

Pakistan must not divert the financial assistance from the US for settling old scores with its neighbours, but use it for the intended purposes. Though, China is providing financial assistance, there is no match between China's contribution and that of the US. Pakistan must show its commitment towards eliminating terrorism by taking honest steps against terrorist groups residing in its territory. In this context, it needs to delink the virtual collaboration between the military and terrorist groups. Pakistan should also understand that the terrorist groups having got shelter in the country became more dangerous to Pakistani people than to others. Taking action against these groups will not only help the country establish friendly relations with the US, but also enhance its prestige across the globe.

Conclusion

In conclusion, though Pakistan and the US are facing a tough time in their bilateral relations, yet the prevailing ground realities seem to indicate that Islamabad and Washington cannot afford having acrimonious relations between themselves. For instance, the US cannot solve issues like terrorism and nuclear proliferation without the active support of Pakistan. Neither can Pakistan fix alone its internal problems like the deteriorating economic conditions, poor functioning of democracy and others. Viewed in this context, both countries should understand that they need each other's help in their respective endeavours, in particular maintaining peace and security at the global level. One way they can reinstate confidence in their bilateral relations is to understand each other's compulsions and limits.

Notes

1. John Rollins, 'Osama bin Laden's Death: Implications and Considerations' (Washington: Congress Research Services-R41809, 5 May 2011), http://www.fas.org/sgp/crs/terrpr/R418098.pdf) (accessed on 5 July 2011), Alex Rodriguez, 'Suspicions Grow over Whether Pakistan Aided Osama Bin Laden', *Los Angeles Times*, 2 May 2011, http://articles.latimes.co/2011/may/02/world/la-fg-bin-laden-pakistan-20110502 (accessed on 8 July 2011); Junaid S. Ahmad, 'Pakistani-US Relations in the post-Osama Era', Al Jazeera Centre for Studies, 31 May 2011, http://www.aljazeera.net/mritems/streams/2011/5/31/1_1065242_1_51.pdf (accessed on 8 July 2011).

2. Reza Sayah and Nick Paton Walsh, 'Pakistan's Prime Minister Warns United States', CNN, 28 November 2011, http://www.cnn.com/2011/11/28/world/asia/paikstan-us/ (accessed on 11 December 2012).
3. Shahid Javed Burki, *Historical Dictionary of Pakistan*, London: The Scarecrow Press, 1999, p. 336.
4. Robert J. McMahon, 'U.S. Policy toward South Asia and Tibet During the Early Cold War', *Cold War Studies*, vol. 8, no. 3, Summer 2006, pp. 131-44.
5. Robert J. McMahon 'United States Cold War Strategy in South Asia: Making a Military Commitment to Pakistan 1947-1954', *American History*, vol. 75, no. 3, December 1988, pp. 812-40.
6. Ibid.
7. Mohammed Ayub Khan, *Friends Not Masters*, London: Oxford University Press, 1967, p. 130.
8. Jayshree Bajoria, 'U.S Involvement in Pakistan', Council on Foreign Relations, 15 February 2008, http://www.cfr.org/publication/15260/uspakistan_relations.html (accessed on 7 April 2011).
9. Sumit Kumar, 'From Estranged Democracies to Pragmatic Partnership: India-US Relations (1998-2008)', M. Phil thesis submitted to Pondicherry University, 2010, Ch.1.
10. Dennis Kux, *The United States and Pakistan 1947-2000: Disenchanted Allies*, Baltimore: Johns Hopkins University Press, 2011, p. 161.
11. Safdar Sial, 'Pak-US: A Balance Sheet of Relations', Islamabad: Pak Institute for Peace Studies, 26 June 2007.
12. Tariq Gilani, 'US-Pakistan Relations: The Way Forward', US Army War College (USAWC) Strategy Research Project, 15 May 2006, http://irnegotiation0708.pbworks.com/f/US-Pakistan+relations.pdf (accessed on 12 August 2011).
13. Jehangir Khan, 'US-Pakistan Relations: The Geo-strategic and Geo-political Factors', *Canadian Social Science*, vol. 6, no. 2, 2010, pp. 61-79.
14. Chandra Chari, *Superpower Rivalry and Conflict the Long Shadow of the Cold War on the Twenty-first Century*, London: Routledge, 2010, pp. 57-71.
15. Samina Ahmed, 'The United States and Terrorism in Southwest Asia: September 11 and Beyond', *International Security*, Winter 2001/2, p. 80.
16. David A. Anderson and Heather Maki, 'Pakistan's Nuclear Defense Ambitions and U.S. Relations: The Global War on Terror in FATA:

Promoting Regional Stability?' *China and Eurasia Forum Quarterly*, vol. 6, no. 3, 2008, pp. 45-64.

17. Khan, 'US-Pakistan Relations: The Geo-strategic and Geo-political Factors, pp. 61-79.
18. Sumit Ganguly, 'India's Pathway to Pokhran II: The Prospects and Sources of New Delhi's Nuclear Weapons Programme', *International Security*, vol. 23, no. 4, Spring 1999, pp. 148-77.
19. Hassan Abbas, *Pakistan's Drift into Extremism: Allah, the Army, and America's War on Terror*, New York: East Gate Book, 2005 p. 189.
20. Anderson and Maki, 'Pakistan's Nuclear Defense Ambitions and U.S. Relations: The Global War on Terror in FATA: Promoting Regional Stability?' pp. 52-3.
21. President Pervez Musharraf s Address to the Nation on 19 September 2001 <http://www.nation.com.pk/daily/Sep-2003/main/top5.asp> (accessed on 13 May 2011), also see, Kanti Bajpai, 'Managing Ambivalence: Pakistan's Relations with the US and China since 2011', in Rajshree Jetly, ed., *Pakistan in Regional and Global Politics* London: Routledge, 2009, pp. 63-97.
22. C. Christine Fair, *The Counter Terror Coalitions*, Washington: RAND Corporation, 2004, pp. 30-3.
23. Owen Bennett Jones, 'Pakistan's Foreign Policy under Musharraf', March 2006, BBC World Service briefing paper, www.bbc.com (accessed on 4 July 2011).
24. Stephen Philip Cohen, 'America and Pakistan: Is the Worst Case Avoidable?' *Current History*, March 2005, p. 132.
25. House Committee on Foreign Affairs Holds a Hearing on 'New Beginnings: Foreign Policy Priorities in the Obama Administration', Washington: The American Congress, 22 April 2009, available on the Internet at http://democrats.foreignaffairs.house.gov/111/48841.pdf (accessed on 13 July 2011), also see, 'Pentagon Chief in Taliban Warning,' http://news.bbc.co.Uk/2/hi/8015604.stm (accessed on 13 July 2011).
26. Ibid.
27. Jayshree Bajoria and Eben Kaplan, 'The ISI and Terrorism: Beyond the Accusations', Council on Foreign Relations, 4 May 2011, http://www.cfr.org/pakistan/isi-terrorism-behind-accusations/pll644 (accessed on 6 July 2011, Augustine Anthony, 'Pakistan Puts Move to Rein in Spies on Ice', *Reuters*, 5 August 2008, http://www.reuters.com/article/2008/08/06/us-pakistan-spies-idUSISL31611520080806 (accessed on 6 July 2011).

28. 'President Obama' Address to the Nation on 'the Way Forward in Afghanistan and Pakistan', 1 December 2011, http://www.whitehouse.gov/the-press-office/remarks-president-address-nation-way-forward-afghanistan-and-Pakistan (accessed on 6 August 2011).
29. K. Alan Kronstadt, 'Pakistan-US Relation', Washington: Congress Research Services- RL33498, 6 February 2009, p. 102. http://fpc.state.gov/documents/organization/127297.pdf (accessed on 28 July 2011).
30. Ibid, pp. 6-9.
31. 'President Obama' Address to the Nation on 'the Way Forward in Afghanistan and Pakistan,' 1 December 2011, http://www.whitehouse,gov/the-press-office/remarks-president-address-nation-way-forward-afghanistan-and-Pakistan (accessed on 6 August 2011).
32. Brian Katulis, and Caroline Wadhams, Center for American Progress, 24 March 2010, http://www.americanprogress.org/issues/2010/03/pakistan__progress.html (accessed on 21 July 2011).
33. K. Alan Kronstadt, 'Pakistan: Key Current Issues and Developments', (Congress Services Report-R 41307, 1 June 2010), https://www.fas.org/sgp/crs/row/R41307.pdf (accessed on 9 August 2011), Chirs Allbriton, 'US Commander Lauds Pakistani Efforts on Militants', Reuters, 23 February 2010, http://in.reuters.com/article/2010/02/23/idINIndia-46409920100223 (accessed on 9 August 2011).
34. Ben Arnoldy, 'Strike on Mehsud Could Spur Stronger US-Pakistan Cooperation', Christian Science Monitor, 7 August 2009, http://connection.ebscohost.com/c/articles/43606307/strike-mehsud-could-spur-stronger-us-pakistan-cooperation (accessed on 10 August 2011), Alex Rodriguez, 'Pakistan Taliban Leader's Purported Death Opens Window of Opportunity', Los Angeles Times, 17 August 2009, http://articles.latimes.com/2009/aug/17/world/fg-pakistan-militants 17 (accessed on 10 August 2011).
35. Joint Statement on 'The US-Pakistan Strategic Dialogue in Washington', 25 March 2010, http://www.america.gov/st/texttrans english/2010/March/ 20100325145715 eaifas0.2140619.html (accessed on 28 July 2011).
36. Ibid.
37. House Committee on Foreign Affairs Holds a Hearing on 'New Beginnings: Foreign Policy Priorities in the Obama Administration,' (Washington: the American Congress, 22 April 2009), available on the Internet at http://democrats.foreignaffairs.house.gOv/l 1 1/48841.pdf (accessed on 13 July 2011).

38. Transcript on 'President Obama's 100th-Day', New York Times, 29 April 2009, http://www.nytimes.com/2009/04/29/us/politics/29text-obama.html?pagewanted=all (accessed on 23 August 2011).
39. Jane Perlez and Eric Schmitt, 'Pakistan Reported to Be Harassing US Diplomats', *New York Times*, 16 December 2009, http://www.nytimes.com/2009/12/17/world/asia/17visa.html?_r=0 (accessed on 23 August 2011), Sabrina Tavernise, 'Pakistan Begins to Ease Backlog of Visas for American Diplomats', *New York Times*, 9 April 2010, http://www.nytimes.com/2010/04/10/world/asia/10pstan.html (accessed on 23 August 2011).
40. 'China PM Vows to Boost Ties with Pakistan', *The Dawn*, 19 December 2010, http://www.dawn.com/news/592130/terrorism-should-not-be-linked-to-any-nation-chinese-pm (accessed on 3 July 2011).
41. K. Alan Kronstadt, *Pakistan-U.S. Relations*, Washington: Congress Research Services- R41832, 24 May 2012, p. 8, http://www.fas.org/sgp/crs/row/R41832.pdf (accessed on 12 June 2012).
42. K. Alan Kronstadt, *Pakistan: Key Current Issues and Developments*, Washington: Congress Research Services-R41307, 1 June 2010), pp. 17–18, https://www.fas.org/sgp/crs/row/R41307.pdf (accessed on 8 June 2011).
43. Adam Entous, 'Drone Warfare in Pakistan under President Barack Obama', Reuters, May 2010, http://static.reuters.com/resources/media/editorial/20100518/Drones.pdf (assessed on 8 June 2011), Huma Yusuf, 'Dealing with Davis: Inconsistencies in the US-Pakistan Relationship', *Asia Pacific Bulletin*, no. 103, 28 March 2011, Greg Bruno, 'U.S. Drone Activities in Pakistan', Council on Foreign Relations, 19 July 2010, http://www.cfr.org/pakistan/us-drone-activities-pakistan/p22659 (accessed on 8 August 2011).
44. Jim Lobe, 'An $800 Million Teaser', Asia Times, 13 July 2011, http://www.atimes.com/atimes/War_and_Terrorl06.html (accessed on 8 August 2011), Rob Crilly 'Pakistan Threatens to Withdraw Troops from Afghan Border over US Aid Reduction', *The Telegraph*, 12 July 2011, http://www.telegraph.co.uk/news/worldnews/asia/pakistan/8632460/Pakistan-threatens-to-withdraw-troops-from-Afghan-border-over-US-aid-reduction.html (accessed on 9 August 2011).

PAKISTAN AND JAMMU & KASHMIR

CHAPTER 20

Pakistan's Changing Policy on Kashmir

Dimensions and Determinants

Samir Ahmad Bhat

IN LATE 1930S, India was undergoing a kind of political furor. Soon the Second World War began. The Indian National Congress put forth the demand for complete freedom of India, while the Muslim League began to raise the slogan for the establishment of a separate homeland – Pakistan – by dividing the country. But the question was how to split the country as the Congress was not ready for that. Nevertheless, all the concerned parties – Congress, Muslim League and the British government reached an agreement and India was effectively divided into two new dominions, India and Pakistan, with a number of issues remaining unsettled between the two independent nations.

The most complex of all these problems has been the issue of political dispensation of the state of Jammu & Kashmir. Of all the princely states (semi-autonomous) Jammu & Kashmir was the only state that in terms of geographical proximity, could join either of the two new dominion governments as it bordered with both the newly-emerging independent countries. This factor combined with the indecisiveness of its then Maharaja, Hari Singh, led to the complications in its future political status. His belated decision of accession to the Indian Union under the challenge of tribal invasion of the state had not helped to settle the issue of the state's political placement effectively and unquestionably. His tardy decision prompted a first military clash between India and Pakistan followed by diplomatic contestations internationally within the United Nations Organization (UNO). The state effectively has got divided between what has been known as India- and Pakistan-controlled parts of Jammu & Kashmir, and has emerged as a major cause of conflict between the two, ever since their independence in 1947.

Both the nations have their own interpretation of the issue. India argues that the state of Jammu & Kashmir has already acceded to the Indian Union through the *Instrument of Accession*, signed between Maharaja Hari Singh and the Indian state under the leadership of Jawaharlal Nehru, the decision which was later ratified by the Jammu & Kashmir state constituent assembly under the leadership of Bakshi Ghulam Mohammad. On the other hand, Pakistan from the very beginning has been opposing the *Instrument of Accession* signed by the Indian state and Maharaja Hari Singh. Pakistan is of the opinion that the accession signed by the Maharaja had violated the 'Stand Still Agreement' which Maharaja Hari Singh had signed with the Government of Pakistan earlier to his signing the accession. Second, this accession was provisional and conditional to the holding of a free and fair referendum under the auspices of the UN, through which the wishes of the people would be ascertained. Since this provision has not been fulfilled, the accession cannot be called legal and valid. Third, Kashmir is geographically more contiguous to Pakistan than to any other country. It has had strong economic, trade and cultural links with Pakistan in the past. Further, Pakistan contests Indian claim that Kashmir being a part of India is necessary for retaining its secular character. Rather, Pakistan says that Kashmir and its Muslim citizens must be part of an Islamic homeland, Pakistan. It is in the light of all these factors that Pakistan is of the opinion that India is in unlawful occupation of Jammu & Kashmir and that it has denied Kashmiris the right to determine their future in accordance with their aspirations.As a result, its defense and foreign policy have been significantly influenced by this attitude and until recently it has made great sacrifices to pursue and hold this stubborn and proactive approach on the issue.

These divergent claims on the state of Jammu & Kashmir and its political future helped in promoting and perpetuating a conflicting relationship between the two countries and thereby, distorting their developmental priorities. Because of this factor the two states have tried to undermine each other, diplomatically, politically, militarily and economically. Over the last six decades, the two countries have got involved in three full-fledged wars, in 1947, 1965, and 1971, the first two of them explicitly over the Kashmir issue. Besides there have been a number of serious localized military confrontations of a very high magnitude, for example, Operation Meghdoot in 1984, operations Brasstacks in 1986, Kargil war in 1999 and Operation Parakaram that was actually in response to the terrorist attack on the Indian parliament on 13 December 2001. However, these have not made any decisive impact on the Kashmir problem. The failure to resolve the issue through military means led the two countries to initiate a number of diplomatic initiatives in the form of a number of bilateral talks, conferences, and agreements such as the Tashkent Agreement, Simla Agreement, Lahore Declaration, Agra Summit, Composite Dialogue and some other official and semi-official negotiations.

However, over the last decade or so there has been a radical shift in Pakistan's strategy on Kashmir in response to developments at the international and regional levels, particularly within the state of Pakistan. These include the, nuclearization of South Asia, Pakistan's rapidly deteriorating political conditions, uncertainty in its civil-military relations, its declining economy, rising ethnic and sectarian conflicts, precarious condition of its democratic institutions, ferociously mounting international pressure to stop sheltering militant groups operating in Kashmir (after the cataclysmic events of 9/11), and most importantly the realization within Pakistan to reduce over-commitment to its military budget and to invest more of its resources on other important sectors like education, health and internal security. Pakistan's earlier position was that Kashmir is the most contentious issue between the two states and no dialogue can move forward unless this issue is resolved by holding a plebiscite under the UN resolution that enables Kashmiris to decide their political future. However, Pakistan has now started realizing a need for moving away from this conventional position on Kashmir so that a workable and mutually acceptable solution to the problem becomes possible. These developments have also gradually led Pakistan to change its policy towards the neighbouring countries.

The main focus and objective of this article is to examine and analyse the various determining factors and developments that took place both at the local and at the international level which ultimately led to a fundamental shift in Pakistan's outlook *vis-à-vis* the Kashmir issue.

Gradual Shift in Pakistan's Kashmir Policy

As mentioned earlier, the last sixty years have seen many ups and downs in the efforts of India and Pakistan to resolve the Kashmir issue. The relations between the two nations have been, at best, cool and at worst, hostile. It has been a two-dimensional relationship which has operated at two levels – conflict and attempts at reconciliation. Their relationship has always been characterized by mutual suspicion and need for trust building. As political rivals, they thrive on unresolved issues that need settlement; at the same time their history is chequered with deep mistrust and suspicion. Initiatives to settle the issues have ranged from a direct military war to bilateral dialogues and discussions at various levels through different channels. However, most of these attempts have been foiled due to the conventional positions held by both the countries *vis-à-vis* the Kashmir issue and thus standing as a major stumbling block in changing the mindset and constraining the prospects for peace and prosperity in the region. But from the mid-1990s a number of developments have coerced Islamabad to show flexibility, seek a path of cooperation and engage in a peace process with India in an attempt to resolve all the issues bedevilling relations between the two states.[1]

A major development in this direction was President Gen. Pervez Musharraf's historic statement that the Government of Pakistan was ready to leave behind its sixty-year long stand that the Kashmir issue should be resolved under the United Nations Security Council resolutions adopted from time to time. Rather, the former president gave a four-point formula, which included identification of the regions; phased withdrawal of the troops; self-governance within each region; and a joint supervision or mechanism involving India, Pakistan and representatives from Kashmir with a soft border connecting the identified regions. He reiterated this proposal in his autobiography *In the Line of Fire* as well.

The foremost step in the four-point formula given by Gen. Pervez Musharraf envisages that the divided state of Jammu & Kashmir consist of five regions, two on the Pakistan side, viz., 'Azad Jammu & Kashmir' and Northern Areas and three on the Indian side, viz. Kashmir, Jammu and Ladakh. What the formula emphasizes is first to identify the regions, then seek demilitarization of the identified regions and finally change their status. These regions could be based on ethno-regional factors, by and large being influenced by language and religion.

The second step is demilitarization of the identified regions. The people of the region have suffered enough over the last sixty years, more particularly during last twenty years of militancy. Therefore, military should be garrisoned in a few places, if not completely moved out. This is not going to be easy process, but Gen. Musharraf asserted that the demilitarization of the area would be a great confidence-building measure and will provide relief to Kashmir and will be an important move to discourage militancy.

Once the process of demilitarization is complete, the people of the region/s should be given maximum autonomy to decide their internal matters themselves, or in other words, there should be self-governance but short of complete independence as it is not acceptable to either India or Pakistan.[2] Gen. Musharraf disapproved the Indian claim that this is providing a form of autonomy in Kashmir which is under its control. In an interview to CNN-IBN news channel he said, 'I did not agree with India's claim that there is already self-governance in the held Kashmir' and claimed that most of the people there do not accept the Indian government. 'If India believed that there was self-governance, we keep sticking to this position, we will never move forward because we do not agree. Therefore, if you want to move forward, we have to leave the stated position.'[3]

The fourth and final step of Musharraf's proposal is the joint management or mechanism. Though, sovereignty would be shared through a mechanism of self-governance, yet there would be residual elements left under the joint management mechanism. It will retain the powers over them to run these affairs jointly. The two states will retain sovereignty over the respective parts of Kashmir.

Genral Musharraf was very positive about the four-point formula. While speaking in a conference organized by the Washington-based think-tank, Pugwash, in March 2006, President Pervez Musharraf said that 'his country's proposal for demilitarization and self-governance offered a practical solution to the Kashmir dispute. An ultimate solution to the problem on these lines would make the Line of Control (LoC) irrelevant and at the same time there won't be need for any drastic change in the current status quo. And such a solution would not require the redrawing of borders.

Gen. Pervez Musharraf is the first leader, civilian or military, in the history of Pakistan who has stated a desire to move away from the demand for the implementation of the United Nations Security Council resolutions as a means to resolving the Kashmir dispute. In fact, earlier also, Pervez Musharraf, on several occasions signaled a shift in Pakistan's conventional approach toward the resolution of the Kashmir issue. Immediately after the suspension of the civilian government in October 1999 Mushrraf announced unilateral de-escalation along the border and expressed a willingness to work with India to take South Asia out of economic deprivation. During the Agra summit in July 2001 he suggested a four-step resolution process whose first and most important step was rejection of any solution that either country found unacceptable; the other three steps were the initiation of dialogue, acceptance of Kashmir as the core issue and exploring the remaining options.[4] On 25 October 2004 in an Iftar party in Islamabad he stressed upon a national debate to explore the feasible options for the resolution of Kashmir issue as he said that plebiscite is not acceptable to either of the two countries, India and Pakistan. In this regard the controversial remarks made by Pakistani President Asif Ali Zardari that 'India does not pose a threat' to Pakistan and his reference to militant groups in Kashmir as 'terrorists' in an interview with the *Wall Street Journal* have not just created a storm in Pakistani domestic politics but highlighted the need for a paradigm shift in both the countries and should be seen as a continuation of the soft policy adopted by the previous military governments of Pakistan over the Kashmir issue. It should not be seen in isolation but rather in the context of the changing global scene.

Let me return to the main focus of the article that explains this radical break with the past in Pakistan's Kashmir policy. Is it only because the Pakistani establishment has realized that it is increasingly losing legitimacy and ground in Kashmir, that the people of Kashmir are no longer looking towards Pakistan for deliverance as they did in the past[5] and there has been growing public participation in the various elections held over the past few years. There are other tangible factors and dimensions to this changing attitude from Islamabad, and each of these factors should be seen in connection with the others.

As already hinted one cannot realistically overlook the changes in geopolitics that the world has witnessed since the last decade of the twentieth century. In this regard the first major and significant change is the end of the Cold War and bipolarity at the world level. As a result, a new order has evolved and new geopolitical equations have been developed in which United States of America (USA) has emerged a new sole super power. In the new equation the USA has dramatically shifted its foreign policy priorities in South Asia from seeking Pakistan's cooperation to non-proliferation and repairing the damage caused to its relations with India due to its Pakistan-Afghanistan policies during the Cold War phase. The USA is no longer willing to support Pakistan's economic development and the modernization of its military institution. This has been starkly manifested through a chain of restrictions the US enacted against Pakistan after the conclusion of the Cold War. In October 1990, US President George Bush (senior) refused to certify that Pakistan did not possess a nuclear explosive device, thereby, triggering the imposition of suspension of aid to Pakistan under the Pressler Amendment (1985) in the Foreign Assistance Act. This disrupted the second assistance package offered in 1987 and discontinued economic assistance and military sales to Pakistan under the package. In addition to this, various military sales and training programme were disrupted and some of the Pakistani military officers under training in the USA were asked to return home. Further, the policy of supporting allies whether they were right or wrong, could no longer work as it could considerably erode the US's legitimacy to intervene in world affairs to promote its interests and ideas. United States could not afford to alienate countries that were likely to become important powers in future. In this context, India's potential both in terms of geopolitics and in terms of its market could not be ignored.[6]

Similarly, other major powers' including China's perception on Kashmir issue has been changing. This was witnessed during the Kargil war, when China, Pakistan's close ally, preferred to remain neutral instead of extending its diplomatic support as it did on several occasions in the past. 'China has changed its stance on Kashmir, it no longer says that there should be plebiscite in Kashmir; rather, it is of the opinion that Kashmir is a matter that needs to be resolved through bilateral negotiations between India and Pakistan.'[7]

In the past, Beijing supported Islamabad's positions on the Kashmir issue to demonstrate solidarity with an 'all weather' ally during periods of Sino-Indian estrangement and hostility. But now normalization of relations with New Delhi has necessitated the adoption of a policy of neutrality to avoid unnecessarily alienating India and running the risk of entrapment.[8] In 1993, the two countries, India and China had signed a peace and tranquility agreement as well as another pact to lessen tensions along the disputed Sino-Indian border. Similarly, in 2003–4 the trade between India and China touched US $7 billion mark and by the end of 2005 the bilateral trade went up to US $18.7 billion, several times larger than the figure a decade ago.[9] China has also changed its position on Kashmir and begun to hint that Pakistan should consider LoC as an international border. China, however, continues to maintain its traditional ties with Pakistan, which is seen less as a counter to India and more as an important factor in Beijing's fight against ethnic separatist problem in Xingjiang and also as a gateway to the Muslim world.

The dawn of globalization with its easy and rapid worldwide trans-border movements, the information technology revolution and the rapid flow of ideas as well as goods[10] has significantly moulded the prism through which Pakistan looked at its neighbouring countries. It started creating imperatives for greater cooperation and strategic partnership at global and regional levels to maximize political, economic, and military gains. The concept of soft border, free flow of trade and information, and economic interdependence are the terms being used in international relations. This has prompted both the countries to engage in an intense process of negotiations and dialogue to promote a stable environment of peace and security rather than the continuation of acrimony and animosity towards each other. This has also brought a realization among the saner elements and some government functionaries within the two countries that the continuation of the problem could be disastrous for the region. The Lahore declaration, signed between Prime Minister Atal Behari Vajpayee and his Pakistan counterpart Prime Minister Nawaz Sharif in February 1999 was in recognition of this fact. The nuclear capabilities acquired by both India and Pakistan had added to their responsibility of avoiding a conflict between the two countries.

In May 1998, both India as well as Pakistan conducted a series of nuclear tests. The explosion of nuclear devices revived international interest in South Asia. The hostile and uncongenial atmosphere between the two newly nuclearized powers, India and Pakistan, was witnessed by the international community with serious concern. Kashmir was seen as a flashpoint of a nuclear conflagration between these two South Asian nuclear powers. The effect was most noticeable in the reaction of the international community during the Kargil war in 1999, after there was a joint incursion by Pakistani troops and Kashmiri militants, who crossed the LoC and occupied strategic mountain peaks in Mushkoh Valley, Dras, Kargil, and Batalik sectors of Ladakh. The main intention of the military operation in the sector was to 'block the Dras-Kargil highway, cut off Leh from Srinagar, trap the Indian forces on the Siachin Glacier, raise the militant's banner of revolt in the Kashmir Valley and take the issue of Kashmir back to the forefront of the international agenda.'[11]

However, Pakistan failed to comprehend that the international community would not support its action and consequently did not anticipate or plan for the unanimous international opprobrium and isolation. The act rather isolated Pakistan completely at the international level and there came a strong diplomatic pressure on it to withdraw all the support to the militants and aid to end the incursion in the mountains. The G-8 countries held Pakistan responsible for the military confrontation in Kashmir and described the Pakistani action to change the status quo through military means as an 'irresponsible and aggressive act'.[12] They called upon Islamabad to withdraw its forces north of the LoC. Similarly, the European Union (EU) publicly called for 'immediate withdrawal of the infiltrators'.[13] The United States also depicted Pakistan as the 'instigator'[14] and insisted that the status quo be unconditionally and unambiguously restored. Under mounting international pressure for the withdrawal of its covert support to the Kargil operation, Pakistan's Prime Minister Nawaz Sharif made a visit to Washington on 4 July 1999 and signed a joint statement with President Clinton, which called for the restoration of 'sanctity' of the LoC in accordance with the Simla Agreement.[15] Pronouncements were made that the international community now viewed military conflict between nuclear armed India and Pakistan as unacceptable and would move against the initiator of the irresponsible military action.[16] During his five-day historic visit to India, followed by a five-hour trip to Pakistan, in March 2000, President Bill Clinton reiterated his earlier call that there could be no military solution to the (Kashmir) dispute. He rather emphasized for a peaceful process of dialogue and negotiations between the two nations. Thus, the option of military adventure or cross-border violence has completely vanished for Pakistan *vis-à-vis* its Kashmir policy.

The Kargil war also uncovered the inherent limitations of Pakistan's strategy to engage in a sub-conventional war against India in the nuclear environment. This also constrained Pakistan to initiate the process of dialogue and reconciliation with India to resolve the Kashmir problem. This was associated with a certain degree of recognition from Pakistan that war scares were neither good for its image as a nuclear power state nor for its economic development and progress in the current international environment.[17] One of the principal lessons of the Kargil crisis is that Pakistan understands that it paid heavily for its adventurism in Kargil and that the international community will not support the use of overt force in future to alter the status quo in the region.

Following the devastating attack on the World Trade Centre on 11 September 2001, there was a change in America's attitude towards Pakistan. Washington added to its list of designated terrorist organizations two Pakistan-based terrorist groups – Lashkar-e-Taiba and Jaish-e-Mohammed, both operating in the state of Jammu and Kashmir, thus sending a strong message to Islamabad about its growing dissatisfaction with Pakistan's Kashmir policy. During this period, a number of events occurred that favoured New Delhi; for instance, the United Nations Resolution 1373 (2001) adopted by the Security Council at its meeting on 28 September 2001, clearly ignored the distinction between freedom movement and terrorism, whereas the US dubbed all resistance movements for the right to self-determination as terrorist campaigns. The change in the international environment combined with the terrorist attack on the Indian parliament on 13 December 2001 invited worldwide condemnation and sympathy. India took advantage of this strategic shift by saying that the attack was part of the same global militancy to which America and the West are opposed, and even linked the attackers to those of 9/11. Consequently, New Delhi could put intense military and a very strong diplomatic pressure on Islamabad to stop providing shelter to armed groups that were active in violent activities in the Indian part of Kashmir. As we could see during his June 2002 visit to Islamabad, the US Deputy Secretary of State, Richard Armitage, managed to extract a pledge from President Musharraf of a 'permanent end' to Islamabad's support to terrorist activities in Kashmir.[18] In response to this Pervez Musharraf banned several militant organizations operating in Kashmir.

Musharraf was forced to abandon support for the Taliban regime in Afghanistan. The use of militancy as an instrument of policy was no longer acceptable under any pretext. Musharraf banned several militant groups and tried to curb cross-border infiltration following a military stand-off with India in 2002. He also restructured the ISI which had been responsible for the covert war in Kashmir.[19]

Thus, under the strong pressure from all corners of the world, military ruler General Pervez Musharraf arrested around 50 members of the two radical Muslim groups which India believe are responsible for the 13 December 2001 terrorist attack on the Indian parliament.

Pakistan ranks 144 out of 170 nations in the physical quality of life index, below even nations like Bangladesh. Between 1997 and 2001, Pakistan's GDP dropped from US $75.3 to 71.5 billion and by 2001 government debt was 82 per cent of its GDP. The huge defense budget of the nation has taken on heavy toll on the nation's economy. The Human Development Centre, Islamabad, in its 'Human Development Report' of 1997 said that Pakistan spent 7 per cent of its GDP on defense, or nearly 27 per cent of the total central government expenditure. This is higher than any other South Asian country.[20]

According to United Nations Human Development Report 2002 on South Asia, Pakistan is continuously spending 6.5 per cent of its GDP on defense compared to mere 2.3 per cent and 0.7 per cent of GDP allocated for the education and health sectors respectively, which is far less than the Millennium Development Goals (MDGs). In the meantime the law and order situation in many parts of the country, especially in the North West Frontier Province (NWFP) and Baluchistan, has become a major stumbling block in the path of many development works in the country. India, on the other hand, is emerging as a global power in terms of its economic and outsourcing potential, its democratic features are being recognized and appreciated worldwide. It has emerged as a major player in the information technology sector and an important source of skilled labour in the international market. The business reached to $4.5 billion in 1988 and climbed to around $27 billion in 2005.[21] USA also recognizes that New Delhi secures its interest in open seas and free movement of the goods and energy supplies through the Indian Ocean. This new attitude has been reflected in a series of military and naval exercises and the US-India nuclear deal signed by the two countries in the recent past. At the same time, brushing off Pakistan, US's close ally against the al-Qaeda and the War on Terror in Afghanistan, is neither possible nor wise.

> Bush's decision to differentiate between the Indian and Pakistani nuclear programmes was rooted in an appreciation of India's importance and its future role in the world that was so different from the traditional views of India in Washington. For decades the US security establishment had seen India through the somewhat limiting prism of South Asia ... Bush sought to alter this by emphasizing the potential global role of India as a rising power....[22]

It is assumed that the nuclear deal would provide India an opportunity to sign similar nuclear arrangements and conventional arms deals with other countries. These will tilt military balance in its favour and would allow it to use its indigenous uranium supplies to expand its nuclear weapons arsenal. India's potential to play a security role in Indian Ocean and Southeast Asia will be another important factor that will enable it to emerge as a major power in international affairs. In fact, some of the US commentators have forecasted that India would sooner or later attain that status. Therefore, US should take note of it while designing its global strategy.[23] As the Under-secretary of State Nicholas Burns predicted, 'within a generation many Americans may view India as one of our most two or three important strategic partners'.[24]

Since its introduction in the United Nations, a number of resolutions have been adopted under Chapter VI of the United Nations charter with regard to and in quest of a permanent settlement of the Kashmir problem. However, because of the non-binding nature of these resolutions both India and Pakistan have refused to abide by them and after more than 60 years the idea of plebiscite has become obsolete. Even the former United Nations Secretary General Kofi Annan, during his visit to India in March 2001, remarked that Kashmir should be resolved mutually by India and Pakistan as it is a bilateral issue in which the UN resolutions had become redundant. In this regard some of the Pakistani analysts observed that General Pervez Musharraf's suggestion of setting aside the UN Security Council resolutions on Kashmir is a pragmatic and realistic approach. Some of the analysts in Pakistan are of the view that there is no reason for Pakistan to stick to the UN resolutions when the UN itself has abdicated the same. The resolutions of the UN Security Council on Kashmir could remain valid until they are either implemented or the Security Council at the joint request of India and Pakistan repeals or replaces them.[25] The Pakistan government has realized the futility of these resolutions and the focus is now on finding other alternatives.

Lastly, there is a feeling in Islamabad that a lot can be expected from India by entering into a cooperative relationship in the economic sphere. Indra Nath Mukherji observes that due to the existence of an 'information gap' and low priority attached by the businessmen of both the countries, even pragmatic business organizations find it hard to expand their bilateral trade and investment relations. Both countries have intra-industry trade in several products at the bilateral level.[26] Firms involved in industries may benefit from joint ventures among them by identifying profitable avenues from intra-industry trade in several products. So, trade and India's technical expertise in areas like information technology, engineering and agriculture are attracting a number of Pakistani businessmen. This has brought about a realization among the stakeholders in Pakistan that instead of adopting hostile attitudes towards neighbouring countries, especially India, economic reconstruction and human development should be given preference. Further, there is a need to trim down the country's over-commitment to military expenditure on its borders and to devote more resources to its economic growth and internal security. In the given situation, it is important for Pakistan's own internal stability and prosperity to have a friendly and peaceful relationship with its neighboring countries, especially India.

All these factors in association with several other issues and events Pakistan is grappling with, like growing extremist forces, assassinations of its political leaders, its current global image as a rogue state and exporter of global terrorism, decline in the support for Pakistan, in the Indian part of Kashmir[27] and the large participation of Kashmiri population in the various elections held in the recent past have diminished Pakistan's hope of changing or redrawing the boundaries in the region through coercion. Similarly, it is palpably clear now that international players don't have any direct stake in the Kashmir issue, rather their policies should be seen in their larger South Asia policy, which in turn is moulded by their global strategic interests.

It is in this context that first, General Pervez Musharraf and later the civil government under the leadership of President Asif Ali Zardari has started realizing a need for moving away from its traditional position on the Kashmir issue so that a workable and mutually acceptable solution to the problem could be reached.

Conclusion

It would not be wrong to say that Kashmir has been put in the back burner while other issues like cross-border trade and travel are the items which have been given substantial importance in the various Indo-Pak bilateral meetings. This has been manifest in the remarks made by the Pakistani foreign minister, Hina Rabbani Khar during her visit to India when she said, 'her country has no interest in allowing its territory to be used by the non-state actors', followed by a very contentious statement by the President of Pakistan, Asif Ali Zardari, when he termed various militant groups operating in Kashmir as terrorists. Simultaneously Pakistani High Commissioner to India invited mainstream politicians from Jammu & Kashmir to an Iftar Party that was attended by Jammu & Kashmir State Congress unit president Saifuddin Soz among others. Even before this, on 18 August 2011, the Pakistani High Commissioner invited Iftikhar Hussain Ansari from People's Democratic Party (PDP) and Engineer Ab Rasheed, an independent candidate and Member of Legislative Assembly (MLA) to attend the Pakistan Day celebrations. There is an urgency that both the countries should come to terms realistically on all the crucial issues including that of Jammu & Kashmir. Most important of all this is the need for addressing the pain and misery of the people of Jammu & Kashmir who have been the worst suffers of this dispute.

The initial steps that can be taken in this direction could be the following:

- Both sides have to be prepared to think anew and revisit their policies and take a serious look at the long-term mutual interests rather than stick to the conventional warfare and conflict.
- Both the countries have to acknowledge the fact that the global scenario has changed and is changing fast. New realities in the international sphere as well as in the subcontinent are influencing local politics. All these developments demand a fresh approach to addressing contentious issues.

- Both the nations must realize that because of its geographical location and historical background, Kashmir can become a means and a bridge for achieving larger economic and political goals in and among the regions, particularly in relation to South Asia and Central Asia.
- Any permanent settlement to the Kashmir issue must take into cognizance the diversity and plural nature of the state.
- Each side must recognize that a politically stable and economically developed neighbour is in the interest of the other.

The future of both the nations largely depends upon how they evolve their relationship with each other in the twenty-first century. It is in the interest of Pakistan's own internal stability, development and strengthening of its democratic institutions to have a peaceful relationship with its neighbouring countries, especially with India. Similarly, for India to become a twenty-first-century economic powerhouse, it is necessary that it resolves the issue of Kashmir and forges a much more friendly and cooperative relationship in its neighbourhood. The aforementioned reasons necessitate a paradigm shift in the policy of Pakistan towards its neighbouring countries.

Notes

1. Talat Masood, 'Pakistan's Kashmir Policy', *China and Eurasia Forum Quarterly*, vol. 4, November 2006, pp. 45-9.
2. A.G. Noorani, 'There is So Much to Gain Mutually', *Frontline*, 25 August-8 September 2006.
3. See 'Musharraf Floats Joint Management Plan for Kashmir', *Dawn*, 10 January 2007.
4. Syed Rifaat Hussain, 'Pakistan's Changing Outlook on Kashmir', *South Asian Survey*, 14 February 2007, pp. 195-205.
5. According to a research report by the author, only 7 per cent of people in Kashmir showed interest in the merger of Kashmir with Pakistan. Samir Ahmad Bhat, 'Musharraff's Four-Point Proposal on Kashmir: A Study in Kashmiri Response', dissertation submitted to the University of Kashmir, Kashmir, 2010, Chap. 5.
6. Ravi Kumar Veena, 'Mediation on Kashmir', in Kanti Bajpai, Afsir Karim and Amitabh Mattoo, eds., *Kargil and After: Challenges For Indian Policy*, New Delhi: Har-Anand, 2001, p. 398.

7. Happymon Jacob, 'Geo-Politics in Southern Asia and its Impact on India-Pakistan Relations', in Amitabh Mattoo, Kapil Kak and Happymon Jacob, eds., *India and Pakistan: Pathways Ahead*, New Delhi: Knowledge World, 2007, p. 24.
8. Wang Guoqiang, 'The Continued Tensions in Indo-Pakistani Relations Cause Serious Consequences for South Asian Security', *Peace and Development*, no. 4, November 1999, pp. 28-32.
9. B. Raman, 'India China Trade: Still Miles to Go', www.rediff.com (4 November 2011).
10. Dipankar Banerjee, ed., *South Asian Security*, Sri Lanka: Regional Center for Strategic Studies, 2002, p. xi.
11. V.P. Malik, *Kargil: From Surprise to Victory*, New Delhi: HarperCollins 2006, p. 64
12. Amit Gupta, 'A Post-Kargil Foreign Policy', in Kanti Bajpai, Afsir Karim and Amitabh Matto, eds., *Kargil and After: Challenges for Indian Policy*, p. 289.
13. Ibid.
14. Pramit Pal Chaudhury,'A Post-Kargil Foreign Policy', in Kanti Bajpai, Afsir Karim and Amitabh Mattoo, eds., *Kargil and After: Challenges for Indian Policy*, p. 327.
15. The Simla Agreement was signed by India and Pakistan after the 1971 War, which resulted in the creation of Bangladesh. Further, under this agreement, Pakistan accepted that any negotiation about Kashmir should be bilateral between India and Pakistan.The implication of this article on Indo-Pakistani relations is that India has never considered any other diplomatic option for the settlement of the dispute after this agreement. The agreement has been effectively used by India as a weapon against further Pakistani efforts to internationalize the Kashmir conflict and to prevent interference by other states such as the United States, China, or other Muslim nations.
16. Alex Ninian, 'Contemporary Review', http/www.usip.org/library/pa.html (4 October 2011).
17. Because of the Kargil war, Pakistan's defense outlay increased by 10.9 per cent during the years 1999-2001 and the rate of economic growth declined drastically.
18. Robert Wirsing, 'Great-Power Foreign Policies in South Asia', in Devin T. Hagerty, ed., *South Asia in World Politics*, Boulder, Co: Rowman and Littlefield, 2005, p. 144.
19. Zahid Hussain, 'Kashmir: The Long Road to Peace', November 2004. www.newslince.com.pk (4 October 2011).

20. Amitabh Mattoo, 'Introduction', in Amitabh Mattoo, Kapil Kak and Happymon Jacob, eds., *India and Pakistan Pathways Ahead,* p. 11.
21. See Asian Development Bank (ADB), 'South Asia's Growth to Remain Strong in 2007-2008, Says ADB' (27 March 2007), available at http://www.adb.org/Media/Articles/2007/11669-south-asian-developmentsoutlooks (10 September 2011).
22. C. Raja Mohan, 'The Great Nuke', in Ira Pande (ed.), *The Great Divide,* New Delhi: HarperCollins, 2009, p. 135.
23. Howard B. Schaffer, 'US Interests in South Asia', in Rafiq Dossani and Henry S. Rowen, eds., *Prospects for Peace in South Asia,* Hyderabad: Orient Longman, p. 341.
24. Nicholas Burns, 'Heady Times for India and the US', *Washington Post,* 29 April, 2007.
25. *Dawn,* 8 January 2004.
26. Indra Nath Mukherji, 'India-Pakistan Trade and Investment Relations: Status and Potential', Draft Paper presented at the seminar 'Contemporary Pakistan in The Changing Global Paradigm', held under the auspices of The Special Area Studies Programme of Pakistani Studies, South Asia Studies Division, School of International Studies, Jawaharlal Nehru University, New Delhi, 24-5 November 2007.
27. Bhat, 'Musharraf's Four-Point Proposal on Kashmir: A Study in Kashmiri Response'.

CHAPTER 21

Pakistan's Incoherent Claim on Kashmir

Deepali Raghunath Khaire

PAKISTAN CLAIMS THE state of Jammu & Kashmir, a Muslim majority state, as an integral part of Pakistan, legitimizing its national identity. Kashmir has become an integral part of Pakistan's imagination as a nation and hence remained a contentious issue for the last six decades. Kashmir becomes central to Pakistan's security and foreign policy as a symbol of the injustice that India has done to Pakistan. Pakistan has taken both overt and covert efforts to gain Kashmir in all these years but the issue remains unresolved. The years since 1999 saw new initiatives for resolving the contentious issue.

There were sustained efforts over the years to bring normalcy in the relations between both the states. The initial phase saw cyclic failures in this process as the Lahore Declaration and Amritsar-Lahore bus service were followed by the Kargil conflict, the failure of the Agra Summit, 13 December 2001 Parliament attack and the 2001-2 military standoff. The tension between the two South Asian nuclear neighbours in Kargil and the 2001-2 military standoff brought the Kashmir issue back into the limelight. From then till November 2008 both the states were working to bring normalcy in relations through confidence building measures (CBMs). Though there were many hurdles the process went smoothly from mid-2004. In all the dialogue processes Kashmir remained a contested issue as Pakistan considered it as the core issue and wanted it to be resolved with priority while India wanted it to discuss state-sponsored terrorism first. These years saw many new initiatives over Kashmir, one of them being Pakistan leaving the traditional stand of conducting United Nations-administered plebiscite in Kashmir as the only solution.

On surface it looked like there were many new possibilities for Kashmir. Both India and Pakistan were ready to discuss what they claimed to be an integral part of their national identity. A close examination of the process shows that understanding of national identity, at least of Pakistan (which is the focus of this article), is much complex and has many tensions. Pakistan largely derives its identity from the concept of Islam; many parts of Pakistan's society and state have rigid and exclusive understanding of Islam. Describing a similar argument, Stephen Cohen writes,

> At their core, nations are ideas and the idea of Pakistan has been in flux since it was first promulgated in the 1930s. We look at three elements of Pakistan's identity: the continuing debate over the meaning of Pakistan and what it means to be a Pakistani, the special difficulty of reconciling this identity with Islam, and regional and sub-national challenges to the idea of Pakistan.[1]

The army is one of Pakistan's stable and influential institutions. Generally hostile towards India but has, however, played an important role in nation-building. The back channel meetings were simultaneous but secret efforts to resolve the Kashmir issue during this period made it clear that Pakistan's army also was ready for normalization and peaceful relations with India. Both the governments were very close to resolving the Kashmir issue but the escalation of the activities of fundamentalist elements in Pakistan resulted in a critical situation due to radicalization of the society. It seemed that fractions of army and the Inter-Services Intelligence (ISI) were not in favour of the peace process. The Mumbai attack of 2008 halted the process for an uncertain time.

The unfolding of events during these years shows an increase in Pakistan's identity crisis where Kashmir is one of the major issues. 'This vexed relationship between Islam and nationalism that has proved deeply problematic and arguably greatest source of ideological uncertainty in Pakistan.'[2] The article will highlight this incoherence of Pakistan's policy towards Kashmir and its effect on Pakistan's claim on Kashmir.

Pakistan: Competing Ideas of Islam

'The history of a nation and the circumstances leading to its birth play an important role in defining the foreign policy of any country.'[3] The 'two nation theory' believed that Muslims of the Indian subcontinent should form a different nation and that led to the creation of Pakistan. Even after the formation of Pakistan on religious grounds not all Muslims migrated to Pakistan, still large numbers of Muslims are residing in India. Pakistan also shared cultural, lingual and ethnic features of identity with India. What then would make Pakistan a different nation was a pertinent question for Pakistan and its leadership. At the time of Partition political leadership could carve out Pakistan by deriving its authority from the power of Islam.

The history of the idea of Pakistan can be traced to the late nineteenth and early twentieth centuries. Indian Muslims adapted the British rule and modern institutions like education and governance yet maintained their distinct religious identity. It got political implication through separate electorates and the right of representation through the Morley-Minto reforms. This suggested that Muslims have different interests than other Indians. Pratap Bhanu Mehta has explained this impasse of religious identity and political representation as, 'In all the negotiations from 1905 onwards about what should be the shape and form of Muslim representation; there was no stable answer to this particular question and dilemma.'[4] The conceptualization of this collective self derives from the image of self as a minority community in a representative democracy. In such a form of governance these two communities are related by majority and minority equation. Such relations where security of one group increases anxieties of another are unstable. The realization that Muslims are in minority and in representative democracies have to live under majority rule constituted the element of 'fear' of Hindu dominance and pressed the need for a separate homeland to protect Muslim interests and identity.

This conception of identity was principally based on the idea of Islam. It varied on large scale as some considered it as religion, some as a faith while some other at a later phase as political ideology. 'The building blocks that shaped the idea of Pakistan – community, nation and power – though largely informed by Islam, were all strongly contested.'[5] The concept of Islam was universal while its interpretations for its followers varied over a large spectrum. At one end of the spectrum was an idea of 'one and only one way' to follow Islam, hence denying different interpretations of it, on the other end was the plural concept of Islam.

Farzana Shaikh in her radio interview 'This Year of India' (5): . . . and the chronic crisis of Pakistan'[6] has put this tension within the conception of the idea of Pakistan as a tussle between 'Pakistan as a secular project' and it as a 'safe haven of Islam'. Such tension is also reflected in all the three constitutions of 1956, 1962 and 1973. This can be seen in debates about the idea of Islam in the collective self of the country. Pakistan portrays itself as a state with moderate Islam but there is no consensus over the concept.

While examining its claim as homeland for Muslims in the Indian subcontinent, Farzana Shaikh draws attention to the fact that Pakistan did not allow all Muslims in the subcontinent the 'right to return', to accommodate them as citizens of Pakistan. The Muslim population was spread across all over India, so when it came to the formation of Pakistan as a nation state there were competing conceptions of it. The major contestation was between the idea of territorial nationalism and Islam. At one level such imagination was 'universalist' and 'extra territorial' while on the other level it was culturally determined and locally grounded. When Pakistan came into existence many people from northern India migrated to Pakistan, resulting in the need for sharing limited resources between local people and the migrated population. This further emphasized the tensions between the vision of Pakistan as a state and Pakistan as an Islamic movement. This ideological diversity resulted in varied and competing claims of nationalism which can be seen in arguments of Muslim intellectuals and ideologues like Muhammad Iqbal, Abul Ala Maududi and Husain Ahmad Madani. The challenges that Pakistan faced to reconcile these contrasting aspirations lead to crisis of identity.

Even after Partition Pakistan had to deal with many other problems like violence and refugees' settlement. The contestation between local Muslim population and Muslim migrants from other regions of India revealed that there were different notions of Pakistan and Pakistani which added to this identity crisis. Pakistan had diverse regions with different ethnicities, cultures and thus it was not easy to sustain the nation by the sole force of Islam. The identity crisis that started then has continued over years till the present.

This has resulted in instability at political and social levels affecting Pakistan's world-view and relations with other nation states. The most important objective of security is survival of the nation state. Along with securing physical borders, it also means protecting the national identity. The two major factors influencing Pakistan's foreign policy in the early years were fear of India undoing the Partition, and seeking 'parity' with India. The constant threats due to fear of India undoing the Partition had its effect on Pakistan's understanding about the 'self'. Pakistan was continuously struggling to find its identity. It has tried to find this answer in the state's version of Islam.

History and geography are important dimensions of foreign policy of any nation state but Pakistan had ideology as the dominant factor in its national identity and foreign policy. Pakistan in its Objectives Resolution of 12 March 1949 declared itself as the Islamic Republic of Pakistan by proclaiming Allah as the sovereign authority and choosing representative democracy.

The second major aspect of Pakistan's foreign policy was seeking parity with India. Muslims were a minority community in British India; this view had immense influence on the political leaders' perception of Pakistan. Though the political leaders could successfully establish Pakistan as a separate nation, the fear of Hindu dominance was further strengthened due to violence at the time of Partition. All these factors had an impact on Pakistan's conception of its security. The need for parity was further consolidated by the sustained fear of India undoing the Partition due to Pakistan's defeat in various wars and at diplomatic levels. The emergence of demand for seeking parity with India and Pakistan's feeling that India will never consider it equal had always influenced Pakistan's policy and its world-view.

This crisis of identity at political, institutional and social levels in Pakistan led to confusion in its policies and action. These confusions about the ideas of 'Islam' and 'Pakistan' had an impact on the country's understanding of modern nation state. One such unresolved issue is of Kashmir. Both India and Pakistan claim Kashmir for legitimizing their national identities.

Kashmir: Injustice by India

Pakistan came into existence with the Partition of British India on religious grounds. While drawing the borders of new states, there were many areas whose fates were still being negotiated at different levels; most of them being princely states. Princely states were under British paramountcy; after the withdrawal of the British, these princely states were to decide whether to be a part of India, Pakistan or to remain independent. Two major guidelines while partitioning such areas were (a) plebiscite in such regions and (b) geographical contiguity of the region with India and Pakistan.

Jammu & Kashmir was the largest princely state bordering both India and Pakistan. It had a Hindu ruler and majority Muslim population. It was a unique situation where the two guidelines were contentious and in addition the maharaja wanted to remain independent and make the state of Jammu & Kashmir the Switzerland of the East. But the state also had a political movement largely against the authoritarian monarchical rule but leaning towards Indian polity. Against such a background Jammu & Kashmir became a part of India by signing the instrument of accession. Pakistan claims Kashmir as an integral part of its national identity and hence its imagination as a nation. It considered the accession of Kashmir to India as an injustice that India has done to both Kashmir and Pakistan. This claim was substantiated by the argument that Kashmir was always an integral part of the idea of Pakistan as the letter K in 'Pakistan' indicates.[7] Pakistan through tribal invasion got de facto control of parts of Jammu & Kashmir known as 'Azad Jammu & Kashmir' (AJK) and 'Northern Areas' (NA).

Pakistan's fear during the early years was that if India could keep Kashmir then it could reabsorb Pakistan as well. 'A feeling of insecurity against a much larger and hostile neighbour was the original source of Pakistani apprehensions about nationhood. The emphasis on seeking to "complete" Pakistan by acquiring Kashmir is directly related to this sense of insecurity.'[8] According to Charles Tilly,

> Territorial conflicts are very important in the formation of nascent states. They provide both internal and international legitimacy to the state (internally for the coercive apparatus and externally among the nations of the world), nurture feelings of nationalism and accelerate the process of centralization of the state.[9]

Over a period of sixty-seven years the Kashmir issue has remained central to Pakistan's national identity as well as foreign and security policy. 'Obtaining justice for Kashmiri Muslims living in the Indian administered parts of the state has been a central goal of Pakistan's foreign policy for five decades.'[10] It also plays a central role in Pakistan's domestic policy and acts as a cohesive force keeping Pakistan together by invoking nationalistic sentiments.

Particularly memorable is Zulfikar Ali Bhutto's speech at the UN

Security Council on the night of 22-3 September 1965, while a war was still on between the two countries. Pakistanis who heard it live on radio were enthralled as Bhutto thundered: 'The people of Jammu and Kashmir are part of the people of Pakistan in blood, in flesh, in life, in culture, in geography, in history, in every form. We will wage a war for a thousand years, a war of defence.'[11]

There are three broad reasons guiding Pakistan's Kashmir policy; they are economic, strategic and ideological. The economic reasons being the state of Jammu & Kashmir having traditional and important trade routes through the Punjab region of Pakistan. The dispute over water sharing is also a source of insecurity for Pakistan. Most of the rivers flowing from the region of Jammu & Kashmir provide water to the then West Pakistan. India's possession of this region means constant fear for Pakistan's agriculture sector. Control over the region and its rivers is also vital for providing energy through the potential for hydroelectric power plants. Both the states signed the Indus Water Treaty in 1960 to share water resources and avoid conflict.

Expropriation of their water resources provides the starkest example of insecurity faced by Pakistan. In a speech to the UN Security Council in 1950, Pakistan's foreign minister, Sir Zafarullah Khan, openly admitted that Kashmir's water resources are central to Pakistan's survival:

> The three rivers beginning at the top of the map – the Indus, the Jhelum and the Chenab, which flow from Kashmir into Pakistan, control, to a very large extent, the agricultural economy of Pakistan itself. . . . If Kashmir were to accede to India, this supply is liable to be cut off altogether. This is not an idle apprehension on the part of Pakistan . . . millions of people would be faced with starvation and extinction. . . . Therefore, to think in terms of Pakistan without Kashmir as an independent country is a complete fallacy.[12]

The water resources are vital for Pakistan and so there are still disputes, like the Wular barrage/Tulbul navigation project where India wants to build a dam on the river Jhelum near the mouth of Wular Lake. India argues that it will help to increase navigation during summer while Pakistan thinks that it is an attempt to divert water resources to harm Pakistan's interest. The project was tabled in 1984 by India while Pakistan considered it a violation of the Indus Water Treaty of 1960 and took the case to the Indus Water Commission in

1986. It complained that this project would have an adverse effect on the triple canal project of Pakistan. Several rounds of talks have been held since then; the issue is still being discussed. Pakistan has made many proposals to resolve the Kashmir issue; most of them include provisions for getting better access to water resources in the Indian region of Kashmir.

The strategic objectives of Pakistan are sharing borders with major powers, gaining strategic depth, securing national interest and influential position in international politics. Accession of Indian-administered Kashmir would have extended Pakistan's territory to share borders with major powers like Soviet Russia and China. It would have increased leverage for Pakistan in international politics. During the Cold War it meant an opportunity to side with the United States of America. At present it will help Pakistan to get access to the Central Asian region, which has rich oil and natural gas resources. Pakistan fears Indian encirclement if Kashmir remains a part of India and also that India by supporting the nationalist movement in Baluchistan would threaten the national integrity of Pakistan. Obtaining Indian administered Kashmir would give Pakistan a much required strategic depth.

The third is ideological – those following the ideology of Islam believe that Kashmiri Muslims should get justice and they should be liberated from the dominance of 'Hindu' India. Supporters of this ideological claim support the notion of *jihad* (holy war) for liberating Kashmir. This has a major impact on Pakistan's identity claims of nationality. This will be discussed in detail further in the article.

Pakistan has tried to attain its objective of wresting Kashmir through overt and covert means, the overt being three wars, in 1948, 1965 and 1971. Though the war of 1971 was not fought in Kashmir, the defeat and disintegration of Pakistan amplified the enmity between the two countries and strengthened the resolution of Pakistan's army to disintegrate India. Thus 'Instead of re-examining its formative ideas, Pakistan responded to this existentialist dilemma by reaffirming one strand within its DNA: Islam.'[13] Kargil conflict was a limited war but due to the nuclear capability of both the states, it attracted much international attention. Covert means included the propagation of religious ideology, militancy and building international pressure on India to discuss the Kashmir issue.

The Simla Agreement signed between India and Pakistan converted the Ceasefire Line (CFL) into the Line of Control (LoC), *de facto* dividing the erstwhile princely state of Jammu & Kashmir between the state of India and Pakistan.

Recently Pakistan has unofficially modified its position in two significant respects. Firstly, the government no longer realistically expects to include the whole of the state (including Ladakh and Jammu) within its borders. . . .

. . . Likewise, despite statements insisting that legally the whole of the state of Jammu and Kashmir belongs to India, the Indian government does not realistically expect to include Azad Jammu and Kashmir and the Northern Areas as part of India. The bone of contention between the two countries is, as it has always been, the status of the valley of Kashmir.[14]

The constitutional status of the region of 'Azad' Jammu & Kashmir and Northern Areas was not clear till the 1970s. 'Azad' Jammu & Kashmir got its right to adult franchise only in the 1970s. The region of Northern Areas was neither included as part of 'Azad' Jammu & Kashmir nor recognized as an independent province in any of Pakistan's constitutions. It had to struggle for forty-seven years to exercise its right to vote. The Ministry of Kashmir Affairs (MKA) formed in 1948 decided issues of governance for 'Azad' Jammu & Kashmir. It was only in the 1970s that 'Azad' Jammu & Kashmir gradually got representative government but it does not have the real power to take decisions. But when there is contestation about any decision, the Ministry of Kashmir Affairs has authority over the local council and legislature. 'Paragraph 156 of its historic judgment stated: No legislation could be placed before the Council (of Ministers) for its approval without obtaining the advice of the Chief Adviser. In case of difference of opinion, the legislation was not to be given effect without prior consultation with the Ministry of Kashmir Affairs.'[15] Northern Areas (currently known as Gilgit-Baltistan) too has a similar fate. Both the regions face discrimination especially in resource allocation. There are many evidences of Pakistan's federal government exploiting the natural resources of the region without giving adequate share of returns.

Over a period of time the ideological element has started dominating Pakistan's world view generally and Kashmir policy particularly. 'The problem is not that most Pakistanis are Muslims and adhere to deep religious beliefs; it is that those beliefs have been exploited by state bureaucracies—notably the army—that support groups whose beliefs they consider ideologically harmonious with theirs and that view militants primarily in instrumental terms, as tools to advance Pakistan's national interests.'[16] The policies started by Gen. Yahya Khan, which were further continued by Zulfikar Ali Bhutto, and further consolidated by Gen. Zia have resulted in the increasing influence of Islam over Pakistan. As Pervez Hoodbhoy has argued in the interview 'Pakistan 3.0: The "CIA Jihad" and the Whirlwind Today', 'Gen. Zia had an agenda to convert Pakistan from a Muslim state to an Islamic state and to use the policy of jihad to win Kashmir through covert war and get strategic depth against India. Muslim state is where majority population living are Muslims but Islamic state is a state ruled by sharia laws, it has changed the whole texture of society.'[17] These conceptions of Islam are not plural or inclusive but believe in exclusive narratives of nationalism. This has been explicitly seen in the disenfranchisement of the Ahmadiya community, which became the root for many future problems.

The army has played a very crucial role in the process of nation-building in Pakistan. It has been one of the most stable factors in the country, and it has ruled for over thirty years. Pakistan has relied on the army rather than on its constitution or other institutions as a correcting mechanism. So whenever there are major questions or tensions for Pakistan as a state, as a nation or society, the army comes forward to give solutions. But the army as an institution is not immune to ideological extremism. It has major influence on Pakistan's foreign policy. Pakistan's army has two major political objectives: protecting Pakistan's identity against India and projecting Pakistan as a nation with a utopian Islamic vision of military expansion with the help of *jihad* or holy war.

Three aspects of the army's centrality are important for Pakistan's future. They are the army's understanding of strategic threats to the country, notably its preoccupation with India; the army's relationship to civilian authority; and, most recently, the army's relationship with militant and extremist groups and radical Islamists, although its use of militants was notable in Kashmir in 1947 and in East Pakistan in 1971.[18]

Pakistan through Operation Gibraltar started infiltrating into Kashmir and Operation Grand Slam resulted in the war of 1965. The defeat in 1971 and the disintegration of the nation state of Pakistan into Bangladesh and Pakistan had an immense psychological impact on Pakistan's army. The invasion by Soviet Union in 1979 of Afghanistan and the Iranian revolution of 1979 added stimulus to Pakistan leaning towards Islam as a faithful ideology to achieve its political goals. The Pakistan army started training Kashmiri youth to fight war against Indian forces. After the end of the war in Afghanistan in 1989 Pakistan diverted the trained Mujahideen to wage *jihad* in Kashmir. During Gen. Zia's regime, Pakistan's policy was to bleed India through a thousand cuts. Pakistan used Islamic extremism as a foreign policy tool to advance its objectives in Afghanistan to achieve strategic depth and freedom for Kashmir. During the early years of insurgency (till the mid-1990s) Kashmiri youth used to cross the border, but in the later phase the militant groups had recruited Mujahideen from the Punjab region of Pakistan. This is a populous region with historical relations and geographical contiguity with Kashmir where the sufferings of Kashmiri Muslims are routinely exploited by religious and nationalistic political parties.

'Pakistan, some argue has not yet arrived at a clear formulation of its foundations, which are rooted in Islam.'[19] Pakistan's political leadership and government have legitimized the exclusionary version of Islam, entitled to one and only one way of Islam, neglecting the pluralistic vision of the religion. This has created the problem of identity struggle between the ideas of 'Islam' and of 'Pakistan' as a modern nation state. Ian Talbot argues that Pakistan has a legacy of historical inheritances from the colonial era that can be seen in the problematic relationship between Islam and Muslim nationalism.[20] Similarly, Farzana Shaikh argues that for Pakistan, 'the problems like failure to withstand military dictatorship, uneven social and economic development, severe ethnic divisions are not causes but symptoms of underlying uncertainty about its identity.'[21]

Kashmir: Over the New Edge

The years since 1999 have seen various new initiatives which raised the hope for the resolution of the Kashmir issue. Pakistan's Kashmir policy has remained dominated by military and strategic understanding than by political understanding. Both India and Pakistan tested their nuclear weapons in 1998, and this built pressure to normalize relations between the South Asian nuclear powers. It resulted in the Lahore declaration of 1999 but was followed by the Kargil war the same year, increasing the divide and also bringing the issue of Kashmir back into focus. The Kargil war raised the tension to the peak, bringing in many international powers to put pressure for peace process. Though there were hurdles it had many positive signs of easing of tension between Pakistan and India. The 11 September 2001 attack on the United States and its policy of 'War on Terror' brought in a major shift. President Gen. Pervez Musharraf followed the policy of supporting the War on Terror and Kashmiri *jihad* simultaneously. Pakistan adopted the policy of selective crackdowns on militant groups. It wanted to maintain the *jihad* as leverage for securing objectives in Kashmir.

Gen. Musharraf while addressing the nation in January 2002 said that 'Kashmir runs in our blood. No Pakistani can afford to sever links with Kashmir. The entire Pakistan and the world know this. We will continue to extend our moral, political and diplomatic support to Kashmiris. We will never budge an inch from our principled stand on Kashmir.'[22]

Such policies could not succeed, as United States invaded Afghanistan in 2001 and started attacking *jihadi* elements and Taliban. This started affecting Pakistan adversely. Around mid-2004 President Musharraf resumed the series of talks through 'composite dialogue' and 'the back channel'[23] efforts showed sincere will to resolve the Kashmir issue.

'Composite dialogues' were confidence building measures to avoid future conflicts between India and Pakistan. They have identified eight issues out of which peace and security, and the Kashmir issue are discussed at the secretary level. Initially both the states were reluctant to leave their traditional positions on Kashmir, resulting in frequent failures. This started changing after 2004 following five rounds of talks from 2004 to 2008. The simultaneous but secret negotiations through 'back channel' also started to discuss and resolve the Kashmir issue. The report 'The Back Channel' by Steve Coll states that 'Negotiators involved in the secret back channel regarded the effort as politically risky and exceptionally ambitious – as one of the officials put it.'[24] It also mentions that President Musharraf drew his generals into a debate about the fundamental definition of Pakistan's national security and the view that Kashmir will not gain freedom without such negotiation with India.

'In Pakistan there are broadly three schools of thought on

Kashmir.'[25] The first is the orthodox school which argues that India is unconditionally hostile towards Pakistan and its creators, not willing to give it equal status. Their traditional stand on Kashmir is the insistence on a United Nations-administered plebiscite. Now during the new peace initiative they are willing to explore other options provided they do not harm Pakistan's claim over Kashmir on moral and legal grounds. The second school is Islamist; it shares the point of a UN-administered plebiscite but further says that India, a Hindu nation, along with Christian nations and Jewish Israel is trying to weaken Muslim Pakistan. The third school is moderate or liberal school which says Pakistan needs to improve relations with India. The increased defence expenditure is a matter of concern for the nation. It also believes Pakistan should not follow policies which will isolate it at the international level. It should work to reduce tension with India to find a solution for Kashmir. There was consensus on leaving the traditional stand of plebiscite and looking for other options resolving the Kashmir issue.

As the peace process made progress and events unfolded over a period of time it showed various trends. One was sustained terrorist attacks on India putting hurdles in the peace process. Second, the level of violence in Kashmir valley started declining and several new initiatives were taken on both sides of the LoC, like opening roads for people and trade. Making borders irrelevant was an effort to find solution. Third, the Pakistan government started taking aggressive action against some *jihadi* groups. In response these groups started targeting major cities in Pakistan like Lahore and Islamabad. The most explicit event was the 2007 episode of the Red Mosque in Islamabad where Pakistan government had to take offensive action against religious fundamentalists. The rise in radicalization of Pakistani society became further evident in the following years. The increasing loss of control over the tribal region has forced Pakistan to act offensively. For instance, over the years it became clear that it could not control the *jihadi* groups. To seek a way out it started signing peace deals with them. Signing of peace deals with fundamentalist elements has deteriorated the efforts of moderate elements to build cohesion in the society.

It is well established that the Mumbai attack of 2008 involved Pakistan's establishment. However, back channel diplomacy showed the willingness of both the governments to work out a solution for Kashmir. The Wikileaks cable dated 28 November 2008 (180571:

Confidential/noforn)[26] mentioned that India and Pakistan were very close to the resolution of Kashmir issue and the 'text' was ready but the military chief Gen. Ashfaq Parvez Kayani, being reluctant, the efforts led nowhere. It leaves space to think that certain factious in the army and ISI were not prepared for the proposed solution of Kashmir and peaceful relations with India.

Pakistan's Incoherent Claim on Kashmir

Pakistan's claim on Kashmir for legitimizing its national identity largely comes from its perception of Islam as a source of identity. 'Islam created Pakistan, but it now divided Pakistan, fuelled ideological passions, diverse social and religious Muslim formations have developed in different parts of the country.'[27] Pakistan's mainstream understanding of Islam is exclusionary and in the case of Kashmir it is exercised through the policy of *jihad* and militancy. 'The army's 25 year-old low-cost, high-impact strategy of covert warfare should have liberated Kashmir and secured Afghanistan from Indian Influence. The tension within Pakistan's society and military fundamentally owe to the underlying confusion about national purpose and identity.'[28] From 2004 onwards there has been a shift in Pakistan's Kashmir policy. On the one hand Pakistan has left behind the traditional stand of United Nations-administered plebiscite for Kashmir as a solution and has taken a liberal position. On the other hand Pakistan has tried to maintain *jihadi* elements. The statement of President Musharraf that 'I don't hold a whistle which I will blow, it will end militancy'[29] reflects the same. As discussed above the increase in terrorist attacks in India and Pakistan depicts that these *jihadi* elements have started operating independently and have spread the ideology deep in society. The Mumbai terrorist attack of 26 November 2008 halted the India-Pakistan peace process abruptly.

The years after 2008 have shown Pakistan's failure to take any positive step towards resolving or even recognizing its identity crisis. 'Overcoming the limitations of this "negative" identity is not only Pakistan's single greatest foreign policy challenge, but also vital to Pakistan's identity. Nowhere has this been more emphatically pursued internationally that in its struggle with India over Kashmir.'[30] The crisis of identity coming from various interpretations of Islam and its clash with the concept of nationalism has resulted in confusion at various levels in Pakistan. This has hampered Pakistan's claim over Kashmir and can be seen in consistent failure to come to any concrete agreement on Kashmir.

Notes

1. Stephen P. Cohen, 'The Future of Pakistan', http://www.brookings.edu/papers/2011/01_pakistan_cohen.aspx (accessed on 13 November 2011), p. 22.
2. Farzana Shaikh, *Making Sense of Pakistan*, New York: Columbia University Press, 2009, p. 2.
3. Aparna Pande, *Explaining Pakistan's Foreign Policy: Escaping India*, New York: Routledge, 2011, p. 4.
4. Pratap Bhanu Mehta, 'Pakistan's Perpetual Identity Crisis'. Interview on *Radio Open Source*, available on the Internet at http://www.radioopensource.org/pratap-mehta-pakistans-perpetual-identity-crisis/ (accessed on 30 July 2011).
5. Shaikh, *Making Sense of Pakistan*, p. 2.
6. Farzana Shaikh, 'This 'Year of India' (5): . . . and the chronic crisis of Pakistan', Interview on *Radio Open Source*. Available on the internet at http://www.radioopensource.org/this-year-of-india-5-and-the-chronic-crisis-of-pakistan/ (accessed on 13 November 2011).
7. Choudhury Rahmat Ali, 'Now or Never. Are We to Live or Perish Forever?' (1933), Available on the Internet at http: //www.chaudhryrahmatali.com/now%20or%20never/index.htm (accessed on 6 October 2011).
8. Husain Haqqani, 'Pakistan's Endgame in Kashmir', in Sumit Ganguly, ed., *The Kashmir Question Retrospect and Prospect*, New York: Frank Cass, 2009, p. 50.
9. Pande, *Explaining Pakistan's Foreign Policy: Escaping India*, p. 19.
10. Stephen P. Cohen, *The Idea of Pakistan*, New Delhi: Oxford University Press, 2005, p. 6.
11. Zaigham Khan, 'Kashmir in Pakistani Politics', *Himal Magazine*, available on Internet at http://www.himalmag.com/component/content/article/2234-Kashmir-in-Pakistani-politics.html (accessed on 7 November 2011).
12. Cited in Khan, *Kashmir Saga*, p. 193, cited in Navnita Chadha Behera, *Demystifying Kashmir*, Washington D.C.: Brookings Institution Press, 2006, p. 189.
13. M.J. Akbar, *Tinderbox: The Past and Future of Pakistan*, New Delhi: HarperCollins, 2011, p. 218.

14. Victoria Schofield, *Kashmir in Conflict: India, Pakistan and the Unending War*, London: I.B. Tauris, 2003, p. XIV.
15. Cited in I. Rammohan Rao, 'POK in Fetters', *Hindustan Times* (New Delhi), 18 May 1996, cited in N. Behera, *Demystifying Kashmir*, p. 179.
16. Cohen, 'The Future of Pakistan', p. 25.
17. Parvez Hoodbhoy, 'Pakistan 3.0: The "CIA Jihad" and the Whirlwind Today', interview on *Radio Open Source*. Available on the Internet at http://www.radioopensource.org/pakistan-3-0-the-cia-jihad-and-the-whirlwind-today (accessed on 12 November 2011).
18. Cohen, 'The Future of Pakistan', p. 28.
19. Behera, *Demystifying Kashmir*, p. 237.
20. Ian Talbot, *Pakistan a Modern History*, New Delhi: Foundation Books, 2009, p. 12.
21. Shaikh, *Making Sense of Pakistan*, p. 9.
22. Haqqani, 'Pakistan's Endgame in Kashmir', p. 34.
23. Steve Coll, 'The Back Channel', *The New Yorker*, New York, 2 March 2009.
24. Ibid.
25. Samina Yasmeen, 'Kashmir: The Discourse in Pakistan', *Economic and Political Weekly*, vol. 37, no. 7, February 2002, pp. 611–13.
26. H. Suroor, 'How the U.K. Saw Kayani as "Obstacle" to Deal on Kashmir', *The Hindu*, available on the internet at http://www.hindu.com/2011/04/03/stories/2011040354791500.htm (accessed on 22 March 2011).
27. Parvez Hoodbhoy, 'Pakistan's Army: Divided It Stands', *Economic and Political Weekly*, vol. XLVI, nos. 26 & 27, 25 June 2011, pp. 67–72.
28. Ibid.
29. Simon Cameron-Moore and K.J.M. Varma, 'India Okayed Hurriyat Trip, Its Breakthrough, Let's Get Started: Gen', *Indian Express*, 25 May 2005 (www.indianexpress.com/res/web/pIe/archive_full_story.php?content_id=71036), cited in N. Behera, *Demystifying Kashmir*, p. 253.
30. Shaikh, *Making Sense of Pakistan*, p. 8.

Index